Debugging
System 360/370 Programs
Using
OS and VS
Storage Dumps

DANIEL H. RINDFLEISCH

USDA Graduate School
Washington, D.C.

PRENTICE-HALL, INC.

Englewood Cliffs, New Jersey

Library of Congress Cataloging in Publication Data

RINDFLEISCH, DANIEL H.
    Debugging system 360/370 programs using OS and VS
    storage dumps.

    Includes index.
    1. IBM 360 (Computer)-Programming.   2. IBM 370 (Computer)
Programming.   3. Debugging in computer science.
    I. Title.
    QA76.8.I12R5   001.6'42   75-43881
    ISBN 0-13-197632-X

PRENTICE-HALL INTERNATIONAL, INC., London
PRENTICE-HALL OF AUSTRALIA PTY. LIMITED, Sydney
PRENTICE-HALL OF CANADA, LTD., Toronto
PRENTICE-HALL OF INDIA PRIVATE LIMITED, New Delhi
PRENTICE-HALL OF JAPAN, INC., Tokyo
PRENTICE-HALL OF SOUTHEAST ASIA PTE. LTD., Singapore

Contents

Preface

Several years ago I began a search for an educational course in debugging OS storage dumps. Being a typical programmer plagued with abnormal terminations and the frightening pages of a memory dump; someone, I presumed, would assist me. I soon found to my dismay that few in my programming surroundings possessed a firm and practical knowledge of storage dump analysis debugging procedures. Unfortunately, this situation persists in most data processing organizations. Yet, storage dumps are a frequent occurrence in all ADP environs. Too often, this printed representation of main storage memory is tossed into a wastepaper basket, rather than be utilized as an effective debugging tool. Since storage dumps are an invaluable aid to the solution of program and file problems resulting in abnormal terminations, the continuing lack of education on this subject in the ever-progressing ADP field is surprising.

How many dumps are simply set aside, while another 'shot' is made, to see if the same problem will occur a second time? And, of course, it does. How many haphazard changes are made to problem programs, on a hope-and-prayer basis, because no one around seems to know how to handle that 'burdensome' print at the end of the job? The answers to the above questions must be staggering in terms of wasted resources.

The purpose of this book is to provide a thorough, yet practical, working knowledge of dump debugging procedures, the most frustrating problem facing application and system programmers and analysts. The objective is to do so in a methodical step-by-step manner making full use of graphic displays. A programmer or analyst can then immediately begin to utilize as well as capitalize upon that portion of a dump of interest to the problem at hand. A liberal use of graphic displays are presented depicting actual computer runs with tape and disk file problems, along with COBOL, FORTRAN, PL1, and generated Assembly and Machine language examples resulting in abnormal terminations. Data base managers, DOS programmers, computer operators, scheduling personnel, and their supervisors alike, will also benefit from the presentation of this material. The book is organized in textbook fashion, utilizing actual computer runs and accompanying workshops, such that it can be readily adapted to classroom use if desired.

Chapter 1 introduces the reader to storage dump terminology and concepts by describing abend procedures, types of main storage dumps, and their format. Chapter 2 discusses the Reference Data Card, numbering systems, and forms of data representation. They are the working tools of a storage dump analyst in all DOS, OS, and VS environments. An accompanying workshop is provided.

Actual debugging procedures for external abends begin in Chapter 3. Step-by-step procedures for debugging file problems external to an application, system, or data base program are methodically presented. Determining the problem file along with pertinent data attributes, and completing the workshop at the end of the chapter will solidify the handling of storage dumps for file problems. The analysis of internal abends or problems resulting in storage dumps are detailed in Chapter 4. COBOL, FORTRAN, and PL1 examples are freely utilized. Assembly language listings are also frequently referenced. Attention is focused on determining the program source statement being executed at the time of the abend. A workshop is provided to obtain a working knowledge of debugging storage dumps for program problems.

Chapter 5 describes procedures for determining the value of pertinent program variables at the time of the abend. COBOL and FORTRAN examples with appropriate maps and assembly language listings are displayed. An extensive workshop is also provided. Appropriate PL1 variables are covered in Chapter 6 along with the breakdown of machine instructions generated by COBOL and FORTRAN programs. A complete description and analysis of instruction formats is accomplished. A final workshop again provides actual hands-on experience. Chapter 7 describes all completion codes and their most probable causes—a most handy and valuable reference in all ADP environments. Finally, workshop answers and a storage dump glossary are provided.

By the way, I never did find that OS storage dump debugging course I was looking for. And so after years of frustration, picking up bits and pieces here and there, gaining experience day by day, and training myself like so many others, I decided to organize the subject matter and begin teaching it myself. Since that first class in the summer of 1972, I have reorganized and refined the course numerous times while presenting it to over 400 students through the U.S. Department of Agriculture Graduate School in Washington, D.C. This textbook is a resultant by-product of that experience.

Debugging System 360/370 storage dumps is a necessary and invaluable programmer debugging tool. And it is not as confusing as most presume! Following a methodical set of step-by-step procedures as described in this text, anyone with a basic understanding of data processing concepts can effectively debug OS and VS main storage dumps. This is a realistically obtainable objective and the primary purpose of this book.

My appreciation is extended to Chuck Tobin for his analytical advice and technical assistance; Charlotte Tsoucalas for her thorough editing and critique; and my wife, Ruth, for her diligent typing and exacting review. I would also like to thank International Business Machines Corporation for permission to reproduce the Reference Data Card. The IBM Programmer's Guide to Debugging Manual as well as the Messages and Codes Manual were also handy references on specific occasions.

DANIEL H. RINDFLEISCH

————————
Reference Data Card reprinted by permission from GX20-1703-9 by International Business Machines Corporation.

1

Storage Dump
Concepts

A. INTRODUCTION

1. Storage Dump Overview

   The Operating System (OS) with or without Virtual Storage (VS)
as well as the Disk Operating System (DOS) provides a programmer with
many debugging and error message facilities. Some, developed directly for use in application, system, and data base programs, display
specific but limited information regarding the status of programs and
files. These types of error messages can be helpful in quickly locating the source of a problem. Too frequently however, the problem
cannot be found, as more information is needed.

   Operating systems also provide a programmer with a more extensive
debugging feature -- storage dumps. A storage dump is simply a printed representation of all, or a significant portion of, main storage
at the time a specific task is interrupted and/or abnormally terminated. It is, in essence, a 'picture' of the contents of main storage. To be an effective programmer, one must learn to utilize dumps to
their fullest advantage. They are an invaluable aid to file and
program problem solving. An OS, OS/VS, or DOS interrupt resulting in

a storage dump provides the complete status of the Operating System as it relates to your program and files at the exact moment the interrupt occurred. Whether beginning programmer or accomplished systems engineer, all facts needed to effectively solve application, data base, and other software file and program problems lie therein.

Although emphasis will be directed towards Multi-programming with a Variable Number of Tasks (MVT) environments, the principles of debugging storage dumps apply to Primary Control Program (PCP) and Multi-programming with a Fixed Number of Tasks (MFT) versions of the Operating System as well.

2. Abnormal Termination Procedures

Although all types of storage dumps will be reviewed, major emphasis must be given to OS and OS/VS Abend Dumps, which provide an extensive yet practical amount of information. When an abnormal termination occurs due to a system, program, or file problem, an Abend macro instruction is issued by the Operating System and a system dump routine called. In order to obtain an Abend dump, however, the pertinent step of a programmer's Job Control Language (JCL) must contain one of the following DD Statements:

```
//SYSUDUMP   DD   SYSOUT=A
            or
//SYSABEND   DD   SYSOUT=A
```

The above DD Statements describe the formatted output file in which the dump will be printed. The SYSUDUMP DD Statement results in a dump containing selected control information and a print of main storage as it relates to the load module. A SYSABEND DD Statement produces a print of the system nucleus in addition to the above. In order to obtain an Abend Dump, either a SYSUDUMP or SYSABEND DD Statement must be present in the JCL for the step being executed at the time of the interrupt. In most cases, the information provided by a SYSUDUMP DD Statement is sufficient to meet the needs of application and system programmers and analysts. Only when severe system problems persist is there a need for a SYSABEND DD Statement. It is for this reason that the author recommends the use of a SYSUDUMP DD Statement, producing a print of main storage as it relates only to the specific load module, rather than the much more lengthly and cumbersome storage dump created by a SYSABEND DD Statement. This recommendation becomes more significant in remote batch communication environments where terminal print time may be a critical performance factor.

B. TYPES OF STORAGE DUMPS

1. Abend or Snap Dumps

Abend and Snap Dumps both provide identical information. For debugging purposes, the terms ABEND and SNAP are interchangeable. An Abend dump is automatically invoked by a macro instruction issued during abnormal termination by the Operating System, provided that the proper storage dump data set has been defined by either a SYSUDUMP or SYSABEND DD Statement. Snap Dumps are usually programmer invoked.

Abend and Snap Dumps are considered the most practical for application programmer use. They do not provide a complete dump of all of main storage from address zero to the end of printable storage; nor do they unnecessarily limit the information printed relating to the load module. Rather they provide all the information needed about the operating status of application, system, and data base programs and files. Abend Dumps are typical of those received by application and system programmers and analysts. For this reason, emphasis in this textbook is given to the analysis of Abend Dumps.

Other than supplying the appropiate DD Statement, a programmer need not provide any other information to evoke an Abend Dump during the execution of most high-level programming languages. When an interrupt resulting in an abnormal termination occurs, the Operating System automatically issues the appropriate instructions for printing the dump.

The format of Abend Dumps will be discussed in detail later in this chapter.

2. Indicative Dumps

Occasionally a programmer will erroneously omit a SYSUDUMP or SYSABEND DD Statement. Or quite possibly, an incorrect specification on the statement will have been made. When this situation occurs under the control of MFT (Multi-programming with a Fixed number of Tasks), an Indicative Storage Dump is issued.

Indicative Dumps provide a very limited amount of information as determined during system generation. Many times the information provided is not extensive enough for debugging purposes, though frequently it is helpful. An Indicative Dump is a means of supplying the programmer with some information relating to the status of the Operating System, even though the programmer may have erroneously omitted the appropriate SYSUDUMP or SYSABEND DD Statement. An Indicative Dump is brief -- a dozen lines or so -- and does provide some debugging assistance. Such items as a completion code indicating the type of interruption, a brief explanation of the completion code, the address of the problem machine instruction, and general register contents are provided. This type of information can be an aid in problem solving until provision is made for an Abend Dump.

The MVT (Multi-programming with a Variable number of Tasks) option of the Operating System does not provide for the issuance of Indicative Storage Dumps. Consequently, this type of dump will not be expanded upon further in this text. However, Abend Dump principles do apply.

3. Stand-alone Dumps

Stand-alone Dumps are, by far, the most extensive type of storage dump. The complete contents of main storage, from the very beginning (address zero) to the end of printable storage, is provided regardless of whether or not a particular area of storage relates to the module of interest.

4

When system failures occur, the Operating System will attempt to recover itself by reinitializing the task which has failed. In this type of unpredictable state, the Operating System continues processing as best it can, while issuing appropiate status and warning messages to the operator. When this occurs, a Stand-alone Dump of the complete contents of main storage is issued. System recovery may or may not be successful; nevertheless, a dump has been provided.

The operator may also, at any time, issue a Stand-alone Dump from the console via a dump command. A service routine will then format and print the dump as appropiate.

As noted, Stand-alone Dumps are issued for potential Operating System failures. As such, they are not particularily pertinent to the problems of application programmers and system analysts.

4. Error Handling and Dump Routines

Error Handling and Dump routines are not storage dumps per se, but are a valuable and closely related feature. They are generally related to specific source program languages.

The FORTRAN Extended Error Handling Facility is one such example. It is covered in detail in Chapter 4. This routine, when activated, usually cancels the dump routine. As a result, it has an impact on a programmer's debugging procedures. Error handling facilities provide a brief description of the error encountered and pertinent register contents. A major disadvantage is that they are limited in scope -- many times the actual cause of the problem cannot be isolated. Values of pertinent variables at the time of abnormal termination cannot be determined. Another disadvantage is that a standard corrective action may be taken each time the error is encountered until a specified maximum number of errors has occurred. The standard corrective action may or may not result in what the programmer originally intended.

Dump commands can also be inserted directly into a source program. With this technique a print of selected program variables is accomplished every time the command is encountered. Abnormal termination does not automatically occur. This type of facility serves as an aid to potential debugging problems.

C. STORAGE DUMP FORMAT

Before such topics as Binary and Hexadecimal Numbering Systems, Data Representation, and Abend Dump procedures are covered, a general overview of storage dump format should be accomplished.

A storage dump will always be located at the end of a job listing as the last item of information. In addition, the following message is also generated in the JCL listing for the step within which the abend occurs:

COMPLETION CODE - SYSTEM = xxx USER = yyyy

The System Completion Code is represented by 'xxx', while 'yyyy' depicts a generated User Code. A completion code is nothing more than a classification of the type of problem encountered. This grouping is a valuable aid to problem solving, as it provides the programmer with a general description of the nature of the problem. Specific completion codes will be described throughout this textbook. In addition, Chapter 7 is devoted to a complete description of all completion codes and their most probable causes. IBM's Messages and Codes Manual is also a good technical reference.

A User Code is generated by the program being executed. The code may have been supplied by a programmer's abend macro instruction, or more frequently, by an error routine automatically called by the program. Error handling facilities are generally tailored to specific source program languages. The FORTRAN Extended Error Handling Facility is one of the most frequently utilized routines of this type. It will be covered in detail in Chapter 4.

Figures 1.1 through 1.6 depict an actual MVT Abend Storage Dump resulting from a typical computer run.

6

Figure 1.1 First Page of OS Storage Dump

```
JOB  RZZO22 ──A   STEP  GO ──B        TIME 160440    DATE 75239                        PAGE 0001 ──E

COMPLETION CODE     SYSTEM = 013 ──F
                                  └─C  └─D
PSW AT ENTRY TO ABEND    FF0400D 50019976 ──G

TCB  037540 ──H
 RBP   0003E8D8    PIE 00000000     DEB 0003781C    TID 0003F180    CMP 80013000    TRN 00000000
 MSS   02043148    PK-FLG 60850400  FLG 00006B6B    LLS 00041208    JLB 00000000    JPQ 80030B40
 FSA   0106DF68    TCB 00036590     TME 00000000    JST 00037540    NTC 00000000    OTC 00039470
 LTC   00000000    IQE 00000000     ECB 00122484    TSF 20000000    D-PQE 00043438  SQS 00036930
 NSTAE 800415D0    TCT 0003F458     USER 00000000   DAR 00000000    RESV 00000000   JSCB 870376BC
 RESV  00000000    IOB 00000000

ACTIVE RBS
PRB  041480 ──I
 RESV  00000000    APSW 00000000    WC-SZ-STAB 00040082    FL-CDE 00041890    PSW FF650013 5004EE38
 Q/TTR 00000000    WT-LNK 00037540

SVRB 042508
 TAB-LN 03E80400   APSW F1F9F9C5    WC-SZ-STAB 0012D002    TQN 00000000    PSW FF04000D 50019976
 Q/TTR  0000120F   WT-LNK 00041480
 RG 0-7    0004E870   0004ED38   000376BC   00039A70   0004E92C   5004F280   0004E870   0004E7E8
 RG 8-15   0004EA88   0004F24E   0004E7E8   0006E7C8   0004ED78   0004E810   0004EF02   0006E7E8
 EXTSA     8004E95C   2106E5E0   0004ED38   0006E7C8   0006E7C8   0006E7E8
           0C011EED

SVRB 042358
 TAB-LN 00980220   APSW F9F0F7C3    WC-SZ-STAB 0012DD02    TQN 00000000    PSW 00040033 50018282
 Q/TTR  03004DDC   WT-LNK 00042508 ──J
 RG 0-7    80000000   4001964A   8004E95C   8004E95C   0004E93C   0004ED38   00000003   0006E7C8
 RG 8-15   0006E7E8   0004E93C   80045E8    00000000   0006E5E0   0000003C   0000003    00037540
 EXTSA     000021BE   8F06DA50   00000000   00000000   FF030000   000423D4   E2E8E2C9
           C5C1F0F1   C9C5C140   C1C2C5D5                                               ──K

SVRB 03EBD8
 TAB-LN 03080308   APSW F1F0F5C1    WC-SZ-STAB 0012DD02    TQN 00000000    PSW FF040117 8006CFA6
 Q/TTR  00003D11   WT-LNK 00042358
 RG 0-7    00000007   0001A318   8001819A   00042358   00037540   04037540   00042358   00042358
 RG 8-15   00037543   8F06DA50   00037540   3F1D8      3F1D8      40017ICC   00042300   00000300
 EXTSA     E2E8E2C9   0006DDEC   1C06E3C0   0006DDEC   0006E5A8   0006E5C8   00000000
           0004C08    FF000000   800193A0

LOAD LIST ──L
 NE 000417D8    RSP-CDE 0203DB40      NE 00041778    NE 000417F8    RSP-CDE 01045808      NE 00041BD0
 NE 00041DF8    RSP-CDE 01045908      NE 00000000    NE 00000000    RSP-CDE 01045988      RSP-CDE 01045888

CDE                                                                                            ──M
 041890   ATR1 0B   NCDE 000000   ROC-RB 00041480   NM MAIN       USE 01   EPA 04E7E8   ATR2 20   XL/MJ 041990
 030B40   ATR1 30   NCDE 03E528   ROC-RB 00000000   NM IGC0A05A   USE 02   EPA 06C858   ATR2 28   XL/MJ 03FFE0
 045808   ATR1 B0   NCDE 0458F8   ROC-RB 00000000   NM IGG019CF   USE 01   EPA 1FC590   ATR2 20   XL/MJ 045888
 045888   ATR1 B0   NCDE 0458C8   ROC-RB 00000000   NM IGG019CL   USE 01   EPA 1FF810   ATR2 20   XL/MJ 045878
 0459C8   ATR1 B0   NCDE 0459F8   ROC-RB 00000000   NM IGG019BA   USE 01   EPA 1FCE40   ATR2 20   XL/MJ 045938
```

Figure 1.2 Second Page of OS Storage Dump

```
045988      ATRI 80   NODE 0459C8   RCC-RB 0000J000   NM IGG0198B   USE 01   EPA 1FCCC8   ATR2 20   PAGE 0002
                                                                                                     XL/MJ 045973

                              LN        ADR           LN        ADR           LN        ADR           LN        ADR

XL  N
    045980   SZ 00000010   NO 00000001   80002018   0004E7E8
    03FFE0   SZ 00000010   NO 00000001   800007A8   0006C858
    045888   SZ 00000010   NO 00000001   80000270   001FC590
    045878   SZ 00000010   NO 00000001   80000040   001FF810
    045898   SZ 00000010   NO 00000001   800001C0   001FCE40
    045978   SZ 00000010   NO 00000001   80000178   001FCCC8

DEB  O
    0377E0   00008660 00008660 00008660 00000000   00008660 001FF810   *14II 013.2D.D4RZ........8.*
    037800   10000000 C8000000 8F000000 01000000   0F000000 04037540   *.............8...*
    037820   0010001 00000000 00000000 0000007D   6B000000 6F06DA50 020377F8 33004C28   *...H........8...*
    037840                                         C2C2C2C1 C3D3C3C6   *...BBBA.LCF....*
    037860   00000000 00000000 00000000 00000000   00000000 00000000   *...Y....*

TIOT  JOB  D4RZZJ22  STEP GO           PGM=*.DD        PROC STEP1
    DD   14040140   00260900            SYSDBOUT         80001944
    DD   14040140   00260A00            SYSDBOUT         80004C08
    DD   14040140   00251600            CARDIN           800045E8
    DD   14040140   00251700            SYSUDUMP         80004C28    P
    DD   14040100   00251800            MSGOUT           80004C48

DATA MANAGEMENT CONTROL BLOCKS   Q

MSS  R   *********** SPQE ***********   ************** DQE **************   ***************** DQE *****************   ******* FQE ********
         FLGS  NSPQE    SPID     DQE    BLK       FQE       LN       DQE   LN       NDQE       NFQE       LN
    043148   00   043D60    251   041998   0004E000 0004E000 00002800 00000000   00000000 00000000   000007E8
    043D60   00   043438    252   041E00   0006E000 0006E000 00000800 00040150   00040800 00000000   00005D8
    043438   CO   000000    000   0408B0   0006D000 0006C800 00000800 0003F400   00000800 00000000   00004F8
    043B80   60   000000    000   041C80   0006C800 0006C800 00000800 00000000   00000000 00000000   00000058
                                          0006D800 0006DA38 00000800 0003FA68   0003FA68 0006D908   00000018
                                                                                          0006D800   00000078
                                          0006C000 0006C000 00000800 00000000   00000000 00000300   000000A8
                                                                                          00000300   00000720

D-PQE 00043438   FIRST 000419E8   LAST 000419E8
PQE 0419E8   FFB 00050800   LFB 00050800   NPQ 00000000   PPQ 00000000
             TCB 00039470   RSI 00020800   RAD 0004E000   FLG 0000
FBQE 050800   NFB 000419E8   PFB 000419E8   SZ 00018800
```

Figure 1.3 Third Page of OS Storage Dump

```
QCB TRACE ——► S
MAJ 03DA08  NMAJ 0003D5F0  PMAJ 00041420  FMIN 0003D638  NM  SYSIEA01


MIN 03D638  FQEL 0003F258  PMIN 0003DA08  VMIN 00000000  NM 60  IEA
            NQEL 00000000  PQEL 0003D638  TCB 00037540  SVRB 0003E8D8

SAVE AREA TRACE ——►
MAIN   WAS ENTERED VIA LINK
SA  06DF58  WD1 00000000  HSA 00000000  LSA 0004EB10  RET 0002C510  EPA 0104E7E8  R0 00000008
            R1 0006DFF8   R2 0003768C   R3 00039A70   R4 00000000   R5 00122408   R6 0003AB38
            R7 0003CCDC   R8 0003A7D0   R9 00121EA0   R10 0003A7F8  R11 00122408  R12 021E00C8
                                AT EP 03 05 08  08  082 09  09        0J80 0  £0J J 0  < I  Z J  -

MAIN   WAS ENTERED VIA CALL
SA  04EB10  WD1 0030C4C2  HSA 0006DF68  LSA 0006DBB0  RET 5004F254  EPA 0004F452  R0 00000001
            R1 0004F390   R2 0003768C   R3 00039A70   R4 00000000   R5 0006DF68  R5 0003AB38
            R7 0003CCDC   R8 8004E7F4   R9 0004F24E   R10 0004E7E8  R11 0004E7E8  R12 0004ED78

INVALID BACK CHAIN
SA  06DBB0  WD1 00000000  HSA 0006D970  LSA 0006DBF8  RET 4004FC06  EPA 0004F780  R0 00000000
            R1 00000000   R2 0006DAB0   R3 0001A318   R4 0001B7DA   R5 00000000  R6 00041500
            R7 00000000   R8 00042508   R9 0006DF68   R10 0006D908  R11 0004F390  R12 4004F992

INTERRUPT AT 04EE38

PROCEEDING BACK VIA REG 13
MAIN   WAS ENTERED VIA CALL
SA  04EB10  WD1 0030C4C2  HSA 0006DF68  LSA 0006DBB0  RET 5004F254  EPA 0004F452  R0 00000001
            R1 0004F390   R2 0003768C   R3 00039A70   R4 00000000   R5 0006DF68  R6 0003AB38
            R7 0003CCDC   R8 8004E7F4   R9 0004F24E   R10 0004E7E8  R11 0004E7E8  R12 0004ED78
                                AT EP 03 05 08  08  082 09  09        0J80 0  £0J J 0  < I  Z J  -
```

Figure 1.4 Fourth Page of OS Storage Dump

```
REGS AT ENTRY TO ABEND <---- U

    FLTR 0-6      0003752800037530   0000000000000008                 C4F4D9E9E9F0F2F2   D3D2C5C440404040

W   REGS 0-7      80000000 80013000  8004E95C 4001964A  V ---> 0006E5E0 0004ED38 0006E7C8 0004ED33
|   REGS 8-15     0006E7E8 0003F1C0  800045E8 0004E93C         0000003C 00000003 00037540 00000020
v                                    X                                                 Y
LOAD MODULE   MAIN                   ^                                                 ^

04E7E0                      90ECD00C 185D05F0   4580F010 C1C3D6D4 D7404040 C1D5E2F4   *...0A. .........0..0.ACOMP   ANS4*
04E800  0700989F F02407FF 96021034 07FE41F0   000107FE 0004F24E 0004E7E8 0004E7E8   *....0.............0.......2...XY..XY*
04E820  0004ED78 0004E810 0004EDFC 0004F20E   40404040 40404040 40404040 4040F0F1   *...............2.             01*
04E840  F0F0F0F5 F0F0F5C1 C1F7F5F0 F5F0F8F7   F5F0F6F0 F9F7F5F0 F7F1F5F7 F5F0F7F1   *0005005AA750508750609750715750 71*
04E860  F5404040 40404040 40404040 00000000   F7F1F5F7 F5F0F7F1 F7F7F5F0 F7F1F5F7   *5           ....715750717750 7157*
04E880  F5F0F7F1 F7F7F5F0 F7F1F5F7 40404040   40404040 40404040 40404040 40404040   *507177507157                    *
04E8A0  40404040 40404040 40404040 40404040   40404040 40404040 40404040 40404040   *                                *
04E8C0  40404040 40404040 F0404040 40404040   40404040 40404040 40404040 40404040   *        0                       *
04E8E0  40404040 40404040 40404040 40404040   40404040 40404040 40404040 40404040   *                                *
     LINE 04E900  SAME AS ABOVE
04E920  40404040 40404040 40404040 00000000   00000000 00000000 00000000 05050232   *            ....................*
04E940  0804E80E 00000001 00000001 00000000   00000000 00000000 80000000 00000000   *..Y.............................*
04E960  00000000 00000000 00000000 00000000   00000001 00004000 00000001 46000001   *..................... ..........*
04E980  9004E92C 00404800 0006E5E0 03004800   00000000 0004FFCE 0001012C 00000000   *..Z.. ....V.....................*
04E9A0  00000000 00000000 00000000 00000050   00000000 00000000 00000000 00000000   *................................*
04E9C0  00000000 00000000 00000000 00000000   00000000 009000F7 00000000 00000000   *.......................7........*
04E9E0  00000000 00000000 05000000 0804E80E   00000001 00000001 00000000 00000000   *..............Y.................*
04EA00  00000000 80000C00 00000000 00000000   00000000 00000000 00000000 00000001   *................................*
04EA20  00004000 00000001 42000001 0004E9D8   D4E2C7D6 E4E34040 02000000 00000000   *.. ...........ZQMSGOUT  ........*
04EA40  00000001 00000A64 00000000 00000000   00000000 00000000 00000085 00000000   *................................*
04EA60  00000000 00000000 00000000 00000000   00000000 00000000 00000000 00000000   *................................*
04EA80  00940040 E6C1E2C8 C9D5C7E3 D6D540E2   E3D9C5C5 E3404040 404040C1 D3C5E7C1   *... WASHINGTON STREET      ALEXA*
04EAA0  D5C4D9C9 C16B40E5 C9D9C7C9 D5C9C140   40404040 40404040 40404040 40404040   *NDRIA. VIRGINIA                 *
04EAC0  40404040 40404040 40404040 40404040   40404040 40404040 40404040 40404040   *                                *
     LINE 04EAE0  SAME AS ABOVE
04EB00  40404040 40404040 40404040 40404040   0030C4C2 0006DF68 0006DBB0 5004F254   *                ..DB...........2.*
04EB20  0004F452 00000001 0004F390 000376BC   00039A70 00000000 0006DF68 0003AB38   *..4........3....................*
04EB40  0003CCDC 8004E7F4 0004F24E 0004E7E8   0004E7E8 0004ED78 3202804B 00000000   *.......X4..2...XY..XY...........*
04EB60  00000000 0004EDFC 00000000 00000000   0004FFCE 0005067C 00000008 0006DFF8   *...............................8*
04EB80  000376BC 00039A70 00000000 0006DF68   0003AB38 0003CCDC 8004E7F4 0004F24E   *..........................X4..2.*
04EBA0  0004E7E8 0004E7E8 0004ED78 F7F5F0F7   F3F1F7F5 F0F7F3F1 F7F5F0F7 F3F1F7F5   *..XY..XY....75073175073175073175*
04EBC0  F0F7F3F1 F7F5F1F0 F3F1F7F5 F1F0F3F1   40F0F0F0 F1F0F0F0 F0F7F5F1 F0F3F140   *0731751031751031 00010000751031 *
04EBE0  40404040 40404040 0604F98C 0004F390   20004040 40404040 40404040 40404040   *        ..9...3...              *
04EC00  40404040 F2F7F6F0 F0F0F0F1 F0F0F0C0   F0F0F0F0 F1F0F0F0 C0404003 15404021   *    276000001000.00001000.  ..  .*
04EC20  C1D3D3D3 C4C1E3C1 C7D9C1D7 C8C9C3E2   6B40C9D5 C34B4040 40404040 40404040   *AL LD T GR PH CS.  NC.          *
04EC40  4040E9F6 F8F0F1F1 F9F3F4F6 F5E240F6   F8F0F1F1 F9F3F4E6 C1F7F6E7 F0F0F1F7   *  Z68011934 65S 68011934WA76X0017*
04EC60  F5F0F7F0 F1C3D7C6 C6E6C1E2 C8C9D5C7   E3D6D5E2 C5D9E5C3 E2404040 40E2D4C1   *50701CPFFW SH NGT NS RVCS    SMA*
04EC80  D3D34040 404040E2 C3C8C1C6 C5D94040   40404040 4040F1E6 C3D660E7 E6C1E3E2   *LL     SCH FER         1WCO.XWATS*
04ECA0  00000000 00000000 404040E3 C5C3C8D5   C9C3C1D3 40C1E200 0004EE02 D5C3C540   *........    T CHN CAL AS.....NCE *
04ECC0  0004E7E8 00000570 0004F390 E2E8E2D6   E4E34040 E3404040 40404040 40404040   *..XY.......3.SYSOUT  T          *
04ECE0  40404040 404040C4 F0F0F0F0 F2404040   40404040 40404040 40404040 40404040   *       D00002                   *
04ED00  40404040 0004E7E8 0004EA88 0004E870   40404040 40404040 40404040 40404040   *    ..XY......Y.                *
04ED20  40404040 40404040 00000000 00000000   40404040 40404040 8004E95C 40404040   *        ........         ..Z.   *
04ED40  40404040 4040F0F0 F0F3F1F9 F9F6F0F0   F0F0F0F0 00000001 00000A26 00000000   *      00031996000000............*
04ED60  0004F2B8 0004F380 0004F38A F0F0F0F0   F2F4F140 C4C1E3C1 0005067C 0004F452   *..2...3...3.0000241 DATA.......4.*
04ED80  0004F462 0004FFCE 00050232 00050252   00050680 0004F17C 0004EEE2 0004EEE8   *..4.....................1....S...Y*
04EDA0  0004EFD8 0004F07C 0004F0DA 0004F138   0004F208 0004E95C 0004EA08 D5DAA933   *...Q..0....0...1...2...Z.....N...*
04EDC0  F0F00000 00020000 00000002 48004805   EF070040 4040C9C4 407E4040 4040D440   *00.................  ID .    M *
04EDE0  7E404040 40D5407E 40C9E3C5 E2E3407E   40D5D6D9 D4C1D340 C5D6D140 58F0C008   *.     N . ITEST . NORMAL EOJ .0..*
04EE00  05EF5810 C03CD203 D060C00C D2021039   D0615810 C03CD201 1032C054 58401024   *......K.....K..........K....... ..*
04EE20  D2024011 C0115010 D2289200 D2289680   D2284110 D2280A13 58F0C008 05EF5810   *K. .....K...K...K...K.....0......*
04EE40  C040D203 D060C00C D2021039 D0615810   C040D201 1032C055 D2031060 C0575840   *. K.....K......... K.....K......  *
04EE60  1024D202 4011C011 5010D228 920FD228   9680D228 4110D228 0A139240 7000D24E   *..K. .....K...K...K...K.... ..K.*
04EE80  70017000 92408000 D2838001 80009240   605DD206 605E605D D2016018 C048D201   *..... ..K...... ..K.....K.....K.*
04EEA0  601AC048 D2016000 C04AD201 6002C04A   D2016004 C04858F0 C00805EF 5810C03C   *....K.....K.....K......0........*
04EEC0  1821D202 2021C021 58F01030 05EF5010   D1F45870 D1F4D24F 60087000 5850C024   *..K......0......J4..J4K.........*
```

Figure 1.5 Intermediate Page of OS Storage Dump

```
                                                                                                                                    PAGE 0006
04F660   00041B00 0A3C12FF 4780C208 9620B001    92190108 182D58F0 D10405EF 47F0C22A   *..........B.......J....OJ....0B.*
04F680   D2039000 CA949104 90484780 C22258F0    00F81850 05EF9620 D2039108 90484710   *K...........B..0.8......K.......*
04F6A0   C23858DD 000494BF B00198EC D00C07FE    9104D203 4710C2D2 9604D203 415091B8   *B..................K...BK..K......*
04F6C0   41F0C986 411090D8 47F0C258 00000FA0    D2031000 C2549220 100841E0 D20850E1   *.OI....Q.OB.....K...3........KQ..*
04F6E0   00049200 10090A04 12FF4780 C28A9610    B0019204 D108182D 58F0D104 05EF47F0   *.............B.......J....OJ....0*
04F700   C22A5810 D2084120 0FA05020 D2DC45E0    C30A4100 C2A247F0 C2AAC9D3 C2D6C4F0   *B...KQ........K...C...3..0B.ILBOD0*
04F720   F1F01B11 0A085000 D2E40700 45F0C2C8    0004F738 00000000 C9D3C2D6 C4F1F0F0   *10.......KU...OBH..7.....ILBOD100*
04F740   0A064150 91B841F0 C9B29110 B0014710    C22A9102 D2034710 C2FE9602 D2034100   *........OI........B...K...B...K...*
04F760   C2EE47F0 C2F6C9D3 C2D6C4F2 F0F01B11    0A085000 D2ED58F0 D2ED05EF 000047F0   *B..OB6ILBOD200.......K..OK.......O*
04F780   C22A4130 01000700 10001000 19234740    C32AD7FF 10001000 41131000 18234720   *B.....P........ C.P...............*
04F7A0   C3141222 4700C336 06204420 C30E07FE    90ECD00C 05B01872 500D704C 41A07048   *C.....C.....C......................*
04F7C0   50AD0008 18DA9601 71FF9108 72024710    B0A09608 72029110 72044710 B068D25F   *..............................K.*
04F7E0   7090B6A2 9280723C 4110723C 94F01000    960F1000 43E10000 41007090 50010000   *..............0..................*
04F800   42E10000 0A139110 70C04710 B0769110    72044780 B0689604 720247F0 B0DE9610   *...............................0....*
04F820   7204D207 7088B7E8 47F0B02E 41107090    58F01030 05EF5610 71081821 50107108   *..K....Y.0........0...............*
04F840   92402000 D2772001 200091FF 71084740    B19847F0 B0DE1B33 58207108 91FF7108   *. ..K........... ...0..............*
04F860   47403198 433071FE 89300002 4140B0BE    1A4307F4 47F0B0DE 47F0B0F0 47F0B100   *. ........... .....4.0...0.0.0..*
04F880   47F0B16A 47F0B16A 47F0B0DA 47F0B186    4540B108 94FE71FF 58D0704C 502D001C   *.0...0... 0...0... ...............*
04F8A0   98ECD00C 07FE4540 B12E9537 72094780    B10847F0 B0DE4540 B12E47F0 B0DED701   *........ ............0... ...0..P.*
04F8C0   72087208 D2782000 710C92F1 20004540    B12ED278 20007185 4540B12E 92F02000   *....K.......1... ..K....... ...0..*
04F8E0   47F0B0DE 48507208 41550001 95602000    4740B14A 41550001 4720B14A 41550001   *.0................ ...............*
04F900   40507208 41107090 58F01030 05EF1821    92402000 D2772001 20005020 710807F4   * .........0........ ..K.............4*
04F920   D21B202F 72EC4540 B12E9240 2000D277    20012000 4140B0DE 47F0B12E 92F12000   *K....... ... ..K....... ...0...1..*
04F940   4140B0DE D7017208 720847F0 B12E5850    71080700 45F0B1B2 0004F960 00000000   *. ..P.......0............0....9......*
04F960   C9D3C2D6 C4C2C5F0 0A069400 71085820    71084140 B0DE47F0 B12ED501 103EF562   *ILBODBEO............ ...0..N...5.*
04F980   4770F010 D201103E 105207FE 90ECD00C    05C04900 C5324770 C04C5822 00005820   *..0.K....................E..............*
04F9A0   20609180 22384780 C0229780 22385810    22380A0E D50322E4 C54A4780 C0304530   *........................N..UE.........*
04F9C0   C2EC921A 210858F0 210405EF 12AA4780    C0461BFF 50FD0010 98ECD00C 07FE18A1   *B.......0..............................*
04F9E0   5880A000 5820B060 50200008 50D20004    18D29110 D2044710 C0A294F3 D2029280   *...............K...K..K.......3K...*
04FA00   D23C4110 D23C43E1 00004100 D0905001    000042E1 00000A14 9610D204 9200D1FE   *K...K.........................K...J.*
04FA20   182D58F0 D10405EF 9104D202 4710C29A    94FED1FF 9140D202 4710C0BA 9140B001   *...0J......K...B...J.. K....... ..*
04FA40   4780C0CA 9101D1FF 4710C29A 920ED108    182D58F0 D10405EF 47F0C280 5890B080   *.......J...B...J....0J....0B......*
04FA60   12994770 C0D85890 A04C45E0 C2C247F0    C0F25899 00041299 4770C0D8 92100108   *.....Q.......BB.0.2..........Q..J.*
04FA80   47F0C0BE 9205D1FE 182D58F0 D10405FF    D20B2000 C57E5850 91B0D207 2010500C   *.0....J.....0J...K...E......K......*
04FAA0   9202D1FE 182D05EF 12AA4770 C1249212    D10847F0 C1CCD503 C54AD230 4780C134   *..J...........A....J..0A.N.E.K....A.*
04FAC0   D207A010 D230D245 2000C58A F3E72019    A010F321 2027A017 9240D2029 D40F2019   *K....K.K....E.3X.....3....... ..M...*
04FAE0   C5FCDC0F 2019C5EC 5800A004 1E001711    8C000000 4900C566 4780C190 12004100   *E.....E.................E....A......*
04FB00   00004770 C1B0D205 202EC568 88100014    4E10A000 F3322047 A00596F0 204A47F0   *.....A.K....E..........3........0....0*
04FB20   C1CC1201 4780C1B0 4110C57A 06101F00    4740C19A 4780C1CC 940FA006 D600A006   *A......A....E....... A....A.......0....*
04FB40   1000F321 2047A005 D4022047 C5FCDC02    2047C5EC 41220004 12004770 C19A182D   *..3......M....E......E...........A...*
04FB60   05EF4150 91B841F0 C45C9108 90484780    C1F49110 B0014710 C22458F0 D2E005EF   *.........0D........A4.......B..0K...*
04FB80   000847F0 C2449102 904847F0 C22458F0    C55E12FF 4780C20C 05EF47F0 C2240700   *...0B..........B...0E......B.....0B...*
04FBA0   45F0C222 0004FBAC 00000000 C9D3C2D6    E2E3D5F0 0A069104 90484780 C2449110   *.0B...........ILBOSTNO..........B...*
04FBC0   D2034710 C24458F0 D0F841FF 0008185D    05EF9610 D203D603 90049004 4780C25E   *K....B...0.8...............K.0...........B.*
04FBE0   58990004 45E0C2C2 47F0C1D8 47F0C244    5820D108 92602000 D21B202F C5D0182D   *........BB.0AQ.0B....J.......K....E...*
04FC00   58F0D104 05EF5890 B0804150 91B841F0    C4989280 D23C4110 D23C43E1 00004100   *.0J.................0D....K....K.........*
04FC20   00905001 000042E1 00000A14 9180D238    4780C2AC 9780D238 5310D238 0A0ED503   *.................K....B....K....K....N.*
04FC40   D2E4C54A 4780C2BA 4530C2EC 58D00004    47F0C03A 18491B55 8C400002 12554780    *KUE....B....B.......0........ .......*
04FC60   C2D89211 D10847F0 C0BED503 9000C57A    477E0004 59B091B8 477E0004 07FE4500    *BQ...J...0...N....E..........................*
04FC80   C2F8C9D3 C2D6C4F0 F1F00A09 4500C306    C9D3C2D6 C4F2F0F0 0A094500 C314C9D3    *B8ILBOD010.....C.ILBOD200.....C.IL*
04FCA0   C2D6C4F2 F2F00A09 4500C322 C9D3C2D6    C4F2F3F0 0A094500 C330C9D3 C2D6C4F2    *BOD220.....C.ILBOD230.....C.ILBOD2*
04FCC0   F4F00A09 07F390EC D06058B0 D1B850D0    B08098EC D06007FE 41EE0000 50E0D1A8    *40...3.......J.........................J.*
04FCE0   07FE90EC D00C0580 189D58B0 91B89640    B00158D0 B060509D 00045000 91A84150    *................ ........................*
04FD00   91B841F0 811658F0 D2E005FF 0004D203    90C481F0 D20790C8 A0001711 431090C9    *....0....0K.......K..D.0K...H........I*
04FD20   541081F8 491081DE 4770804E D2059000    81EA47F0 8054C205 90D081E4 431090C8    *...8..........K........0...K.....0....H*
```

Figure 1.6 Last Page of OS Storage Dump

```
06DB80  40404040 40404040 40404040 40404040  40404040 40404040 40404040 40404040  *................*
06DBA0  40404040 40404040 4006DB63 40000005  40404040 40006970 0006DBF8 4004FC06  *..........R..8 .*
06DBC0  0004F7B0 00000000 00000000 0006DAB0  0001A318 0001B7DA 00000000 00041500  *..7.............*
06DBE0  00000000 00042508 0006DF68 0006D908  0004F390 4004F992 00000000 0006DBB0  *....R..3..9.....*
06DC00  00000000 00000000 00000000 4004F90E  921FCC48 00000000 0006DC40 0006DB30  *..........9.....*
06DC20  00000034 A004F8AA 0000000D 000415D0  0006DBB0 00042508 501FCC98 001FDA00  *......8.........*
06DC40  00000030 00070000 00000000 00000001  00480000 0006DAA8 00004000 00000001  *................*
06DC60  0400D001 9404FEB8 E2E8E2C4 C2D6F4E3  02000048 00000001 07000D01 00300000  *.....N..SYSDBOUT*
06DC80  00000000 00000000 00000001 07000001  00000079 00000001 00000000 00000000  *................*
06DCA0  00000000 00000000 00000079 0004F7B0  00000000 0004F7B0 0006DAB3 40404040  *...........7....*
06DCC0  40404040 40404040 40404040 40404040  40404040 40404040 40404040 40404040  *................*
        LINES 06DCE0-06DD80 SAME AS ABOVE
06DDA0  40404040 40404040 40404040 00400100  40404040 40404040 00000000 00000000  *................*
06DDC0  00000000 00000000 00000000 00000000  00002800 00000000 F0000000 00000000  *.......0........*
06DDE0  00000000 00000000 80060C40 00000000  11111111 11111111 11111111 11111111  *...........0....*
06DE00  11111111 11111111 11111111 11111111  11111111 11111111 11111111 11111111  *................*
        LINES 06DE20-06DE60 SAME AS ABOVE
06DE80  11111111 11111111 00000000 00000000  00000000 00000000 00000000 00000000  *................*
06DEA0  00000000 00000000 00000000 11111111  00000000 00000000 11111111 11111111  *................*
06DEC0  11111111 11111111 11111111 11111111  11111111 11111111 11111111 11111111  *................*
        LINES 06DEE0-06DF40 SAME AS ABOVE
06DF60  11111111 00000008 00000000 00000000  11111111 00000008 0104E7E8 00000008  *..............XY*
06DF80  0006DFF8 0003768C 00039A70 0003A7D0  00122408 0003AB38 0003CCDC 0003A7D0  *...8....H.......*
06DFA0  0012EA00 0003A7F8 00122408 021E00C8  02020000 00000000 00000000 00000000  *.....8.....H....*
06DFC0  0006D4E4 00020510 0104EA00 0002ED80  00122408 000376BC 00039A70 00000000  *..MU............*
06DFE0  80060FE4 0D1A23C5 E36BD3C9 E2E368E7  D9C5C66B E2C9E9C5 80060DFC 003DC5E3  *...U..LET.LIST.XREF.SIZE....ET*
06C720  7F000000 00200000 8F06DA50 0006C77C  0006D988 00000000 00000000 00000000  *........G....R..*
06C740  00000000 00000000 4006CB88 001FCCC8  00019104 0006C720 0006C740 0036CB1C  *........H....G..*
06C760  00037540 9006C9A8 00036901 00036938  00036901 00000000 00000000 00810000  *...I..H......J..*
06C780  00700000 40F0F6C3 F7F6F040 4040F0F0  F0F3F7F5 F4F040F9 F0F0F6C3 F9C1F840  *...06C760   00037540 9006C9A8 *
06C7A0  C6F7C6F6 C6F0F4F0 40F4F0F4 F0C6F0C6  F0404040 40C6F0C6 F3C6F7C6 F540C6F4  *F7F6F040 4040F0F0  F0F3F7F5 F4*
06C7C0  C3F6C6F0 C3F6C6C6 F7C3F640 F7C3F640  C6F5F4F0 40C6F6F4 4040405C C6F7C6F6  *C6F0C6 F3C6F7C6 F540C6F4  .F7F6*
06C7E0  C3F64DC6 F3C3F6C6 F7C3F640 C6F5F4F0  C3F6C6F4 40404048 C6F7C6F6 5C060000  *.C6 F3C6F7C6 F540C6F4  .F7F6...*

        END OF DUMP ——> N
```

1. Problem Identification

A problem overview can be found on the first page of a storage dump. See Figure 1.1.

The Jobname as coded by the programmer on the Job Statement in the JCL can be found at letter 'A'. The Jobname for this run is RZZ022. The Stepname for the step in which the abend occurred, as called by the programmer on the EXEC Statement in the JCL, can be located at letter 'B'. The Stepname is GO. The precise time when the abend occurred is provided in military fashion, including seconds, at letter 'C'. The time was 1604 hours and 40 seconds. The year and Julian day of the run is shown at letter 'D'. The page number of the dump is printed at letter 'E' and in the upper right-hand corner of every page thereafter. The Completion Code, denoting the nature of the problem, is located at letter 'F'. The 13 Group of completion codes and others will be discussed in detail throughout the text.

The right-most three bytes, or six hexadecimal characters, of the PSW AT ENTRY TO ABEND on systems with Virtual Storage provides the programmer with the address of the next machine instruction to be executed. See letter 'G'. The Program Status Word (PSW) for this run is 019976.

The Task Control Block (TCB) contains six lines of information relating to the task (or step) which was being executed at the time of the abend. See letter 'H'.

A general identification of the problem at hand is the first step when debugging storage dumps.

2. Active Request Blocks

The Active Request Blocks (RBS) portion of a storage dump is also referenced quite frequently.

The Active Program Status Word (APSW) is located in the first line of the Program Request Block (PRB) within the RBS. See Figure 1.1, letter 'I'. On systems without Virtual Storage, the APSW contains the address of the next machine instruction to be executed, similar in function to the previously mentioned PSW AT ENTRY TO ABEND.

The Supervisor Request Block (SVRB) also contains pertinent storage dump information. A SVRB is created when various requests by the supervisor control program are issued. A programmer accesses the SVRB area of a storage dump to locate information pertaining to the problem file. For example, the right-most three bytes in Register 2 of a SVRB contain the starting address of Data Control Block (DCB) information. See letter 'J'. The value 04E95C in Register 2 of the second SVRB is an example of a DCB address. Likewise, Unit Control Block (UCB) information can be found in the right-most three bytes of Register 10 of a SVRB. This register points to information about the unit (or device) on which the file is actually located. See letter 'K'. The value 0045E8 in Register 10 of the second SVRB is an example of a valid UCB.

The Load List area refers to modules called by a load macro instruction and contains identifying information about them. See letter 'L'.

The text will be referring quite frequently to the Active RBS area; in particular, the APSW and Registers 2 and 10 of the pertinent SVRB.

3. Contents Directory Entry

The Contents Directory Entry (CDE) contains one line of information for each load module associated with the task being executed. See Figure 1.1.

The first line of the CDE contains specific information about the actual program module. The Entry Point Address (EPA) of the load module can be located at letter 'M'. The right-most three bytes, or 04E7E8, provides the starting address in main storage of the program of concern. This is particularily useful because in a multi-programming environment programs are loaded in available, but different, locations in main storage each time they are executed. The EPA points to that starting address. Subtracting the EPA from the Active Program Status Word (APSW) obtained previously gives the relative length into the program module at which the abend occurred. Because compiler and linkage editor output is expressed in terms of relative addresses, the above calculation permits us to relate to that output. The actual source statement being executed can then be determined. This is a tremendous aid to the programmer faced with internal program problems.

Referring to Figure 1.2, the Extent List (XL) can be located at letter 'N'. This area is an extension of the CDE.

The Data Extent Block (DEB) describes auxiliary storage locations for data sets which were open at the time of the abend. See letter 'O'.

Reference to the Contents Directory Entry will be made primarily to obtain the Entry Point Address of the processing program.

4. Task Input Output Table

The Task Input Output Table (TIOT) contains one line of information for each input and output file associated with the program module.

The TIOT is most often referenced for storage dump file problems. It contains the UCB alluded to earlier in Register 10 of the pertinent SVRB, and as such points to the ddname of the problem file. See Figure 1.2, letter 'P'. The pertinent UCB in the right-most portion of the TIOT is 0045E8. Finding the UCB which points to the problem ddname is an invaluable aid to an application programmer confronted with file problems.

The OS Data Management Control Block area points to additional file information. See letter 'Q'. References to the DEB, DCB, UCB, and Input Output Block (IOB), can be found here. The IOB provides information relating to Input/Output requests.

The Main Storage Supervisor (MSS) contains information pointing to the Subpool Queue Elements (SPQE), Descriptor Queue Elements (DQE), and Free Queue Elements (FQE). See Figure 1.2, letter 'R'.

15

Storage control information is provided here.

The Queue Control Block (QCB) trace area contains information relating to requests for system resources. See Figure 1.3, letter 'S'. It is further sub-divided into major and minor areas for each resource requested by the task.

The TIOT is the most frequently accessed item in this general area of a storage dump.

5. Save Area Trace

The Save Area Trace portion of a storage dump is actually a program tracing aid.

The trace area keeps track of the chain of requested load modules. This can be particularily valuable to an application programmer when it is determined that a system load module, such as an Input/Output routine, was being executed at the time of the abend. Register contents in this area of the dump provide a chain (or trace) from the statement in the routine at which the abend occurred to the statement in the source module which called the routine. As such, an Entry Point Address (EPA) and a Return Address (RET) are provided. See Figure 1.3, letter 'T'. The RET contains the address of the statement in the load module which called the current active module. Tracing backwards, one can eventually locate the original program module which called these system routines. More importantly, it actually points to the source statement which called the routine.

This procedure is similar in technique to that mentioned previously when the actual instruction being executed was located within the programmer's original load module. A starting address is subtracted from the address of the instruction being executed, giving the relative location of the problem statement. In tracing however, this procedure may be repeated a number of times until the program module is reached and the appropiate source statement identified.

In many cases this area trace 'rescues' a programmer from a confusing course of internal program events.

6. Registers at Entry to Abend

    The Registers At Entry To Abend area of a storage dump displays
the contents of the Floating Point Registers as well as the 16 General Registers.

    General Register 2 is of particular interest to a programmer with
file problems, as it contains the starting address of the file's
Data Control Block (DCB) information. See Figure 1.4, letter 'U'.
The starting address of DCB information in main storage is 04E95C.
This address corresponds to the information found in Register 2 of
the pertinent SVRB discussed previously. After locating this point
in storage and displacing various lengths from that location a programmer will be able to determine the characteristics of the problem file. Such information as the block count, tape density, TIOT
offset, maximum block size, address of next record, logical record
length, and physical record length can be determined.

    Likewise, General Register 4 contains the starting address of label
information if the label was actually being processed at the time the
abend occurred. See letter 'V'. For this run the starting address
of the label (standard or otherwise) as it resides in main storage
is 06E5E0. Accessing this point in storage, it is possible to pin-
point such items as the volume serial number, data set name, DCB
characteristics, and other information, all of which will be expanded upon later in this text.

    As will be seen, the contents of General Registers 2 and 4
provide a programmer with insight into the problem associated with
a given file.

7. Main Storage

    Finally, with most of the significant information having been
formatted and displayed for us, a printed representation of main
storage begins. See Figure 1.4, letter 'W'. The starting address
of the programmer's load module is 04E7E8 or eight bytes greater

than the printed address 04E7E0. These addresses, incremented by hexadecimal 20 bytes, proceed to increase as one moves down the left-hand side of the dump. This is because each print line of main storage contains 20 hexadecimal bytes of information.

The printed representation consists of two parts. First, a print of all storage is provided to the right of the storage addresses in hexadecimal form. See letter 'X'. Actually, all data is stored internally in binary. Because a binary print would be very hard and cumbersome to interpret, a hexadecimal representation of the binary data is provided. This technique speeds up the analysis of main storage contents.

The second part of the print of main storage consists of a decimal interpretation of that portion of storage which can be interpreted as such. See letter 'Y'. The only data which can be meanfully printed in decimal form is that which has been defined in Character Format. Character Format is also referred to as Zoned Decimal, Unpacked Format, or External Decimal representation. This area of storage is a basic aid to the interpretation of programmer defined data values. Actual machine instructions are not interpreted in decimal form.

An intermediate page of main storage is shown in Figure 1.5. The amount of storage printed, of course, varies with the size of the program module and buffer areas. This particular dump generated 12 pages of print before an END OF DUMP message was given. See Figure 1.6, letter 'Z'.

8. Format Summary

The previous overview of storage dump format was not intended to create a debugging 'expert' out of the reader. Rather, it was to provide a general overview of the contents of a main storage dump.

Many technical terms were introduced. Some will not be expanded upon further in this textbook. They are inconsequential to effective storage dump analysis for application and system programmers and analysts.

Other terminology will be expanded upon in a methodical step-by-step manner. There is no need to understand many of the engineering

18

technicalities of the Operating System. Rather, a practical course of action to the solution of a storage dump problem will be pursued.

A problem solution for the storage dump depicted in this chapter can be found at the end of Appendix A. Debugging of this dump should not be accomplished, however, until Chapter 3 and the accompanying workshop have been completed.

2

Data Identification

A. REFERENCE DATA CARD

1. Overview

The IBM Reference Data Card, sometimes referred to as the 'green card', is a necessary programmer tool. Used by all, from beginning programmer to accomplished system engineer, it contains a host of machine-oriented technical information. Because of its frequent utilization in OS, OS/VS, and DOS installations, in application, system, and data base environments, its contents should be reviewed prior to discussion of debugging procedures.

Figures 2.1 through 2.7 display the IBM System 360 Reference Data Card. The card is appropriate to System 370 as well.

The reference card depicts all machine instructions and their respective codes, operands, and format, along with proper boundary alignments. Assembler instructions are also displayed in addition to condition and program interruption codes. The card also includes a very frequently utilized hexadecimal to decimal conversion table. Additionally, the breakdown and format of various program and channel status words are displayed. A table of permanent storage assignments

Figure 2.1 Reference Data Card (panels 1 and 2)

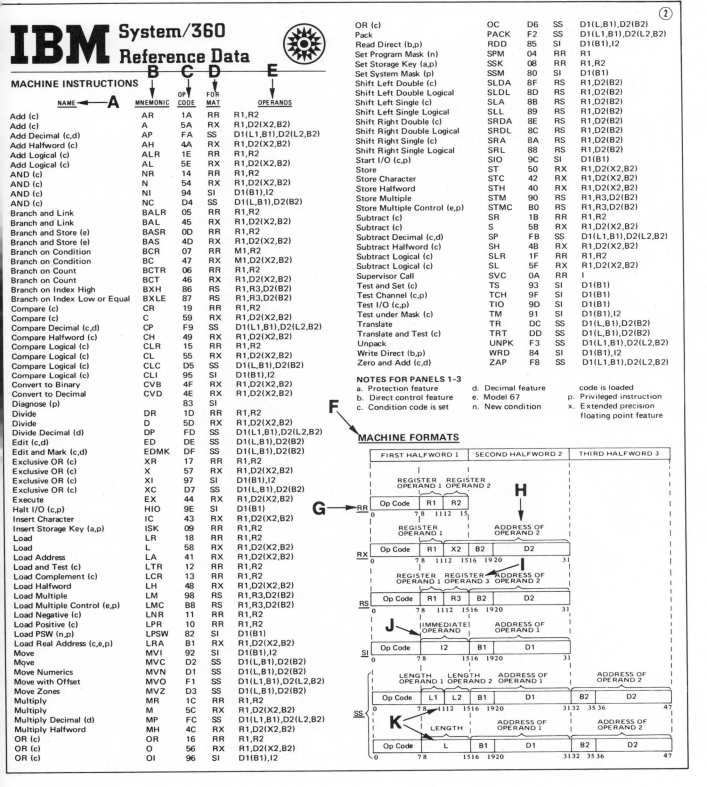

Figure 2.2 Reference Data Card (panels 3 and 4)

FLOATING-POINT FEATURE INSTRUCTIONS ③

Add Normalized, Extended (c,x)	AXR	36	RR	R1,R2
Add Normalized, Long (c)	ADR	2A	RR	R1,R2
Add Normalized, Long (c)	AD	6A	RX	R1,D2(X2,B2)
Add Normalized, Short (c)	AER	3A	RR	R1,R2
Add Normalized, Short (c)	AE	7A	RX	R1,D2(X2,B2)
Add Unnormalized, Long (c)	AWR	2E	RR	R1,R2
Add Unnormalized, Long (c)	AW	6E	RX	R1,D2(X2,B2)
Add Unnormalized, Short (c)	AUR	3E	RR	R1,R2
Add Unnormalized, Short (c)	AU	7E	RX	R1,D2(X2,B2)
Compare, Long (c)	CDR	29	RR	R1,R2
Compare, Long (c)	CD	69	RX	R1,D2(X2,B2)
Compare, Short (c)	CER	39	RR	R1,R2
Compare, Short (c)	CE	79	RX	R1,D2(X2,B2)
Divide, Long	DDR	2D	RR	R1,R2
Divide, Long	DD	6D	RX	R1,D2(X2,B2)
Divide, Short	DER	3D	RR	R1,R2
Divide, Short	DE	7D	RX	R1,D2(X2,B2)
Halve, Long	HDR	24	RR	R1,R2
Halve, Short	HER	34	RR	R1,R2
Load and Test, Long (c)	LTDR	22	RR	R1,R2
Load and Test, Short (c)	LTER	32	RR	R1,R2
Load Complement, Long (c)	LCDR	23	RR	R1,R2
Load Complement, Short (c)	LCER	33	RR	R1,R2
Load, Long	LDR	28	RR	R1,R2
Load, Long	LD	68	RX	R1,D2(X2,B2)
Load Negative, Long (c)	LNDR	21	RR	R1,R2
Load Negative, Short (c)	LNER	31	RR	R1,R2
Load Positive, Long (c)	LPDR	20	RR	R1,R2
Load Positive, Short (c)	LPER	30	RR	R1,R2
Load Rounded, Extended to Long (x)	LRDR	25	RR	R1,R2
Load Rounded, Long to Short (x)	LRER	35	RR	R1,R2
Load, Short	LER	38	RR	R1,R2
Load, Short	LE	78	RX	R1,D2(X2,B2)
Multiply, Extended (x)	MXR	26	RR	R1,R2
Multiply, Long	MDR	2C	RR	R1,R2
Multiply, Long	MD	6C	RX	R1,D2(X2,B2)
Multiply, Long/Extended (x)	MXDR	27	RR	R1,R2
Multiply, Long/Extended (x)	MXD	67	RX	R1,D2(X2,B2)
Multiply, Short	MER	3C	RR	R1,R2
Multiply, Short	ME	7C	RX	R1,D2(X2,B2)
Store, Long	STD	60	RX	R1,D2(X2,B2)
Store, Short	STE	70	RX	R1,D2(X2,B2)
Subtract Normalized, Extended (c,x)	SXR	37	RR	R1,R2
Subtract Normalized, Long (c)	SDR	2B	RR	R1,R2
Subtract Normalized, Long (c)	SD	6B	RX	R1,D2(X2,B2)
Subtract Normalized, Short (c)	SER	3B	RR	R1,R2
Subtract Normalized, Short (c)	SE	7B	RX	R1,D2(X2,B2)
Subtract Unnormalized, Long (c)	SWR	2F	RR	R1,R2
Subtract Unnormalized, Long (c)	SW	6F	RX	R1,D2(X2,B2)
Subtract Unnormalized, Short (c)	SUR	3F	RR	R1,R2
Subtract Unnormalized, Short (c)	SU	7F	RX	R1,D2(X2,B2)

NOTES

EXTENDED MNEMONIC INSTRUCTION CODES ④

GENERAL

Extended Code		Machine Instruction		Meaning
B	D2(X2,B2)	BC 15,	D2(X2,B2)	Branch Unconditionally
BR	R2	BCR 15,	R2	Branch Unconditionally
NOP	D2(X2,B2)	BC 0,	D2(X2,B2)	No Operation
NOPR	R2	BCR 0,	R2	No Operation (RR)

AFTER COMPARE INSTRUCTIONS (A:B)

BH	D2(X2,B2)	BC 2,	D2(X2,B2)	Branch on A High
BL	D2(X2,B2)	BC 4,	D2(X2,B2)	Branch on A Low
BE	D2(X2,B2)	BC 8,	D2(X2,B2)	Branch on A Equal B
BNH	D2(X2,B2)	BC 13,	D2(X2,B2)	Branch on A Not High
BNL	D2(X2,B2)	BC 11,	D2(X2,B2)	Branch on A Not Low
BNE	D2(X2,B2)	BC 7,	D2(X2,B2)	Branch on A Not Equal B

AFTER ARITHMETIC INSTRUCTIONS

BO	D2(X2,B2)	BC 1,	D2(X2,B2)	Branch on Overflow
BP	D2(X2,B2)	BC 2,	D2(X2,B2)	Branch on Plus
BM	D2(X2,B2)	BC 4,	D2(X2,B2)	Branch on Minus
BZ	D2(X2,B2)	BC 8,	D2(X2,B2)	Branch on Zero
BNP	D2(X2,B2)	BC 13,	D2(X2,B2)	Branch on Not Plus
BNM	D2(X2,B2)	BC 11,	D2(X2,B2)	Branch on Not Minus
BNZ	D2(X2,B2)	BC 7,	D2(X2,B2)	Branch on Not Zero

AFTER TEST UNDER MASK INSTRUCTIONS

BO	D2(X2,B2)	BC 1,	D2(X2,B2)	Branch if Ones
BM	D2(X2,B2)	BC 4,	D2(X2,B2)	Branch if Mixed
BZ	D2(X2,B2)	BC 8,	D2(X2,B2)	Branch if Zeros
BNO	D2(X2,B2)	BC 14,	D2(X2,B2)	Branch if Not Ones

CNOP ALIGNMENT

Double Word							
Word				Word			
Half Word		Half Word		Half Word		Half Word	
Byte	Byte	Byte	Byte	Byte	Byte	Byte	Byte
0,4		2,4		0,4		2,4	
0,8		2,8		4,8		6,8	

EDIT AND EDMK PATTERN CHARACTERS (in hex)

20–digit selector	40–blank	5C–asterisk
21–start of significance	4B--period	6B--comma
22–field separator	5B--dollar sign	C3D9--CR

SUMMARY OF CONSTANTS (OS and DOS Assemblers)

TYPE	IMPLIED LENGTH, BYTES	ALIGNMENT	FORMAT	TRUNCA-TION/PADDING
C	–	byte	characters	right
X	–	byte	hexadecimal digits	left
B	–	byte	binary digits	left
F	4	word	fixed-point binary	left
H	2	halfword	fixed-point binary	left
E	4	word	short floating-point	right
D	8	doubleword	long floating-point	right
L	16	doubleword	extended floating-point	right
P	--	byte	packed decimal	left
Z	–	byte	zoned decimal	left
A	4	word	value of address	left
Y	2	halfword	value of address	left
S	2	halfword	address in base-displacement form	--
V	4	word	externally defined address value	left
Q*	4	word	symbol naming a DXD or DSECT	left

*OS only

Figure 2.3 Reference Data Card (panels 5 and 6)

⑤

ASSEMBLER INSTRUCTIONS

Source: GC24-3414 for DOS
GC28-6514 for OS

Function	Mnemonic	Meaning
Data definition	DC	Define constant
	DS	Define storage
	CCW	Define channel command word
Program sectioning and linking	START	Start assembly
	CSECT	Identify control section
	DSECT	Identify dummy section
	DXD*	Define external dummy section
	CXD*	Cumulative length of external dummy section
	COM	Identify blank common control section
	ENTRY	Identify entry-point symbol
	EXTRN	Identify external symbol
	WXTRN	Identify weak external symbol
Base register assignment	USING	Use base address register
	DROP	Drop base address register
Control of listings	TITLE	Identify assembly output
	EJECT	Start new page
	SPACE	Space listing
	PRINT	Print optional data
Program control	ICTL	Input format control
	ISEQ	Input sequence checking
	PUNCH	Punch a card
	REPRO	Reproduce following card
	ORG	Set location counter
	EQU	Equate symbol
	OPSYN*	Equate operation code
	LTORG	Begin literal pool
	CNOP	Conditional no operation
	COPY	Copy predefined source coding
	END	End assembly
Macro definition	MACRO	Macro definition header
	MNOTE	Request for error message
	MEXIT	Macro definition exit
	MEND	Macro definition trailer
Conditional assembly	ACTR	Conditional assembly loop counter
	AGO	Unconditional branch
	AIF	Conditional branch
	ANOP	Assembly no operation
	GBLA	Define global SETA symbol
	GBLB	Define global SETB symbol
	GBLC	Define global SETC symbol
	LCLA	Define local SETA symbol
	LCLB	Define local SETB symbol
	LCLC	Define local SETC symbol
	SETA	Set arithmetic variable symbol
	SETB	Set binary variable symbol
	SETC	Set character variable symbol

*OS only

⑥

CONDITION CODES

	0	1	2	3
Condition Code Setting	0	1	2	3
Mask Bit Position	8	4	2	1

Floating-Point Arithmetic

	0	1	2	3
Add Normalized S/L/E	zero	<zero	>zero	--
Add Unnormalized S/L	zero	<zero	>zero	--
Compare S/L (A:B)	equal	A low	A high	--
Load and Test S/L	zero	<zero	>zero	--
Load Complement S/L	zero	<zero	>zero	--
Load Negative S/L	zero	<zero	--	--
Load Positive S/L	zero	–	>zero	--
Subtract Normalized S/L/E	zero	<zero	>zero	--
Subtract Unnormalized S/L	zero	<zero	>zero	--

Fixed-Point and Decimal Arithmetic

	0	1	2	3
Add H/F/Dec.	zero	<zero	>zero	overflow
Add Logical	zero, no carry	not zero, no carry	zero, carry	not zero, carry
Compare H/F/Dec. (A:B)	equal	A low	A high	–
Load and Test	zero	<zero	>zero	--
Load Complement	zero	<zero	>zero	overflow
Load Negative	zero	<zero	--	--
Load Positive	zero	–	>zero	overflow
Shift Left Single/Double	zero	<zero	>zero	overflow
Shift Right Single/Double	zero	<zero	>zero	–
Subtract H/F/Dec.	zero	<zero	>zero	overflow
Subtract Logical	–	not zero, no carry	zero, carry	not zero, carry
Zero and Add	zero	<zero	>zero	overflow

Logical Operations

	0	1	2	3
AND	zero	not zero	--	--
Compare Logical (A:B)	equal	A low	A high	–
Edit	zero	<zero	>zero	--
Edit and Mark	zero	<zero	>zero	--
Exclusive OR	zero	not zero	--	--
OR	zero	not zero	–	--
Test under Mask	zero	mixed	–	one
Translate and Test	zero	incomplete	complete	–

Input/Output Operations

	0	1	2	3
Halt I/O	interruption pending	CSW stored	halted	not oper
Start I/O	started	CSW stored	busy	not oper
Test I/O	available	CSW stored	busy	not oper
Test Channel	available	interruption pending	burst mode	not oper

Miscellaneous Operations

	0	1	2	3
Test and Set	zero	one	--	--
Load Real Address (Mod. 67)	successful	segment unavailable	page unavailable	--

NOTES

23

Figure 2.4 Reference Data Card (panels 7 and 8)

CODES FOR PROGRAM INTERRUPTION

Interruption Code Dec	Hex	Program Interruption Cause	Interruption Code Dec	Hex	Program Interruption Cause
1	0001	Operation	10	000A	Decimal overflow
2	0002	Privileged operation	11	000B	Decimal divide
3	0003	Execute	12	000C	Exponent overflow
4	0004	Protection	13	000D	Exponent underflow
5	0005	Addressing	14	000E	Significance
6	0006	Specification	15	000F	Floating-point divide
7	0007	Data	16 *	0010	Segment translation
8	0008	Fixed-point overflow	17 *	0011	Page translation
9	0009	Fixed-point divide			

*Model 67

HEXADECIMAL AND DECIMAL CONVERSION

From hex: locate each hex digit in its corresponding column position and note the decimal equivalents. Add these to obtain the decimal value.

From decimal: (1) locate the largest decimal value in the table that will fit into the decimal number to be converted, and (2) note its hex equivalent and hex column position. (3) Find the decimal remainder. Repeat the process on this and subsequent remainders.

Note: Decimal, hexadecimal, (and binary) equivalents of all numbers from 0 to 255 are listed on panels 11-14.

N **M** **L**

HEXADECIMAL COLUMNS

	6		5		4		3		2		1
HEX	= DEC	HEX	= DEC	HEX	= DEC	HEX	= DEC	HEX	= DEC	HEX	= DEC
0	0	0	0	0	0	0	0	0	0	0	0
1	1,048,576	1	65,536	1	4,096	1	256	1	16	1	1
2	2,097,152	2	131,072	2	8,192	2	512	2	32	2	2
3	3,145,728	3	196,608	3	12,288	3	768	3	48	3	3
4	4,194,304	4	262,144	4	16,384	4	1,024	4	64	4	4
5	5,242,880	5	327,680	5	20,480	5	1,280	5	80	5	5
6	6,291,456	6	393,216	6	24,576	6	1,536	6	96	6	6
7	7,340,032	7	458,752	7	28,672	7	1,792	7	112	7	7
8	8,388,608	8	524,288	8	32,768	8	2,048	8	128	8	8
9	9,437,184	9	589,824	9	36,864	9	2,304	9	144	9	9
A	10,485,760	A	655,360	A	40,960	A	2,560	A	160	A	10
B	11,534,336	B	720,896	B	45,056	B	2,816	B	176	B	11
C	12,582,912	C	786,432	C	49,152	C	3,072	C	192	C	12
D	13,631,488	D	851,968	D	53,248	D	3,328	D	208	D	13
E	14,680,064	E	917,504	E	57,344	E	3,584	E	224	E	14
F	15,728,640	F	983,040	F	61,440	F	3,840	F	240	F	15
0 1 2 3		4 5 6 7		0 1 2 3		4 5 6 7		0 1 2 3		4 5 6 7	
BYTE				BYTE				BYTE			

POWERS OF 2

2^n	n
256	8
512	9
1 024	10
2 048	11
4 096	12
8 192	13
16 384	14
32 768	15
65 536	16
131 072	17
262 144	18
524 288	19
1 048 576	20
2 097 152	21
4 194 304	22
8 388 608	23
16 777 216	24

POWERS OF 16

	16^n	n
$2^0 = 16^0$	1	0
$2^4 = 16^1$	16	1
$2^8 = 16^2$	256	2
$2^{12} = 16^3$	4 096	3
$2^{16} = 16^4$	65 536	4
$2^{20} = 16^5$	1 048 576	5
$2^{24} = 16^6$	16 777 216	6
$2^{28} = 16^7$	268 435 456	7
$2^{32} = 16^8$	4 294 967 296	8
$2^{36} = 16^9$	68 719 476 736	9
$2^{40} = 16^{10}$	1 099 511 627 776	10
$2^{44} = 16^{11}$	17 592 186 044 416	11
$2^{48} = 16^{12}$	281 474 976 710 656	12
$2^{52} = 16^{13}$	4 503 599 627 370 496	13
$2^{56} = 16^{14}$	72 057 594 037 927 936	14
$2^{60} = 16^{15}$	1 152 921 504 606 846 976	15

PROGRAM STATUS WORD

System Mask*	Key	AMWP*	Interruption Code
0 7	8 11	12 15	16 23	24 31

ILC	CC	Program Mask*	Instruction Address
32 34 36 39			40 47	48 55	56 63
33 35			

0 Channel 0 mask	13 Machine check mask (M)
1 Channel 1 mask	14 Wait state (W)
2 Channel 2 mask	15 Problem state (P)
3 Channel 3 mask	32-33 Instruction length code (ILC)
4 Channel 4 mask	34-35 Condition code (CC)
5 Channel 5 mask	36 Fixed-point overflow mask
6 Mask for channel 6 and up	37 Decimal overflow mask
7 External mask	38 Exponent underflow mask
12 ASCII-8 mode (A)	39 Significance mask

*A one-bit equals on, and permits an interrupt.

CHANNEL ADDRESS WORD

Key	0000	Command Address
0 3	4 7	8 15	16 23	24 31

CHANNEL COMMAND WORD

Command Code	Data Address
0 7	8 15	16 23	24 31

Flags	000	////	Byte Count
32 36	37 39	40 47	48 55	56 63

CD—bit 32 (80) causes use of address portion of next CCW.
CC—bit 33 (40) causes use of command code and data address of next CCW.
SLI—bit 34 (20) causes suppression of possible incorrect length indication.
Skip—bit 35 (10) suppresses transfer of information to main storage.
PCI—bit 36 (08) causes a channel Program Controlled Interruption.

CHANNEL STATUS WORD

Key	0000	Command Address
0 3	4 7	8 15	16 23	24 31

Status	Byte Count
32 39	40 47	48 55	56 63

32 (8000) Attention	40 (0080) Program-controlled interruption
33 (4000) Status modifier	41 (0040) Incorrect length
34 (2000) Control unit end	42 (0020) Program check
35 (1000) Busy	43 (0010) Protection check
36 (0800) Channel end	44 (0008) Channel data check
37 (0400) Device end	45 (0004) Channel control check
38 (0200) Unit check	46 (0002) Interface control check
39 (0100) Unit exception	47 (0001) Chaining check

Byte Count: bits 48-63 form the residual count for the last CCW used.

Comments about this card may be sent to the Technical Publications Department at the White Plains address below. All comments and suggestions become the property of IBM.

IBM ®

International Business Machines Corporation
Data Processing Division
1133 Westchester Ave., White Plains, N.Y. 10604
(U.S.A. only)

IBM World Trade Corporation
821 United Nations Plaza, New York, New York 10017
(International)

Printed in U.S.A. GX20-1703-9

Figure 2.5 Reference Data Card (panels 9 and 10)

PERMANENT STORAGE ASSIGNMENTS ⑨

Dec	Hex	Length	Purpose
0	0	double word	Initial program loading PSW
8	8	double word	Initial program loading CCW1
16	10	double word	Initial program loading CCW2
24	18	double word	External old PSW
32	20	double word	Supervisor Call old PSW
40	28	double word	Program old PSW
48	30	double word	Machine-check old PSW
56	38	double word	Input/output old PSW
64	40	double word	Channel status word
72	48	word	Channel address word
76	4C	word	Unused
80	50	word	Timer (uses bytes 50, 51 & 52)
84	54	word	Unused
88	58	double word	External new PSW
96	60	double word	Supervisor Call new PSW
104	68	double word	Program new PSW
112	70	double word	Machine-check new PSW
120	78	double word	Input/output new PSW
128	80	(1)	Diagnostic scan-out area

(1) The size of the diagnostic scan-out area depends on the particular model and I/O channels; for models 30 through 75, maximum size is 256 bytes.

CHANNEL COMMANDS

2314, 2311/2321 DASD
Source: GA26-3599, GA26-5988

Command for CCW‡		Count	MT Off	MT On†
Control	Seek	6	07	
	Seek Cylinder	6	0B	
	Seek Head	6	1B	
	Set File Mask	1	1F	
	Space Count	3	0F	
	Recalibrate (Note 1)	Not zero	13	
	Restore (2321 only)	Not zero	17	
Sense	Sense I/O	6	04	
	Release Device } (Note 2)	6	94	
	Reserve Device	6	B4	
Search	Home Address EQ	4 (usually)	39	B9
	Identifier EQ	5 (usually)	31	B1
	Identifier HI	5 (usually)	51	D1
	Identifier EQ or HI	5 (usually)	71	F1
	Key EQ	1 to 255	29	A9
	Key HI	1 to 255	49	C9
	Key EQ or HI	1 to 255	69	E9
	Key & Data EQ		2D	AD
	Key & Data HI	Number	4D	CD
	Key & Data EQ or HI	of bytes	6D	ED
Continue	Search EQ	in search	25	A5
Scan	Search HI	argument,	45	C5
	Search HI or EQ	including	65	E5
	Set Status Modifier*	mask bytes.	35	B5
	Set Status Modifier*	(Special	75	F5
	No Status Modifier	feature.)	55	D5
Read	Home Address	5	1A	9A
	Count	8	12	92
	Record 0		16	96
	Data	Number	06	86
	Key & Data	of bytes	0E	8E
	Count, Key & Data	transferred	1E	9E
	IPL		02	
Write	Home Address	5 (usually)	19	
	Record 0	8+KL+DL of R0	15	
	Count, Key & Data	8+KL+DL	1D	
	Special Count, Key & Data	8+KL+DL	01	
	Data	DL	05	
	Key & Data	KL+DL	0D	
	Erase	8+KL+DL	11	

1. For 2311 or 2314 only.
2. Two-channel switch required except for a 2314/2844 combination.
*Sense byte determines command used.
†Code same as MT Off except as listed.
‡See also standard commands, panel 10.

CHANNEL COMMANDS (Contd) ⑩

Standard Command Code Assignments (CCW bits 0-7) for I/O Operations

xxxx 0000	Invalid	†††† ††01	Write
†††† 0100	Sense	†††† ††10	Read
xxxx 1000	Transfer in Channel	†††† ††11	Control
†††† 1100	Read Backward	0000 0011	Control No Operation

x—Bit ignored.   †Modifier bit for specific type of I/O device

1052 CONSOLE
Source: GA22-6877

Read Inquiry BCD	0A	Sense	04
Write BCD, Auto Carrier Return	09	Alarm	0B
Write BCD, No Carrier Return	01		

2540 CARD READ PUNCH
Source: GA24-3312

Command	Type	Code	Bit	Meanings
Read, Feed, Select Stacker	AA	SSD0 0010	SS	Stacker
Read	AB	11D0 0010	00	R1 or P1
Read, Feed (1400 Compatibility*)	—	11D1 0010	01	R2 or P2
Feed, Select Stacker	BA	SS10 0011	10	RP3
PFR* Write, Feed, Select Stacker	BA	SSD0 1001	D	Data Mode
Write, Feed, Select Stacker	BB	SSD0 0001	0	1-EBCDIC
Sense	—	0000 0100	1	2-Col. binary*

1442-N1 CARD READ PUNCH
Source: GA21-9025

Write	01	Read	02
Write, Select Stacker 2	41	Read, Select Stacker 2	42
Write, Feed	81	Read Card Image	22
Write, Feed, Select Stacker 2	C1	Read Card Image, Sel Stkr 2	62
Write Card Image*	21	Read 1442 Compatibility*	12
Write Card Image, Sel Stkr 2	61	Read 1442 Compat, Sel Stkr 2	52
Write Card Image, Feed	A1	Control Feed	83
Write Card Image, Feed, Sel Stkr 2	E1	Control Feed, Select Stkr 2	C3
Sense	04	Control Select Stacker 2	43

1403, 1443 PRINTERS
Source: GA24-3312, GA24-3120

	After Write	Immed		
Skip to Channel 1	89	8B	Diagnostic Data Read	02
Skip to Channel 2	91	93	Diagnostic Check Read	06
Skip to Channel 3	99	9B	UCS Gate*	EB
Skip to Channel 4	A1	A3	1403 only { UCS Load (No Folding)*	FB
Skip to Channel 5	A9	AB	UCS Load (Folding)*	F3
Skip to Channel 6	B1	B3	Block Data Check*	73
Skip to Channel 7	B9	BB	Reset Block Data Check*	7B
Skip to Channel 8	C1	C3	Write without Spacing	01
Skip to Channel 9	C9	CB	Sense	04
Skip to Channel 10	D1	D3		After Write	Immed
Skip to Channel 11	D9	DB	Space 1 Line	09	0B
Skip to Channel 12	E1	E3	Space 2 Lines	11	13
			Space 3 Lines	19	1B

2400-SERIES MAGNETIC TAPE

Note: Refer to GA22-6866 for operation of specific models, special features required, mode resets, and precedence of commands.

		Density	Parity	DC	Trans	Cmd
Sense	04					
Read Backward	0C				on { off	13
Write	01		odd	off { off	33
Read	02	200		{ on	3B
Rewind (REW)	07		even	off { off	23
Rewind-Unload (RUN)	0F			{ on	2B
Erase Gap (ERG)	17			on { off	53
Write Tape Mark (WTM)	1F		odd	off { off	73
Backspace Block (BSB)	27	556		{ on	7B
Backspace File (BSF)	2F		even	off { off	63
Forward Space Block (FSB)	37			{ on	6B
Forward Space File (FSF)	3F			on { off	93
Request Track in Error (TIE)	1B		odd	off { off	B3
Diagnostic Mode Set	0B	800		{ on	BB
Set Mode 2 (9-track), 1600 bpi	C3		even	off { off	A3
Set Mode 2 (9-track), 800 bpi	CB			{ on	AB

(7-track, Set Mode 1)

*Special feature required.

Figure 2.6 Reference Data Card (panels 11 and 12)

O P Q ⑪

Decimal	Hexadecimal	Instruction Mnemonic (RR Format)	Graphic & Control Symbols (5) BCDIC	EBCDIC	7-Track Tape BCDIC	Punched Card Code	System/360 8-bit Code
0	00			NUL		12-0-1-8-9	0000 0000
1	01			SOH		12-1-9	0000 0001
2	02			STX		12-2-9	0000 0010
3	03			ETX		12-3-9	0000 0011
4	04	SPM		PF		12-4-9	0000 0100
5	05	BALR		HT		12-5-9	0000 0101
6	06	BCTR		LC		12-6-9	0000 0110
7	07	BCR		DEL		12-7-9	0000 0111
8	08	SSK				12-8-9	0000 1000
9	09	ISK				12-1-8-9	0000 1001
10	0A	SVC		SMM		12-2-8-9	0000 1010
11	0B			VT		12-3-8-9	0000 1011
12	0C			FF		12-4-8-9	0000 1100
13	0D	BASR(4)		CR		12-5-8-9	0000 1101
14	0E			SO		12-6-8-9	0000 1110
15	0F			SI		12-7-8-9	0000 1111
16	10	LPR		DLE		12-11-1-8-9	0001 0000
17	11	LNR		DC1		11-1-9	0001 0001
18	12	LTR		DC2		11-2-9	0001 0010
19	13	LCR		TM		11-3-9	0001 0011
20	14	NR		RES		11-4-9	0001 0100
21	15	CLR		NL		11-5-9	0001 0101
22	16	OR		BS		11-6-9	0001 0110
23	17	XR		IL		11-7-9	0001 0111
24	18	LR		CAN		11-8-9	0001 1000
25	19	CR		EM		11-1-8-9	0001 1001
26	1A	AR		CC		11-2-8-9	0001 1010
27	1B	SR		CU1		11-3-8-9	0001 1011
28	1C	MR		IFS		11-4-8-9	0001 1100
29	1D	DR		IGS		11-5-8-9	0001 1101
30	1E	ALR		IRS		11-6-8-9	0001 1110
31	1F	SLR		IUS		11-7-8-9	0001 1111
32	20	LPDR		DS		11-0-1-8-9	0010 0000
33	21	LNDR		SOS		0-1-9	0010 0001
34	22	LTDR		FS		0-2-9	0010 0010
35	23	LCDR				0-3-9	0010 0011
36	24	HDR		BYP		0-4-9	0010 0100
37	25	LRDR		LF		0-5-9	0010 0101
38	26	MXR		ETB		0-6-9	0010 0110
39	27	MXDR		ESC		0-7-9	0010 0111
40	28	LDR				0-8-9	0010 1000
41	29	CDR				0-1-8-9	0010 1001
42	2A	ADR		SM		0-2-8-9	0010 1010
43	2B	SDR		CU2		0-3-8-9	0010 1011
44	2C	MDR				0-4-8-9	0010 1100
45	2D	DDR		ENQ		0-5-8-9	0010 1101
46	2E	AWR		ACK		0-6-8-9	0010 1110
47	2F	SWR		BEL		0-7-8-9	0010 1111
48	30	LPER				12-11-0-1-8-9	0011 0000
49	31	LNER				1-9	0011 0001
50	32	LTER		SYN		2-9	0011 0010
51	33	LCER				3-9	0011 0011
52	34	HER		PN		4-9	0011 0100
53	35	LRER		RS		5-9	0011 0101
54	36	AXR		UC		6-9	0011 0110
55	37	SXR		EOT		7-9	0011 0111
56	38	LER				8-9	0011 1000
57	39	CER				1-8-9	0011 1001
58	3A	AER				2-8-9	0011 1010
59	3B	SER		CU3		3-8-9	0011 1011
60	3C	MER		DC4		4-8-9	0011 1100
61	3D	DER		NAK		5-8-9	0011 1101
62	3E	AUR				6-8-9	0011 1110
63	3F	SUR		SUB		7-8-9	0011 1111

R ⑫

Decimal	Hexadecimal	Instruction Mnemonic (RX Format)	Graphic & Control Symbols (5) BCDIC	EBCDIC	7-Track Tape BCDIC (1)	Punched Card Code	System/360 8-bit Code
64	40	STH		SP	(2)	no punches	0100 0000
65	41	LA				12-0-1-9	0100 0001
66	42	STC				12-0-2-9	0100 0010
67	43	IC				12-0-3-9	0100 0011
68	44	EX				12-0-4-9	0100 0100
69	45	BAL				12-0-5-9	0100 0101
70	46	BCT				12-0-6-9	0100 0110
71	47	BC				12-0-7-9	0100 0111
72	48	LH				12-0-8-9	0100 1000
73	49	CH				12-1-8	0100 1001
74	4A	AH		¢		12-2-8	0100 1010
75	4B	SH	.	.	BA8 21	12-3-8	0100 1011
76	4C	MH	⌷	<	BA84	12-4-8	0100 1100
77	4D	BAS(4)	[	(	BA84 1	12-5-8	0100 1101
78	4E	CVD	<	+	BA842	12-6-8	0100 1110
79	4F	CVB	‡	|	BA8421	12-7-8	0100 1111
80	50	ST	& +	&	BA	12	0101 0000
81	51					12-11-1-9	0101 0001
82	52					12-11-2-9	0101 0010
83	53					12-11-3-9	0101 0011
84	54	N				12-11-4-9	0101 0100
85	55	CL				12-11-5-9	0101 0101
86	56	O				12-11-6-9	0101 0110
87	57	X				12-11-7-9	0101 0111
88	58	L				12-11-8-9	0101 1000
89	59	C				11-1-8	0101 1001
90	5A	A		!		11-2-8	0101 1010
91	5B	S	$	$	B 8 21	11-3-8	0101 1011
92	5C	M	°	*	B 84	11-4-8	0101 1100
93	5D	D	]	)	B 84 1	11-5-8	0101 1101
94	5E	AL	;	;	B 842	11-6-8	0101 1110
95	5F	SL	Δ	¬	B 8421	11-7-8	0101 1111
96	60	STD	-	-	B	11	0110 0000
97	61		/	/	A 1	0-1	0110 0001
98	62					11-0-2-9	0110 0010
99	63					11-0-3-9	0110 0011
100	64					11-0-4-9	0110 0100
101	65					11-0-5-9	0110 0101
102	66					11-0-6-9	0110 0110
103	67	MXD				11-0-7-9	0110 0111
104	68	LD				11-0-8-9	0110 1000
105	69	CD				0-1-8	0110 1001
106	6A	AD		|		12-11	0110 1010
107	6B	SD	,	,	A8 21	0-3-8	0110 1011
108	6C	MD	% (	%	A84	0-4-8	0110 1100
109	6D	DD	ɣ	_	A84 1	0-5-8	0110 1101
110	6E	AW	\\	>	A842	0-6-8	0110 1110
111	6F	SW	⧻	?	A8421	0-7-8	0110 1111
112	70	STE				12-11-0	0111 0000
113	71					12-11-0-1-9	0111 0001
114	72					12-11-0-2-9	0111 0010
115	73					12-11-0-3-9	0111 0011
116	74					12-11-0-4-9	0111 0100
117	75					12-11-0-5-9	0111 0101
118	76					12-11-0-6-9	0111 0110
119	77					12-11-0-7-9	0111 0111
120	78	LE				12-11-0-8-9	0111 1000
121	79	CE	`			1-8	0111 1001
122	7A	AE	ƀ	:	A	2-8	0111 1010
123	7B	SE	# =	#	8 21	3-8	0111 1011
124	7C	ME	@ '	@	84	4-8	0111 1100
125	7D	DE	:	'	84 1	5-8	0111 1101
126	7E	AU	>	=	842	6-8	0111 1110
127	7F	SU	√	"	8421	7-8	0111 1111

NOTES FOR PANELS 11-14

1. Add C (check bit) for odd or even parity as needed, except as noted
2. For even parity use CA
3. Decimal feature
4. Model 67
5. EBCDIC graphics shown are standard bit pattern assignments. For specific print train/chain see printer manual.

RR FORMAT

Op Code	R₁	R₂

0   78 1112 15

RX FORMAT

Op Code	R₁	X₂	B₂	D₂

0   78 1112 1516 1920   31

R1, D2 (X2, B2) or R1, S2 (X2)
R1, D2 (0, B2) or R1, S2

Figure 2.7 Reference Data Card (panels 13 and 14)

Panel 13 — T

Decimal	Hexadecimal	Instruction Mnemonic (Var. Formats)	Graphic & Control Symbols (5) BCDIC	EBCDIC	7-Track Tape BCDIC	Punched Card Code	System/360 8-bit Code
128	80	SSM				12-0-1-8	1000 0000
129	81			a		12-0-1	1000 0001
130	82	LPSW		b		12-0-2	1000 0010
131	83	(Diagnose)		c		12-0-3	1000 0011
132	84	WRD		d		12-0-4	1000 0100
133	85	RDD		e		12-0-5	1000 0101
134	86	BXH		f		12-0-6	1000 0110
135	87	BXLE		g		12-0-7	1000 0111
136	88	SRL		h		12-0-8	1000 1000
137	89	SLL		i		12-0-9	1000 1001
138	8A	SRA				12-0-2-8	1000 1010
139	8B	SLA				12-0-3-8	1000 1011
140	8C	SRDL				12-0-4-8	1000 1100
141	8D	SLDL				12-0-5-8	1000 1101
142	8E	SRDA				12-0-6-8	1000 1110
143	8F	SLDA				12-0-7-8	1000 1111
144	90	STM				12-11-1-8	1001 0000
145	91	TM		j		12-11-1	1001 0001
146	92	MVI		k		12-11-2	1001 0010
147	93	TS		l		12-11-3	1001 0011
148	94	NI		m		12-11-4	1001 0100
149	95	CLI		n		12-11-5	1001 0101
150	96	OI		o		12-11-6	1001 0110
151	97	XI		p		12-11-7	1001 0111
152	98	LM		q		12-11-8	1001 1000
153	99			r		12-11-9	1001 1001
154	9A					12-11-2-8	1001 1010
155	9B					12-11-3-8	1001 1011
156	9C	SIO				12-11-4-8	1001 1100
157	9D	TIO				12-11-5-8	1001 1101
158	9E	HIO				12-11-6-8	1001 1110
159	9F	TCH				12-11-7-8	1001 1111
160	A0					11-0-1-8	1010 0000
161	A1			~		11-0-1	1010 0001
162	A2			s		11-0-2	1010 0010
163	A3			t		11-0-3	1010 0011
164	A4			u		11-0-4	1010 0100
165	A5			v		11-0-5	1010 0101
166	A6			w		11-0-6	1010 0110
167	A7			x		11-0-7	1010 0111
168	A8			y		11-0-8	1010 1000
169	A9			z		11-0-9	1010 1001
170	AA					11-0-2-8	1010 1010
171	AB					11-0-3-8	1010 1011
172	AC					11-0-4-8	1010 1100
173	AD					11-0-5-8	1010 1101
174	AE					11-0-6-8	1010 1110
175	AF					11-0-7-8	1010 1111
176	B0	STMC (4)				12-11-0-1-8	1011 0000
177	B1	LRA (4)				12-11-0-1	1011 0001
178	B2					12-11-0-2	1011 0010
179	B3					12-11-0-3	1011 0011
180	B4					12-11-0-4	1011 0100
181	B5					12-11-0-5	1011 0101
182	B6					12-11-0-6	1011 0110
183	B7					12-11-0-7	1011 0111
184	B8	LMC (4)				12-11-0-8	1011 1000
185	B9					12-11-0-9	1011 1001
186	BA					12-11-0-2-8	1011 1010
187	BB					12-11-0-3-8	1011 1011
188	BC					12-11-0-4-8	1011 1100
189	BD					12-11-0-5-8	1011 1101
190	BE					12-11-0-6-8	1011 1110
191	BF					12-11-0-7-8	1011 1111

Panel 14 — U

Decimal	Hexadecimal	Instruction Mnemonic (SS Format)	Graphic & Control Symbols (5) BCDIC	EBCDIC	7-Track Tape BCDIC (1)	Punched Card Code	System/360 8-bit Code
192	C0		?	{	B A 8 2	12-0	1100 0000
193	C1		A	A	B A 1	12-1	1100 0001
194	C2		B	B	B A 2	12-2	1100 0010
195	C3		C	C	B A 2 1	12-3	1100 0011
196	C4		D	D	B A 4	12-4	1100 0100
197	C5		E	E	B A 4 1	12-5	1100 0101
198	C6		F	F	B A 4 2	12-6	1100 0110
199	C7		G	G	B A 4 2 1	12-7	1100 0111
200	C8		H	H	B A 8	12-8	1100 1000
201	C9		I	I	B A 8 1	12-9	1100 1001
202	CA					12-0-2-8-9	1100 1010
203	CB					12-0-3-8-9	1100 1011
204	CC		♪			12-0-4-8-9	1100 1100
205	CD					12-0-5-8-9	1100 1101
206	CE		Ч			12-0-6-8-9	1100 1110
207	CF					12-0-7-8-9	1100 1111
208	D0		!	}	B 8 2	11-0	1101 0000
209	D1	MVN	J	J	B 1	11-1	1101 0001
210	D2	MVC	K	K	B 2	11-2	1101 0010
211	D3	MVZ	L	L	B 2 1	11-3	1101 0011
212	D4	NC	M	M	B 4	11-4	1101 0100
213	D5	CLC	N	N	B 4 1	11-5	1101 0101
214	D6	OC	O	O	B 4 2	11-6	1101 0110
215	D7	XC	P	P	B 4 2 1	11-7	1101 0111
216	D8		Q	Q	B 8	11-8	1101 1000
217	D9		R	R	B 8 1	11-9	1101 1001
218	DA					12-11-2-8-9	1101 1010
219	DB					12-11-3-8-9	1101 1011
220	DC	TR				12-11-4-8-9	1101 1100
221	DD	TRT				12-11-5-8-9	1101 1101
222	DE	ED (3)				12-11-6-8-9	1101 1110
223	DF	EDMK (3)				12-11-7-8-9	1101 1111
224	E0		∓	\	A 8 2	0-2-8	1110 0000
225	E1					11-0-1-9	1110 0001
226	E2		S	S	A 2	0-2	1110 0010
227	E3		T	T	A 2 1	0-3	1110 0011
228	E4		U	U	A 4	0-4	1110 0100
229	E5		V	V	A 4 1	0-5	1110 0101
230	E6		W	W	A 4 2	0-6	1110 0110
231	E7		X	X	A 4 2 1	0-7	1110 0111
232	E8		Y	Y	A 8	0-8	1110 1000
233	E9		Z	Z	A 8 1	0-9	1110 1001
234	EA					11-0-2-8-9	1110 1010
235	EB					11-0-3-8-9	1110 1011
236	EC		н			11-0-4-8-9	1110 1100
237	ED					11-0-5-8-9	1110 1101
238	EE					11-0-6-8-9	1110 1110
239	EF					11-0-7-8-9	1110 1111
240	F0		0	0	8 2	0	1111 0000
241	F1	MVO	1	1	1	1	1111 0001
242	F2	PACK	2	2	2	2	1111 0010
243	F3	UNPK	3	3	2 1	3	1111 0011
244	F4		4	4	4	4	1111 0100
245	F5		5	5	4 1	5	1111 0101
246	F6		6	6	4 2	6	1111 0110
247	F7		7	7	4 2 1	7	1111 0111
248	F8	ZAP (3)	8	8	8	8	1111 1000
249	F9	CP (3)	9	9	8 1	9	1111 1001
250	FA	AP (3)		|		12-11-0-2-8-9	1111 1010
251	FB	SP (3)				12-11-0-3-8-9	1111 1011
252	FC	MP (3)				12-11-0-4-8-9	1111 1100
253	FD	DP (3)				12-11-0-5-8-9	1111 1101
254	FE					12-11-0-6-8-9	1111 1110
255	FF					12-11-0-7-8-9	1111 1111

RS FORMAT

Op Code	R1	R3	B2	D2

0 7 8 11 12 15 16 19 20 31

R1, R3, D2 (B2) or R1, R3, S2: BXH, BXLE, LM, LMC, STM, STMC
R1, D2 (B2) or R1, S2: All shift instructions

SI FORMAT

OP Code	I2	B1	D1

0 7 8 15 16 19 20 31

D1 (B1) or S1: LPSW, SSM, HIO, SIO, TIO, TCH, TS
D1 (B1), I2 or S1, I2: MVI, CLI, NI, OI, XI, TM, WRD, RDD

SS FORMAT

Op Code	L1	L2	B1	D1	B2	D2

0 7 8 11 12 15 16 19 20 31 32 35 36 47

D1 (L, B1), D2 (B2) or S1 (L), S2: { NC, OC, XC, CLC, MVC, MVN, MVZ, TR, TRT, ED, EDMK }
D1 (L1, B1), D2 (L2, B2) or S1 (L1), S2 (L2): { PACK, UNPK, MVO, AP, CP, DP, MP, SP, ZAP }

and the complete series of channel commands are also provided. Finally, a complete list of mnemonic codes for assembler instructions, BCDIC and EBCDIC symbols, punch card code representation, and respective 8-bit codes are depicted.

A programmer need not understand all aspects of the Reference Data Card to effectively debug storage dumps. Those portions of the card vital to debugging procedures will be expanded upon and frequently referenced throughout the text.

2. Machine Instructions and Formats

Panels 1 and 2 of the Reference Data Card display machine instructions and their format. (See Figure 2.1.) Reference Data Card panel numbers are printed in the upper right-hand corner. When it is necessary to locate and breakdown machine instructions as they reside in main storage, it is this instruction table which will be used.

The name of each machine instruction is located in the left-hand column. See letter 'A'. The listing, which continues onto a second panel, depicts all operations allowed by machine language conventions and indicates a mnemonic code for each function to be performed. See letter 'B'. These English-like operation codes, used when programming in Assembly Language, provide the programmer with an abbreviated name for each instruction. The middle column depicts the actual Operation Code, or Op Code, as it exists in machine form. See letter 'C'. When a programmer locates a machine instruction residing in main storage, the first byte (two hexadecimal characters) of that instruction will always be the Op Code. Utilizing the Reference Data Card, the Op Code can then be related back to the appropriate mnemonic code and machine instruction name to determine the function performed. In addition, an abbreviated format of the complete machine instruction can be determined from the fourth column. See letter 'D'. Having determined instruction format, a detailed breakdown of the instruction can be made. Finally, Assembly Language operands and their required coding sequence can be determined from the fifth column. See letter 'E'. The operands are depicted in the actual form in which they should be coded by the programmer -- not as they necessarily exist in main storage.

The relationship of the Op Code and operands to main storage will be discussed next. Detail machine formats can be found at the bottom of panel 2 of the Reference Data Card. See letter 'F'. The five basic machine formats consist of RR for Register To Register, RX for Register To Index, RS for Register To Storage, SI for Storage Immediate, and SS for Storage To Storage. These formats are the abbreviated form described in the fourth column at letter 'D'. Machine formats vary in length and are depicted in terms of a first halfword, second halfword, and third halfword. On System 360/370:

1 Word = 4 Bytes = 32 Bits   or   1 Byte = 8 Bits

A word is represented in print form by 8 hexadecimal characters.

As can be seen, machine instructions consist of two main parts -- an Op Code and associated operands. See letter 'G'. Note that the Op Code is always located in the left-most byte. Two or three operands which vary in length exist for each Op Code, depending upon the machine format utilized. The field descriptors consist of R for Register, X for Index, B for Base, D for Displacement, and L for Length. The suffixes 1, 2, and 3 relate to the first, second, and third operands, respectively.

In the case of RR Format, the two operand values are located at addresses specified by two register numbers stored in R1 and R2 of the machine instruction. As an example, an Add Instruction in RR Format may reside in main storage as follows:

1 A 6 8

Op Code 1A stands for mnemonic AR, or an Add Instruction. The value stored in Register 8 is to be added to the value stored in Register 6. With this format, the sum is stored in Register 6, overlaying its contents.

RX Format is similar in principle to RR and other formats, except that in order to determine the address of the value of the second operand, the contents of three locations must be added. See letter 'H'. The contents of the specified Index Register (X2) must be added to the contents of the specified Base Register (B2), this total then being added

29

to the Displacement (D2) which is actually located in the machine instruction itself. This final total provides the address of the second operand.

For RS Format, a third operand is provided in terms of a register number. See letter 'I'. The address of the second operand is calculated by adding the contents of the specified Base Register to the Displacement.

In SI Format, the value of an immediate operand actually located in the machine instruction itself. See letter 'J'. The address of the first operand is calculated by adding the contents of the Base Register to the Displacement.

With SS Format, the length of each operand is specified in the machine instruction. In addition, two optional forms exist. See letter 'K'. Although in all previous formats, the length of the Index and Base Register values has been assumed to be four bytes, or occasionally two; with SS Format, operand value length may vary substantially. Depending upon which option is utilized, the length of Operands 1 and 2 are represented either individually, or as a single length which applies to both of the operands. The starting address of both operands is calculated by adding the contents of the Base Register to the Displacement. Once this calculation is located in main storage, the appropriate length can be marked off.

The breakdown and analysis of machine instructions is covered in Chapter 6. This portion of the Reference Data Card will then be referred to in detail.

3. Hexadecimal Decimal Conversion Table

The Hexadecimal Decimal Conversion Table is located in the middle of panel 7 on the Reference Data Card. See Figure 2.4. This table is utilized when converting a value from hexadecimal to decimal or vice versa. As such it is a handy reference, utilized quite frequently in the analysis of storage dumps.

The Hexadecimal Decimal Conversion Table consists of six columns from minor (right-hand) to major (left-hand), each being further subdivided into a hexadecimal column indicated by the abbreviation HEX

and a decimal column indicated by the abbreviation DEC. See letter
'L'. Column 1 depicts a basic comparison of the Hexadecimal Numbering System with the Decimal Numbering System. As shown, a Hexadecimal zero equals a Decimal zero. Continuing down the column, Hexadecimal F equals Decimal 15. Moving to the second column, it can be
seen that a Hexadecimal 1 in the second (next to minor) position of
a hexadecimal number is equal to a Decimal 16. See letter 'M'. Continuing down the column, a Hexadecimal F in the second position
equals a Decimal 240. As an example, Hexadecimal FB can be converted to Decimal as follows:

        Hexadecimal: F   B
        Decimal: 240 + 11 = 251

Hexadecimal FB is equal to Decimal 251. Moving all the way to
the left of the Hexadecimal Decimal Conversion Table, a Hexadecimal
F in the major (sixth) position equals Decimal 15,728,640 and so on.
See letter 'N'.

Likewise, the opposite conversion from Decimal to Hexadecimal
can be made. It will be necessary to discuss both conversions in
more detail later in this chapter.

4. Data Codes

The third and last portion of the Reference Data Card accessed
when debugging storage dumps is the data codes area depicted on
panels 11 through 14. See Figures 2.6 through 2.7.

The two left-hand columns depict the decimal numbers from 0 to
255 and their hexadecimal equivalent from 00 to FF. See Figure 2.6,
letter 'O'. A valid mnemonic code is represented, whenever appropiate, along with graphic and control symbols for the Binary Coded
Decimal Interchange Code (BCDIC) and the Extended Binary Coded Decimal Interchange Code (EBCDIC). See letter 'P'. BCDIC and EBCDIC
are two types of data coding systems.

Of particular interest to a programmer debugging a storage dump
is the punched card code. See letter 'Q'. Punched card code is
represented in Character Format as discussed in Chapter 1. This

type of data representation is sometimes referred to as External Decimal, Zoned Decimal, and Unpacked Format. The punched card column provides a programmer with the punched card code for a character string located in storage provided it is described in Character Format. For example, a Hexadecimal 40 residing in main storage and programmer defined in Character Format is found to equal a blank (no punches) in the punched card code. See letter 'R'. Similarly, a Hexadecimal F1 residing in core and programmer defined as External Decimal is equal to a Decimal 1 in the punched card code. See Figure 2.7, letter 'S'. Alpha and special characters defined in Character Format are depicted. See letter 'T'. Equivalent 8-bit codes are also provided. See letter 'U'.

This area of the Reference Data Card will be utilized quite frequently by programmers wishing to interpret values located in the main storage area of a dump.

B. NUMBER SYSTEMS

1. Comparisons

The methods used to store data within main storage does not readily lend itself to the Decimal Numbering System. All information is represented in Binary; that is, via two codes -- either a 0 or a 1. The Binary Numbering System is the most basic of all forms of data representation. Storage dumps, however, are printed utilizing the Hexadecimal Numbering System, which consists of 16 codes from 0 to F. If storage dumps were printed in Binary, the dump would virtually be impossible to interpret in a reasonable length of time. The Hexadecimal Numbering System and the Binary Numbering System actually complement each other. Binary numbers can easily be converted to hexadecimal, and vice versa.

Basically, the only difference between numbering systems of any kind is the value of the Base of that numbering system, which is equal to the total number of allowable codes. The Binary Numbering System has a Base of 2 -- two codes, either a 0 or a 1. The Decimal

Numbering System consists of Base 10 -- ten codes, from 0 to 9. The
Hexadecimal Numbering System Base equals 16 -- sixteen codes, from
0 to F.

The four basic types of arithmetic manipulation (that is, addition, subtraction, multiplication, and division) can be performed
quite readily in any numbering system; however, only addition and
subtraction are actually necessary for dump analysis purposes. In
the Decimal Numbering System, Base 10 is the factor for 'borrowing'
and 'carrying' from one column to another. In the Hexadecimal System, a Base of 16 is utilized, and in Binary, the Base 2 is used for
this purpose.

The Base, and its relationship to the number of codes utilized,
is the only essential difference between numbering systems of any
type.

Following is a side-by-side comparison of the three numbering
systems most frequently utilized by programmers during the debugging
of storage dump problems.

Figure 2.8   Binary, Decimal, and Hexadecimal Comparison

BINARY	DECIMAL	HEXADECIMAL
00000000	0	0
00000001	1	1
00000010	2	2
00000011	3	3
00000100	4	4
00000101	5	5
00000110	6	6
00000111	7	7
00001000	8	8
00001001	9	9
00001010	10	A
00001011	11	B
00001100	12	C
00001101	13	D
00001110	14	E
00001111	15	F
00010000	16	10
.	.	.
.	.	.
.	.	.
00011111	31	1F
.	.	.
.	.	.
.	.	.
11111111	255	FF

a. Binary Numbering System

The Binary Numbering System with Base 2 can be used to represent any desired value from zero to near infinity, using only the codes 0 to 1, and assigning a geometrically increasing value to each sucessive column (or position). The decimal value assigned to each binary position, from right to left, consists of 1, 2, 4, 8, 16, 32, 64, 128, etc. The value of the previous position is multiplied by the Base to determine the value assigned to the next highest position. Suppose the following string of binary characters were printed as follows.

        Character String: 1 0 1 0
        Assigned Value: 8 4 2 1

Because only the second to the right and left-most characters (or bits) are 'on', as represented by a 1 for the values 8 and 2 respectively, Binary 1010 is equal to 8 + 2 or Decimal 10. Likewise Binary 1111, with all bits on, is equal to 8 + 4 + 2 + 1 or Decimal 15. Similarily, Binary 0000 equals zero as no bits are turned 'on' in any of the four positions.

Assigned values to each position of a binary number increase by a multiple of the Base. Consider the following.

        Character String: 0   0   0   1   0   0   0   0
        Assigned Value: 128   64 32 16   8   4   2   1

In this example, Binary 00010000 is equal to a Decimal 16 as only the fifth position with an assigned value of 16 is 'on'. Likewise, Binary 00011111 equals 16 + 8 + 4 + 2 + 1 or Decimal 31. Similarly, Binary 11111111 is equal to 128 + 64 + 32 + 16 + 8 + 4 + 2 + 1 or Decimal 255. Binary character strings of any appreciable size are very cumbersome and time consuming to interpret in our familiar decimal form. Because all data resides in main storage in binary form, however, a conversion to a more readable numbering system is necessary. A most convenient expression of binary data can be found in the Hexadecimal Numbering System.

b. Hexadecimal Numbering System

The Hexadecimal Numbering System with Base 16 can also be used
to represent any number from zero to near infinity, but in a more
readable fashion than Binary. This system consists of the sixteen
codes 0, 1, 2, 3, 4, 5, 6, 7, 8, 9, A, B, C, D, E, and F. Note
from the comparisions in Figure 2.8 that a Decimal 10 equals an A
in Hexadecimal; 15 is equal to F; and so on.

Binary numbers are represented in hexadecimal as follows.

        Character String: 1 0 1 0
        Assigned Value: 8 4 2 1

Binary 1010 equal 8 + 2 or Decimal 10 or Hexadecimal A. Likewise,
Binary 1111 equals 8 + 4 + 2 + 1 or Decimal 15 or Hexadecimal F, the
highest allowable one-position code in the Hexadecimal Numbering System. In other words, the highest value in a 4-bit binary string can
be fully represented in hexadecimal with only one character.

2. Hexadecimal Arithmetic

The only two forms of hexadecimal arithmetic required to effectively debug storage dumps are addition and subtraction.

a. Addition

Whenever two decimal numbers are added, and the sum of an individual column is less than or equal to 9, the highest allowable code,
the sum can be directly recorded in that same column. No values need
be carried. For example:

        Column: 2 1
                   2 4   4 + 5 = 9 in Column 1.
                 + 1 5   No Carry.
                   3 9   2 + 1 = 3 in Column 2.

A Decimal nine is entered in Column 1 by adding 4 + 5 = 9. Because nine is less than or equal to nine, the highest allowable code in the Decimal Numbering System, it can be directly entered as the sum for Column 1. No carry is necessary to Column 2. A three is then entered in Column 2 by adding 2 + 1 = 3. Likewise, whenever two hexadecimal numbers are added, and the sum of an individual column is less than or equal to F, the highest allowable code, the sum can be directly recorded in that individual column. No values need be carried. For example:

```
Column:     2  1
            1  4    4 + B (or 11) = F (or 15) in Column 1.
          + 3  B    No Carry.
            4  F    1 + 3 = 4 in Column 2.
```

A Hexadecimal F is entered in Column 1 by adding 4 + B = F, where B = 11 and F = 15. Because F is less than or equal to F, the highest allowable code in the Hexadecimal Numbering System, it can be directly entered as the sum for Column 1. No carry is necessary to Column 2. A four is then entered in Column 2 by adding 1 + 3 = 4.

Whenever two decimal numbers are added and the sum of an individual column is greater than 9, the Base 10 must first be subtracted from the column total. The remainder is then recorded in the respective column. An offsetting 'carry' must then be made to the next column. For example:

```
Column:     2  1
            3  8    8 + 9 = 17 - Base 10 = 7 in Column 1.
          + 1  9    Carry 1 to Column 2.
            5  7    1 + 3 + 1 = 5 in Column 2.
```

A Decimal seven is entered in Column 1 by adding 8 + 9 = 17 followed by subtracting the Base 10 such that 17 - 10 = 7. The subtraction is necessary because 17 is greater than 9 and therefore cannot be entered directly. A one is carried to Column 2 to offset the effect of the previous subtraction such that 1 + 3 + 1 = 5. Likewise, whenever two hexadecimal numbers are added, and the sum of an individual column is greater than F, the Base 16 must first be subtracted from the column total. The remainder is then recorded in the respective column. An offsetting 'carry' must then be made to the next column.

For example:

```
Column:    2  1
           B  D   D (or 13) + F (or 15) = 28 - Base 16 = 12
          +2  F       (or C) in Column 1.
           E  C   Carry 1 to Column 2.
                  1 + B (or 11) + 2 = 14 (or E) in Column 2.
```

A Hexadecimal C is recorded in Column 1 by adding D + F = 28 where
D = 13 and F = 15, followed by subtracting the Base 16 such that 28 -
16 = 12 where 12 = C. The subtraction is necessary because 28 is
greater than F and therefore cannot be entered directly. A one is
carried to Column 2 to offset the effect of the previous subtraction
such that 1 + B + 2 = E where B = 11 and E = 14.

Most addresses in main storage consist of five or six hexadecimal
digits while many displacements contain two or three hexadecimal
digits. The technique of hexadecimal addition remains the same. For
example:

```
Column:   5  4  3  2  1
          4  F  6  B  C   C (or 12) + E (or 14) = 26 - Base 16 =
         +      7  4  E       10 (or A) in Column 1.
          4  F  E  0  A   Carry 1 to Column 2.
                          1 + B (or 11) + 4 = 16 - Base 16 = 0
                              in Column 2.
                          Carry 1 to Column 3.
                          1 + 6 + 7 = 14 (or E) in Column 3.
                          No Carry.
                          F + 0 (blank) = F in Column 4.
                          No Carry.
                          4 + 0 (blank) = 4 in Column 5.
```

Hexadecimal A is recorded in Column 1 by adding C + E = 26 where
C = 12 and E = 14, followed by subtracting the Base 16 such that 26 -
16 = 10 where 10 = A. Carrying 1 to Column 2, a zero is recorded in
Column 2 by adding 1 + B + 4 = 16 where B = 11, followed by subtracting the Base 16 such that 16 - 16 = 0. Carrying 1 to Column 3,
a Hexadecimal E is recorded in Column 3 by simply adding 1 + 6 + 7 =
14 where 14 = E. With no carry the F and 4 can be directly recorded
in Columns 4 and 5 respectively.

b. Subtraction

Whenever two decimal numbers are subtracted, and the upper character (minuend) is greater than or equal to the lower character (subtrahend), the remainder can be directly recorded in the respective column. No value need be 'borrowed'. For example:

```
Column:  2  1
         7  9   No Borrow.
       - 6  2   9 - 2 = 7 in Column 1.
         1  7   7 - 6 = 1 in Column 2.
```

A Decimal seven is entered in Column 1 by subtracting 9 - 2 = 7. Because nine is greater than or equal to two, borrowing is not necessary and the remainder, seven, can be directly entered in Column 1. In the same manner a one is entered in Column 2 by subtracting 7 - 6 = 1. Likewise, whenever two hexadecimal numbers are subtracted, and the minuend is greater than or equal to the subtrahend, the remainder can be directly recorded in the respective column. No value need be 'borrowed'. For example:

```
Column:  2  1
         E  F   No Borrow.
       - 3  D   F (or 15) - D (or 13) = 2 in Column 1.
         B  2   E (or 14) - 3 = 11 (or B) in Column 2.
```

A Hexadecimal two is entered in Column 1 by subtracting F - D = 2 where F = 15 and D = 13. Because F is greater than or equal to D, borrowing is not necessary and the remainder, two, can be directly entered in Column 1. A Hexadecimal B is entered in Column 2 by subtracting E - 3 = B where E = 14 and B = 11. E is greater than or equal to 3; borrowing was not necessary prior to subtraction.

Whenever two decimal numbers are subtracted, and the minuend is less than the subtrahend, the Base 10 must be 'borrowed' from the next column prior to the subtraction. For example:

```
Column:  2 1
         7 2   Borrow Base 10 from Column 2.
       - 4 8   10 + 2 = 12 - 8 = 4 in Column 1.
         2 4   7 - 1 = 6 - 4 = 2 in Column 2.
```

A Decimal four is entered in Column 1 by borrowing the Base 10 from
Column 2 and subtracting 12 - 8 = 4. Borrowing is necessary as two
is less than eight and cannot be subtracted directly. A Decimal two
is entered in Column 2 by reducing the seven to a six as a result of
the previous borrow, and subtracting 6 - 4 = 2. Likewise, whenever
two hexadecimal numbers are subtracted, and the minuend is less than
the subtrahend, the Base 16 must be 'borrowed' from the next column
prior to the subtraction. For example:

```
Column:  2 1
         D A   Borrow Base 16 from Column 2.
       - 3 F   16 + A (or 10) = 26 - F (or 15) = 11 (or B)
         9 B       in Column 1.
                 D (or 13) - 1 = C (or 12) - 3 = 9 in Column 2.
```

A Hexadecimal B is entered in Column 1 by borrowing the Base 16 from
Column 2 and subtracting 26 - F = B where F = 15 and B = 11. Borrowing is necessary as A is less than F and cannot be subtracted directly. A Hexadecimal nine is entered in Column 2 by reducing the D to
a C as a result of the previous borrow, and subtracting C - 3 = 9
where C = 12. Regardless of the size of fields to be subtracted, the
technique of hexadecimal subtraction remains the same. For example:

```
Column:  5 4 3 2 1
         2 F 1 C B   Borrow Base 16 from Column 2.
       - 2 B 6 D E   16 + B (or 11) = 27 - E (or 14) = 13
         3 A E D         (or D) in Column 1.
                     Borrow Base 16 from Column 3.
                     C (or 12) - 1 = B (or 11) + 16 = 27 - D
                         (or 13) = 14 (or E) in Column 2.
                     Borrow Base 16 from Column 4.
                     1 - 1 = 0 + 16 = 16 - 6 = 10 (or A) in
                         Column 3.
                     No Borrow.
                     F (or 15 - 1 = E (or 14) - B (or 11) = 3
                         in Column 4.
                     2 - 2 = 0 (blank) in Column 5.
```

A Hexadecimal D is entered in Column 1 by borrowing the Base 16 from Column 2 and subtracting 27 - E = D where E = 14 and D = 13. A Hexadecimal E is entered in Column 2 by reducing the C to a B as a result of the previous borrow, then borrowing Base 16 from Column 3 and subtracting 27 - D = E where D = 13 and E =14. Hexadecimal A is entered in Column 3 by reducing the one to a zero as a result of the previous borrow, then borrowing Base 16 from Column 4 and substracting 16 - 6 = A where A = 10. A Hexadecimal 3 is entered in Column 4 by reducing the F to an E as a result of the previous borrow, and subtracting E - B = 3 where E = 14 and B = 11. A blank can remain in Column 5 as a result of subtracting 2 - 2 = 0.

Hexadecimal addition and subtraction are frequently used when debugging storage dumps. With practice, it can be mastered relatively easily. A workshop is provided at the end of this chapter for that purpose.

C.   DATA REPRESENTATION

1.   Data Addressing

Locating data addresses in main storage is a technique required in all data processing environments. Once found, an interpretation of field contents at that location can be made. Figure 2.9 illustrates a schematic diagram of main storage print. It will be used to find the location of a data item given its address.

The left-hand column in the main storage portion of a dump contains a series of addresses incremented by Hexadecimal 20. See letter 'A'. These addresses refer to the starting point of each print line. Actual data beginning at Address 1BC00, for example, can be found at letter 'B'. The string of x's following each address refer to the actual contents of main storage. The interpretation of data at a particular address depends upon the type of data representation utilized. Note that eight hexadecimal digits (or four bytes) are grouped together for print purposes, and are commonly referred to as

one word. Each line contains the equivalent of eight words, i.e.,
32 bytes or 64 hexadecimal digits. Note from letter 'C' that a
larger gap exists for ease in readability between the fourth and
fifth words.

The problem, as shown in Figure 2.9, is to locate Address
1BC3A in main storage. Finding Address 1BC20 and 1BC40 in the left-
hand column, indicates that the location of 1BC3A lies between 1BC20
and 1BC40, or at some point on the line beginning with Address 1BC20.
See letter 'D'.

The gap provided at letter 'C' can now be conveniently used to
locate Address 1BC30, or the half-way point between Address 1BC20
and 1BC40. An example of what a programmer might find on the remainder of this line is shown at the bottom of Figure 2.9. The
four groups of x's refer to four groups of data. Having located
Address 1BC30, it is necessary now to count A (or 10) bytes from
that point to locate Address 1BC3A. Remember that each byte contains two hexadecimal characters and that the count must begin
with Hexadecimal zero, as shown in this example at letter 'E',
because Address 1BC30 ends with zero. It is then a simple procedure
to count to the right the significant number of bytes until the
address of interest, 1BC3A, is located. This is illustrated at
letter 'F'.

If it were determined that the length of the field starting at
Address 1BC3A was one byte, then the represented value of the data
at that location would be F1. Similarily, if field length were
two bytes, F1F5 would be the appropiate value to interpret, etc.

The procedure described above, which locates addresses in main
storage, soon becomes second nature to programmers and analysts.
Determination of field lengths will be made throughout the text
as actual debugging problems are encountered. The interpretation of
character strings found at various storage locations will be covered
next.

The techniques discussed in this chapter are utilized in all OS,
OS/VS, and DOS installations. Storage dumps resulting from application,
system, and data base problems are no exception.

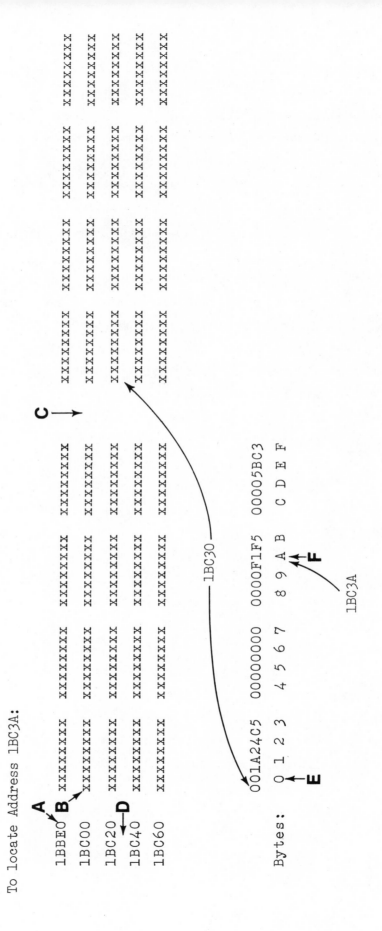

Figure 2.9   Schematic Diagram of Main Storage

42

2. Interpretation

Once the location of various addresses has been determined, an interpretation of the respective field must be made. Programmers define data fields in many forms. As a result, character strings found at any particular location must be related to their actual usage as defined in the program being executed.

a. External Decimal

Often referred to as Character Format, Zoned Decimal, and Unpacked Format, External Decimal representation is one of the most frequently used forms of data representation. COBOL's Usage DISPLAY with Picture 9's and FORTRAN's Read/Write Statements in Integer Format are two ways of defining data fields in External Decimal. Each digit of a particular number is represented by two hexadecimal characters (one byte). The high-order hexadecimal character represents a zone (or sign) field, while the low-order hexadecimal character represents the actual value of the digit. The letter F in the zone position is equivalent to a non-printing plus (+) sign, a C to the internal presence of a plus sign, while a D is equal to a minus (-) sign. A blank is represented by the character 40. For example:

```
F1     =  +1    =  +1    =      1
40     =  b     =  blank =
C2C5   =  +2+5  =  +25   =    +25
40F7F6 =  b+7+6 =  +76   =     76
D1D2D3 =  -1-2-3 = -123  =   -123
```

In this manner, given an appropiate field length, any string of External Decimal characters can be readily interpreted.

b. Internal Decimal

Often referred to as Packed Format, Internal Decimal representation is most frequently generated during the compilation process to handle arithmetic manipulations and tests. The sign is contained in the low-order hexadecimal position. An 04 is equal to a blank. For example:

```
1F   = 1+   = +1     =    1
04   = b    = blank  =
25C  = 25+  = +25    =  +25
076F = 076+ = +76    =   76
123D = 123- = -123   = -123
```

Although it is possible to define a given field as Internal Decimal in some programming languages, such as COBOL's Usage COMP-3, this
form of data representation is usually derived from a compiler-generated External Decimal conversion (or packing) operation. An External
Decimal field is packed by moving the sign in the low-order zone position to the low-order sign position of the Internal Decimal field.
Actual values within the External Decimal field are then brought for-
ward, in order of occurrence, to the left of the sign. For example:

```
F1        40        C2C5        40F7F6        D1D2D3
 |         |          |            |             |
 v         v          v            v             v
1F        04         25C         076F          123D
```

The packing of data fields saves storage space. The unpacked character string D1D2D3 requires three bytes of storage, while the packed
equivalent 123D requires only two bytes.

c. Binary

The Binary form of data representation is also a frequently used
technique. COBOL's Usage COMP and FORTRAN Integer fields are two
methods of defining data in Binary. Binary fields are printed as hexadecimal in a storage dump and can be directly interpreted as such.
For example:

Binary		Hexadecimal		Decimal
0000 0000 0000 1111	=	000F	=	15
0000 0000 0100 0000	=	0040	=	64
0000 0000 1111 0001	=	00F1	=	241
0000 0111 0110 1111	=	076F	=	1903
0001 0010 0011 1101	=	123D	=	4669

Negative numbers, if desired, can be interpreted in binary though they
appear in the two's complement form. A one in the sign (high-bit)

```
```

position means the number is negative, while a zero signifies the number to be positive. For example:

FEB4 = 1111 1110 1011 0100 in binary two's complement form.
         ↑
         1 = minus (-) sign.

Remaining bits converted to positive plus one (opposite of two's complement):

Binary: 000 0001 0100 1011
Hexadecimal: 0   1   4   B plus 1 = 14C

A Hexadecimal 14C equals Decimal 332, or in this case -332 due to the negative binary expression.

d. External Floating Point

Although External Floating Point is not as frequently used as other forms of data representation, it is exemplified in COBOL's Usage DISPLAY with an E Picture. An External Floating Point item consists of a signed decimal number, the letter E, and an exponent with a sign indication. The exponent is a power of ten to be applied to the decimal number. As such, a very large number can be represented in a relatively small amount of storage space in External Floating Point. For example:

$$+67.89Eb02 = +67.89 \times 10^2 = +6789.$$
$$+67.89E-02 = +67.89 \times 10^{-2} = +.6789$$
$$-67.89Eb02 = -67.89 \times 10^2 = -6789.$$
$$-67.89E-01 = -67.89 \times 10^{-1} = -6.789$$
$$+67.89Eb11 = +67.89 \times 10^{11} = +6789000000000.$$

External Floating Point data fields are sometimes converted to Internal Floating Point items via compiler-generated instructions. As such, a programmer may find that a given data value is represented in Internal

Floating Point in main storage even though the initial variable had been described as External Floating Point in the original program. This is similar to the automatic packing of some values from External Decimal to Internal Decimal as mentioned earlier.

e. Internal Floating Point

Internal Floating Point is a common form of data representation. COBOL's Usage COMP-1 and COMP-2 along with FORTRAN Real fields are two methods of representing data in Internal Floating Point. An Internal Floating Point item consists of a characteristic developed from the exponent, and a fraction. A one in the high-bit position means the number is negative, while a zero signifies the number to be positive. A very large number can be represented in a relatively small amount of storage space as in External Floating Point. Internal Floating Point, however, is generally more difficult to interpret. For example:

> 4430AF40 = Characteristic of 44 (first byte)
> and
> Fraction of .30AF40 (remaining bytes)

To determine the Exponent:

> Hexadecimal 44 = Binary 0100 0100
>
> 0 = plus (+) sign; the number is positive.

Ignoring the left-most bit,

> Binary 100 0100 = Hexadecimal 44 = Decimal 68

Because the Characteristic is stored in 'excess 64' arithmetic form, the Exponent is equal to:

> 68 - 64 = an Exponent of 4

To determine the value:

.30AF40 with an Exponent of 4 = 30AF.40

Hexadecimal 30AF = Decimal 12463
Hexadecimal .40 = Decimal .25

A Hexadecimal .40 is converted to a Decimal .25 by multiplying the number to be converted by 10/16, the ratio of the Base of the Decimal Numbering System to the Base of the Hexadecimal Numbering System.

.40 X 10/16 = 4/16 = 1/4 = .25

Finally, both portions of the converted fraction are added.

Decimal 12463 + Decimal .25 = Decimal 12463.25

The Internal Floating Point expression 4430AF40 is equal to 12463.25 in decimal. The result is positive rather than negative as determined earlier from the initial left-most bit.

The following workshop is provided to assist in working with numbering systems and the basic forms of data representation. After this practice exercise is completed, the actual debugging of storage dumps can begin.

D. WORKSHOP PROBLEMS

Utilizing the Reference Data Card where appropriate, perform the following hexadecimal arithmetic, conversions, and data representation interpretations. Problem solutions can be found in Appendix A.

Reference Data Card on pp. 21-27 reprinted by permission from GX20-1703-9© by International Business Machines Corporation.

Arithmetic:

1. Hexadecimal Addition

```
  2          4          3          5          B
  4          7          B          F          D
  _          _          _          _          _


  E          42         4CF        ABCD       A94FC
  F          8F         BAD        EFAB       ACB1
  _          __         ___        ____       ____
```

2. Hexadecimal Subtraction

```
  6          D          D          A0         B3
  4          6          B          4          D
  _          _          _          _          _


  DA         C72        F123       1ABCD      C4000
  AD         AB8        ABC        CDEF       C3ABC
  __         ___        ___        ____       _____
```

Conversion:

1. Hexadecimal to Decimal

C = _____   35 = _____   6B = _____

54C = _____   DEF = _____   7CB3 = _____

5AD2 = _____   46C4C = _____   FBFCA = _____

2. Decimal to Hexadecimal

11 = _____   48 = _____   237 = _____

1035 = _____   2000 = _____   3484 = _____

12380 = _____   65535 = _____   200000 = _____

3. Hexadecimal to Binary

       4 = _____   F = _____   1B = _____

     ABC = _____   D7E = _____

   F159D = _____

Decimal Interpretation:

1. External Decimal

      F9 = _____   C4 = _____   40 = _____

    C1C8 = _____   D6D2 = _____   F3F4 = _____

  40F4F7 = _____   C9C7C5 = _____   40D9D8 = _____

2. Internal Decimal

      8F = _____   6D = _____   04 = _____

     24C = _____   37F = _____   64D = _____

   267F = _____   814D = _____   974C = _____

3. Binary

      04 = _____   0F = _____   F1 = _____

      40 = _____   06D = _____   7BC = _____

   03F4 = _____   F23B = _____   A67F = _____

4. External Floating Point

   +01.00Eb00 = _____   -123.4Eb01 = _____   +4.567E-01 = _____

   -.74620E-02 = _____   +01.000Eb05 = _____   -12.120Eb05 = _____

   +000.310E-04 = _____   -187224.E-06 = _____   +.999999Eb10 = _____

5. Internal Floating Point

    44A45B40 = _____   43AB4800 = _____

    C2FB0000 = _____   C35CC120 = _____

3

External Abends

A. DESCRIPTION

In the previous two chapters it was determined that a storage dump
is, in essence, nothing more than a snapshot of the contents of main
storage. Storage Dumps, however, fall into two broad classifications:

1. External Abends
2. Internal Abends

An External Storage Dump is the result of an abend which occurred
external to program execution; that is, when the program was not being
executed. Perhaps a command to mount a particular tape has been issued
to the operator and the system is awaiting a response. Or, a block of
data is being transferred from the buffer area to a physical device.
Perhaps a program for the next job step is being fetched and about to
be loaded into main storage. In situations such as these, the program
of concern is not being executed. When a system abend occurs under
this circumstance, external to the program to be executed, the dump is
classified as External.

Conversely, an Internal Abend occurs when the program is actually
being executed at the time of abnormal termination. This is not to
say that Internal Abends are strictly program problems while External
Abends are always file problems, though generally this is true. Erroneous file descriptions within a program can cause an External Abend.
Likewise, faulty data can cause an Internal Abend. The terms 'external' and 'internal' refer only to the status of the program at the
precise moment the abend occurs.

Storage Dumps are classified for the purpose of indicating which
set of debugging procedures need be followed; one, file oriented (External); another, program oriented (Internal). The abend classification is easily discerned from the completion code or abend grouping as
follows:

1. External Abends
   a. 001
   b. 13 Group
   c. 22 Group (excluding 322)
   d. 37 Group
2. Internal Abends
   a. 0C Group (includes User Code 240)
   b. 322

Other completion codes have not been classified because of their
infrequent occurrence. Though generally external by nature, debugging
procedures as relate to application and system programmers and analysts
are usually minimal. This notion will be expanded in Chapter 7's description of completion codes and their most probable causes.

The principles of debugging External Abends relate not only to
application program files, but to system and data base files as well.

B. ABEND GROUPINGS

1. 001 Completion Code

This completion code denotes a noncorrectable Input/Output (I/O)
error. A damaged tape, a system problem while accessing a disk data

51

set, improper file descriptions, and the like, can cause an 001 Completion Code. Determining the problem file and its attributes are basic to instituting corrective action.

2. 13 Group

Completion codes ending with the numerals 13, i.e., 213, 813, etc., refer to a type of problem in which the system cannot locate the data set as defined. Perhaps a file in a step calling for that particular data set cannot be located, or, an erroneous file specification has been made. Again, determination of the problem file is of utmost importance.

3. 22 Group

Completion codes in the 22 Group with the exception of a 322 are also classified as External and refer, in general, to the violation of installation standards and/or system limitations. When an operator anxiously reports that the system went into a Wait State, this denotes that the Operating System is awaiting response to a query, request, or command of some type and the response is not forthcoming. Operator errors and system and programmer errors to which the system and/or operator cannot respond usually cause abends of the 22 Group. External reference to the problem file must be made.

4. 37 Group

Completion codes in this group, such as B37, D37, etc., refer to end of file problems. Errors in trailer label processing, exceeding space allocations, and other end of file or volume problems cause abends of the 37 Group. Analysis of the problem file is a necessity.

C. DEBUGGING PROCEDURES

1. Computer Run Overview (001)

A distinct set of step-by-step procedures need be followed to effectively debug an External Abend. Utilizing a Job Control Language

(JCL) listing in addition to the storage dump, the problem file for an External Abend can easily be determined as well as the location of Data Control Block (DCB) attributes. Equipped with this information, the programmer can then isolate the source of the problem and take appropriate corrective action.

The computer run depicted in the following pages consists of selected pertinent pages of a typical job which has abended with an 001 Completion Code in the execution of a COBOL program. The specific programming language utilized is of little consequence when debugging External Abends.

A Job Control Language listing is a necessary reference when debugging External Abends primarily because it provides a description of pertinent file characteristics. A program listing is also helpful, especially when the completion code indicates that file attributes as described by the programmer may be in conflict. As far as the storage dump itself is concerned, only the first and second page plus the first page of main storage are necessary. An intermediate page may also be desired. Figures 3.1 through 3.6 depict these pertinent pages.

Figure 3.1 Job Control Language Listing (001)

```
//STEP1    EXEC  PGM=IEBGENER
//SYSUT1      DD   *
/*
//SYSIN       DD   DUMMY
//SYSUT2      DD  UNIT=SYSDA,DISP=(NEW,PASS),
//               DSN=&&GRD123,SPACE=(080,12,RLSE),
//               DCB=(RECFM=FB,LRECL=080,BLKSIZE=560)
//SYSPRINT   DD  SYSOUT=A
//SYSUDUMP   DD  SYSOUT=A
/*
//STEP2    EXEC COBUCLG,PARM.COB='DMAP,PMAP',
//               REGION.GO=30K,TIME.GO=(.20)
//COB.SYSIN   DD   *
/*
//GO.INPUT1   DD  UNIT=SYSDA,DISP=(OLD,DELETE),
//               DSN=&&GRD123,
//               DCB=(RECFM=FB,LRECL=080,BLKSIZE=0560)
//GO.CDINPUT1 DD   *
/*
//GO.OUTPUT1  DD UNIT=SYSDA,DISP=(NEW,DELETE),
//               DSN=&&GRD456,SPACE=(0080,12,RLSE)
//GO.OUTPUT2  DD UNIT=SYSDA,DISP=(NEW,DELETE),
//               DSN=&&GRD789,SPACE=(0080,12,RLSE)
//GO.MSGOUT    DD  SYSOUT=A
//GO.SYSUDUMP  DD  SYSOUT=A
//
```

Figure 3.2   Portion of COBOL Source Program Listing (001)

```
00001      101    IDENTIFICATION DIVISION.
00002      102    PROGRAM-ID.   'A5558'.
00003      104    REMARKS.
00004      105       DIVIDE A FILE INTO TWO PARTS FOR INPUT TO PROGRAM 4204.
00005      106    ENVIRONMENT DIVISION.
00006      107    CONFIGURATION SECTION.
00007      108    SOURCE-COMPUTER.    IBM-370.
00008      109    OBJECT-COMPUTER.    IBM-370.
00009      110    INPUT-OUTPUT SECTION.
00010      111    FILE-CONTROL.
00011      112       SELECT INPUT       ASSIGN TO UT-S-INPUT1.  ←———— R
00012      113       SELECT OUTPUT1     ASSIGN TO UT-S-OUTPUT1.
00013      114       SELECT OUTPUT2     ASSIGN TO UT-S-OUTPUT2.
00014      115       SELECT CDINPUT1    ASSIGN TO UT-S-CDINPUT1.
00015      1151      SELECT TERM-FILE ASSIGN UT-S-MSGOUT.
00016      116    DATA DIVISION.
00017      1161   FILE SECTION.
00018      117    FD  INPUT
00019      118        RECORDING MODE IS F
00020      119        LABEL RECORDS STANDARD
00021              RECORD CONTAINS 070 CHARACTERS  ←———— V
00022              BLOCK CONTAINS 560 CHARACTERS   ←———— S
00023      121        DATA RECORD IS INRCD.
00024      122    01  INRCD PIC X(70).
00025      2 1    FD  OUTPUT1
00026      2 2        RECORDING MODE F
00027      2 3        LABEL RECORD STANDARD
00028      2 31       RECORD CONTAINS 080 CHARACTERS
00029                 BLOCK CONTAINS 0560 CHARACTERS
00030      2 4        DATA RECORD IS OUTRCD1.
00031      2 5    01  OUTRCD1 PIC X(80).
00032      2 71   FD  OUTPUT2
00033      2 72       RECORDING MODE F
00034      2 73       LABEL RECORD STANDARD
00035                 RECORD CONTAINS 080 CHARACTERS
00036                 BLOCK CONTAINS 0560 CHARACTERS
00037      2 74       DATA RECORD IS OUTRCD2.
00038      2 75   01  OUTRCD2 PIC X(80).
00039      217    FD  CDINPUT1
00040      218        RECORDING MODE F
00041      219        LABEL RECORDS OMITTED
00042      220        RECORD CONTAINS 080 CHARACTERS
00043      221        DATA RECORD IS CD-IN.
00044      222    01  CD-IN PIC X(80).
00045      276    FD  TERM-FILE
00046      277        LABEL RECORDS STANDARD
00047      278        RECORDING MODE F
00048      279        DATA RECORD IS TERM-RECORD.
00049      280    01  TERM-RECORD PIC X(133).
00050      3 1    WORKING-STORAGE SECTION.
00051      3 2    77  STATE4 PICTURE  9(7).
00052             77  X  PICTURE 99.
00053             01  INREC.
00054                 02 IDENT1      PICTURE 9(7)  OCCURS 10 TIMES.
00055                 02 FILLER PIC X(10).
00056             01  OUTREC1.
00057                 02 IDENT2   PICTURE 9(8)  OCCURS 10 TIMES.
```

Figure 3.3 First Page of 001 Storage Dump

```
JOB  DZZ137 ──A  STEP GO ──B   TIME 115721
COMPLETION CODE.    SYSTEM = 001 ──C
PSW AT ENTRY TO ABEND  FF04000D 50016A6A

TCB 037D30  RHP 00041970   PIE 00000000    DER 00038F4    TIO 00037A98   CMP 80001000   TRN 00000000
            MSS 0203ABC0   PK-FLG 60850400 FLG 00006A6B   LLS 0003F7F0   JLB 00000000   JPQ 800391E0
            FSA 011FF768   TCR 0003361A    TME 00000000   JST 00037D30   NTC 00000000   OTC 0003A10A
            LTC 00000000   IOE 00000000    ECB 002174A4   TSF 20000000   D-PQE 00038F90 SQS 00035110
            NSTAE A003AF28 TCT 00036D28    USER 00000000  DAR 00000000   RESV 00000000  JSCB 870347BC
            RESV 00000000  IOR 00000000

ACTIVE RBS

PRR 038D78  RESV 00000000   APSW 00000000   WC-SZ-STAB 00040082  FL-CDE 00039558  PSW FF650037 502FDDFE
            Q/TTR 00000000  WT-LNK 00037D30

SVRB 041C40 TAB-LN 00380400  APSW F5F5F1C4   WC-SZ-STAB 00120002  TQN 00000000  PSW FF04000D 50016A6A
            Q/TTR 00001721   WT-LNK 00038D78
            RG 0-7  001FE2B0  001E0234  001E0234  001E0AEA  901E02B0  001E0028  001FE51A
            RG 8-15 001FD8A0  001FD440  001FF1E8  001FF080  001E07C8  602FDDF0  0E1E1BC6
            EXTSA   001E0234  40016732  001FFDE0  411FE284  001FFE2B0 B02D73DE  001FD440
                    5002411A  C0036044  001E2B0   001E0560

SVRB 041730 TAB-LN 009A0220  APSW F9F0F1C3   WC-SZ-STAB 00120002  TQN 00000000  PSW 00040033 50018282
            Q/TTR 0004D0C    WT-LNK 00041C40
            RG 0-7  80000000  80000001  001E0234  40016732  001FFE34  001FFDE8  001FFD70
            RG 8-15 00041C40  0037AD8   58003744  C0036044  001E0560  001FFF44  6001EC32
            EXTSA   00021BE   8F1FF250  00000000  C4F90010  FF030000  000417AC  E2E8E2C9
                    C5C1F0F1  C9C5C130  C1C2C5D5

SVRB 041970 TAB-LN 00D803D8  APSW F1F0F5C1   WC-SZ-STAB 00120002  TQN 00000000  PSW FF04000C 401FCFA6
            Q/TTR 00003D11   WT-LNK 00041730
            RG 0-7  00105BB0  00041790  8001819A  0001A318  00037D30  04037D30  00041730
            RG 8-15 0037D30   400180E2  0037D30   9F1FF250  00037840  400417B4  40017614  00000000
            EXTSA   E2E8E2C9  C5C1F0F1  C9C7C3F0  F1F0F7C2  0001CF30  5001A460  00000000
                    00028740  00000000  C4E24040  00000000

LOAD LIST

NE 00041278  RSP-CDE 020391E0   NE 00041100  RSP-CDE 0104589A   NE 00041110  RSP-CDE 0104589A
NE 00041230  RSP-CDE 01045908   NE 00038DF0  RSP-CDE 01045988   NE 00038E88  RSP-CDE 02045ACA
NE 00038ED8  RSP-CDE 03045A28   NE 00038F90  RSP-CDE 01045A58   NE 00039208  RSP-CDE 03038DCA
NE 00039200  RSP-CDE 01045AF8   NE 00039208  RSP-CDE 02045A98   NE 00039230  RSP-CDE 02045ACA
NE 00039280  RSP-CDE 02045828   NE 00039378  RSP-CDE 01045898   NE 00039308  RSP-CDE 0304595A
NE 00000000  RSP-CDE 03045AF8

CDE

039558  ATR1 08  NCDE 000000  ROC-RB 0003AD78  NM MAIN  USE 01  EPA 1DFFA0  ATR2 20  XL/MJ 039510
```

55

Figure 3.4   Second Page of 001 Storage Dump

```
035BB0  00008660 001FE888 00008660 002FD298   00008660 00000000 00000115 00010EE0   *....Y......K....*
035BA0  11000000 05037D30 10035C34 E8000000   0F000000 00000000 6B000000 6F1E038C   *........Y......Y.*
035BC0  04035B80 10001B44 0000001E 00000020   00120039 00010001 00000000 00000000   *....ARAIFNCICD..*
035BE0  00000050 C1D9C1C9 C6D5C3C9 C3C40000   00000000 00000000 00000000 00000000   *......Y.....K..*
035C00  00000000 60400000

DEB

035C00  00008660 00000000 00000116 00010EE0   00008660 001FE888 00008660 002FD298   *....Y......K....*
035C20  0F000000 01000000 6B000000 6F1E02E0   11000000 05037D30 10036044 E8000000   *........Y......Y.*
035C40  00120039 00010001 00000000 00000000   04035C10 10001B44 00000021 00000023   *....ARAIFNCICD..*
035C60  00000000 00000000 00000000 00000000   00000050 C1D9C1C9 C6D5C3C9 C3C40000   *.........0......*
035C80  00000000 00000000

DEB

036020  002FD978 001FE888 00008660 002FD298   00008660 00000000 00000112 00010EE0   *....R...Y......K*
036040  11000000 06037D30 10037864 68000000   00000000 01FFFFFF 6B000000 6F1E0234   *..............*
036060  04036020 58003744 00000018 0012001B   00110039 00010001 00000000 00000000   *....AQAAFNCHCICC*
036080  00000046 C1D8C1C1 C6D5C3C8 C3C9C3C3   00000000 00000000 00000000 00000000   *..............*
0360A0  00000000 00000000

DEB

037840  00008660 00000000 00008660 00008660   00008660 00000000 00000000 00010EE0   *..............*
037860  0F000000 03037D30 10000000 C8000000   00000000 01000000 6B000000 6F1E0438   *..............H.*
037880  02037840 33004688 00010001 00000000   00000000 00000050 C1D8C1C1 C3C30000   *....AQAACC..*
0378A0  00000000 00000000 00000000 00000000
```

```
TIOT   JOB RODZZ137   STEP GO              PROC STEP2
DD     14040140   PGM=*.DD     0026D700   80003544
DD     14040140   SYSDROUT     0026D800   80004C08
DD     14040140   INPUT1       0026D900   80003744
DD     14040140   CDINPUT1     0026DA00   80004688
DD     14040140   OUTPUT1      0026DB00   80001B44
DD     14040140   OUTPUT2      0026DC00   80004C28
DD     14040140   MSGOUT       0026DD00   80004C28
DD     14040140   SYSUDUMP     0026DE00   80004C48
```

DATA MANAGEMENT CONTROL BLOCKS

```
MSGOUT  DEB 036474   04037D30 10035BA4 CA000000 0F000000   01000000 6B000000 6F1E04E4 02036450
                     33004C28 00010001 00000000 00000000   00000085 C1D9C1C9 C3D3C3C5 00000000
                     00000000 00000000 00000000 00000000   00000000 000363B0 00000080 00008660

        DCB 1E04E4   00000000 00000000 00000000 00000000   00480000 21FF078 00004000 00000001
                     46000001 801E04B4 00900048 00036474   922FCDC0 002FDC98 071E1BC6 00090085
                     28022828 421FE790 001FF105 001FF105   00000085 00000001 00000000 002FCB10
```

Figure 3.5 First Page of UUI Main Storage

REGS AT ENTRY TO ABEND ——▶ M

FLTR 0-6   00001BE007000000   00035BE800035204   0000000000000000   0000000000000000

REGS 0-7   80000000 80001000 01E0234   40016732   001FFDE0 001FFE34 001FFDE8 001FFD70
REGS 8-15   001E087A 00041C40 00003AD8 58003744   C0036044 001FFFA4 001E0560 6001EC32

LOAD MODULE   MAIN

1DFFA0	90ECD00C 185D05F0 4580F010 C1F5F5F5	F8404040 C1D5E2F4 0700989F F02407FF	*......0...A5558 ANS4....n...*
1DFFC0	96021034 07FE41F0 000107FE 001E0E60	001DFFA0 001D0FFA0 001E07C8 001E0560	*........................H....*
1DFFE0	001E087A 001E0E20 40404040 40404040	40404040 40404040 40404040 40404040	*..............*
1E0000	40404040 40404040 001F9ACC E3E7F0F0	F0F6F2F2 F040F0F0 40404040 F2F9F1F1	*........TX0006220 001 M 2911*
1E0020	40C140C1 00000000 F0F0F0F0 F0F0F1F1	F140F24B F0404040 F2F1F4F3 F667F3F4	*A A....00000111 2.0 2143f734*
1E0040	F1F1F1F1 F1F1F1F1 F1F2F2F2 F2F2F2F2	F2F0F0F0 F0F0F0F1 F6F9F3F9 F1F4F9F4	*1111111222222200000169391494*
1E0060	F9F3F4F1 F3F5F7F8 F4F4F9F0 F4F1F3F4	F2F0F0F1 F2F3F4F5 F5F94040 40404040	*93413578419449041342901123459*
1E0080	40404040 40404040 F0F2F1F4 F3F6F7F3	F0F4F1F1 F1F1F1F1 F1F0F1F1 F1F22222	*021436730411111101112222*
1E00A0	F0F2F2F2 F2F0F0F0 F0F1F6F9 F3F0F9F3	F9F4F9F3 F0F4F1F3 F5F7F8F3	*2222200000169309149493041357837*
1E00C0	F0F4F4F9 F4F4F1F3 F4F2F9F0 F0F1F2F3	F3F4F5F9 F0F6F1F1 F8F8F1F4	*041449004134290011234590611814*
1E00E0	F0F3F2F3 F2F1F4F3 F0F6F7F3 F4F1F1F0	F1F1F1F1 F1F1F2F2 F2F2F2F2	*03232143067341110111112202222222*
1E0100	F0F0F0F0 F0F0F0F1 F0F6F9F3 F9F1F4F9	F0F4F9F3 F4F1F3F5 F0F7F8F3 F4F1F4	*000000010693914904934135078341*
1E0120	F0F4F9F0 F4F1F3F4 F0F0F0F0 F0F0F140	04904134 0000001	*049041340000n01*
1E0140	40404040 40404040 40404040 40404040	40404040 40404040 40404040 40404040	*......*
1E0160	40404040 40404040 00000000 00004000	40404040 40D9C5C3 D6D9C4E2	*......RECORDS*
1E0180	40D6D540 E3C1D7C5 40F1407E 40F0F0F0	F0F0F1F4 40D9C5C3 D6D9C4E2 40D6D540	*ON TAPE 1 . 0000014 RECORDS ON*
1E01A0	E3C1D7C5 40F2407E 00000001 00000000	4005D6D5 D4C1D340 C5D5C440 D6C640D1	*TAPE 2 . 0000002 NORMAL END OF J*
1E01C0	D6C24040 40404040 40404040 40404040	40404040 40404040 40404040 40404040	*0B......*
1E01E0	40404040 40404040 40404040 40404040	40404040 40404040 40404040 40404040	*......*
1E0200	001FA08C 00000000 00000000 051E1E2A	00000000 081DFFC6 00000000 00180012	*........F.......*
1E0220	000C0394 0029336D 021FE328 0E1E1BC6	00000000 461E0A26 901E0204 0404040	*......T....F.....*
1E0240	006044 122FE808 002FDDA8 00000000	00000001 38000000 901E240 001FE560	*..........V*
1E0260	001FE51A 40F2407E 00000046 00909090	00090230 00000000 00000000 00000000	*..M8...*
1E0280	00000000 00000000 0010FFC6 00000001	002FD4F8 00000000 00000000 00000000	*.V.F.......V*
1E02A0	051E1E2A 00000000 00210000 00000001	00000000 00004000 00000001 80000000	*.......F...C*
1E02C0	00000000 38000000 00210000 0201C394	021FDB98 00004000 00000001 00000000	*.......C*
1E02E0	901E0280 00680048 002FDC98 00035C34	002FDC98 0D1E1A8C 00090230 002FD9F8	*.......0.......F.*
1E0300	001FE168 001FDDB0 00000050 00000001	00000050 00000001 00000000 00000000	*.......2...R8*
1E0320	0050 001FE560 00000000 051E1E2A	00000000 00900000 00000000 00000000	*........2*
1E0340	05EF0000 00000000 00000000 00000000	001DFFC6 00000001 00000000 00000000	*.......F...*
1E0360	00000000 00000000 80000000 00000000	00000000 001E0000 0001C394 0029336D	*.......F...*
1E0380	021FD398 00004000 00000001 46000000	38000000 007C0048 00035BA4 922FCDC0	*.......F.....C*
1E03A0	002FDC98 0D1E1BC6 00090230 30060050	421FE090 001FD5D0 001FD490 00000050	*.....F...F....N..M*
1E03C0	00000001 00000000 002FD9F8 05EF0000	00004000 00000001 461E09E0 801E0408	*.......R8......*
1E03E0	00544800 00037864 122FE808 002FDDA8	061E1BC6 00090050 002FD4F8 001FF048	*.....F.......0*
1E0400	00000000 00000000 00000000 00000000	00000000 051E1E2A 081DFFC6 00000000	*.......F*
1E0420	00000001 00000001 00000000 00000000	80000000 00004000 00000000 00000000	*......*
1E0440	00000000 00000000 00410000 00000001	00004000 461E09E0 801E0408 00000000	*.....N.M...*
1E0460	00000000 00037864 122FE808 002FDDA8	061E1BC6 00090050 28022828 001FF048	*......F...0*
1E0480	001FF238 001FF1E8 00000000 00000050	00000000 002FD4F8 00000000 00000000	*....Y...F...0*
1E04A0	00000000 00000000 051E1E2A 081DFFC6	00000040 00000000 00000000 00000000	*.......F*
1E04C0	80000000 00000000 46000001 001DFFC6	00000001 00000000 021FF078 00000000	*.......F...0.*
1E04E0	00000001 46000001 801E0484 00900048	00480000 021FF078 00000000 00000000	*.......0..*
1E0500	00000000 00000000 004100000 021FF190	002FDC98 00036474 922FCDC0 071E1BC6	*.....R8*
1E0520	00090085 28022828 421FE790 001FF105	00000085 00000000 002FDC98 00000000	*.......X...1*
1E0540	002FC810 05EF0000 001FFC6 00000000	00000000 501E0A08 122FE808 90009124	*.......F..Y...1*
1E0560	0030C4C2 001FF768 001FF3B0 501E0E66	001E104A 501E0A08 00000046 002FDDA8	*DB..7..3....Y...*
1E0580	001E0234 001E0234 001FE280 001FE560	001FE560 00000046 001E087A 00000000	*...S...V...V..*
1E05A0	402FE840 002FDDA8 32028048 00000000	0003478C 00003A108 001E087A 00000000	*.Y.......*
1E05C0	001E1BC6 001E1E7C 00000000 001FF7F8	0003478C 00000000 00000000 001FF768	*.......F...78..*
1E05E0	0003A080 0003C5AC 801DFFAC 00000000	001DFFAC 001D0FFAC 001E07C8 F140F0F0	*.....E.......H1 00*
1E0600	F640D440 F2F9F1F1 40D740C1 E5C440F0	F0F4F0F0 40404040 4040F948 F0C84040	*6 M 2911 P AvD 00400 9.nH*

57

Figure 3.6 Intermediate Page of 001 Main Storage

```
1FE020                                         01AC0000 000004B1 00000000 00000000  *................................*
1FE040  001FF3B0 001FF3F8 801FEF76 001E13A8   00000060 001FE030 001FF330 001E0F77  *..3...38...................3.....*
1FE060  0000017C 001FF3B0 0000004B 00000001   001E0EF5 001E07B0 001E0560 001FECF8  *......3............5...........8*
1FE080  001FE030 00000000 00000000 0000001C   011FE0F8 7F000000 00000000 001FE094  *...................8............*
1FE0A0  00000000 00000000 001FE0C0 001E038C   00000000 00000000 00000000 1E000000  *................................*
1FE0C0  231FE160 40000001 311FE0BB 40000005   081FE0C8 00000230 1D1FE0F0 A0000008  *.... ....... ......H.......0....*
1FE0E0  001FD3A0 40000230 221FE161 00000001   00000000 00000000 001FE090 7F000000  *..L. ...........................*
1FE100  00000000 001FE0FC 00000000 00000000   001FE128 001E038C 00000000 00000000  *................................*
1FE120  00000000 1E000000 231FE160 40000001   311FE123 40000005 081FE130 00000230  *............ ....... ...........*
1FE140  1D1FE158 A0000008 001FD5D0 40000230   221FE161 00000001 00000000 00000000  *..........N. ...................*
1FE160  00000000 00000000 411FE1D0 7F000000   00000000 7F1FE16C 001FE1C8 0C000000  *...........................H....*
1FE180  401FE198 001E02E0 00000000 00000000   00000000 21000000 231FE238 40000001  * ..........................S. ...*
1FE1A0  311FE193 40000005 081FE1A0 00000230   1D1FE1C8 A0000008 001FDBA0 40000230  *.... ..............H........ ...*
1FE1C0  221FE239 00000001 00210000 01000230   401FE168 7F000000 00000000 7F1FE1D4  *..S............. ..............M*
1FE1E0  001FE230 0C000000 401FE200 001E02E0   00000000 00000000 00000000 21000001  *..S..... .S.....................*
1FE200  231FE238 40000001 311FE1FB 40000005   081FE208 00000230 1D1FE230 A0000008  *..S. ....... .....S.......S.....*
1FE220  001FDDD0 40000230 221FE239 00000001   00210000 02000230 09090000 00000000  *.... .....S.....................*
1FE240  011FE2B0 48000000 00000000 481FE244   00000000 00000000 001FE270 001E0234  *..S...........S...........S.....*
1FE260  00000000 00000000 00000000 18001203   231FE320 40000001 311FE26B 40000005  *..................T. .....S. ...*
1FE280  081FE278 00000230 081FE290 70000001   921FE2A8 40000008 861FE330 60000230  *..S.......S.......S. .....T.....*
1FE2A0  221FE321 00000001 00180012 02000230   901FE240 41000000 04000000 411FE2B4  *..T...............S ..........S.*
1FE2C0  001FE310 0C4000F0 401FE2E0 001E0234   00000000 00000000 00000000 18001202  *..T.. .0 .S.....................*
1FE2E0  231FE320 40000001 311FE2DB 40000005   081FE2E8 00000230 081FE300 70000001  *..T. .....S. .....SY......T.....*
1FE300  921FE318 40000008 861FE560 60000230   221FE321 00000001 00180012 03000140  *..T. .....V.......T............ *
1FE320  10100000 00000000 00000000 00020230   F6F1F1F8 F8F1F4F3 F2F3F2F1 F4F3F6F7  *................6118814323214367*
1FE340  F3F4F1F1 F1F1F1F1 F1F1F1F2 F2F2F2F2   F2F2F2F0 F0F0F0F0 F0F1F6F9 F3F9F1F4  *34111111111222222220000001693914*
1FE360  F9F4F9F3 F4F1F3F5 F7F8F3F4 F1F9F4F4   F9F0F4F1 F3F4F2F9 F0F1F1F2 F3F4F5F9  *94934135783419449041342901123459*
1FE380  F6F1F1F8 F8F1F4F3 F2F3F2F1 F4F3F6F7   F3F4F1F1 F1F1F1F1 F1F1F1F2 F2F2F2F2  *61188143232143673411111111122222*
1FE3A0  F2F2F2F0 F0F0F0F0 F0F1F6F9 F3F9F1F4   F9F4F9F3 F4F1F3F5 F7F8F3F4 F1F9F4F4  *22200000016939149493413578341944*
1FE3C0  F9F0F4F1 F3F4F2F9 F0F1F1F2 F3F4F5F9   F6F1F1F8 F9F1F4F3 F2F3F2F1 F4F3F6F7  *90413429011234596118914323214367*
1FE3E0  F3F4F1F1 F1F1F1F1 F1F1F1F2 F2F2F2F2   F2F2F2F2 F0F3F6F1 F5F4F6F9 F3F9F1F4  *34111111111222222222036154693914*
1FE400  F9F4F9F3 F4F1F3F5 F7F8F3F4 F1F9F4F4   F9F0F4F1 F3F4F2F9 F0F1F1F2 F3F4F5F9  *94934135783419449041342901123459*
1FE420  F6F1F1F8 F9F1F4F3 F2F3F2F1 F4F3F6F7   F3F4F1F1 F1F1F1F1 F1F1F1F2 F2F2F2F2  *61189143232143673411111111122222*
1FE440  F2F2F2F2 F0F3F6F1 F5F4F6F9 F3F9F1F4   F9F4F9F3 F4F1F3F5 F7F8F3F4 F1F9F4F4  *22220361546939149493413578341944*
1FE460  F9F0F4F1 F3F4F2F9 F0F1F1F2 F3F4F5F9   F6F1F1F8 F9F1F4F3 F2F3F2F1 F4F3F6F7  *90413429011234596118914323214367*
1FE480  F3F4F1F1 F1F1F1F1 F1F1F1F2 F2F2F2F2   F2F2F2F2 F0F3F6F1 F5F4F6F9 F3F9F1F4  *34111111111222222222036154693914*
1FE4A0  F9F4F9F3 F4F1F3F5 F7F8F3F4 F1F9F4F4   F9F0F4F1 F3F4F2F9 F0F1F1F2 F3F4F5F9  *94934135783419449041342901123459*
1FE4C0  F6F1F1F8 F8F1F4F3 F2F3F2F1 F4F3F6F7   F3F4F1F1 F1F1F1F1 F1F1F1F2 F2F2F2F2  *61188143232143673411111111122222*
1FE4E0  F2F2F2F0 F0F0F0F0 F0F1F6F9 F3F9F1F4   F9F4F9F3 F4F1F3F5 F7F8F3F4 F1F9F4F4  *22200000016939149493413578341944*
1FE500  F9F0F4F1 F3F4F2F9 F0F1F1F2 F3F4F5F9   F6F1F1F8 F8F1F4F3 F2F3F2F1 F4F3F6F7  *90413429011234596118814323214367*
1FE520  F3F4F1F1 F1F1F1F1 F1F1F1F2 F2F2F2F2   F2F2F2F0 F0F0F0F0 F0F1F6F9 F3F9F1F4  *34111111111222222220000001693914*
1FE540  F9F4F9F3 F4F1F3F5 F7F8F3F4 F1F9F4F4   F9F0F4F1 F3F4F2F9 F0F1F1F2 F3F4F5F9  *94934135783419449041342901123459*
1FE560  F6F1F1F8 F8F1F4F3 F2F3F2F1 F4F3F6F7   F3F4F1F1 F1F1F1F1 F1F1F1F2 F2F2F2F2  *61188143232143673411111111122222*
1FE580  F2F2F2F0 F0F0F0F0 F0F1F6F9 F3F9F1F4   F9F4F9F3 F4F1F3F5 F7F8F3F4 F1F9F4F4  *22200000016939149493413578341944*
1FE5A0  F9F0F4F1 F3F4F2F9 F0F1F1F2 F3F4F5F9   F6F1F1F9 F1F1F4F3 F2F3F2F1 F4F3F6F7  *90413429011234596119114323214367*
1FE5C0  F3F4F1F1 F1F1F1F1 F1F1F1F2 F2F2F2F2   F2F2F2F2 F0F3F6F1 F5F4F6F9 F3F9F1F4  *34111111111222222222036154693914*
1FE5E0  F9F4F9F3 F4F1F3F5 F7F8F3F4 F1F9F4F4   F9F0F4F1 F3F4F2F9 F0F1F1F2 F3F4F5F9  *94934135783419449041342901123459*
1FE600  F6F1F1F9 F1F1F4F3 F2F3F2F1 F4F3F6F7   F3F4F1F1 F1F1F1F1 F1F1F1F2 F2F2F2F2  *61191143232143673411111111122222*
1FE620  F2F2F2F2 F0F3F6F1 F5F4F6F9 F3F9F1F4   F9F4F9F3 F4F1F3F5 F7F8F3F4 F1F9F4F4  *22220361546939149493413578341944*
1FE640  F9F0F4F1 F3F4F2F9 F0F1F1F2 F3F4F5F9   F6F1F1F9 F1F1F4F3 F2F3F2F1 F4F3F6F7  *90413429011234596119114323214367*
1FE660  F3F4F1F1 F1F1F1F1 F1F1F1F2 F2F2F2F2   F2F2F2F2 F0F3F6F1 F5F4F6F9 F3F9F1F4  *34111111111222222222036154693914*
1FE680  F9F4F9F3 F4F1F3F5 F7F8F3F4 F1F9F4F4   F9F0F4F1 F3F4F2F9 F0F1F1F2 F3F4F5F9  *94934135783419449041342901123459*
1FE6A0  F6F1F1F8 F8F2F4F3 F2F3F2F1 F4F3F6F7   F3F4F1F1 F1F1F1F1 F1F1F1F2 F2F2F2F2  *61188243232143673411111111122222*
1FE6C0  F2F2F2F2 F0F3F6F1 F5F4F6F9 F3F9F1F4   F9F4F9F3 F4F1F3F5 F7F8F3F4 F1F9F4F4  *22220361546939149493413578341944*
1FE6E0  F9F0F4F1 F3F4F2F9 F0F1F1F2 F3F4F5F9   F6F1F1F8 F8F2F4F3 F2F3F2F1 F4F3F6F7  *90413429011234596118824323214367*
1FE700  F3F4F1F1 F1F1F1F1 F1F1F1F2 F2F2F2F2   F2F2F2F2 F0F3F6F1 F5F4F6F9 F3F9F1F4  *34111111111222222222036154693914*
1FE720  F9F4F9F3 F4F1F3F5 F7F8F3F4 F1F9F4F4   F9F0F4F1 F3F4F2F9 F0F1F1F2 F3F4F5F9  *94934135783419449041342901123459*
1FE740  F6F1F1F8 F8F1F4F3 F2F3F2F1 F4F3F6F7   F3F4F1F1 F1F1F1F1 F1F1F1F2 F2F2F2F2  *61188143232143673411111111122222*
1FE760  F2F2F2F0 F0F0F0F0 F0F1F6F9 F3F9F1F4   F9F4F9F3 F4F1F3F5 F7F8F3F4 F1F9F4F4  *22200000016939149493413578341944*
1FE780  F9F0F4F1 F3F4F2F9 F0F1F1F2 F3F4F5F9   011FF7C8 7F000000 40000000 001FE794  *9041342901123459..XH.... .....X.*
1FE7A0  00000000 00000000 001FE7B8 001E04E4   00000000 00000000 031FF080 40000085  *..........X....U..........0. ...*
1FE7C0  09000000 20000000 001FE790 7F000000   40000000 001FE7CC 00000000 00000000  *..........X..... .....X.........*
1FE7E0  001FE7F0 001E04E4 00000000 00000000   031FF108 40000085 09000000 20000000  *..X0...U..........1. ...........*

1FDA80  7F000000 C4200000 8F1FF250 001FDADC   001FD868 00000000 00000000 00000000  *....D.....2.....................*
```

2. Problem File Determination

A problem overview can be found on the first page of all storage dumps. See Figure 3.3. The name assigned to this job is DZZ137. See letter 'A'. The name of the step in which the abend occurred is GO. See letter 'B'. The Completion Code is 001. See letter 'C'.

Before proceeding, the nature of the completion code should be described. An 001 Completion Code refers to an Input/Output (I/O) error which has been determined to be noncorrectable by the Operating System. As a result, the job is terminated and the dump routine called. DCB conflicts, damaged tape, and disk and drive malfunctions are typical 001 Storage Dump causes. A more detailed description of all completion codes can be obtained from IBM's Messages and Codes Manual as well as Chapter 7 of this text.

a. Short Hand Method

Either the Short Hand Method or Long Hand Method may be used to determine the problem file; however, the Long Hand Method need only be used when the Short Hand Method does not provide exact information as to which specific file was active at the time the problem occurred. Insufficient information is likely, for example, when concatenating data sets in which a series of separate files are strung together for the purpose of processing. The Short Hand Method does not indicate whether the 1st, 2nd, or 5th, etc., data set of a concatenation was being processed when the abend occurred.

The first step in the Short Hand Method of debugging External Abends is to locate Unit Control Block (UCB) information for the problem ddname, which can be found in the right-most three bytes of Register 10 of a Supervisor Request Block (SVRB). The SVRBs contain control information relating to program files. A valid UCB contains either three or four hexadecimal characters and points to the problem ddname. Looking down the left hand side of the first page of the dump, three SVRBs can be noted. See Figure 3.3, letter 'D'. To the right and below SVRB can be found RG 8-15. See letter 'E'. Checking the three right-most bytes in Register 10 of the first SVRB, the

hexadecimal characters 1FF1E8 are located. See letter 'F'. Being
larger than three or four characters, it can be presumed that this is
a high address in storage and not a UCB. Checking Register 10 of
the second SVRB, the hexadecimal characters 3744 are located. See letter 'G'. This four character value is a valid UCB and should be noted.
In this example, therefore, the third SVRB need not be checked. The
appropriate UCB is usually found in the next to last SVRB.

Next, the Task Input Output Table (TIOT) need be referenced. See
Figure 3.4, letter 'H'. The TIOT contains one line of information for
each file to be processed. It is possible to locate the UCB value
3744 obtained above by looking down the right hand portion of the TIOT.
See letter 'I'. Moving to the left two columns, the problem ddname is
found to be INPUT1. See letter 'J'. Having narrowed the problem file
to a specific ddname, the JCL listing can be referenced and the appropriate DD Statement analyzed. See Figure 3.1, letter 'K'. The DD
Statement for INPUT1 is:

```
//GO. INPUT1 DD  UNIT=SYSDA,DISP=(OLD,DELETE),
//         DSN=&&GRD123,
//         DCB=(RECFM=FB,LRECL=080,BLKSIZE=0560)
```

The problem disk file was created previously in STEP1 and passed to
STEP2 as input to the GO or execute step of the catalogued procedure
COBUCLG. This procedure compiles, links, and executes ANS COBOL programs. A JCL listing also provides information about the assigned
attributes of a data set. Quite often a programmer will be able to
solve the problem at this point. A JCL error, an erroneous program
specification, an invalid file description, and other similar causes
can be determined here. However, in the above example no apparent JCL
discrepancies can be uncovered and the problem file, as described in
the JCL, appears appropriate. A breakdown of DCB information later in
this chapter will shed more light on this type of problem.

b. Long Hand Method

Before proceeding to locate and analyze actual DCB information in
main storage, the Long Hand Method of determining the problem file

60

should be described. In spite of the fact that this method need only
be used when the Short Hand Method does not provide the programmer with
the specific file which was being processed at the time of the abend;
as mentioned earlier, it must be used when more than one line of the
TIOT contains the valid UCB, such as when data sets have been con-
catenated. Whereas the Short Hand Method always points to the problem
ddname, the Long Hand Method not only points to the problem ddname, but
in addition indicates to the programmer which file of a concatenation
is directly related to the storage dump problem.

Recall that a valid UCB of 3744 was found in Register 10 of the
second SVRB via the Short Hand Method. The starting address of Data
Control Block (DCB) information must be determined to utilize the
Long Hand Method, and can be found directly above the valid DCB in
Register 2 of the pertinent SVRB. The DCB Address in this example is
1E0234. See Figure 3.3, letter 'L'. This same address can also be
found in Register 2 of the REGS AT ENTRY TO ABEND. See Figure 3.5,
letter 'M'. Either location provides the appropriate DCB Address.

The next step involves locating the TIOT Offset in main storage.
This offset, or displacement from the starting point determined above,
will be used to calculate the position of the problem file in the TIOT.
To locate the TIOT Offset, a Hexadecimal 28 must be added to the DCB
Address as follows:

```
        DCB Address              1E0234
        Relative Location     +      28
        TIOT Offset Address      1E025C
```

TIOT Offset Address 1E025C can now be located in main storage.
First, page down the left hand side of the print of main storage until
the nearest address is found which does not exceed TIOT Offset Address
1E025C. This would be 1E0240 since the next line with 1E0260 exceeds
the address of interest. See Figure 3.5, letter 'N'. Reviewing the
technique of locating addresses as described in Chapter 2, the first
character encountered at Address 1E025C is a zero. Marking off a
length of two bytes for the length of the TIOT Offset, a hexadecimal
value of 0040 is found. See letter 'O'.

Next, a conversion which can be verified by referencing the Hexadecimal Decimal Conversion Table as discussed in the previous chapter,
from Hexadecimal 40 to Decimal 64 is accomplished. Finally, subtract
24, divide the result by 20 truncating any remainder, and add 1 as
follows:

$$64 - 24 = 40$$
$$40 / 20 = 2$$
$$2 + 1 = 3$$

The answer is the actual number of lines into the TIOT Table at which
the problem file can be found. Go to the TIOT Table and count down
three lines as indicated. At that point is the same UCB of 3744 which
was determined by the Short Hand Method. See Figure 3.4, letter 'I'.
The storage dump problem can now continue to be traced in the same
manner as employed by the Short Hand Method.

If, for example, the JCL for ddname INPUT1 had depicted a concatenation of six data sets, six lines with an identical UCB of 3744 would
have been generated for ddname INPUT1 in the TIOT. The Long Hand
Method would have pointed to the specific file, 1st, 2nd, 5th, etc.
Only when two or more data sets contain the same UCB value in the TIOT
is the Long Hand Method necessary.

The TIOT Offset is actually part of the DCB information which can
be located in main storage for the problem file. A description and
breakdown of pertinent elements of the Data Control Block is the next
concern.

3. Problem File Breakdown

a. DCB Initialization

The Operating System must determine Data Control Block (DCB) information for all files prior to actual processing. Each DCB describes
the attributes of a given data set. This includes such information as
Record Length, Blocksize, Block Count, Density, etc. DCB data is
obtained from a combination of specifications in the Program, JCL, and

Header Label. Locating the value of actual DCB attributes in main storage can be an aid in the debugging of many External Abends.

The Operating System actually determines DCB information by checking the Program first, the JCL second, and in the case of an input file, the Label third. DCB attributes must be specified in one or more of these sources. Subsequently, if DCB information is specified in more than one source, it should not conflict with previous specifications. Figure 3.7 below depicts a typical DCB initialization procedure.

Figure 3.7 DCB Initialization Process

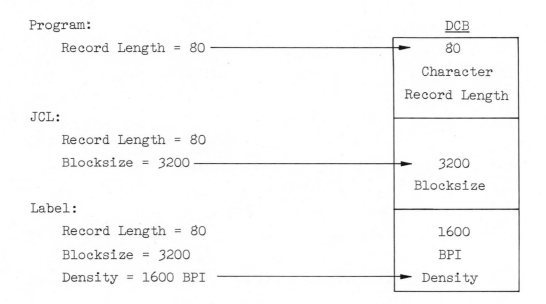

Note in the previous example that the record length specification in the JCL as well as the record length and blocksize specifications in the label were not referenced for building the DCB since these items had already been previously obtained. Locating DCB values in main storage can be a valuable aid in the debugging of abends caused by conflicting DCB specifications.

b. DCB Location

Figure 3.8 illustrates the location of pertinent DCB information relating to the problem file.

Figure 3.8   DCB Attribute Location

DCB Address plus:

		Field Length
Hexadecimal 0 = Block Count		(4 bytes)
12 = Density		(1 byte)
28 = TIOT Offset		(2 bytes)
3E = Maximum Blocksize		(2 bytes)
4C = Address of Next Record		(4 bytes)
52 = Logical Record Length		(2 bytes)
5A = Physical Record Length		(2 bytes)

The Block Count contains the number of complete blocks which have been processed up to the time of the abend and thus provides an indication of how far into the file actual processing has proceeded prior to abnormal termination.   The field is four bytes in length.

The one byte Density field contains a DCB tape density indication for 200 Bits Per Inch (BPI), 556 BPI, 800 BPI, 1600 BPI, and so on. Incorrect DCB Density specifications often occur when 'outside' tapes are brought into an installation for processing.

The TIOT Offset was referenced earlier in this chapter in the Long Hand Method of determining the problem file.   A decimal value of 64 was used in calculating the location of the problem ddname in the Task Input Output Table.   Field length is two bytes.

Maximum Blocksize refers to the programmer specified blocksize as coded in the program, JCL, or Label for each file.   This value must be greater than or equal to the actual size of the current block being processed.   If a block is encountered which exceeds the specified Maximum Blocksize, an External Abend will occur.   A field of two bytes is utilized.

The four byte Address of Next Record provides a programmer with the starting address of the next record to be processed.   This can be particularly helpful when attempting to determine which record was being processed at the time of the abend.

Logical Record Length refers to the programmer specified record length as coded in the program, JCL or Label for each file. Values in this two byte field must be equal to the size of any fixed length records to be processed. If a fixed length record exceeds the Logical Record Length, and/or the Maximum Blocksize for fixed length records is not a multiple of the Logical Record Length, an External Abend is likely to result. Logical Record Length for variable length records can exceed actual record size.

Physical Record Length refers to the actual blocksize of the data currently being processed. When DCB conflicts arise relating to blocksize specifications during processing, the value in this two byte field can be compared with Maximum Blocksize to determine erroneous program or JCL specifications.

DCB problems usually result in an 001 or 013 Completion Code. Debugging of the 001 Storage Dump depicted earlier in this chapter can now proceed.

Realizing that an improper file description can cause an 001 Dump, a programmer would be interested in determining the DCB attributes for the previously determined problem ddname INPUT1. Specifications for Maximum Blocksize and Logical Record Length would be of particular interest as they are most frequently involved in DCB conflicts. Locating the next record to be processed will also be covered.

To locate Maximum Blocksize, a Hexadecimal 3E must be added to the DCB Address or starting point of DCB information in main storage. Recall that DCB Address 1E0234 was found in Register 2 of the pertinent SVRB as well as Register 2 of the Registers At Entry To Abend. See Figures 3.3 and 3.5, letters 'L' and 'M', respectively. Hexadecimal 3E is added as follows:

DCB address	1E0234
Relative Location	+ 3E
Maximum Blocksize Address	1E0272

Address 1E0272 can now be located in storage. Paging down the left hand side of the print of main storage. Address 1E0260 and 1E0280 are encountered in Figure 3.5. The address of interest, 1E0272, is contained within the print line beginning at Address 1E0260. See letter 'P'. Moving to the right and using Chapter 2's technique of locating addresses in main storage, the first character encountered at Address 1E0272 is found to be a zero. Marking off a field length of two bytes, a Hexadecimal value of 0230 is found to reside at that point. See letter 'Q'. Converting Hexadecimal 230 to Decimal, it can be determined that the Maximum Blocksize for problem ddname INPUT1 is 560 characters. This agrees with the blocksize specification as coded in the JCL's DD Statement for INPUT1. See Figure 3.1, letter 'K'.

The Source Program listing should also be referenced for ddname INPUT1. See Figure 3.2, letter 'R'. Detail characteristics of the problem file can be found in the file section of the program. See letter 'S'. The Maximum Blocksize specification of 560 characters appears appropriate.

Logical Record Length should be determined next. A Hexadecimal 52 is added to the DCB Address as follows:

```
DCB Address                          1E0234
Relative Location                  +     52
                                   ──────────
Logical Record Length Address        1E0286
```

Again, paging down the left hand side of Figure 3.5, Address 1E0280 and 1E02A0 are soon encountered. The address of interest, 1E0286, is contained within the print line beginning at Address 1E0280. See Figure 3.5, letter 'T'. Moving to the right the required number of bytes, the first character encountered at Address 1E0286 is a zero. Marking off a field length of two bytes, a hexadecimal value of 0046 is found to reside at that point. See letter 'U'. Converting Hexadecimal 46 to Decimal, it can be determined that the Logical Record Length for problem ddname INPUT1, as described in the DCB, is 70 characters. Referring back to the DD Statement for problem ddname INPUT1, however; it is found that the specified record length is 80 characters. See Figure 3.1, letter 'K'.

From where did Logical Record Length 70 as found in main storage originate? Remembering that the Operating System first references the program during the DCB initialization process, a record length

specification of 70 characters can be found. See Figure 3.2, letter
'V'. As a result, the Record Length recorded in the JCL was bypassed,
or simply not used to build the DCB for the file referenced by ddname
INPUT1. Referring to ddname SYSUT2 in STEP1, it is found that the output file as created and passed to STEP2's GO step contains a Record
Length of 80 characters. See Figure 3.1, letter 'W'. DCB conflicts
of this nature lie at the heart of many External Abend storage dump
problems.

4. Buffer Location

An analysis of data stored within the Buffer Area for the problem
file can also be made. The size of a buffer is equivalent to the
Blocksize specification. If it has been loaded into main storage at
the time of the abend, it can easily be located. An examination of
the current and next record to be processed can then be made.

To determine the Address of the Next Record to be processed, a
Hexadecimal 4C is added to the DCB Address as follows:

DCB Address	1E0234
Relative Location	+ 4C
Address of Next Record	1E0280

Paging down the left hand side of Figure 3.5, Address 1E0280 is
soon encountered. See letter 'T'. Marking off a four byte field, the
Address of the Next Record to be processed is found to be 1FE51A. See
letter 'X'. This address can now be located in the Buffer Area of
main storage.

Paging down the left hand side of Figure 3.6, Address 1FE500 comes
closest to but does not exceed the address of interest. See letter
'Y'. Counting to the right the required number of bytes, the first
character encountered at Address 1FE51A is F. See letter 'Z'. This
is the beginning of the next record to be processed. Noting such
character strings as F2, F1, etc., and reviewing Chapter 2's technique
of data interpretation, it is apparent that the data contained within
the problem file is defined in Character Format. This could be

verified by a check of the processing program. The absence of the USAGE Clause in the COBOL program's File Section assumes DISPLAY. F2 can be interpreted to be a +2 or 2; F1 a +1, or 1; etc. In other words, columns 1 and 2 of the next record to be processed are equal to a 2 and 1, respectively. The same technique can be utilized to interpret remaining columns, if desired. The current record being processed could be found by moving back a number of bytes equivalent to the record length from the Address of the Next Record, 1FE51A, previously located.

All data represented in Character Format is interpreted in the right-most portion of the print of main storage. A Decimal interpretation of the next record to be processed can be found. See Figure 3.6, number '1'. This is a Decimal interpretation of Column 1 in the next record and is equivalent to that stored at letter 'Z' in main storage. The beginning of this particular buffer for the problem file is somewhat obvious. See number '2'. This is the beginning of External Decimal interpretations. A complete review of the data, including the current and next record to be processed, will assist the analysis of many abends.

5. Problem Analysis

For interest's sake, the values for Block Count and Physical Record Length can be determined. They are 00000000 (a complete block has not yet been processed) and 0000 (not yet determined), respectively.

In retrospect, what actually happened to cause this particular storage dump was as follows:

a. Program IEBGENER in STEP1 created an output file for ddname SYSUT2 with a Logical Record Length of 80 characters as specified in the JCL. This IBM utility does not specify record length and blocksize within the program itself, but rather relies on JCL specifications. The file was then correctly passed as input to STEP2's GO step.

b. A user program called by catalogued procedure COBUCLG in STEP2 was referenced by the Operating System for DCB attributes. The system obtained a Logical Record Length of 70 from the program's File Section.

    c. The Operating System, therefore, bypassed record length information contained within the JCL and Label when setting up a DCB for that file.

    d. The abend occurred after the Operating System began processing under the designated DCB specifications. A conflict between actual and expected records lengths was encountered.

    This type of external abend is one of the most perplexing to debug. It was used as an example because of the extensive procedures one must go through to effectively locate the cause. Whether JCL and Label DCB specifications are correct and the program wrong, or vice versa, would of course, depend upon the programmer's original intention.

    For most External Abends the Short Hand Method is sufficient. Nevertheless, on occasion the Long Hand Method is necessary. For DCB conflicts, a breakdown of pertinent DCB information is required. The preceding example has successfully utilized all three phases of External Storage Dump debugging procedures.

D. LABEL PROCESSING

1. Computer Run Overview (813)

    Abnormal terminations while processing label records are a frequent occurrence. Prior to the DCB Initialization process and actual processing of data, the volume and header label must pass a series of validity checks. Label processing is accomplished to ensure that the correct volume has been mounted and that the data set name for the file to be processed agrees with the data set name as coded in the JCL.

    The Volume Serial number is internally recorded in the Volume Label record. When an output file is created, the Data Set name as coded in the JCL's DD Statement for that particular file is placed in a Header Label record. Upon completion of processing, similar identifying information is placed in the Trailer Label records. Later, when used as input, the Volume Serial number and Data Set name contained within the Label is compared to that of the JCL. Discrepancies result in an 813 Storage Dump.

With abends of this nature, the specific programming language utilized is again of no consequence. Only the JCL listing and Storage Dump itself need be referenced.

Figures 3.9 through 3.14 depict pertinent pages of an 813 Storage Dump.

Figure 3.9   Job Control Language Listing (813)

```
//STEP1   EXEC  PGM=IEBGENER
//SYSUT1  DD  UNIT=2400,DISP=(OLD,KEEP),
//          DSN=AMASTER,VOL=SER=OS2219,
//        D DCB=(RECFM=FB,LRECL=080,BLKSIZE=560)
//SYSIN    DD  DUMMY
//SYSUT2   DD  UNIT=SYSDA,DISP=(NEW,PASS),
//          DSN=&&GRD123,SPACE=(080,12,RLSE),
//          DCB=(RECFM=FB,LRECL=080,BLKSIZE=560)
//SYSPRINT  DD  SYSOUT=A
//SYSUDUMP  DD  SYSOUT=A
/*
//STEP2    EXEC COBUCLG,PARM.COB='DMAP,PMAP',
//          REGION.GO=30K,TIME.GO=(,20)
//COB.SYSIN    DD  *
/*
//GO.INPUT1   DD  UNIT=SYSDA,DISP=(OLD,DELETE),
//          DSN=&&GRD123,
//          DCB=(RECFM=FB,LRECL=080,BLKSIZE=0560)
//GO.CDINPUT1  DD  *
/*
//GO.OUTPUT1  DD UNIT=SYSDA,DISP=(NEW,DELETE),
//          DSN=&&GRD456,SPACE=(0080,12,RLSE)
//GO.OUTPUT2  DD UNIT=SYSDA,DISP=(NEW,DELETE),
//        DSN=&&GRD789,SPACE=(0080,12,RLSE)
//GO.MSGOUT     DD  SYSOUT=A
//GO.SYSUDUMP   DD  SYSOUT=A
//
```

Figure 3.10 First Page of 813 Storage Dump

```
JOB  RZZ126  (A) STEP STEP1                TIME 185743
COMPLETION CODE   SYSTEM = 813
PSW AT ENTRY TO ABEND  FF04000D 50016616

TCB 0351F0   RBP   00042368   PIE    00000000   DEB   00035FAC   CMP   80813000   TRN   00000000
             MSS   02040A28   PK-FLG D085040D   FLG   0005F5B    JLB   00000000   JPQ   0003F848
             FSA   0108E768   TCB    00036868   TME   00000000   NTC   00000000   DTC   0003C2D0
             LTC   00000000   IQE    00000000   ECB   0003561C   D-PQE 00041560   SQS   00034F80
             NSTAE 00000000   TCT    80035DD8   USER  00000000   RESV  00000000   JSCB  87037E40
             RESV  00000000   ICB    00000000

ACTIVE RBS

PRB  037CF0  RFSV  00000000   APSW   00000000   WC-SZ-STAB 00040082  FL-CDE 00037F10  PSW FFD50013 50082D9E
             Q/TTR 00000000   WT-LNK 00035F10

SVRB 042638  TAB-LN 00280400  APSW   F1F9F9C5   WC-SZ-STAB 0C12D002  TQN    00000000  PSW FF04000D 50016616
             Q/TTR  0000101D   WT-LNK 00037CF0
             RG 0-7  0000280   9C082D98   CC082BD8   0008E588   0008E088   00035338   0003D890
             RG 8-15 00000000  00035DD8   00035620   00037998   0000000C   4007FC7A   00082BD8
             EXTSA 800833DC    2208EDE0   00027A08   0008EFC8   0008EFE8   0008EFE8   000352E4
                   00011BE0    90081B60   00000000   001DEB52

SVRB 041F78  TAB-LN 00480220  APSW   F9F0F1C3   WC-SZ-STAB 0012D002  TQN    00000000  PSW 00040033 50016D1A
             Q/TTR  00004629   WT-LNK 00042638
             RG 0-7  80000000  80813000   4C0162EA(E) 0808EDE0(H) 0027A08   90082D98
             RG 8-15 0008EFE8  00035200   0008EE44   0008EE4B   0008EE44   00000004
             EXTSA 000021BF    8F08DD28   00000000   FF030000   00041FF4   E2E8E2C9
                   C5C1F0F1    C9C5C1F0   C1C2C5D5(B) C4F98130

SVRB 042308  TAB-LN 008803D8  APSW   F1F0F5C1   WC-SZ-STAB 0012D002  TQN    00000000  PSW FF04000C 40080D7A6
             Q/TTR  00003801   WT-LNK 00041F78
             PG 0-7  00000007  80016C32   0C01A318   0C0351FC   04C351F0   00041F78
             RG 8-15 000351F0  0001687A   8F08DD28   00041FFC   4001940C   00000000
             EXTSA E2E8E2C9    C5C1F0F1   00000000   F9000000   0000C378   00040004

LCAD LIST

NE 0003FB40  RSP-CDE 0203F848   NE 0003FB50  RSP-CDE 01045C8    NE 0003FB60  RSP-CDE 01045888
NE 0003FB68  RSP-CDE 01045C8    NE 0003EB98  RSP-CDE 01045988   NE 0003FB38  RSP-CDE 010 58C8
NE 0003F938  RSP-CDE 01045888   NE 0003F940  RSP-CDE 01045B58   NE 00000000  PSP-CDE 01045AF8

CDE
037F10  ATR1 08  NCDE C00000  FOC-RB 00037CF0  NM TERGENER  USE 01  EPA 07FAC0  ATR2 20  XL/MJ 037AA8
03F848  ATR1 30  NCDE 037F10  POC-RB 00000000  NM IGC0A05A  USE 02  EPA C8D058  ATR2 28  XL/MJ 03F988
0458C8  ATR1 80  NCDE 0458F8  ROC-RP 00000000  NM IGG019CF  USE 01  EPA 1FC590  ATR2 20  XL/MJ 045888
```

Figure 3.11 Second Page of 813 Storage Dump

```
045888   ATR1 BO   NCDE 0458C8   RQC-RB 00000000   USE 01   NM IGG019CL   RQC-RB 00000000   EPA 1FF810   ATR2 20   XL/MJ 045878
0459C8   ATR1 BO   NCDE 0459F8   RQC-RB 00000000   USE 01   NM IGG019BA   RQC-RB 00000000   EPA 1FCE40   ATR2 20   XL/MJ 0459B8
045988   ATR1 BO   NCDE 0459C8   RQC-RB 00000000   USE 01   NM IGG019BB   RQC-RB 00000000   EPA 1FCCC8   ATR2 20   XL/MJ 045978
045858   ATR1 BO   NCDE 045888   RQC-RB 00000000   USE 01   NM IGG019AK   RQC-RB 00000000   EPA 1FDD58   ATR2 20   XL/MJ 045848
045AF8   ATR1 BO   NCDE 045828   RQC-RB 00000000   USE 01   NM IGG019AR   RQC-RB 00000000   EPA 1FDAD0   ATR2 20   XL/MJ 045AE8

XL          SZ                NO                      LN         ADR          LN         ADR          LN         ADR
037AA8   SZ 00000010   NO 00000001   80006540   0007FAC0
03F988   SZ 00000010   NO 00000001   800007A8   0008D058
045888   SZ 00000010   NO 00000001   80000270   001FC590
045878   SZ 00000010   NO 00000001   80000040   001FF810
0459B8   SZ 00000010   NO 00000001   800001C0   001FCE40
045978   SZ 00000010   NO 00000001   80000178   001FCCC8
045848   SZ 00000010   NO 00000001   800000E0   001FDD58
045AE8   SZ 00000010   NO 00000001   80000110   001FDAD0

DEB
035F80                                00008660 001FF810   00008660 00008660 00000000   *...H.........8....*
035FA0   00000000 00002BE0 0F000000 04035IF0   100350F4 C8000000 01000000   *.......O...4H.....*
035FC0   5B000000 DF08DD28 02035F88 33004DA8   00010001 00000000 0000007D   *.................*
035FE0   C2C2C2C1 C3D3C3C6 00000000 00000000   00000000 00000000 00000000   *BBBACLCF.........*

DEB
0350C0                                00008660 001FF810   00008660 00008660 00008660   *...........8.....*
0350E0   000C8660 00000000 00000000 00011BF0   0F000000 040351F0 10000000 C8000000   *.........O...H..*
035100   0F000000 01300000 00000079 5B000000   02035DD0 33004C88 00010001 00000000   *.....ARAKLCF.....*
035120   00000000 00000079 C1D9C1D2 C3D3C3C6   00000000 00000000 0000C000   *.........8......*
035140   00000000 00000000

TIOT   JOB D3RZZ126   STEP STEP1
  DD    14060140   SYSUT1     C0612200           80C4164
  DD    14C00040   SYSIN      00612800   00000000
  DD    14040100   SYSUT2     C0612A00   80001944
  DD    14040140   SYSPRINT   00620100   80004D88
  DD    14040140   SYSUDUMP   00620300   80004DA8   ← C

DATA MANAGEMENT CONTROL BLOCKS

SYSPRINT   DEB   0350F4   040351F0 10000000 C8000000 0F000000   01000000 5B000000 DF080300 02035DD0
                          33004D88 00C10001 0C0C0000 00000000   00000079 C1C9C1D2 C3D3C3C6 00000000
                          00000000 00000000 0C0C00C0 00000000   0C0C0000 00000000 00000080 00008660

           DCR   080300   0C0C0000 30CC0000 0C0C0000 00000000   C4080000 0208E66C 00004000 00000001
                          04000001 84C7FE8C 0C540050 000350F4   921FDD58 001FDAD0 0707FE46 04090079
                          28022828 4308E628 0008E761 0008E761   00000079 00000001 00000000 001FC590
```

72

Figure 3.12 First Page of 813 Main Storage

```
                NQEL 00000000    PQEL 0003EBA8   TCB 00035IF0    SVRB 00042368

SAVE AREA TRACE

IEBGENER WAS ENTERED VIA LINK

SA  08E768  WD1 00000000   HSA 00000000   LSA 00000000   RET 00020510   FPA 0107FAC0   R0 F0000008
            R1  0008E7F8    R2  00000000   R3  5C035620   R4  00030520   R5  0003C200   R6  00035338
            R7  00038890    R8  000355F8   R9  00035DD8   P10 00035620   P11 00037998   R12 401FE102

INTERRUPT AT C82D9E

PROCEEDING BACK VIA REG 13

SA  083A30  WD1 60004770   HSA 0007FE9C   LSA 60004550   RET 92869540   EPA 70004780   R0 92869101
            R1  98604710    R2  92749102   R3  98604710   R4  92749268   R5  8C0041B8   R6 0001926B
            R7  B0000207    R8  80017000   R9  50809862   P10 96049860   P11 41F08008   R12 45E092A2

REGS AT ENTRY TO ABEND

    FLTR 0-6   0000001200080012      0C0B00041B001944      000000C1200C0012      000D00021B001944

    REGS 0-7   80000000   80813000   8CC833DC   400162EA     0808EDE0   00027A08   0008EFC8   90382D98
    REGS 8-15  0008EFE8   00035200   8CC04164   0008EE44     0008EE4B   0008EF44   00000004   00000004
                                          F                      I

LCAD MODULE  IEBGENER

07FAC0  90ECD00C 052090DE 23CE41DC 23069200   27260727 24222422 58310000 95801000   *........O....P....*
07FAE0  47802088 58410004 12444780 20644884   00001288 47C02064 41900048 19894740   *.........K.......*
07FB00  203E1889 41900020 1B890680 42802048   D2272422 40221B88 5980242A 47802064   *.....K.....K.....*
07FB20  4180283A D2078028 242A9580 10044780   20885851 00084885 00041190 00041989   *...K.........K...*
07FB40  47402088 D2032481 500247F0 208E0203   248124C5 41800000 89800002 5A8025C6   *.K.....O.K....E.*
07FB60  58880000 D227244A 80000700 45102OAE   8F080300 0A1341E0 283A9110 E0304ICO   *........O.K.....*
07FB80  000C4780 226A9110 23CA4780 21284100   02004110 244445E0 26344110 0C138910   *..........6...O.*
07FBA0  00084190 00131A19 41F02548 05EF41C0   000C0700 45102OF6 80080300 0A144110   *............O...O*
07FBC0  283A58F0 10149601 10171B6E 43E0F005   4CE0F006 4100F008 9140F004 47E021IF   *...O....O...O...O*
07FBE0  4100E010 4110F000 0A0A47F0 22644100   02004110 244445E0 26341B44 4883O000   *...O...O...O.....*
07FC00  194847F0 2158411O 00018910 00084190   00021A19 41F02548 05EF47F0 23424100   *..O........N.....*
07FC20  00684510 21600A0A 5010241E 41400002   19844740 217AD5O1 30022403 47802A2    *......O.....N..C.*
07FC40  47F02182 0008IC68 4510218A 0007FEE8   58F0217E 05EF47F0 21984770 23425830   *.Y.O....O.......*
07FC60  241ED267 30001000 411024IE 47F021AE   00082BD8 58F021AA 05EF18CF 45102IBE   *..K.........Y.O.*
07FC80  80080300 0A144110 283A58F0 10149601   10171B6E 43E0F005 4CE0F006 4100E008   *.........O...O...*
07FCA0  9140F004 47E021E6 4100E010 4110F000   0A0A5830 241E1233 4780226A 91FF2836   *...O.........O...*
07FCC0  4710225E 48530060 12554780 22145813   0040180S 41110000 0A0A4853 00621255   *.K.....O...W....O*
07FCE0  47802232 58130044 41400008 1B144105   00084111 0000OA0A 48530064 12554780   *...........K.....*
07FD00  22485813 00481805 41110000 0A0A4853   00661255 4780225E 58130O4C 18054111   *...........O.....*
07FD20  0000OA0A 18134100 00684111 00000A0A   18FC98DE 23C982C D0IC07FE 4180283A   *................*
07FD40  4850803E 12554780 229C1B44 00080C68   1D461244 078E9210 23CAD201 803E8052   *.K.......K.......*
07FD60  07FE9279 803FO7FE 47FO22AA 00081C68   4510228E 8007FEE8 58F022A6 05EF5840   *.........Y.O....*
07FD80  241E96FF 28364190 00081998 47802336   41303O0A 16885983 00004770 22E69240   *.............W...*
```

73

Figure 3.13 Intermediate Page of 813 Main Storage

```
082EE0  47F02214 91012F94 47102D0C 91022F94 47102D30 94002F27 58102804 41502804  *.0......4...0...0*
082F00  41602864 91082DE8 47102734 94002F27 47F02320 00085050 58F0231C 05EF45E0  *......Y....0.....0*
082F20  27F849F0 2F224780 276649F0 2F204780 27664110 28049110 10304780 23520700  *.8.0.....0.....0*
082F40  45102350 800833DC 0A145840 2F2C1244 47802364 41402E21 45E02784 95FF2F10  *.0....0..9..0...0*
082F60  92F02359 47F02378 41F02F8C 47F021FA 92022F27 96802EF9 92002DE9 58402DF0  *.9...Z....0*
082F80  41440000 50402F4C 41102864 91101030 4780240E 451023A4 8008343C 0A149104  *....0....0....0.0*
082FA0  2DE847E0 24E04110 280458F0 10149601 10171BEE 43E0F005 4CE0F006 91011020  *.Y......0...0.0*
082FC0  47102304 4100E008 47F023D8 4100E010 4110F000 0A0A4110 286458F0 10149601  *.M...0.Q....0.0*
082FE0  10171BEE 43E0F005 4CE0F006 91011020 47102404 4100E008 47F02408 4100E010  *...0....0.0.0*
083000  4110F000 0A0A5840 2F341244 47802420 41402E2F 45E02784 95FF2F10 92F02415  *....0....4...0*
083020  47702434 41F02F84 47F021FA 581020F4 12114780 24484100 02804111 00000A0A  *....0....0....0*
083040  581020DEC 12114780 245C4100 02804111 00000A0A 581020F0 12114780 24704100  *.0....0.....0*
083060  28044160 2864D501 503E2F98 47702461 960A503F D2015052 2F9A9601 2F94D501  *.Y..0.*
083080  50522F98 477024EE 91485024 47F025E4 91405024 471024D2 91105024 471024E4  *..0...K...K...U*
0830A0  D2015052 503E47F0 24EE4130 00044845 003E1B43 40450052 47F024EE D2015052  *.0...K...K.*
0830C0  503E9601 2F94D501 603E2F98 47702532 D5016052 60245024 41100033 41110034  *.K...N...K..*
0830E0  2532D201 603E503E D2016052 5052D200 60245024 471024D2 960A603F D2016052  *.0...N..K...N*
083100  58F02F0C 05EF47F0 25AAD501 603E2F98 4770254A 960A603F D2016052 2F9A9602  *.0...N*
083120  2F94D501 60522F98 477025AA 91486024 47102594 47102570 91106024 91106052  *.N....0*
083140  47102594 47F025A4 91FF2EEC 47802582 D2016052 50524770 251C4130 00044846  *.0...K...0*
083160  003E1B43 40460052 47F025AA 91FF2EEC 47802578 96022F94 D2016052 47802614  *.K...N...0*
083180  603E4130 2D0C9140 50244710 25F49110 25CCD501 5052503E 47802614 920C300B  *...4...N...0*
0831A0  47F025DE 1B884895 003E4845 00521D84 12884780 2614D201 5052503E 920C300B  *....K...0*
0831C0  920B3013 96012F94 47F02614 95024 41990004 4995003E  *...M..*
0831E0  47D02614 4095003E 47F025E4 19564780 26281856 41302030 920225ED 47F025AE  *...0.U...U...0*
083200  41502804 91485024 47102640 91486024 47102684 47F02CC8 D5006024 50244770  *...K...0.HN*
083220  2684D501 60525052 47702684 D501603E 503E4770 2684918F 2EEC4780 26849280  *...N...0.*
083240  2F264110 00228910 008A4111 002258F0 2F0C05EF 96082DE8 47F02CC8 91805052  *...0.Y.0.H*
083260  47802644 41100010 89100008 41400010 41000C01 45E02784 47F02214 91806052  *...0.8.0*
083280  4710268C 91202875 47802604 95002874 47802CC8 41100014 89100008 41400014  *...Y.0.H*
0832A0  41F0000C 45E027F8 41F0000C 41F0000C 47802740 95002814 2EEC4780 41100015  *...0.8.0*
0832C0  89100008 41400015 41F0000C 45E027F8 47F02214 59022EE0 47802F1C 48002F18  *...0.8.0*
0832E0  4000282E 48002F1A 4000288E 960C2DE8 47F02CC8 41100010 89100008 4140001D  *...Y.0.H*
083300  41F0000C 45E027F8 47F02214 94002F27 47F02740 00084058 58F0273C 05EF45E0  *...0....0...0*
083320  27F849F0 2F224780 276649F0 2F204780 276647F0 233A1A14 58F02F0C 05EF48F0  *.8.0.....0...0*
083340  2F129400 2C4C9680 2C4C9940 2C3C9680 2C3C9680 233A1000 47F0233A 50E02EF0  *...0....0*
083360  58102DFC 1BEE43E0 2DE941EE 00F042E1 0000D20D 100B4000 41100018 89100008  *....Z...K*
083380  41400001C1A1458F0 2F0C05EF 18551B44 43502E04 4130000A 1D435810 2E004144  *...0.Z...*
0833A0  00F0415C C00F0425 00154241 00164110 00198910 00084140 00191A14 58F02F0C  *.0.Z....0*
0833C0  05EF9200 2DE99200 2E04580 2EF007FE 49F02F12 074E40F0 2F1207FE 00000000  *.Z.....0*
0833E0  00000000 00000000 00000000 00000000 00000001 00004000 00083358 00083358  *.0...0*
083400  00083814 00182000 00000000 0008EDE0 03002000 00000000 00083358 00000000  *.9...0*
083420  00000001 00000000 00000001 00000000 00000000 00000000 00000000 00000000  *.0...0*
083440  00000001 00083820 E2E8E2E4 E3F24040 02000024 00000000 00083358 00000000  *.SYSUT2*
083460  00000000 00000000 00000000 00000000 00000001 00C00000 41300084 00000001  *...0*
083480  1BF3182F 50E02EF0 92042DEA 91801008 18444340 2DF44144 00014240 41300804  *.3...0...D*
0834A0  12FF4780 29185831 00001233 47802918 47F0291E 91012F27 47802918 47802918  *...0...F.0*
0834C0  2DF8D24F 41440050 50402DF8 58E02EF9 07FE5831 00001233 47802962 47802962  *...4....4*
0834E0  91B02EEE 47802A58 41440000 0000D24F 47003034 91B02EE9 47802962 43402DEC  *.8K....9..0*
083500  95F13003 47702934 96802EF9 91F02F27 48E02EF9 00505040 2E389180 2EF94780  *.1.....9.K.*
083520  41440001 42402DEC 58402F38 D24F4000 30004144 00054040 42E02DE9 2E0491F0  *....K.....0*
083540  29A858F0 2DE941EE 00142E09 2DE905EF 4JE0E001 42E02DE9 05EF42F0 2E0491F0  *.Z...9...0*
083560  2F274780 29869138 2EEE4780 2DEA47F0 4780029A8 49F02F20 47702800 96802EF5  *.Z...Z...0*
083580  947F2EF9 1BFF43F0 2DEA47F0 28E049F0 478029A8 28E096FF 2F1047F0 28E04140  *...9....0*
0835A0  2E0545E0 2B8047F0 29624130 09D21BF3 182F50E0 2EF09204 2DEA9180 1008.4710  *.9...0.0*
0835C0  2A805831 00001233 47802A58 47F02F11 47102A36 92F02F11 584020F0 58402DE4  *...K.3....0*
0835E0  91B02EEE 47802A58 91801004 47E02A58 91F02F11 47102A36 00014240 2F4C5831  *.9.....Z*
083600  41440000 50402F4C 1B444240 2DF04340 2DF04144 00014240 2DF05840 2F4C5831  *.....0....0*
083620  0000D24F 47003000 41440050 50407F4C 91802EF9 478029A8 58F02F2C 12FF4780  *.K...9...0*
083640  29A843E0 2DE941EE 00014260 2DE905EF 42E02E04 47F0298E 41402E21 45E02BB0  *.K...Z...9*
083660  47F02A58 41300A8C 1BF3182F 50E02EF0 92082DEA 91801008 47102B12 91012F27  *.0...3....0*
083680  47802AE2 1B444340 2DEC1244 4780280A 58310000 12334780 2AE20640 42402DEC  *.0.....S....0*
0836A0  58402F38 D24F3000 00004144 00505040 2F389180 2EF94780 29A858F0 2F3012FF  *...K....9*
0836C0  478029A8 43E02DE9 41EE0001 42E02DE9 05EF42F0 2E0491F0 2EF74780 29864780  *.Z....Z...0*
0836E0  298E9200 2DEA47F0 2AE24130 0B1E1BF3 182F50E0  *.0.S....S....3*
```

74

Figure 3.14 Label Residing in 813 Main Storage

```
                                                                                                          N
                                                                                           HDR1E110BACK
J                                                                 L                    75177        OS2219000010000
→                                                              K  ↓   O  AMASTER            P→ OS2219
08EDC0  C8C4D9F1 C5F1F1F0 C2C1C3D2 40404040   40404040 40D6E2F2 90082D98 8008EEF4  *..HDR1E110BACK....OS2.....0..8........8......OS221900010*
08EDE0  F0F0F140 40404040 F0F0F0F0 F0F0F0F0   F0F0F0F0 F0F0F0F0 F2F1F9F0 F0F0F1F0  *001.........75177.........75177....0000000000000.....*
08EE00  00000000 00000000 00000000 80003138   80003138 00000000 F0F0F0F0 00000000  *............................................*
08EE20  00000000 C1D4C1E2 E3C5D940 40404040   40404040 4B00E000 0F08EF20 C3004164  *....AMASTER.............................YC..*
08EE40  40404040 40404040 40404040 40404040   40404040 00002000 00008EE8 00000000  *......................................*
08EE60  00000000 00000200 00010000 00002000   4B00E000 00000040 00000000 00000000  *......................................*
08EE80  0000C300 00000000 90000230 00000000   00000000 0001D6E2 F2F2F1F9 00000000  *...........................OS2219.....*
08EEA0  40404040 40404040 40404040 40404040   40404040 40404040 00000000 00000000  *......................................*
08EEC0  00000000 00000000 00000100 7F000000   7F000000 02000000 7F08EEF4 00000000  *.C................................4*
08EEE0  0008EF58 08000050 4008EF20 00000000   00000000 0F08EF20 00008EE8 6B000222  *............................................*
08EF00  00000000 00000000 00000000 01000000   00000000 00008EE8 C3004164 00000000  *.........................YC..*
08EF20  00000166 00000177 00120156 2708EDE0   2708EDE0 00000050 2008EF50 00000000  *...............................*
08EF40  0608EE44 00000080 2308EF80 40000001   40000001 0808EF50 00000000 0008EF1C  *...............................*
08EF60  5F000000 00000000 000352D0 80004164   80004164 0008EE48 00000004 00004164  *.......8.5H4F....H....OS2219..*
08EF80  0008EEF8 00F5C8F4 C6000813 8008EFC8   D6E2F2F2 1D08EDD8 0000C379 00000000  *.........IFG0199E.........Q..C.*
08EFA0  00000000 00000000 C9C6C7F0 F1F9F9C5   F1F9F9E4 00000010 1D08EDD8 0000C379  *.......8N...................*
08EFC0  00060000 F8D5D010 0808EDE0 00000000   00000000 00000000 00000000 00000100  *...........................*

SP 006
08E000  005100FF 0008E010   10C8C4D9 F1C5F1F1   F1F0C2C1 C3D2E8E2  D2404040  *........HDR1E110BACK*
08E020  40404040 40D6D6E2   F2F2F1F9 F0F0F0F1   F0F0F0F1 40404040 F5F1F7F7  *.OS221900010001    75177*
08E040  40F0F0F0 F0F0F0F0   00000000 00000000   00000000 04004040 40404040  *.00000000000............*
08E060  00000000 40404040   40404040 40404040   813E0414 40404040 40404040  *......................*
08E080  00000000 00000000   40404040 00000200   40404040 40404040 40404040  *....................*
08E0A0  40404040 4B00E000   00000000 00000000   40404040 40404040 40404040  *.....A..............*
08E0C0  00000000 000000C1   00000000 04004040   40404040 40404040 40404040  *........A.........*
08E0E0  00000000 00000000   40404040 40404040   40404040 40404040 00000100  *................*
08E100  40404040 D9C9D5E3   00000000 04010004   00000000 00000000 00612B00  *....SYSPRINT.......*
08E120  00612903 E2E8E2D7   D9C9D5E3 00000000   00000000 00D00000 00000000  *..SYSPRINT........*
08E140  00620100 00000000   00000000 00000000   40404040 00000000 00000000  *..................*
08E160  00000000 40404040   40404040 40404040   40404040 00000000 40404040  *..................*
08E180  00000000 40404040   40404040 40404040   40404040 40404040 40404040  *..................*
08E1A0  40404040 40404040   E2E8E2F7 F5F2F2F4   4BE3F0F6 F5F6F3F1 F5F6F3F1  *........SYS75224.T065631*
08E1C0  4BD9E5F0 F0F04BC4   C7D9C4F1 F2F34040   4BE3F0F6 F5F6F3F1 40404040  *.RV000.D3RZ1Z6.GRD123*
08E1E0  40404040 00000203   00000000 00000200   40404040 40404040 40404040  *................A.....*
08E200  4B00E000 00000000   00000000 90000230   00500000 40404040 40404040  *.....A.....*
08E220  0001D6E2 E2C3D9F1   40404040 40404040   40404040 40404040 00500100  *.OSSCR1...........*
08E240  40404040 00000C40   00000000 00000000   00000000 00000000 00620200  *..................*
08E260  40404040 C4E4D4D7   E2E8E2E4 C4E4D4D7   00000000 00000000 00000000  *....SYSUDUMP.SYSUDUMP.....*
08E280  00612B03 E2E8E2E4   D9C9D5E3 05010004   00000000 00000000 00000000  *..SYSUDUMP......*
08E2A0  00620300 00000000   00000000 00000000   40404040 40404040 40404040  *................*
08E2C0  00000000 40404040   40404040 40000000   00000000 40404040 40404040  *................*
08E2E0  00000000 40404040   40404040 40404040   40404040 40404040 40404040  *................*
08E300  40404040 4B00E000   40404040 40404040   4B00E000 40404040 40404040  *.....A.......A....*
08E320  40404040 F0F04BC4   F5F2F2F4 F5F2F2F4   4BE3F0F6 F5F6F3F1 40404040  *.....SYS75224.T065631*
08E340  4BD9E5F0 F0F04BC4   D9F0F0F0 F7F2F6F0   40404040 40404040 40404040  *.RV000.D3RZ1Z6.R0007260*
08E360  40404040 00000000   00000000 00000200   00000000 00000000 40404040  *...............A.....*
08E380  4B00E000 000000C1   00000000 00000000   00000000 00000000 00000100  *.....A..........*
08E3A0  00000000 00004040   40404040 40404040   40404040 40404040 40404040  *................*
08E3C0  00000000 E2E8E2D3   C9D5F040 40404040   00000000 00000000 00D082A00  *....SYSLIN......*
08E3E0  00620203 E2E8E2D3   C9D5F040 01010014   00000000 00000100 00082A00  *....SYSLIN.........Q..*
08E400  00620500 00000000   00000000 00000000   E2E8E2C4 00000200 E2E8E2C4  *....SYSD....SYSD*
```

2. Problem File Determination

Realizing that an 813 Storage Dump refers to a conflict between the Volume Serial number and Data Set name contained within the Label and the JCL, the problem ddname should first be determined.

A Jobname, Stepname, and Completion Code of RZZ126, STEP1, and 813, respectively, can be determined from the first page of the dump. See Figure 3.10, letter 'A'.

Utilizing the Short Hand Method, a valid UCB of 4164 can be found in Register 10 of the second SVRB. See letter 'B'. The problem ddname SYSUT1 can be determined by referencing the appropriate UCB of 4164 in the TIOT Table. See Figure 3.11, letter 'C'. The DD statement for problem ddname SYSUT1 can be found in the JCL listing for STEP1. See Figure 3.9, letter 'D'. Having narrowed the problem to a specific file, a brief analysis of the JCL can be accomplished. At this point, however, no apparent JCL errors can be found.

Verifying the problem file via the Long Hand Method, a DCB Address of 0833DC can be found in Register 2 of the pertinent SVRB as well as Register 2 of the Registers At Entry To Abend. See Figure 3.10, letter 'E', and Figure 3.12, letter 'F'. Adding Hexadecimal 28 to the DCB Address, a TIOT Offset Address of 083404 is calculated. Locating this address in the print of main storage and marking off two bytes, a value of 0018 is found. See Figure 3.13, letter 'G'. Converting to Decimal 24, subtracting 24, dividing by 20 and truncating any remainder, and finally adding 1, verifies the location of the problem ddname in the TIOT as the first print line. See Figure 3.11, letter 'C'.

3. Label Information

DCB information other than the TIOT Offset need not be referenced because an 813 Storage Dump is not caused by DCB conflicts. In fact, Data Control Blocks are not completely set up until after label processing is completed.

Because the Header Label was being processed when the abend occurred, it can be located in main storage and analyzed. The starting address for label information can be found in Register 4 of the pertinent SVRB. Checking that register, a Label Address of 08EDE0 is determined. See Figure 3.10, letter 'H'. This same address can also be located in Register 4 of the Registers At Entry To Abend. See Figure 3.12, letter 'I'. Label information at Address 08EDE0 can now be referenced. The label's starting address can be found on the print line beginning with 08EDE0. See Figure 3.14, letter 'J'. There is no need to decipher main storage contents at that point, for it is printed in the right-most portion of the page. As previously mentioned, all data represented in Character Format can be readily interpreted. See letter 'K'. This is the beginning of a printed representation of data located at Address 08EDE0.

The first four characters identify a Standard Label as follows:

        VOL1 - Volume Record Number 1

        HDR1 - Header Record Number 1

        HDR2 - Header Record Number 2

        EOV1 - End of Volume Record Number 1

        EOV2 - End of Volume Record Number 2

        EOF1 - End of File Record Number 1

        EOF2 - End of File Record Number 2

As can be seen, the specific label record being processed at the time of the abend was HDR1 or Header Record Number 1. See letter 'L'.

The Data Set name contained within the Header Record is always found immediately to the right of the label identifier HDR1. The Data Set name as recorded in the label is E110BACK. See letter 'M'. The Volume Serial number as recorded internally in the label to the right of the Data Set name is OS2219. See letter 'N'.

Similarly, these same two items of information as coded in the JCL can also be located in main storage. Three lines directly below the Data Set name located in the Header Label can be found the Data Set name recorded in the JCL, that is, AMASTER. See letter 'O'. Likewise, six lines below the Volume Serial number in the Header Label can be found the Volume Serial number in the JCL, that is, OS2219. See letter 'P'.

As can be seen, a conflict exists between the data set names recorded in the Label and JCL as follows:

```
                                        Label      JCL
Data Set Name .....................  E110BACK   AMASTER
Volume Serial Number .............   OS2219     OS2219
```

A thorough problem analysis can now be accomplished. The programmer's
log of files created and associated characteristics must be reviewed
in addition to the possibility of keypunch error.

4. Problem Analysis

The fact that the Volume Serial number recorded in the Label and
the JCL agree with each other indicates that the computer operator has
mounted the correct file as requested. This does not mean that the
programmer has keypunched the correct volume, however. Certainly a
keypunch error in the JCL could have caused the 'wrong' volume to be
mounted. This would result in a conflict between the expected Data
Set name as coded in the JCL and the actual Data Set name as recorded in the Label.

Assuming that the programmer has specified the correct volume in the
JCL, 813 main storage indicates that the appropriate volume has been
mounted. With this assumption, the disagreement between Data Set
names becomes significant. This type of conflict suggests two
possibilities:

a. The Data Set name as recorded in the JCL is incorrect. This
could have resulted from two possible causes - a simple keypunch error,
or, an incorrect entry in the programmer's log.

b. The file has been accidently scratched and used for another
job. A backup file need be referenced or the original file recreated.
A check with the tape librarian should be made.

For all occurrences of an 813 Storage Dump, a conflict between the
Label and the JCL as regards Data Set name and/or Volume Serial number
can be assumed. First, the problem file must be isolated via the
Short Hand or Long Hand Method. Next, the appropriate DD Statement
within the JCL should be studied. Finally, the Label need be broken

down and analyzed as it resides in main storage. From this information, a correct solution to the storage dump problem can be made.

E.   EXTERNAL STORAGE DUMP SUMMARY

External Storage Dumps are those which occurred external to the program being executed. They are denoted by Completion Codes 001, 13 Group, 22 Group (excluding 322), and 37 Group. The following set of step-by-step procedures apply to all External Abends.

1.   Determine Jobname, Stepname, and Completion Code from top of first page of storage dump.

2.   Obtain detail description of Completion Code by referencing the IBM Messages and Codes Manual and/or Chapter 7 of this textbook.

3.   Utilize Short Hand Method to isolate problem ddname and file.

    a.   Locate valid UCB in Register 10 of SVRB.

    b.   Find UCB in TIOT; associate with problem ddname.

    c.   Refer to JCL listing and analyze appropriate DD Statement file.

4.   Utilize Long Hand Method to isolate problem ddname and file if valid UCB occurs more than once in TIOT.

    a.   Determine DCB Address from Register 2 of pertinent SVRB or Registers At Entry To Abend.

    b.   Add 28 to DCB Address and locate two byte TIOT Offset in main storage.

    c.   Convert TIOT Offset to Decimal, subtract 24, divide by 20 truncating remainder, and add 1.

    d.   Count down indicated number of lines in TIOT; associate with problem ddname.

    e.   Refer to JCL listing and analyze appropriate DD Statement file.

5.   Determine DCB attributes for Completion Codes relating to DCB conflicts.

    a.   Determine DCB Address from Register 2 of pertinent SVRB or Registers At Entry To Abend; then add:

```
 0 - Block Count              (4 bytes)
12 - Density                  (1 byte)
28 - TIOT Offset             (2 bytes)
3E - Maximum Blocksize       (2 bytes)
4C - Address of Next Record  (4 bytes)
52 - Logical Record Length   (2 bytes)
5A - Physical Record Length  (2 bytes)
```

    b. Locate DCB attributes in main storage; convert to Decimal.

    c. Refer to Program File Descriptions.

6. Analyze Label contents for storage dumps which occurred during Label processing.

    a. Determine Label Address from Register 4 of pertinent SVRB or Registers At Entry To Abend.

    b. Locate Label in main storage; compare Data Set Name and Volume Serial Number with JCL.

7. Complete thorough problem analysis. Determining the value of pertinent program variables at the time of the abend, as discussed in Chapter 5, may also be of assistance.

A workshop is now provided to solidify a working knowledge of External Storage Dump debugging procedures.

Although the above procedures are specific to OS and OS/VS environments, the principle of debugging file problems resulting in external abends, and locating addresses and values in main storage can be applied to DOS applications as well. The nature of the program to be executed is of little concern. File problems resulting in external storage dumps are often encountered when attempting to execute COBOL, FORTRAN, PL1 and Assembly language programs in all application, system, and data base environments.

F. WORKSHOP PROBLEMS

1. 213 Storage Dump

a. Description

Figures 3.15 through 3.18 consist of pertinent pages of a job which has abended with a 213 Storage Dump.

Figure 3.15   Job Control Language Listing (213)

```
// EXEC  PL1LFCLG,PARM.PL1L='LIST,LOAD,NODECK,NOSTMT,EXTDIC',
//        REGION.GO=96K,TIME.GO=(,20)
//PL1L.SYSIN DD *
/*
//GO.READIT  DD  UNIT=3330,DISP=(OLD,KEEP),
//        DSN=GOODDATA,VOL=SER=TS0001,
//        DCB=(RECFM=FB,LRECL=120,BLKSIZE=3120)
//GO.SYSOUT   DD  SYSOUT=A
//GO.SYSUDUMP  DD  SYSOUT=A
//
```

Completion Codes of the 13 Group are classified as External. They refer to situations in which the system cannot determine or locate the problem file as described. In particular, a 213 Storage Dump indicates a type of problem in which the system cannot locate a disk data set to be processed.

Illogical JCL specifications are many times the cause of a 213 Dump. Sometimes, the cause of the problem can be found in the preceding job or step. Perhaps the previous job or step did not create the data set as expected. As a result, the system could not locate the data set to be processed in the following job or step, i.e., it simply doesn't exist.

Procedures for debugging a 213 Storage Dump are similar to that of other External Abends except that DCB attribute determinations are usually of little value. First, determine the problem file via the Short Hand Method. Next, analyze JCL specifications, in particular, those relating to the problem ddname. Having accomplished these tasks, a complete problem analysis can be made.

A problem solution can be found in Appendix A.

Figure 3.16 First Page of 213 Storage Dump

```
JOB  RZZ414        STEP GO        TIME 210005

COMPLETION CODE    SYSTEM = 213

PSW AT ENTRY TO ABEND  FF04000D 50017FC6

TCB 0323B8  R3P   00041980  PIE    00000000  DEB  000312F4  TIO  00034320  CMP   80213000  TRN  00000000
            MSS   02046E38  PK-FLG 8085D400  FLG  0005F5B   LLS  0003CCF8  JLB   00000000  UPQ  80036E18
            FSA   011CCF68  TCB    00030B10  TME  00000000  JST  00032388  NTC   00000000  OTC  0003BF80
            LTC   00000000  IQE    00000000  ECB  0003429C  TSF  20000000  D-PQE 00045DF8  SQS  0002FF48
            NSTAE A0046808  TCT    80036A28  USER 00000000  DAR  00000000  RESV  00000000  USCB 87036F60
            RESV  00000000  IOB    00000000


ACTIVE RBS

PRB  037710  RESV 00000000  APSW   00000000  WC-SZ-STAB 00040082  FL-CDE 00033DB0  PSW FF030006 4E1C1B16
             Q/TTR 00300000 WT-LNK 00032388

PRB  037680  RESV 00000000  APSW   00000000  WC-SZ-STAB 00040002  FL-CDE 00037150  PSW FF030013 7E1C901C
             Q/TTR 00000000 WT-LNK 00037710

SVRB 037498  TAB-LN 00880400 APSW  F1F9F9C5  WC-SZ-STAB 0012D002  TQN 00000000  PSW FF040000 50017FC6
             Q/TTR  0030120F WT-LNK 00037680
   RG 0-7   FF850000  001CC35C  001C0200  001C9EC8  001C9F00  001CC35C  001CBA58
   RG 8-15  00000000  001C1720  011C8FA8  001C8BD8  001C8908  00020513  011C8FA8
   EXTSA    901C9F00  221CD5E0  00027A08  001CD7C8  001CC35C  001CD7E8  0003434C
            00001EE0  001C97DC  00000000  002DEB52

SVRB 03841B  TAB-LN 00780220 APSW  F9F0F1C3  WC-SZ-STAB 0012D002  TQN 00000000  PSW 00040033 500179F2
             Q/TTR  0004D0C  WT-LNK 00037498
   RG 0-7   80000000  80213000  901C9F00  4001C9A   0032/A08  001CD7C8  001CC35C
   RG 8-15  001CD7E8  00034360  80003DC4  0001A318  A02DF684  00030000  00000004
   EXTSA    00002IBE  8F1CCDC8  00000000  00033494  0003849C  E2E8E2C9
            C5C1F0F1  C9C5C1BB  C1C2C5D5  C4F92130

SVRB 041980  TAB-LN 00C80308 APSW  F1F0F5C1  WC-SZ-STAB 0012D002  TQN 00000000  PSW FF030000 401C8F4E
             Q/TTR  0003D11  WT-LNK 00038418
   RG 0-7   0105SB0   00038478  8001790A  0001A318  00038418  04032388  00038418
   RG 8-15  00032388  40017852  0003238B  8F1CCDC8  0003349C  40016D84  00000000
   EXTSA    E2E8E2C9  C5C1F0F1  151CD3C0  001C838C  001CD5A8  001CD5C8  00000000
            0004E08   000312F4  80018F58  40400FFE


LOAD LIST

NE 00042678  RSP-CDE 02036E18  NE 000431A0  RSP-CDE 01045BC8  NM GO      RSP-CDE 01045898
NE 00043948  RSP-CDE 01045 9C8 NE 00000000  RSP-CDE 01045988  NM IHEOPPA


CDE

038DB0  ATR1 0B  NCDE 000000  ROC-RB 00037710  USE 01  EPA 1C01F0  ATR2 20  XL/MJ 046940
037150  ATR1 39  NCDE 0375C0  ROC-RB 00037680  USE 01  EPA 1C8FA8  ATR2 28  XL/MJ 037318
```

82

Figure 3.17 Second Page of 213 Storage Dump

```
036E18  ATR1 30  NCDE 034E18  ROC-RB 00000000  NM IGG0A05A  USE 02  EPA 1C9300  ATR2 28  XL/MJ 0376D0
0453C8  ATR1 B0  NCDE 0458F8  ROC-RB 00000000  NM IGG019CF  USE 01  EPA 2FC3A0  ATR2 20  XL/MJ 045888
045898  ATR1 B0  NCDE 0458C8  ROC-RB 00000000  NM IGG019CL  USE 01  EPA 2FF008  ATR2 20  XL/MJ 045888
0459C8  ATR1 B0  NCDE 0459F8  ROC-RB 00000000  NM IGG019BA  USE 01  EPA 2FCE40  ATR2 20  XL/MJ 045988
045988  ATR1 B0  NCDE 0459C8  ROC-RB 00000000  NM IGG019BB  USE 01  EPA 2FD300  ATR2 20  XL/MJ 045978

XL                                LN          ADR          LN       USE        ADR          LN       ADR

046940  SZ 00000010  NO 00000001  80006DE0  001BE720
037318  SZ 00000010  NO 00000001  80000858  001C8FA8
0375D0  SZ 00000010  NO 00000001  800007A8  001C8800
045888  SZ 00000010  NO 00000001  80000270  002FC8A0
0459B8  SZ 00000010  NO 00000001  80000040  002FF008
045978  SZ 00000010  NO 00000001  800001C0  002FCE40
                                  80000178  002FD800

DEB
0312C0  0000B660  00000000  00000000  00002BE0
0312E0  00008660  00000000  00000000  00008660  002FF008  00008650  00008660          *....O.......*
0313D0  8F000000  01000000  5B000000  8F1CCDC8  0F000000  04532388  10000000  C8000000 *.........H..*
031300  00000000  00000000  C2C2C2C1  C3D3C3C6  02031200  33004C00  00100031  00000000 *....H.......*
031340  00000000  00000000                      00000000  00000000  00000000          *...BBBACLCF.*
                                                                                       *....Y.......*
                                                                                       *.....GBSWY117*

TIOT  JOB  DARZZ414  STEP GO
DD  14040140  PGM=*.DD   01910500  80002D44
DD  14040140  SYSPRINT   01910F00  80004E08
DD  14040140  READIT     010C1E00  80003DC4
DD  14040100  SYSOUT     010C2100  80004E48
DD  14040140  SYSUDUMP   010C2300  80004E68

DATA MANAGEMENT CONTROL BLOCKS

MSS     ************ SPQE ************    ************** DQE **************    ****** FQE *******
        FLGS  NSPQE    SPID  DQE          BLK       FQE       LN        NDQE      NFQE     LN
046E38  00    046CD0   001   046C48       001C8800  00000000  00001000  00037390  00000000 000006C0
046CD0  00    046CE8   251   0468C8       001C9800  001C9800  00003800  00000000  00000000 00000720
046CE8  00    046A80   252   03A160       001BE000  001BE000  00006800  000375E0  00000000 000005D8
                                          001CD000  001CB000  00000800  00038FC0  00000000 000000A0
                                          001CA000  001CA000  00001000  00036EF8  00000000 000001D0
                                          001C8800  00000000  00001000  00000000  001CCD00 00000020
046A80  C0    000000   000   0401E0       001CC800  001CCF48  00000800  00000000  001CC800 00000018
0401E0  60    000000   000   03A140                                               00000000 00000418

D-PQE 00046DF8  FIRST 00039080  LAST 00039080
PQE   039080  FFB 001C4800  LFB 001C4800  NPQ 00000000  PPQ 00000000
```

Figure 3.18 First Page of 213 Main Storage

```
INTERRUPT AT 1C901C

PROCEEDING BACK VIA REG 13

GO      WAS ENTERED VIA CALL

SA  1CB3D8  WD1 63000000  HSA 001CBA08  LSA 00000000  RET 7E1CA7FA  EPA 001CC9A   R0 00000010
            R1  001C8920   R2  001CC340   R3  00000000   R4  00000004   R5  001CC200   R6  001CBA58
            R7  001CBA58   R8  00000000   R9  001C1720   R10 001CA7C8   R11 001C83D9   R12 00000000

REGS AT ENTRY TO ABEND

FLTR 0-6   00000050C1D9C1C9  C6D5C3C9C3C40000  00000000000000000  00000000000000000

REGS 0-7   80000000  30213000  90109F00  40017C9A  231CD5E0  00027A03  001CD7C8  001CC35C
REGS 8-15  001CD7E8  00034360  80003DC4  0001A318  00034370  A02DF684  00000000  00000004

LOAD MODULE  GO

1BE720  4FF0F014  05E0D7D9  E2F14015  000003C4  001BFC38  9CEBD00C  58B0F010  5800F00C  *.00..SPRSL .....D.....0.*
1BE740  58F03020  05EF5540  4190D363  50DC000C  58B0B098  41E08000  50E0D058  9288D059  *.J.............*
1BE760  9288D05C  92820000  D25FD0A0  B36C58E0  D0A81AED  50E0D0A8  58E0D030  1AED50E0  *........K.......*
1BE780  D0B058E0  D0B81AED  D25FD0A0  B36C58E0  D0B058E0  D0C81AED  50E0D0C8  50E0D0E0  *........H......H*
1BE7A0  58E0D0D0  1AED50E0  D0D058E0  D0D81AED  50E0D0D8  58E0D0E0  D0E058E0  D0E058E0  *.............H.*
1BE7C0  D0E81AED  50E0D0E8  58E0D0F0  1AED50E0  D0F058E0  D0F81AED  50E0D0F8  D257D10J  *.Y...Y..0...8..8K.J*
1BE7E0  B3CC58E0  D1001AED  50E0D100  58E0D108  1AED50E0  D10858E0  D1101AED  50E0D110  *.........J...J*
1BE800  5BE0D118  1AED50E0  D11858E0  D1201AED  50E0D120  58E0D128  1AED50E0  D1285BE0  *.J...J...J...J.*
1BE820  D1301AED  50E0D130  58E0D138  1AED50E0  D13858E0  D1401AED  50E0D140  59E0D148  *.J...J...J...J.*
1BE840  1AED50E0  D1485BE0  D1501AED  50E0D150  58E0D158  B4241FF0  D15DD217  D15BD217  *.J...J...J..0J.K.J*
1BE860  D1U0842C  58E0D160  1AED50E0  D16058E0  D1681AED  50E0D168  58E0D170  1AED50E0  *J..K.J...OJ..OJ..0.*
1BE883  D170D207  D17BB444  41F0D1DC  50F0D178  D2071AED  50E0D178  DIDE50F0  D180D207  *.J.K.J..JJ..K.J..K.J.*
1BE8A0  D1888454  41F0D1E0  50F0D188  D2070190  B45C41F0  D1E250F0  D190D237  D1988464  *J..K.J..JJ..K.J..OJ..K.J.*
1BE8C0  41F0D1E4  50F0D198  D2070100  B46C41F0  D1E85FF0  D1A041F0  D08C50F0  D0A0D203  *J..K.J..OJ..0J..0..0..K.*
1BE8E0  D1AC8UA8  41F0D1F3  50F0D1A8  41AOA1A8  D202D180  B368D200  D183B338  D202D186  *J..JJ..JJ..K.J.K.J.*
1BE900  B368D202  D1B98368  D202D1B8  B368D202  D1BFB368  D20201C2  B368D202  D1C5B363  *..K.J..K.J..K.JB..K.JE.*
1BE923  D202D1C8  B368D202  DICEB363  4180D0A0  5080D088  4110D088  58F0B094  05EFD205  *K.J4..J..<..0.....K.*
1BE940  D1D1D08C  41F0D158  41800D88  D2078000  B55C50F0  80001818  58F0B038  05A10573  *JJ...J.....0......K.*
1BE960  A0944110  D1704120  B5A10573  4110D160  4120B5A1  05784110  D1684120  B5A10573  *..J...J...J...J.*
1BE980  4FF0A0BC  4130B116  58F0B064  18E7058F  4130B116  58F0B064  18E7058F  4130B116  *.0...X....X....X.*
1BE9A0  53F0B064  18E7058F  47F0A094  58F0B084  05EFD202  D1D7B365  D201D1DA  B362D201  *.0.X...0...K.JP..K..K.*
1BE9C0  D1DCB35D  D2011D8E  B35DD206  D201D1E2  B350D206  DIE4B356  D2070IE3  D2E4B356  *J..K.J..K..JS..K.JU..K.J.*
1BE9E0  B34E41F0  D05894C7  F004D202  F005804D  4110B53C  58F0B080  05EFD201  D2E4835F  *J..J.<.0........K.KU.*
1BEA00  D213D088  B58C4180  D1A85080  D08C4110  D08858F0  B08C05EF  D500D209  B3614770  *K....J...N.K....*
1BEA20  A138D050  D20AB118  4790A110  D500D1E2  B3614770  A14CD500  DIE3B118  4790A4AA  *.....N.JS..N.JT..*
1BEA40  D501D1DA  DIF34790  AF704110  B53058F0  B07C05EF  4180A1F8  4110D199  4120B5A0  *JJ.......8..J.*
1BEA60  05784110  D1A04120  B5A00578  4120B5A0  05784110  D1A04120  B5A00578  4120B5A0  *.J...J...*
1BEA80  05784110  D1984120  B5A00578  4110D198  4120B5A0  05784110  D1984120  05784110  *.J...J....J.*
1BEAA0  D1A04120  B5A00578  4110D1A0  4120B5A0  05784110  D1984120  B5A00578  D1984120  *.J...J...J.*
1BEAC0  4120B5A0  05784110  D1A04120  B5A00578  4110D1A0  4120B5A0  05784110  D1984120  *.J...J...J.*
1BEAE0  B5A00578  47F0A2AA  58F0B064  18E7058F  58F0B060  18E7058F  50109020  4110B116  *.0...X....X....X.*
1BEB00  53F0B058  05EF4130  B10A58F0  B06818E7  58109020  05F84130  B10658F0  B06818E7  *.0.X....0.X.*
1BEB20  058F4130  B10658F0  B06818E7  058F4130  B10658F0  B06818E7  058F4130  B10A58F0  *..X....X....X.*
1BEB40  B06818E7  058F4130  B10658F0  B06818E7  058F4130  B10658F0  B06818E7  058F41B0  *..X....X....X.*
1BEB60  B10258F0  B06818E7  058F4130  B10658F0  B06818E7  058F47F0  B10658F0  B06818E7  *..X....X..0..X.*
1BEB80  058F4130  B10658F0  B06818E7  058F47F0  B06018E7  058F47F0  A1F858F0  B07805EF  *..X....X..0..X..0.8.0.*
1BEBA0  4110B524  58F0B07C  05EF4180  A3264110  B3404120  B5A00578  4110D1B0  4120B5A2  *..J...0.8.0..J.*
1BEBC0  05784110  D1B34120  B5A20578  4110D1B6  4120B5A2  05784110  D1DB94120  B5A20578  *.J...J...J.*
1BEBE0  4110D1BC  4120B5A2  05784110  D1BF4120  B5A20578  4110D1C2  4120B5A2  05784110  *.J...J...JB..J.*
1BEC00  D1C54120  B5A20578  057847F0  A4525010  90244110  B0FE58F0  B0FE58F0  05EF41B0  *JE...0.X...0.*
1BEC20  B05805EF  4130B060  18E75810  9024058F  50109024  4110B0FA  58F0B058  05EF41B0  *...0.X....0.*
1BEC40  B03858F0  B0701BE7  58109024  50109024  90244110  B0FF58F0  B05805EF  4130B038  *.0.X...2.0.*
1BEC60  58F0B070  18E75810  9024058F  50109024  4110B0F2  58F0B058  05EF4130  B03858F0  *.0.X...0.*
```

b. Workshop

    1. Problem Overview

                Completion Code _____

        Jobname _____   Stepname _____

    2. Short Hand Method

        Valid UCB _____   Problem Ddname _____

        Problem File JCL DD Statement:

        _____

        _____

        _____

    3. Problem Analysis

    Summarize your findings. Analyzing all JCL associated with the
problem file; and assuming the Data Set name and Volume Serial number
to be correctly specified, what would your problem solution be?

        _____

        _____

        _____

2. D37 Storage Dump

a. Description

    Figures 3.19 through 3.23 consist of pertinent pages of a job
which has abended with a D37 Storage Dump.
    Completion Codes of the 37 Group are classified as External. They
refer to situations in which end of volume or end of file problems

occur. In particular, a D37 Dump indicates a problem concerned with space allocations. An output file has exceeded the amount of space allocated to it.

The Space Parameter in the JCL's DD Statement did not specify enough space in terms of tracks or cylinders to completely hold the data set. Perhaps, the programmer under-estimated the size of an output file. Or quite possible, the program being executed was in an endless loop encircling a Write Statement. In either case, the abend occurred when data was being transferred from the buffer area to a physical device, i.e., external to the program being executed.

Procedures for debugging a D37 Storage Dump are similar to that of other External Abends. First determine the problem file via the Short Hand or Long Hand Method. Next, analyze JCL specifications, in particular, those relating to space allocations. Third, verify DCB attributes as desired. Having accomplished these tasks, a complete problem analysis can be made.

A problem solution can be found in Appendix A.

Figure 3.19   Job Control Language Listing (D37)

```
//STEP1      EXEC PGM=IEBGENER
//SYSUT1 DD *
/*
//SYSUT2 DD   UNIT=3330,DISP=(NEW,PASS),
//           DSN=GOODDATA,VOL=SER=TSO001,
//           SPACE=(1600,4),
//           DCB=(RECFM=FB,LRECL=080,BLKSIZE=1600)
//SYSIN   DD DUMMY
//SYSPRINT DD SYSOUT=A
//SYSUDUMP DD SYSOUT=A
/*
//STEP2      EXEC PGM=IEBPTPCH
//SYSUT1 DD UNIT=3330,DISP=(OLD,DELETE),
//           DSN=GOODDATA,VOL=SER=TSO001,
//           DCB=(RECFM=FB,LRECL=080,BLKSIZE=1600)
//SYSUT2 DD SYSOUT=A
//SYSIN   DD *
/*
//SYSPRINT DD SYSOUT=A
//SYSUDUMP DD SYSOUT=A
//
```

Figure 3.20 First Page of D37 Storage Dump

```
JOB  RZZ455            STEP STEP1           TIME 161703

COMPLETION CODE        SYSTEM = D37

PSW AT ENTRY TO ABEND  FF04000D 500172EE

TCB 036798   RBP  00035EA8   PIE  00000000   DEB  00035B84   TIO 00036DA8   CMP  80D37000   TRN 00000000
             MSS  02040E90   PK-FLG A0850400 FLG  0005F58    LLS 0003F0C8   JLB  00000000   JPQ 0003DBC8
             FSA  01090F68   TCB  00036880   TME  00000000   JST 0036798    NTC  00000000   OTC 0003C230
             LTC  00000000   IQE  00000000   ECB  00036F5C   TSF 20000000   D-PQE 00040EB0  SQS 000358E8
             NSTAE 00000000  TCT  8003C098   USER 00000000   DAR 00000000   RESV 00000000  JSCB 8703EA68
             RESV 00000000   IOB  00000000

ACTIVE RBS

PRB 03F1F8   RESV 00000000   APSW 00000000   WC-SZ-STAB 00000000    FL-CDE 00040648   PSW FFA50037 601FCD06
             Q/TTR 00000000  WT-LNK 00036798

SVRB 041F68  TAB-LN 00580400 APSW F5F5F9C5   WC-SZ-STAB 0012D002    TQN 00000000      PSW FF04000D 500172EE
             Q/TTR 0001001D  WT-LNK 0003F1F8
             RG 0-7  00000000  00087C54  00087850  00090D88  00000000  0008F330  00090000  00000050
             RG 8-15 00000640  00008F9C0 00085C3C  0003E1F0  80087AE6  000886C0  40087BEC  001FCCC8
             EXTSA   8008C53C  0C0915E0  00027A08  00091788  000917F4  00091708  00040004  00000000
                     00041FC8  00000000  00000000  404007FE

SVRB 046470  TAB-LN 00D80220 APSW F9F0F1C3   WC-SZ-STAB 0012D002    TQN 00000000      PSW 00040033 500193A2
             Q/TTR 00004629  WT-LNK 00041F68
             RG 0-7  80000000  80D37000  80085C3C  40016FC2  0F0915E0  00027A08  00091788  000917F4
             RG 8-15 00091708  00036DD4  80003984  0036700C  0003670C  00000001  00000000  00000004
             EXTSA   000021BE  8F090478  00000000  00000000  FF030000  000464EC  000464F4  E2E8E2C9
                     C5C1F0F1  C9C5D5    C1C2C5D5  C4F9D370

SVRB 035EA8  TAB-LN 00280308 APSW F1F0F5C1   WC-SZ-STAB 0012D002    TQN 00000000      PSW FF04000C 4008E7A6
             Q/TTR 00003801  WT-LNK 00046470
             RG 0-7  00000007  000464D0  8001928A  0001A318  00036798  00046470  04036798  00046470
             RG 8-15 00036798  40019202  00036798  8F090478  00036E14  00464F4   40019C9C  00000000
             EXTSA   E2E8E2C9  C5C1F0F1  0000F0F2  0000F0F2  F9000000  000C378   00000000  00000000
                     00035F08  00000000  00000000

LOAD LIST

NE 0003DDA8  RSP-CDE 0203DBC8   NE 0003EE78  RSP-CDE 01045BC8   NE 0003EE80  RSP-CDE 01045888
NE 0003EE88  RSP-CDE 010459C8   NE 0003F300  RSP-CDE 01045A98   NE 0003F318  RSP-CDE 01045A98
NE 0003F320  RSP-CDE 0103E1F8   NE 0003F3F8  RSP-CDE 01045AC8   NE 0003F440  RSP-CDE 02045A28
NE 0003F660  RSP-CDE 0103F1A0   NE 0003FA68  RSP-CDE 0204S9C8   NE 0003FC58  RSP-CDE 02045988
NE 0003FE68  RSP-CDE 01045BC8   NE 0003FF80  RSP-CDE 01045888   NE 00040630  RSP-CDE 01045858
NE 00000000  RSP-CDE 01045AF8

CDE

040648  ATR1 0B  NCDE 000000  ROC-RB 0003F1F8  NM IEBGENER  USE 01  EPA 0822C0  ATR2 20  XL/MJ 03FFF8
```

Figure 3.21 Second Page of D37 Storage Dump

```
036900  00008660 00000000 00000000 00011BE0   00008660 001FF810 00008660 00008660   *........8.....*
036920  0F000000 01000000 58000000 AF082800   0F000000 04036798 10000000 C8000000   *.........H...*
036940  00000000 00000079 C109C1D2 C3D3C3C6   02036910 33004C68 00010001 00000000   *......ARAKCLCF.....*
036980  00000000 00000000                                                            *...HCCB      USER*

TIOT  JOB  D4RZZ455  STEP  STEP1
      DD   14040140  SYSUT1    01492100    80004608
      DD   14040140  SYSUT2    01492600    80003984
      DD   14000040  SYSIN     01492900    00000000
      DD   14040140  SYSPRINT  01492800    80004C68
      DD   14040140  SYSUDUMP  014A0200    80004C88

DATA MANAGEMENT CONTROL BLOCKS

SYSUT1   DEB  03668C   04036798 1003670C C8000000 00000000   01000000 5B000000 AF085BDC 02036668
                       33004608 00010001 00000000 00000000   00000050 C2C2C2C1 C3C9C3C3 00000000
                       00000000 00000000 00000000 00000000   00000000 00036908 00000090 00008660

         DCB  085BDC   00000000 00000000 00000000 00000000   00410000 00000001 00504000 00000001
                       040881FA 90086014 00182000 0003668C   121FCE40 001FCCC8 06088250 00000050
                       28022828 21090550 011FD4F8 001FD4F8   00000050 00000001 00000000 00000001

         IOB  090550   21090550 7F000000 00000000 7F08802C   00090580 0C000000 21090578 00085BDC
                       21090578 00000000 0208F2E0 20000050   B0001000 45E09278 95401008 47809324
                       9268B000 D2078001 10084 5E0 927858F0  001058F0 F0949108 F0894710 933C9140

         UCB  004608   0000FF88 06030038 00370903 00F6F0F3   50000801 00000000 00000000 00000000
                       0000FF80 06040038 00380903 00F6F0F4   50000801 00000000 00000000 00000000

SYSUT2   DEB  03670C   06036934 10036798 C8000000 0F000000   01000000 5B000000 AF085C3C 040366E8
                       18003984 00000014 00080014 00080001   00010001 00000000 00000000 00000050
                       C2C2C2C1 C6D5C3C9 C3C4C2C3 00000000   00000000 00000000 00000000 00000000
                       D8000000 00037258 000000E8 5B000000   AF084DDC 04036740 10001944 00000038

         DCB  085C3C   00000000 38000000 00140008 0701C394   002903FC 00000001 06404000 00000001
                       04000001 90086020 002C0024 0003670C   961FCE40 001FCCC8 0D08828C 00000640
                       30060050 41090818 011FD830 011FD830   00000050 000911F8 00000000 00000001

         IOB  090818   41090818 50090818 02000000 80087C54   00090878 00000000 41090848 00085C3C
                       00000000 00000000 00000640 14000806   23090880 40000001 31090843 40000005
                       08090850 00000640 1D090878 A0000008   0008F380 40000640 22090881 00000001

         UCB  003984   0009FFA8 03910028 01FD0600 04F3F9F1   30702009 65880000 1800FA88 D7E4C2D3
                       F0F40402 00010100 00000000 00000000   00000000 75000001 04000000 0000FA50

SYSPRINT DEB  036934   04036798 10000000 C8000000 0F000000   01000000 5B000000 AF082800 02036910
                       33004C68 00010001 00000000 00000000   00000079 C109C1D2 C3D3C3C6 00000000
                       00000000 00000000 00000000 00000000   00000000 000382A8 000800C8 C3C3C240
```

Figure 3.22 First Page of D37 Main Storage

```
SA  090F68  WD1 00000000  HSA 00000000  LSA 00000000  RET 00020510  EPA 01082200  R0  FD000008
            R1  00090FF8   R2  00000000  R3  5C036F60  R4  0003D2C8  R5  0003C230   R6  00036E28
            R7  0003C2F8   R8  00036F38  R9  0003C098  R10 0003F60   R11 0003E1F0   R12 401FE102

INTERRUPT AT 1FCD06

PROCEEDING BACK VIA REG 13

IEBGENER WAS ENTERED VIA CALL

SA  0886C0  WD1 40404040  HSA 40404040  LSA 0002E401  RET 400879D2  EPA 000867F8  R0  40087BEC
            R1  001FCCC8   R2  00090818  R3  0085C3C   R4  00085C3C  R5  00090820   R6  00087C54
            R7  001FCCC8   R8  00000000  R9  00000050  R10 00000640  R11 00090818   R12 0085C3C

REGS AT ENTRY TO ABEND

FLTR 0-6   5B000000AF084DDC   040367A010001944              000000380000003C   0012005F00010001

REGS 0-7   80000000  80D37000  80000000  8085C3C   40016FC2   0F0915E0   00027A08   00091788
REGS 8-15  000917D8  0003DD4   0003984   0003670C  0003670C   0003670C   00000001   00000004

LOAD MODULE  IEBGENER

0822C0  90ECD00C 052090DE 23CE41D0 23D69200  2726D727 24222422 58310000 95801000  *........0....P....*
0822E0  47802088 58410004 12444780 20644884  00001288 47C02064 41900048 19894740  *.................*
082300  203E1889 41900020 1B890680 42802048  D2272422 40221888 5980242A 47802064  *........K........*
082320  4180283A D2078028 242A9580 10044780  20885851 00084885 00004190 00041989  *.K..........K....*
082340  47402088 D2032481 500247F0 208ED203  24B124C5 41800000 89800002 5A8025C6  *.K..0..K..E.....F*
082360  58880000 D227244A 80000700 451020AE  8F082B00 0A1341E0 283A9110 E03041C0  *.K..0..K.........*
082380  000C4780 22649110 23CA4780 21284100  02004110 000C0700 451020F6 00138910  *..........6......*
0823A0  00084190 00131A19 41F02548 05EF41C0  00C0700 451020F6 80082B00 0A144110  *...0...0......6..*
0823C0  283A58F0 10149601 10171BEE 43E0F005  4CE0F006 244A45E0 9140F004 47E0211E  *..0...0...0......*
0823E0  4100E010 411 0F000 0A0A47F0 2264A100  02004110 244A45E0 26341B44 48830000  *...0...0....0....*
082400  194847F0 2158411 0 00018910 00084190  0021A19 41F02548 05EF47F0 23424100  *.0...0....0....0.*
082420  00684510 21600A0A 5010241E 41400002  19847440 217AD501 300224C3 478022A2  *.0...N...C.......*
082440  47F02182 00084468 4510218A 000826E8  58F0217E 05EF47F0 219847F0 23425830  *...0.....Y.0..0.0*
082460  241ED267 30001000 4110241E 47F021AE  00085308 10171BEE 43E0F005 4510218E  *.0..K..0..Q.0....*
082480  80082B00 0A144110 283A58F0 10149601  10171BEE 41E1233 4780226A 91FF2836  *.0...0...0.......*
0824A0  9140F004 47E021E6 4100E010 4110F000  0A0A5830 41110000 0A0A4853 00621255  *.0..W...0...0....*
0824C0  4710225E 48530060 12554780 22145813  00401805 00000A0A 48530064 12554780  *.....0...........*
0824E0  47802232 58130044 41400008 18144105  00084111 0000A0A 4780225E 58130040  *........K....0...*
082500  22485813 00481805 41110000 0A0A4853  00661255 4780225E 58130040 18054111  *.K....0..........*
082520  0000A0A  18134100 00684111 00000A0A  18FC98DE 23CE982C D01C07FE 4180283A  *..........Y......*
082540  48508030E 12554780 229C1B44 48608052  1D461244 078E9210 23CAD201 803E8052  *..K..........K...*
082560  07FE9279 803F07FE 47F022AA 00084468  45102282 80082E8  58F022A6 05EF5840  *...0........Y.0..*
082580  241E96FF 28364190 00081998 47802336  18885983 00004770 22E69240 22E69240  *.K..0...K....W...*
0825A0  4000D23E 40019000 47F022F0 58930000  D23F4000 9000D20F 40403004 D701405D  *K.......0....K..P*
0825C0  405D5984 00404780 23089202 405E5984  00484770 231496F0 405D5984 0044960F  *...0........0..O.*
0825E0  405D4770 21A2D23E 40014000 D70F4040  40400701 405D405D 47F021A2 92404000  *.K..P..O..P....O.*
082600  1B8847F0 22FC0700 451023A 80082B00  0A144110 283A58F0 10149601 10171BEE  *..0..O.....0.....*
082620  43E0F005 4CE0F006 4100E008 9140F004  47E02372 4100E010 4110F000 0A0A41F0  *..0...0....O....0*
```

Figure 3.23   Intermediate Page of D37 Main Storage

```
085680  47F0275E 91802F25 478022CC 41F00010 45E027F8 41100016 89100008 41400016  *.0...........0....8...*
0856A0  47F02214 91202EEE 478022EC 41F00008 45E027F8 41100017 89100008 41400017  *.0...........0....8...*
0856C0  47F02214 91012F94 4710200C 91022F94 47102030 94002F27 58102EF4 41502804  *.0.......4........4...*
0856E0  41602864 91082DE8 47102734 94002F27 47F02320 00087850 58F0231C 05EF45E0  *.........Y........0...*
085700  27F849F0 2F224780 276649F0 2F204780 27664110 28049110 10304780 23520700  *.8.0..........0...Y...*
085720  45102350 80085BDC 0A145840 2F2C1244 47802364 41402E21 45E02784 95FF2F10  *.......................*
085740  92F02359 47702378 41F02F8C 47F021FA 92022F27 96802EF9 92002DE9 584020F0  *...........9...Z..0...*
085760  41440000 50402F4C 41102864 91101030 47802E40 451023A4 80085C3C 0A149104  *.......................*
085780  2DE847E0 240E4110 280458F0 47F023D8 4100E010 43E0F005 4CE0F006 91011020  *.Y............0...0...*
0857A0  47102DD4 4100E008 47F023D8 4100E010 4110F000 0A0A4110 28645BF0 10149601  *.M......0.....0...0...*
0857C0  10171BEE 43E0F005 4CE0F006 91011020 41102404 4100E008 47F02408 4100E010  *......0..Q........0...*
0857E0  4110F000 0A0A5840 2F341244 47802420 41402E2F 45E02784 95FF2F10 92F02415  *.0.....0...4...........*
085800  47702434 41F02F84 47F021FA 58102DF4 12114780 24484100 02804111 00000A0A  *...............4...........*
085820  58102DEC 12114780 245C4100 02804111 00000A0A 58102DF0 12114780 24704100  *.......................*
085840  02804111 00000A0A 58DD0004 48F02F12 58ED0004 980CD014 07FE9640 2DE84150  *...............N.......Y..*
085860  28044160 2864D501 503E2F98 47702498 960A503F D2015052 2F9A9601 2F94D501  *...N....K.......K...K..*
085880  50522F98 47702AEE 91485024 471024EA 91405024 471024D2 91105024 471024E4  *.......................*
0858A0  D2015052 503E4720 24EE4130 00044845 003E1843 40450052 47024EE0 2F015052  *.K....K....................*
0858C0  503E9601 2F94D501 603E2F98 47702532 D5016052 2F984770 25329100 60244770  *......K...K....N.....K..*
0858E0  2532D201 603E503E D2016052 50520200 60245024 41100033 89100008 41110034  *.K....K.....K....N.....K..*
085900  58F02F0C 05EF4720 25AAD501 603E2F98 4770254A 960A603F D2016052 2F9A9602  *.0.....K....................*
085920  2F94D501 60522F98 4770255A 91486024 47102594 91406024 47102570 91106024  *.K....................*
085940  47102594 47F025AA 91FF2EEC 47802582 D2016052 5052A4F0 251C4130 00044846  *...0.........K.....0......*
085960  003E1B43 40460052 47F025AA 47702532 478025A0 47F02578 96022F94 D2016052  *....... .0..........K..*
085980  603E4130 50244710 25F49110 50244710 12884780 26140201 25CCD501 5052503E  *......................*
0859A0  47F025DE 1B884895 003E4845 00521D84 47702614 26140201 25329100 920C300B  *.0.....N..........U.......*
0859C0  92083013 96022F94 47F02614 91885024 47702614 48950052 41990004 4995003E  *......0....................*
0859E0  47D02614 4095003E 47F025E4 19564780 2F0C05EF 96082DE8 47F02CC8 91805052  *.....U...0....N...Y.HN.*
085A00  41502804 91485024 47102640 91486024 41F0000C 41100014 47F02214 91806052  *.......................*
085A20  2684D501 60525052 47702684 D501603E 478026D4 41100014 89100008 41400014  *.N...K.............M....*
085A40  2F264110 00228910 00084111 00022580 2F0C05EF 96082DE8 47F02CC8 91805052  *....................*
085A60  47802684 4110001C 89100008 4140001C 41F0000C 41100014 89100008 41400014  *......................*
085A80  4710268C 91202875 478026D4 95002874 478026D4 41100014 89100008 41400015  *......M.........8.....0*
085AA0  41F0000C 45E027F8 47F02214 91202815 478026FC 95002814 478026FC 41100015  *....8...0....8........*
085AC0  89100008 41400015 41F0000C 45E027F8 47F02214 95022EED 4780271C 48002F18  *........8...0...Y.0.H..*
085AE0  4000282C 48002F1A 4000288E 960C2DE8 47F02CC8 41100010 4780271D 4140001D  *......Y.0.H...........*
085B00  41F0000C 45E027F8 47F02214 94002F27 47F02740 00086858 58F0273C 05EF45E0  *....8...0........0....*
085B20  27F849F0 2F224780 276649F0 2F204780 276647F0 2C3C47F0 58F02F0C 05EF48F0  *.8.0......0...0...0...0*
085B40  2F129400 2C4C9680 2C4C9400 2C3C9680 0000D20D 233A1A14 47F0233A 50E02EF0  *..............K....0..0*
085B60  58102DFC 1BEE43E0 2DE941EE 00F042E1 0000D20D 100B4000 41100018 89100008  *.....Z...K...........*
085B80  41400018 1A1459F0 2F0C05EF 1B551B44 43502E04 4130000A 1D435810 2E004144  *......0....K.....*
085BA0  00F04155 00F04251 00154241 00164110 00198910 00084140 00191A14 58F02F0C  *.0...0...........0...0*
085BC0  05EF9200 2DE99200 2E0458E0 2F1207FE 49F02F12 074E4AF0 F1207FE8 00000000  *...Z...Z....0....M8.M8.*
085BE0  00000000 00000000 00410000 00000001 00504000 00000000 00000000 040881FA  *................H....*
085C00  90086014 00182000 00036B8C 121FCE40 001FCCC8 06088250 00000050 28022828  *...........C.......*
085C20  21090550 011FD4F8 001FD4F8 00000050 001FCCC8 00000001 00000000 00000000  *....M.....M8........*
085C40  38000000 00140008 0701C394 00290393FC 00000001 06440000 00000001 04000001  *.........C.....*
085C60  90086020 002C0024 0003670C 961FCE40 001FCCC8 0D08828C 00000640 30060050  *...........H...*
085C80  41090818 011FD830 001FD830 00000050 000911F8 00000000 00000001 413008C4  *.........8...0...D*
085CA0  1BF3182F 50E02EF0 92042DEA 96802EF9 471029C6 47F0291E 91012F27 47802918  *.3....0....Q...9.0.*
085CC0  12FF4780 29185831 00001233 47802918 18444340 2DF44144 00014240 2DF45840  *....K....4....*
085CE0  2DF8024F 40003000 50402DF8 58E02EF0 07FE5831 00001233 00001233 47802962  *......8...0*
085D20  95F13003 47702934 96802EF9 91802EE6 471029C6 91802EEE 47802962 43402DEC  *....9.0*
085D40  41440001 424020EC 58402F38 D24F4000 30004144 00505040 2F389180 2EF94780  *.K.......Z...9.*
085D40  29A858F0 2F2812FF 478029A8 43E02DE9 41EE0001 42E02DE9 05EF42F0 2E0491F0  *.0......Z.....0...0*
```

90

b. Workshop

    1. Problem Overview

        Completion Code _____

        Jobname _____   Stepname _____

    2. Short Hand Method

        Valid UCB _____   Problem Ddname _____

        Problem File JCL DD Statement?

        _____

        _____

        _____

        _____

    3. Long Hand Method

        DCB Address .... _____
        DCB + Hexadecimal 28 .... _____
        Hexadecimal TIOT Offset Value .... _____
        Decimal TIOT Offset Value .... _____
        Subtract 24, Divide 20 .... _____
        Truncate, Add 1 .... _____
        Problem Ddname .... _____

        Is the Problem Ddname the same as that obtained in the Short
        Hand Method? _____ If not, recheck both methods.

4. DCB Characteristics

   Maximum Blocksize?

        DCB Address .... _____

        DCB + Hexadecimal 3E .... _____

        Hexadecimal Blocksize Value .... _____

        Decimal Blocksize Value .... _____

   Logical Record Length?

        DCB + Hexadecimal 52 .... _____

        Hexadecimal Record Length Value ..... _____

        Decimal Record Length Value .... _____

   Block Count?

        DCB + Hexadecimal 0 .... _____

        Hexadecimal Block Count Value .... _____

        Decimal Block Count Value .... _____

   What is the significance of the obtained value for Block
   Count?

   _____

   _____

   _____

5. Problem Analysis

   Summarize your findings. Analyzing all JCL associated with
   the problem file; and assuming that the program is not in a
   loop, what would your problem solution be?

   _____

   _____

4

Internal Abends

A. DESCRIPTION

The previous chapter discussed the debugging of External Abends; that is, abends which occurred when the program of interest was not being executed, a condition external to the problem program. Conversely, this chapter will direct attention to debugging Internal Abends; that is, abends which occurred while the application, system, or data base program of interest was being executed, a condition internal to the problem program. Although storage dump format remains the same, the procedures for debugging Internal Abends are quite different from the external class.

A further distinction need be made. Although an abnormal termination may occur while a program is being executed, this does not necessarily mean that the cause of the problem is internal to the particular program. Faulty data can cause an Internal Abend, for example. Strictly speaking, an Internal Abend means only that the program was being executed at the time the abend occurred. In most cases, however, it can be assumed that an Internal Abend reflects a genuine problem within the source program. In either case, the internals of the program must be analyzed. This will be expanded upon later in this chapter and with the accompanying workshop problems.

An Internal Abend is easily discernable in the Abend Grouping. Completion Code 322 and those of the OC Group, such as OC5, OC7, OCB, etc., are classified as Internal. A distinct set of debugging procedures, therefore, need be followed. Though the following procedures are specific to OS and OS/VS environments, the principle of debugging Internal Abends and locating the problem source statement can be applied to DOS applications as well.

B. ABEND GROUPINGS

1. OC Group (includes User Code 240)

The OC Group refers to those completion codes beginning with the characters OC and ending with a hexadecimal number from 0 to F. All abends prefixed by the letters OC should be debugged as an Internal Abend. In general, completion codes in the OC Group refer to the calculation of invalid data and/or storage addresses; calculations if allowed to continue would locate and destroy pertinent data and/or programs not related to the specific intent. Attempting to execute privileged operations, exceeding the bounds of a program and/or available storage as well as performing illogical arithmetic functions, are examples which can cause an abend of the OC Group. The Operating System attempts to protect itself and the programmer from errors of this type; processing is discontinued, and the dump routine called.

2. 322 Completion Code

A 322 Completion Code refers to those situations in which a specified CPU time limit has been exceeded. Either the program is in an endless loop, or the respective Time Parameter in the JCL for the program being executed should be increased. Because the program module was being executed, that is, the Central Processing Unit was being utilized at the moment CPU time was exceeded, this abend should also be viewed as internal to the problem program.

95

C. DEBUGGING PROCEDURES (COBOL)

1. Computer Run Overview (OC7)

In order to effectively debug an Internal Storage Dump, a programmer must follow a patterned set of step-by-step procedures. Utilizing a Source Program listing and the compiler-generated Assembly Language listing, the actual source statement which was being executed at the time the abend occurred can be determined. In order to isolate the problem source statement with minimum difficulties, it is strongly recommended that a Source Program listing and related Assembly or Condensed listing be generated each time a program is re-compiled.

The computer run depicted in Figures 4.1 through 4.4 consists of selected pertinent pages of a typical computer run which has abended with an OC7 Completion Code. An OC7 Storage Dump results when a program attempts to manipulate one or more non-numeric characters in a field described to contain numeric characters only. Somehow, the program has transferred one or more blanks, alpha, or special characters to a numeric field being operated upon by an arithmetic or test statement.

This particular example depicts the execution of an ANS COBOL program. Differences in storage dump analysis between COBOL and other programming languages will be covered later in this chapter. Source Program and Assembly Language listing formats differ slightly among various programming languages and levels. The procedure for locating the problem source statement remains the same, however. Techniques for determining the value of pertinent program variables will be covered in Chapter 5.

2. Source Statement-Determination

A problem overview can be found on the first page of the dump. See Figure 4.4. The name assigned to this job is, RZZ765. See letter 'A'. The name of the step in which the abend occurred is GO. See letter 'B'. The Completion Code is OC7. See letter 'C'.

Figure 4.1   Portion of COBOL Source Program Listing (OC7)

```
00023     2 1   FD    OUTPUT1
00024     2 2         RECORDING MODE F
00025     2 3         LABEL RECORD STANDARD
00026     2 31        BLOCK CONTAINS 4000 CHARACTERS
00027     2 4         DATA RECORD IS OUTRCD1.
00028     2 5   01    OUTRCD1 PIC X(80).
00029     2 71  FD    OUTPUT2
00030     2 72        RECORDING MODE F
00031     2 73        LABEL RECORD STANDARD
00032     2 74        DATA RECORD IS OUTRCD2.
00033     2 75  01    OUTRCD2 PIC X(80).
00034     217   FD    CDINPUT1
00035     218         RECORDING MODE F
00036     219         LABEL RECORDS OMITTED
00037     220         RECORD CONTAINS 080 CHARACTERS
00038     221         DATA RECORD IS CD-IN.
00039     222   01    CD-IN PIC X(80).
00040     276   FD    TERM-FILE
00041     277         LABEL RECORDS STANDARD
00042     278         RECORDING MODE F
00043     279         DATA RECORD IS TERM-RECORD.
00044     280   01    TERM-RECORD PIC X(80).
00045     3 1   WORKING-STORAGE SECTION.
00046     3 2   77    STATE4 PICTURE  9(7).
00047           01    INREC.
00048                 02   IDENT1        PICTURE 9(7)   OCCURS   5 TIMES.
00049                 02   STATE-DATA    PICTURE 9(7).
00050                 02   IDENT2        PICTURE 9(7)   OCCURS   5 TIMES.
00051                 02   FILLER PIC X(3).
00052           01    CARDIN.
00053                 02   STATE2    PICTURE X(7).
00054                 02   FILLER        PICTURE X(73).
00055     3 3   01    COUNTS.
00056     3 4         02   FILLER PICTURE X(21) VALUE ' RECORDS ON TAPE 1 = '.
00057     3 5         02   CNT1 PICTURE   9(7) VALUE ZEROS.
00058     3 6         02   FILLER PICTURE X(21) VALUE ' RECORDS ON TAPE 2 = '.
00059     3 7         02   CNT2 PICTURE   9(7) VALUE ZEROS.
00060     3 8         02   FILLER PICTURE X(24) VALUE ' NORMAL END OF JOB        '.
00061     4 1   PROCEDURE DIVISION.
00062     4 2         OPEN INPUT CDINPUT1 INPUT1 OUTPUT OUTPUT1 OUTPUT2 TERM-FILE.
00063     4 3         READ CDINPUT1 INTO CARDIN AT END GO TO NORMAL-EOJ.
00064   J 4 4         MOVE STATE2 TO STATE4.
00065   ↗ 4 5   PRO-2.
00066     4 6         READ INPUT1 INTO INREC AT END GO TO NORMAL-EOJ.
00067     4 7         IF STATE-DATA = STATE4 GO TO PRO-3.
00068     4 8         WRITE OUTRCD1 FROM INREC.
00069     4 9         ADD 1 TO CNT1.
00070     410         GO TO PRO-2.
00071     411   PRO-3.
00072     412         WRITE OUTRCD2 FROM INREC.
00073     413         ADD 1 TO CNT2.
00074     415         GO TO PRO-2.
00075     416   NORMAL-EOJ.
00076                 WRITE TERM-RECORD FROM COUNTS.
00077     418         CLOSE INPUT1 OUTPUT1 OUTPUT2 TERM-FILE CDINPUT1.
00078     419         STOP RUN.
```

Figure 4.2 Portion of Assembly Language Listing (OC7)

```
                    0008EA  18 21                      LR    2,1
                    0008EC  D2 02 2 021 C 025          MVC   021(3,2),025(12)              GN=01+1
                    0008F2  58 F0 1 030                L     15,030(0,1)
                    0008F6  05 EF                      BALR  14,15
                    0008F8  50 10 D 204                ST    1,204(0,13)         BL =4
                    0008FC  58 A0 D 204                L     10,204(0,13)        BL =4
                    000900  D2 4F 6 058 A 000          MVC   058(80,6),000(10)   DNM=1-360     DNM=1-202
                    000906  58 50 C 028                L     5,028(0,12)         GN=02
                    00090A  07 F5                      BCR   15,5
63      GO          00090C                    GN=01    EQU   *
                    00090C  58 10 C 020                L     1,020(0,12)         PN=03
                    000910  07 F1                      BCR   15,1
64      MOVE        000912                    GN=02    EQU   *
                    000912  D2 06 6 000 6 058          MVC   000(7,6),058(6)     DNM=1-263     DNM=1-379
                    000918  96 F0 6 006                OI    006(6),X'F0'        DNM=1-263+6
65      *PRO-2
                    00091C                    PN=01    EQU   *
66      READ        00091C  58 F0 C 008                L     15,008(0,12)        V(ILBODBG4)
                    000920  05 EF                      BALR  14,15
                    000922  58 10 C 054                L     1,054(0,12)         DCB=1
                    000926  18 21                      LR    2,1
                    000928  D2 02 2 021 C 02D          MVC   021(3,2),02D(12)                  GN=03+1
                    00092E  58 F0 1 030                L     15,030(0,1)
                    000932  05 EF                      BALR  14,15
                    000934  50 10 D 1F8                ST    1,1F8(0,13)         BL =1
                    000938  58 70 D 1F8                L     7,1F8(0,13)         BL =1
                    00093C  D2 4F 6 008 7 000          MVC   008(80,6),000(7)    DNM=1-279     DNM=1-92
                    000942  58 50 C 030                L     5,030(0,12)         GN=04
                    000946  07 F5                      BCR   15,5
66      GO          000948                    GN=03    EQU   *
                    000948  58 10 C 020                L     1,020(0,12)         PN=03
                    00094C  07 F1                      BCR   15,1
67      IF          00094E                    GN=04    EQU   *
                    00094E  F2 76 D 210 6 02B          PACK  210(8,13),02B(7,6)  TS=01         DNM=1-313
                    000954  F2 76 D 218 6 000          PACK  218(8,13),000(7,6)  TS=09         DNM=1-263
                    00095A  F9 33 D 214 D 21C          CP    214(4,13),21C(4,13) TS=05         TS=013
                    000960  58 F0 C 034                L     15,034(0,12)        GN=05
                    000964  07 7F                      BCR   7,15
67      GO          000966  58 10 C 01C                L     1,01C(0,12)         PN=02
                    00096A  07 F1                      BCR   15,1
68      WRITE       00096C                    GN=05    EQU   *
                    00096C  58 F0 C 008                L     15,008(0,12)        V(ILBODBG4)
                    000970  05 EF                      BALR  14,15
                    000972  D2 4F 8 000 6 008          MVC   000(80,8),008(6)    DNM=1-127     DNM=1-279
                    000978  58 10 C 058                L     1,058(0,12)         DCB=2
                    00097C  18 21                      LR    2,1
                    00097E  92 00 2 07A                MVI   07A(2),X'00'
                    000982  58 40 2 024                L     4,024(0,2)
                    000986  92 00 4 014                MVI   014(4),X'00'
                    00098A  58 10 C 058                L     1,058(0,12)         DCB=2
                    00098E  58 00 1 04C                L     0,04C(0,1)
                    000992  58 F0 1 030                L     15,030(0,1)
                    000996  44 00 1 060                EX    0,060(0,1)
                    00099A  58 20 C 058                L     2,058(0,12)         DCB=2
                    00099E  91 40 2 07A                TM    07A(2),X'40'
                    0009A2  92 00 2 07A                MVI   07A(2),X'00'
                    0009A6  58 30 C 044                L     3,044(0,12)         GN=09
                    0009AA  07 13                      BCR   1,3
                    0009AC  50 10 D 1FC                ST    1,1FC(0,13)         BL =2
                    0009B0  58 80 D 1FC                L     8,1FC(0,13)         BL =2
                    0009B4                    GN=09    EQU   *
69      ADD         0009B4                    GN=06    EQU   *
                    0009B4  F2 76 D 218 6 0BD          PACK  218(8,13),0BD(7,6)  TS=09         DNM=1-442
                    0009BA  FA 40 D 21B C 068          AP    21B(5,13),068(1,12) TS=012        LIT+0
                    0009C0  F3 64 6 0BD D 21B          UNPK  0BD(7,6),21B(5,13)  DNM=1-442     TS=012
                    0009C6  96 F0 6 0C3                OI    0C3(6),X'F0'        DNM=1-442+6
```

98

Figure 4.3 Control Section of Cross Reference Table (OC7)

```
F88-LEVEL LINKAGE EDITOR OPTIONS SPECIFIED LET,LIST,XREF,SIZE=(,),LET
    DEFAULT OPTION(S) USED - SIZE=(90112,8192)
    SYSPRINT DEFAULT BLOCKING USED  1 - 1

                         CROSS REFERENCE TABLE

CONTROL SECTION               ENTRY

NAME      ORIGIN  LENGTH  G   NAME      LOCATION  NAME      LOCATION  NAME      LOCATION  NAME      LOCATION

A5558       00    D33
ILBOCOM0*   D38    BA        ILBOCOM    D38

ILBODBG *   DF8   860        ILBODBG0   DFA       ILBODBG1   DFE      ILBODBG2   E02       ILBODBG3   E06
                             ILBODBG4   E0A       ILBODBG5   E0E

ILBOERR *  1958   27B        ILBOERR0  195A       ILBOERR1  195E      ILBOERR2  1962       ILBOERR3  1966
                             ILBOERR4  196A       ILBOERR5  196E      ILBOERR6  1972       ILBOERR7  1976

ILBOEXT *  1BD8    1C        ILBOEXT0  1BDA

ILBOSRV *  1BF8   1B7        ILBOSRV0  1C2C       ILBOSRV1  1C30      ILBOSRV2  1C34       ILBOSRV3  1C38


LOCATION  REFERS TO SYMBOL  IN CONTROL SECTION    LOCATION  REFERS TO SYMBOL  IN CONTROL SECTION

  738     ILBOSRV0                                  73C     ILBOSRV           ILBODBG
  740     ILBODBG4                                  744     ILBODBG           ILBOERR
  748     ILBOEXT0                                  74C     ILBOEXT           ILBOSRV
  698     ILBOCOM0                                 188C     ILBOCOM0          $UNRESOLVED(W)
 1890     ILBOFLW2                                 1894     $UNRESOLVED(W)    $UNRESOLVED(W)
 1898     ILBOSTN0                                 1D98     $UNRESOLVED(W)    ILBOCOM0


ENTRY ADDRESS   00
TOTAL LENGTH   1DB0

****MAIN    DOES NOT EXIST BUT HAS BEEN ADDED TO DATA SET
```

Figure 4.4 First Page of OC7 Storage Dump

```
JOB  RZZ765  ——A  STEP GO ——B    TIME 132747
COMPLETION CODE    SYSTEM = 0C7 ——C
PSW AT ENTRY TO ABEND  FFF5000D C0096BB0  ——F

TCB 036CD8  RBP   00042520  PIE    00000000  DEB  00036RR4  TIO 00037880  CMP   800C7000  TRN  00000000
            MSS   0203F670  PK-FLG F0850400  FLG  0005F5R   LLS 0003ACE0  JLB   00000000  JPQ  80037F10
            FSA   0109D768  TCB    000369D0  TME  00000000  JST 00000000  NTC   00000000  OTC  0003D078
            LTC   00000000  IQE    00000000  ECB  00037A64  TSF 20000000  D-PQE 00043B50  SQS  00036IE8
            NSTAE 8003E088  TCT    8003A7D8  USER 00000000  DAR 00000000  RESV  00000000  JSCR 87030928
            RESV  00000000  IOB    00000000

ACTIVE RBS

PRB 03D308  RESV  00000000  APSW   C0096BB0  WC-SZ-STAR 00040082  FL-CDE 0003E748  PSW FFF5000D C0096BB0  ——E
            Q/TTR 00000000  WT-LNK 00036CDR

SVRB 042250 TAB-LN 00080220  APSW   F9F0F1C3  WC-SZ-STAR 0012D002  TQN 00000000  PSW 00040033 50015BFA
            Q/TTR  00004629   WT-LNK 0003D30R
            RG 0-7  0000000A  0009D140  00096404  0009652C  00096B9E  0009D140
            RG 8-15 0009A0C0  8F09D250  0009D1E8  00096730  50096R84  001FDBE0
            EXTSA   000021BE  C9C5C1D8  00000000  00042?CC  00042?D4  E2E8E2C9
                    C5C1F0F1

SVRB 042520 TAB-LN 00A803D8  APSW   F1F0F5C1  WC-SZ-STAR 0012D002  TQN 00000000  PSW FF04000C 4009FA6
            Q/TTR  00003801   WT-LNK 00042250
            RG 0-7  00000007  00042280  0001A318  00036CD8  04036CD8  00042250
            RG 8-15 00036CD8  40015A5A  8F09D250  00037C28  40017EA4  00000000
            EXTSA   E2E8E2C9  C5C1F0F1  1509DE0   0009D5EC  0009DFE8  00000000
                    00?04C08  00036BB4  80015BF8

LOAD LIST
  NE 0003ADC0  RSP-CDE 02037F10  NE 0003AF28  ROC-RB 0003D308  RSP-CDE 01045BC8  NE 00003B548  RSP-CDE 01045888
  NE 0003BD88  RSP-CDE 01045?C8  NE 0003D9D8  ROC-RB 00000000  RSP-CDE 01045988  NE 0003DAB0  RSP-CDE 02045ACA
  NE 0003DF98  RSP-CDE 02045A28  NE 0003E080  ROC-RB 00000000  RSP-CDE 02030488  NE 0003E3B8  RSP-CDE 01045BFA
  NE 0003E6C8  RSP-CDE 02045A98  NE 0003E6F0  ROC-RB 00000000  RSP-CDE 02045B88  NE 0003F598  RSP-CDE 02045B?A
  NE 0003F6E8  RSP-CDE 01045888  NE 00040EF0  ROC-RB 00000000  RSP-CDE 03045958  NE 00000000             ——D

CDE
  03E748  ATR1 0B  NCDE 000000  NM MAIN      USE 01  EPA 096250  ATR2 20  XL/MJ 03E0A8
  037F10  ATR1 30  NCDE 03CE00  NM IGC0A05A  USE 02  EPA 099858  ATR2 28  XL/MJ 037AE8
  0458C8  ATR1 B0  NCDE 0458F8  NM IGG019CF  USE 01  EPA 1FC590  ATR2 20  XL/MJ 045A88
  045888  ATR1 B0  NCDE 0458C8  NM IGG019CL  USE 01  EPA 1FF810  ATR2 20  XL/MJ 045A78
  0459C8  ATR1 80  NCDE 0459F8  NM IGG019BA  USE 01  EPA 1FCE40  ATR2 20  XL/MJ 045988
  045988  ATR1 B0  NCDE 0459C8  NM IGG019BB  USE 01  EPA 1FCCC8  ATR2 20  XL/MJ 045978
  045AC8  ATR1 B0  NCDE 045AF8  NM IGG019CD  USE 01  EPA 1FD830  ATR2 20  XL/MJ 045A88
  045A28  ATR1 B0  NCDE 045A58  NM IGG019CI  USE 01  EPA 1FD298  ATR2 20  XL/MJ 045A18
```

An OC7 Completion Code refers to a situation in which a numeric field to be tested or manipulated was found to contain non-numeric characters. The job was terminated and the dump routine called. A more detailed description of completion codes and their most probable causes can be obtained from the IBM Messages and Codes Manual as well as Chapter 7 of this text.

a. Address Location

The first step in debugging Internal Abends is to determine the Entry Point Address (EPA) of the program module, that is, the address of the beginning point of the executable load module as it resides in main storage. Every time a relocatable program is called, it is loaded in a different area of storage as determined by the Operating System. The EPA for this run can be found in the first line of the Contents Directory Entry (CDE). See Figure 4.4, letter 'D'. The starting address of the load module is 096250. Other lines within the CDE refer to those load modules attached to the program module during the linkage process. For all practical purposes they can be ignored.

Next, one must locate the Interrupt Address (IA); that is, the address of the actual machine instruction to be executed at the time the abend occurred. For System 360/370 OS, the IA can be found in the Active Program Status Word (APSW) near the top of the first page of the dump. The right-most three bytes, 096BB0, is the address at which the abend occurred. See Figure 4.4, letter 'E'. The machine language statement located at this address in main storage is one of a complete set of machine language statements generated by the compiler for the source statement being executed. Our objective is to locate that source statement.

To accomplish this objective we must first subtract, in hexadecimal, the EPA 096250 from the IA 096BB0, giving the Relative Length into the program module at which the abend occurred (096BB0 - 096250 = 000960). This calculation of Relative Length into the program module is necessary because the generated Assembly Language listing, soon to be referenced, begins at Relative Address zero and increases as increments into the program module are made. This concept is depicted in Figure 4.5.

Figure 4.5 Load Modules as Stored within Main Storage

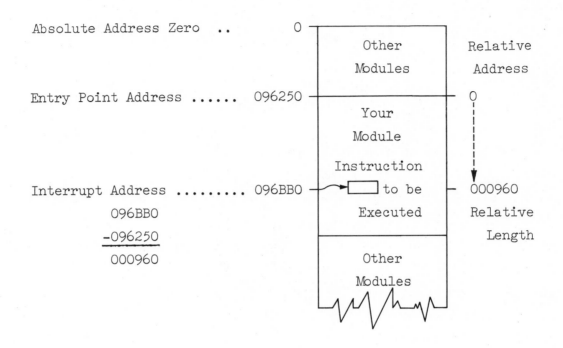

Absolute Address Zero ..   0   Other   Relative
                                          Modules   Address

Entry Point Address   096250   0

                                          Your
                                          Module

                                          Instruction
Interrupt Address ....   096BB0   to be   000960
          096BB0   Executed   Relative
         -096250   Length
          000960   Other
                                          Modules

The Interrupt Address for System 370 OS/VS is located nearer the
top of the first page at PSW AT ENTRY TO ABEND, not in the APSW. See Figure 4.4, letter 'F'. On Systems without Virtual Storage, this register
does not necessarily provide a programmer with the appropriate IA.
Rather, it must be obtained from the APSW as stated previously.

b. Control Section

Now that the Relative Length into the load module at which the
abend occurred has been determined, it will be fairly easy to locate
the instruction being executed. Before doing so, however, a quick reference to the Control Section of the Cross Reference Table should be
made. The Cross Reference Table is an output of the linkage process.
The linkage editor program calls various routines, such as those which
perform Input/Output functions, and attaches (links) them to the

program module. This table provides information about the origin and relative length of the program of interest as well as each module linked to that program.

As can be seen in Figure 4.3, letter 'G', the origin of the program module named A5558 is Relative Address zero. Its total length is D33; consequently Relative Length 960 calculated earlier falls within the program module as expected. This verification should always be made, as it is quite possible that the calculated length could have fallen outside the bounds of the main part of the program. When this occurs it simply means that the instruction being executed is located in a routine which was called by the program. This routine could have been either programmer-written or one of the many system routines attached during the linkage process. When the Relative Length calculated above falls outside the bounds of the main program, another subtraction would need to be made to find the length into the actual routine which was being executed. This condition will be explained more fully in the FORTRAN example later in this chapter. For now we need not be further concerned with Control Section information as Relative Length 960 falls within the bounds of the main program (00 to D33).

c. Assembly Language Listing

Having verified the actual length into the program at which the abend occurred, the next reference will be to the compiler-generated Assembly Language listing. It is important to note that one need not be an Assembly Language programmer to successfully interpret an Assembly Language listing to debug internal abends. Each listing begins at Relative Address zero and increments by the length of each instruction as one pages through the instruction list. Examining the third column from the left in Figure 4.2, letter 'H', one can locate Relative Address 000960 relatively easily. The information to the right of this address is a representation of the machine and assembly language statement to be executed. The breakdown and analysis of machine instructions is the topic of Chapter 6.

What is important in achieving our objective of locating the problem source statement is the information to the left of Address 000960.

Moving up and to the left it is found that Source Statement #67 was being executed when the program abnormally terminated. See Figure 4.2, letter 'I'. The problem has been narrowed to a single source statement. This is a significant piece of information in terms of 'zeroing in' on the problem area. It can also be seen that the compiler has generated five machine instructions for the IF Statement portion of the source statement (Address 00094E to and including 000964). The GO portion of Source Statement #67 generated two machine instructions (Address 000966 to and including 00096A). However, the instruction located at Relative Address 000960 was the one to be executed when the abend occurred.

With Source Statement #67 in mind, we can now proceed to the Source Program listing and isolate the appropriate source statement. The actual statement which was being executed at the time the OC7 Storage Dump occurred is IF STATE-DATA = STATE4. See Figure 4.1, letter 'J'. As determined from the Assembly Language listing, the GO portion of the source statement was not being executed and therefore can be ignored.

3. Problem Analysis

Realizing that an OC7 Dump implies the existence of non-numeric characters in a field described as numeric, and knowing the actual source statement being executed at the time the abend occurred, one may not have to proceed much further in the analysis of the problem. Assuming familiarity with the program, a programmer would probably know how the variables STATE-DATA and STATE4 are defined, and quite possibly, where the non-numeric characters originated from. Corrective action can then be taken by changing either the program or the data to prevent this error from re-occurring. Various program checks could be made to ensure that non-numeric data is not moved to numeric fields. Or, the programmer may decide to initially process the raw data through a special pre-edit program, thus 'cleaning up' the data prior to execution of the program.

As can be seen, external file data can cause an Internal Abend, though program edit changes should probably be made. Regardless, once the source statement is located, it is quite possible that the problem can be solved without proceeding much further in the process of debugging internal storage dumps.

In the next chapter the value of pertinent variables, such as STATE-DATA and STATE4, will be determined from main storage contents. One should always accomplish this after the problem statement has been located, especially if the actual source of the problem has not yet been determined. Nevertheless, narrowing the problem to one source statement is a significant accomplishment in the analysis of Internal Abends.

D. FORTRAN COMPARISON

1. Computer Run Overview (322)

Internal Abend debugging procedures for FORTRAN programs are the same as those for COBOL. A comparison with other programming languages will find a slightly different format in the Assembly Language listing; however, identical information is contained therein.

The Control Section is generally more frequently referenced for FORTRAN program problems because FORTRAN programmers have a much higher tendency to utilize programmer-written subroutines and functions as compared to their use in other programming languages. As a result, the Control Section must be referenced to determine if the abend occurred in a programmer-written subroutine outside the main part of the program. If it did, another subtraction must be made to determine the length into the routine at which the abend occurred. The Assembly Language listing for the appropriate routine can then be referenced to determine the problem source statement. If the routine of interest is not programmer-written, the Trace Area must first be accessed to determine the length into the module which called the routine. The computer run depicted in Figures 4.6 through 4.11 consists of selected pertinent pages of a computer run which has abended with a 322 Completion Code. A 322 Storage Dump results when a specified CPU time limit has been exceeded. Perhaps a Time Parameter in the JCL should be increased, but more important, the program could be in an endless loop. In this case, increasing the time specification would only result in another 322 Storage Dump! In either case, the source statement being executed should be isolated and analyzed.

2. Control Section

The Control Section of the Cross Reference Table contains the starting point and length of each routine attached to the main program during the linkage process. It will be used to assist in locating the source statement being executed at the time of the abend.

Before proceeding, however, a problem overview should be obtained from the first page of the dump. The Jobname, Stepname, and Completion Code are RZZ124, GO, and 322, respectively. See Figure 4.10, letter 'A'.

As with all Internal storage dumps, the Relative Length into the load module must be determined. The Entry Point Address (EPA), 0B4C10, is obtained from the first line of the Contents Directory Entry (CDE). See letter 'B'. On System 360/370 OS, the Interrupt Address (IA), 0B4F26, is obtained from the Active Program Status Word (APSW) near the top of the first page of the dump. See letter 'C'. If this job were run on System 370 OS/VS, the same IA, 0B4F26, would have been obtained from the PSW AT ENTRY TO ABEND nearer the top of the first page

Figure 4.6   FORTRAN Source Program Listing for MAIN and COMP (322)

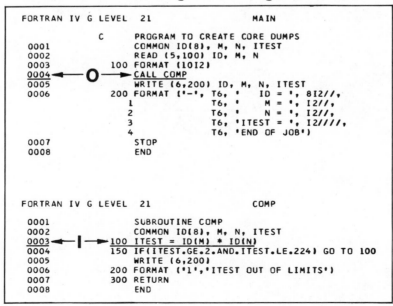

```
FORTRAN IV G LEVEL  21                    MAIN

               C      PROGRAM TO CREATE CORE DUMPS
     0001             COMMON ID(8), M, N, ITEST
     0002             READ (5,100) ID, M, N
     0003        100 FORMAT (10I2)
     0004            CALL COMP
     0005            WRITE (6,200) ID, M, N, ITEST
     0006        200 FORMAT ('-', T6, '   ID = ', 8I2//,
               1                 T6, '    M = ', I2//,
               2                 T6, '    N = ', I2//,
               3                 T6, 'ITEST = ', I2////,
               4                 T6, 'END OF JOB')
     0007            STOP
     0008            END




FORTRAN IV G LEVEL  21                    COMP

     0001            SUBROUTINE COMP
     0002            COMMON ID(8), M, N, ITEST
     0003        100 ITEST = ID(M) * ID(N)
     0004        150 IF(ITEST.GE.2.AND.ITEST.LE.224) GO TO 100
     0005            WRITE (6,200)
     0006        200 FORMAT ('1','ITEST OUT OF LIMITS')
     0007        300 RETURN
     0008            END
```

106

Figure 4.7   Portion of Assembly Language Listing for MAIN (322)

```
FORTRAN IV G LEVEL  21                    MAIN

LOCATION    STA NUM    LABEL    OP        OPERAND              BCD OPERAND
000000                          BC        15,12(0,15)
000004                          DC        06D4C1C9
000008                          DC        D5404040
00000C                          STM       14,12,12(13)
000010                          LM        2,3,40(15)
000014                          LR        4,13
000016                          L         13,36(0,15)
00001A                          ST        13,8(0,4)
00001E                          STM       3,4,0(13)
000022                          BCR       15,2
000024                          DC        00000000             A4
000028                          DC        00000000             A20
00002C                          DC        00000000             A36
000138               A36        L         13,4(0,13)
00013C                          L         14,12(0,13)
000140                          LM        2,12,28(13)
000144                          MVI       12(13),255
000148                          BCR       15,14
00014A               A20        L         15,100(0,13)         IBCOM#
00014E                          LR        12,13
000150                          LR        13,4
000152                          BAL       14,64(0,15)
000156                          LR        13,12
000158     2                    L         15,100(0,13)         IBCOM#
00015C                          BAL       14,0(0,15)
000160                          DC        00000005
000164                          DC        0000009C
000168                          BAL       14,12(0,15)
00016C                          DC        00000000
000170                          DC        04500008
000174                          L         10,72(0,13)
000178                          BAL       14,8(0,15)
00017C                          DC        0450A020
000180                          BAL       14,8(0,15)
000184                          DC        0450A024
000188                          BAL       14,16(0,15)
00018C     4                    LA        1,0(0,0)
000190                          L         15,104(0,13)         COMP
000194                          BALR      14,15
000196                          BC        0,4(0,0)
00019A     5                    L         15,100(0,13)         IBCOM#
00019E                          BCR       0,0
0001A0                          BAL       14,4(0,15)
0001A4                          DC        00000006
0001A8                          DC        000000A2
0001AC                          BAL       14,12(0,15)
0001B0                          DC        00000000
0001B4                          DC        04500008
0001B8                          BAL       14,8(0,15)
0001BC                          DC        0450A020
0001C0                          BAL       14,8(0,15)
0001C4                          DC        0450A024
0001C8                          BAL       14,8(0,15)
0001CC                          DC        0450A028
0001D0                          BAL       14,16(0,15)
0001D4     7                    L         15,100(0,13)         IBCOM#
0001D8                          BAL       14,52(0,15)
```

N ↓

M

Figure 4.8   Portion of Assembly Language Listing for COMP (322)

```
FORTRAN IV G LEVEL  21                     COMP

LOCATION   STA NUM    LABEL    OP        OPERAND              BCD OPERAND
 000000                        BC        15,12(0,15)
 000004                        DC        06C3D6D4
 000008                        DC        D7C4040
 00000C                        STM       14,12,12(13)
 000010                        LM        2,3,40(15)
 000014                        LR        4,13
 000016                        L         13,36(0,15)
 00001A                        ST        13,8(0,4)
 00001E                        STM       3,4,0(13)
 000022                        BCR       15,2
 000024                        DC        00000000             A4
 000028                        DC        00000000             A20
 00002C                        DC        00000000             A36
 000108              A20       BALR      2,0
 00010A                        L         3,6(0,2)
 00010E                        BCR       15,3
 000110                        DC        0000000C             A52
 000114              A36       L         1,4(0,13)
 000118                        L         1,24(0,1)
 00011C                        L         13,4(0,13)
 000120                        L         14,12(0,13)
 000124                        LM        2,12,28(13)
 000128                        MVI       12(13),255
 00012C                        BCR       15,14
 00012E      3       100       L         10,72(0,13)
 000132                        L         8,32(0,10)           M
 000136                        SLA       8,2(0)
 00013A                        A         8,200(0,13)
 00013E                        L         1,0(8,10)            ID
 000142                        L         9,36(0,10)           N
 000146                        SLA       9,2(0)
 00014A                        A         9,200(0,13)
 00014E                        M         0,0(9,10)            ID
 000152                        ST        1,40(0,10)           ITEST
 000156      4       150       L         0,40(0,10)           ITEST
 00015A                        C         0,204(0,13)
 00015E                        L         0,208(0,13)
 000162                        BALR      14,0
 000164                        BC        11,6(0,14)
 000168                        SR        0,0
 00016A                        L         1,40(0,10)           ITEST
 00016E                        C         1,212(0,13)
 000172                        LA        1,1(0,0)
 000176                        BALR      14,0
 000178                        BC        13,6(0,14)
 00017C                        SR        1,1
 00017E                        NR        1,0
 000180                        LTR       1,1
 000182                        L         14,100(0,13)         100
 000186                        BCR       7,14
 000188      5                 L         15,112(0,13)         IBCOM#
 00018C                        BAL       14,4(0,15)
 000190                        DC        00000006
 000194                        DC        000000A4
 000198                        BAL       14,16(0,15)
 00019C      7       300       SR        15,15
 00019E                        L         1,0(0,13)
```

G

H

Figure 4.9 Control Section of Cross Reference Table (322)

F88-LEVEL LINKAGE EDITOR OPTIONS SPECIFIED XREF,LET,LIST
DEFAULT OPTION(S) USED - SIZE=(90112,8192)

CROSS REFERENCE TABLE

CONTROL SECTION

NAME	ORIGIN	LENGTH
MAIN	00	1E2 ← E
COMP	1E8	1A4
IHNECCMH*	390	F8C ← F
IHNCOMH2*	1320	715
IHNFCVTH*	1A38	B6F
IHNEFNTH*	25A8	548
IHNEFIOS*	2AF0	FF8
IHNFIOS2*	3AE8	5B8
IHNUOPT *	40A0	318
IHNFCONI*	43B8	2E5
IHNFCONQ*	46A0	4A2
IHNERRM *	4B48	5FC
IHNUATBL*	5148	638
IHNFTEN *	5780	198
IHNETRCH*	5918	2A6
$BLANKCOM	5BC0	2C

ENTRY

NAME	LOCATION	NAME	LOCATION	NAME	LOCATION	NAME	LOCATION
IBCOM#	3BC	FDIOCS#	478	INTSWTCH	12F6		
SEQDASD	174E						
ADCON#	1A38	FCVAOUTP	1A38	FCVLOUTP	1AE2	FCVZOUTP	ICCE
FCVIOUTP	2076	FCVEOUTP	2168	FCVCOUTP	1B72	INT6SWCH	2528
ARITH#	25A8	ADJSWTCH	2944		22B2		
FIOCS#	2AF0	FIOCSBEP	2AF6				
FQCONI#	4388						
FQCONQ#	46A0						
ERRMON	4848	IHNERRE	4860				
FTEN#	5780						
IHNTRCH	5918	ERRTRA	5920				

LOCATION	REFERS TO SYMBOL	IN CONTROL SECTION
16C		
78	COMP	COMP
98	IBCOM#	IHNECCMH
288	IHNCOMH2	IHNCOMH2
4D0	FIOCS#	IHNEFIOS
1F4	ADJSWTCH	IHNEFNTH
1220	IHNCMSE	$UNRESOLVED(W)
1318	FCVLOUTP	IHNFCVTH
1208	FCVCOUTP	IHNFCVTH
1210	FCVZOUTP	IHNFCVTH
1218	IHNCOMH2	IHNCOMH2
11D4		

LOCATION	REFERS TO SYMBOL	IN CONTROL SECTION
1B0		
94	IBCOM#	IHNECOMH
260		
478	SEQDASD	IHNCOMH2
11FC	ADCON#	IHNFCVTH
1200	ARITH#	IHNEFNTH
121C	IHNUOPT	IHNUOPT
1204	FCVEOUTP	IHNFCVTH
120C	FCVIOUTP	IHNFCVTH
1214	FCVAOUTP	IHNFCVTH
11A8	IHNERRE	IHNERRM
11D8	IHNERRM	IHNERRM

Figure 4.10   First Page of 322 Storage Dump

```
                                        TIME 184518

JOB  RZZ124 —A—  STEP GO
COMPLETION CODE  SYSTEM = 322
PSW AT ENTRY TO ABEND  FF75000D 62084F26 —D

TCB 0365D0  RBP    000421B8  PIE    00000000  DEB  000363EC  TIO 00036CD0  CMP   80322000  TRN  00000000
            MSS    020414F8  PK-FLG 70854400  FLG  0000FBFB  LLS 0003F4F0  JLB   00000000  JPQ  0003E5A0
            FSA    010BDF68  TCB    0003DAC8  TME  00000000  JST 00036500  NTC   00000000  QTC  0003BE48
            LTC    00000000  IQE    00000000  ECB  0003C104  TSF 20000000  D-PQE 00041 4F8 SQS  00035510
            NSTAE  0003EC78  TCT    80036708  USER 00000000  DAR 00000000  RESV  00000000  JSCB 8703E250
            RESV   00000000  IOB    00000000

ACTIVE RBS

PRB 03E580   RESV  00000000  APSW 62084F26   WC-SZ-STAB 00040082  FL-CDE 0003FAF0  PSW FF75000D 62084F26  —C
             Q/TTR 00000000  WT-LNK 000365D0

SVRB 042098  TAB-LN 30780220  APSW F9F0F1C3   WC-SZ-STAB 0012D002  TQN 00000000  PSW 00040033 500179F2
             Q/TTR  00004629  WT-LNK 0003E580
             RG 0-7  00000001  00000001  42084F02  00B4C40   0003BE48  00036D64  0003E4D0
             RG 8-15 000021BE  00000008  000BA700  0003E588  00084C40  00084F26  00B4DF8
             EXTSA   C5C1F0F1  8F0BDAE0  00000000  00000000  FF030000  0004211C  E2E8E2C9

SVRB 0421B8  TAB-LN 00B803D8  APSW F1F0F5C1   WC-SZ-STAB 0012D002  TQN 00000000  PSW FF04000C 400BD7A6
             Q/TTR  00003801  WT-LNK 00042098
             RG 0-7  00000007  000420F8  8001790A  0001A318  00042098  04036500  00042098
             RG 8-15 000365D0  40017852  00036500  8F0BDAE0  0004211C  4001693C  00000000
             EXTSA   E2E8E2C9  C5C1F0F1  C9C7C3F5  F4F0F3C4  0003C0E0  E2E3C1C5  00000000
                     C0001944  00000000  00000000  00000000

LCAD LIST
NE 0003F4F8  RSP-CDE 0203E5A0  NE 0003F990  RSP-CDE 01045BC8  NE 0003F998  RSP-CDE 01045888
NE 0003FC20  RSP-CDE 01045 9C8 NE 0003F9A8  RSP-CDE 01045988  NE 0003FB50  RSP-CDE 01045BF8
NE 0003FC10  RSP-CDE 01045A98  NE 0003FD58  RSP-CDE 01045A28  NE 0003FD78  RSP-CDE 01045BC8
NE 000403E0  RSP-CDE 01045888  NE 000406A0  RSP-CDE 02045 9C8  NE 00000000  RSP-CDE 02045988

CDE                                                                                                    —B
03FAF0  ATR1 0B  NCDE 000000  ROC-RB 0003E580  NM MAIN     USE 01  EPA 0B4C10  ATR2 20  XL/MJ 03F958
03E5A0  ATR1 30  NCDE 03FAF0  ROC-RB 00000000  NM IGC0A05A USE 02  EPA 0BD058  ATR2 28  XL/MJ 03EC40
045BC8  ATR1 B0  NCDE 0458F8  ROC-RB 00000000  NM IGG019CF USE 01  EPA 1FC590  ATR2 20  XL/MJ 045BB8
045888  ATR1 B0  NCDE 0458C8  ROC-RB 00000000  NM IGG019CL USE 01  EPA 1FF810  ATR2 20  XL/MJ 045878
0459C8  ATR1 B0  NCDE 0459F8  ROC-RB 00000000  NM IGG019BA USE 01  EPA 1FCE40  ATR2 20  XL/MJ 045988
045988  ATR1 B0  NCDE 0459C8  ROC-RB 00000000  NM IGG019B3 USE 01  EPA 1FCCC8  ATR2 20  XL/MJ 045978
0458F8  ATR1 B0  NCDE 045928  ROC-RB 0C000000  NM IGG019CE USE 01  EPA 1FC998  ATR2 20  XL/MJ 0458E8
045A98  ATR1 B0  NCDE 045AC8  ROC-RB 00000000  NM IGG019CC USE 01  EPA 1FD4F8  ATR2 20  XL/MJ 045A88
045A28  ATR1 B0  NCDE 045A58  PCC-RB 00000000  NM IGG019CI USE 01  EPA 1FD298  ATR2 20  XL/MJ 045A18
```

Figure 4.11 Save Area Trace Portion of 322 Storage Dump

```
MAJ 046740   NMAJ 00035B88   PMAJ 00027DB8   FMIN 00046718   NM  SYSDSN
MIN 040628   FQEL 0003FF28   PMIN 0003EC08   NMIN 0003FC68   NM FF SYS1.FORTLIB
             NQEL 00041590   PQEL 80040628   TCB  0003BE48   SVRB 00042368

MIN 03FC68   FQEL 000402A8   PMIN 00040628   NMIN 0003FA20   NM FF SYS2.SYSLIB
             NQEL 0003D468   PQEL 8003FC68   TCB  0003BE48   SVRB 00042368

MAJ 03E3A8   NMAJ 00000000   PMAJ 00035B88   FMIN 0003E2E0   NM  SYSIEA01
MIN 03E2E0   FQEL 0003E328   PMIN 0003E3A8   NMIN 00000000   NM 70 IEA
             NQEL 00000000   PQEL 0003E2E0   TCB  000365D0   SVRB 000421B8


SAVE AREA TRACE ──────J

MAIN   WAS ENTERED VIA LINK        AT EP MAIN ──────

SA   0BDF68   WD1 00000000   HSA 00000000   LSA 000B4C40   RET 00020510   EPA 010B4C10   R0  FD000008
             R1  000BDFF8   R2  0003C218   R3  5C03C108   R4  0003C520   R5  0003BE48   R6  00036D64
             R7  0003E4D0   R8  0003C0E0   R9  000367D8   R10 0003C108   R11 0003E588   R12 401FE102

MAIN   WAS ENTERED VIA CALL   00004  AT EP COMP ──────
                                                                                            ↑L
SA   0B4C40   WD1 000B4D48   HSA 000BDF68   LSA 000B4E28   RET 420B4DA6   EPA 000B4DF8   R0  FD000008
             R1  00000000   R2  00084D5A   R3  0008404B   R4  000BDF68   R5  0003BE48   R6  00036D64
             R7  0003E4D0   R8  0003C0E0   R9  000367D8   R10 000BA7D0   R11 0003E588   R12 000B4C40

SA   0B4E28   WD1 000B4F0C   HSA 000B4C40   LSA 540A4208   RET CA0C5803   EPA CA0C1601   R0  D230C8AE
             R1  CA14CA0C   R2  6C165620   R3  840FB20E   R4  1C0E9807   R5  CC04CC14   R6  C832A009
             R7  0425B618   R8  1255CC04   R9  3A30CC14   R10 CA0C340D   R11 CA0C1602   R12 4C4C58E0

INVALID BACK CHAIN

SA   0A4208   WD1 00000000   HSA 00000000   LSA 45227068   RET 46305105   EPA 448E300B   R0  441E16E5
             R1  42262666   R2  42204AC5   R3  4278F24A   R4  428DBC9E   R5  00000000   R6  42341381
             R7  4419A49D   R8  45460DF2   R9  436D11CF   R10 43E2775D   R11 41D7F1C    R12 41126031

INTERRUPT AT 0B4F26

PROCEEDING BACK VIA REG 13

SA   0B4E28   WD1 000B4F0C   HSA 00084C40   LSA 540A4208   RET CA0C5803   EPA CA0C1601   R0  D230C8AE
             R1  CA14CA0C   R2  6C165620   R3  840FB20E   R4  1C0E9807   R5  CC04CC14   R6  C832A009
             R7  0425B618   R8  1255CC04   R9  3A30CC14   R10 CA0C340D   R11 CA0C1602   R12 4C4C58E0

REGS AT ENTRY TO ABEND
```

K

111

of the dump. See letter 'D'. Subtracting the EPA from the IA, a
Relative Length into the load module of 316 is determined (0B4F26 -
0B4C10 = 000316).

The Control Section need now be referenced. As can be seen in
Figure 4.9, letter 'E', the Origin of the program module named MAIN
is zero. Its total length is 1E2. As a result, Relative Length 316
calculated above falls outside the bounds of the main portion of the
program. Checking the next line of the Control Section, it can be
determined that Address 316 falls within the bounds of programmer-
written Subroutine COMP. See letter 'F'. The Origin of COMP is 1E8.
Its length is 1A4. The Origin of the next module, IHNECOMH, is 390.
It can be seen, therefore, that Relative Address 316 falls within Subroutine COMP, i.e., between Address 1E8 and 390. Subtracting the
Origin of Subroutine COMP, 1E8, from Relative Length 316 provides a
length of 12E into the actual subroutine which was being executed
(316 - 1E8 = 12E). This concept is depicted in Figure 4.12 below
using the above addresses.

Figure 4.12   Load Module Stored within Main Storage

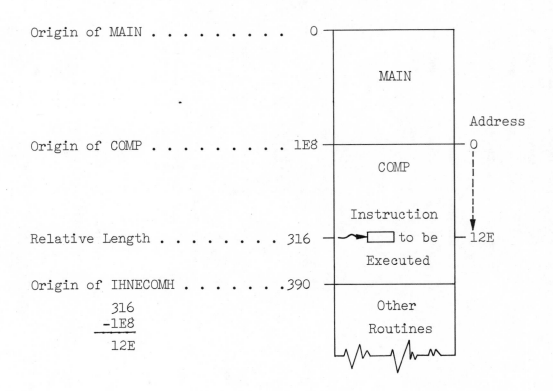

112

The extra subtraction to determine the length into the actual routine which was being executed must be accomplished because the Assembly Language listings for MAIN, COMP, and other routines each begin at Address zero. A length of 12E has been determined to be the length into Subroutine COMP at which the abend occurred. The Assembly Language listing for COMP can now be referenced.

3. Assembly Language Listing

Compiler-generated Assembly Language listings for FORTRAN contain the same information as that of other languages. The only essential difference is that the print format of the listing itself varies somewhat.

Address 12E, obtained previously from the Control Section, can now be referenced in the Assembly Language listing for Subroutine COMP. See Figure 4.8, letter 'G'. The information to the right of this address is a representation of the machine or assembly language statement to be executed. The breakdown and analysis of machine instructions is the subject of Chapter 6.

Our objective now, however, is to locate the source statement being executed at the time of the abend. Moving up and to the right it can be determined that Source Statement #3 was being executed when the job was abnormally terminated. See letter 'H'. The problem has been successfully narrowed to a select area of the source program. It can also be seen that the compiler has generated 10 assembly instructions for Source Statement #3 (Address 00012E to and including 000152). However, the machine instruction located at Address 12E in Subroutine COMP was the one to be executed when the abend occurred.

With Source Statement #3 in mind, one can now proceed to the Source Program listing for Subroutine COMP and isolate the appropriate source statement. The actual statement that was being executed at the time the 322 Storage Dump occurred is 100 ITEST = ID(M) * ID(N). See Figure 4.6, letter 'I'. A review and analysis of the problem statement can now be made.

4. Problem Analysis

A 322 Storage Dump indicates that a specified CPU time has been exceeded. Quite possibly, the cause of the problem could be a program loop. Knowing the actual source statement that was being executed at the time the abend occurred, one may not have to proceed much further in the analysis of this particular problem.

Assuming familiarity with the program itself, a programmer would probably understand how the variable ITEST was created as well as the source of its components. A review of program logic may uncover an endless loop whereby corrective action can then be taken. The Time Parameter in the JCL should only be increased after the programmer has attained complete confidence that a loop within the program does not exist.

Assurance of this fact can be made by determining the value of pertinent variables at the time of the abend. Now that the problem has been narrowed to a single source statement, the value of the program variable, ITEST, would be a logical choice to locate in main storage. Determining the value of pertinent variables is the subject of the next chapter.

Regardless, it is quite possible that the problem can be solved without proceeding much further in the process of debugging internal abends. The source statement being executed at the time of the dump would be part of a program loop. Isolating the cause to a single source statement or problem area is a significant accomplishment when debugging Internal Abends.

5. Trace Area

In the previous example, the abend occurred during execution of a programmer-written subroutine called COMP. As a result, the Source Program and Assembly Language listings were readily available. After a calculation to determine the length into the appropriate routine was accomplished, it was then an easy matter to reference the listings to determine the problem source statement.

Suppose however, that Subroutine COMP was not a programmer-written routine, but rather a routine provided by the Operating System. For propietary reasons, the Source Program and Assembly Language listings may not be available. This is particularly true for programs which interface with data base and other software packages. As a result, they cannot be accessed to determine the problem source statement. And even if they were, what could we do with it? Programmers have no control over the maintenance of many routines supplied by vendors to perform specific functions. This is when the Trace Area of a storage dump becomes significant in the analysis of Internal Abends. It will be used to determine the length into the calling routine.

Figure 4.11 depicts that portion of a dump called SAVE AREA TRACE. This area provides information relating to those instructions which called the problem routine for which we have no listing. If the source statement which called the routine can be determined, the problem has essentially been isolated to a programmer-written statement within the program of interest for which Source Program and Assembly Language listings are available. In the following example, assume then, that Subroutine COMP is a system routine outside the bounds of the main program for which little information is available.

Recall that after subtracting the Entry Point Address from the Interrupt Address, a Relative Length of 316 into the load module was determined. Referencing the Control Section it was found that the problem instruction is located at Address 12E in Subroutine COMP, outside the bounds of MAIN. This concept can be reviewed in Figure 4.12.

Assuming that the listings for Subroutine COMP are not available, the SAVE AREA TRACE portion of a storage dump must be accessed. See Figure 4.11, letter 'J'. This area is located on the page just prior to the beginning of the print of main storage. Noting that portion of the Trace Area relating to the name of the program module, MAIN, an EPA of OB4C1O can be obtained. See letter 'K'. This is the entry point of the programmer-written module which called the problem routine.

A Return Address (RA), the address of the instruction in the program module which called the problem routine, is determined next. It can be found in the return area called RET relating to the name of the problem routine, COMP. The RA is found to be OB4DA6. See letter 'L'. Subtracting the EPA from the RA, a length into the program module of 196 is determined (OB4DA6 - OB4C1O = OOO196). The Assembly Language listing for MAIN can now be referenced at Address 196. See Figure 4.7, letter 'M'. Moving up and to the right, it can be determined that Source Statement #4 in MAIN called Subroutine COMP which was being executed when the abend occurred. See letter 'N'. The problem has been narrowed to the source statement which called the problem routine. The Source Program listing for MAIN can now be referenced. The statement which called the routine is CALL COMP. See Figure 4.6, letter 'O'.

The SAVE AREA TRACE portion of a storage dump can be a valuable aid in the analysis of Internal Abends. This is especially true when the instruction which was being executed is located outside the bounds of the program or the Interupt Address (IA) is invalid. The specific programming language utilized is of little consequence.

6. H-Level Differences

Various compiler levels within a given programming language are readily available. Differences among programming levels usually relate to various features and extensions which become available at the next higher level.

The previous FORTRAN example utilized the G-Level compiler. This is perhaps the most frequent FORTRAN programming level for testing purposes as the compiler demands less storage space than the respective H-Level, and also produces a more easy to read Assembly Language listing. However, it also produces a less efficient object module for execution purposes. H-Level FORTRAN, on the other hand, utilizes more of main storage during the compilation process, but produces a more efficient object module. This is because the H-Level compiler attempts to streamline the object module, thus creating a more economical program which requires less storage space than that of G-Level. As a result, the Assembly Language listing, which has been compacted and economized in certain areas, is more difficult to interpret.

A clear distinction cannot always be made between machine instructions generated by a particular source statement, and those generated by another nearby. Utilizing a reasonable level of common sense in relating the Assembly Language listing to the Source Program listing, the problem statement can always be approximated and usually isolated.

Figures 4.13 and 4.14 on the following pages depict a Source Program and Assembly Language listing as generated by the FORTRAN H-Level compiler. It is comparable to that generated for Subroutine COMP by the G-Level compiler in the previous example. An essential difference will be noted, however.

Suppose that after referencing the Control Section, a length into Subroutine COMP of FA was determined. Reference can be made to the Assembly Language listing in Figure 4.14, letter 'A'. Moving two columns to the right and up, program label 150 is found. See letter 'B'. This column contains programmer-coded as well as compiler-generated program labels. They are not statement numbers as determined previously. Compiler-generated labels are those containing six characters, i.e., 200001, 100002, etc.

Referring to the Source Program listing for Subroutine COMP, Source Statement #5 with a label of 150 can be found. See Figure 4.13, letter 'C'. The statement being executed at the time of the abend was 150 IF(ITEST.GE.2.AND.ITEST.LE.224) GO TO 100. Reliance must be placed on programmer-coded labels rather than source statement numbers when referring to a FORTRAN H-Level Assembly Language listing.

If the calculated length into the executable routine was determined

Figure 4.13   FORTRAN Source Program Listing (H-Level)

```
LEVEL 21.7                                OS/360   FORTRAN H

          COMPILER OPTIONS - NAME=  MAIN,OPT=00,LINECNT=60,SIZE=0000K,
                             SOURCE,EBCDIC,LIST,NODECK,LOAD,MAP,NOEDIT,ID,XREF
                C      PROGRAM TO CREATE CORE DUMPS
  ISN 0002             COMMON ID(8), M, N, ITEST
  ISN 0003             READ (5,100) ID, M, N
  ISN 0004      100 FORMAT (10I2)
  ISN 0005             CALL COMP
  ISN 0006             WRITE (6,200) ID, M, N, ITEST
  ISN 0007      200 FORMAT ('-', T6, '   ID = ', 8I2//,
               1                 T6, '   M = ', I2//,
               2                 T6, '   N = ', I2//,
               3                 T6, 'ITEST = ', I2////,
               4                 T6, 'END OF JOB')
  ISN 0008             STOP
  ISN 0009             END



LEVEL 21.7                                OS/360   FORTRAN H

          COMPILER OPTIONS - NAME=  MAIN,OPT=00,LINECNT=60,SIZE=0000K,
                             SOURCE,EBCDIC,LIST,NODECK,LOAD,MAP,NOEDIT,ID,XREF
  ISN 0002             SUBROUTINE COMP
  ISN 0003             COMMON ID(8), M, N, ITEST
  ISN 0004      100 ITEST = ID(M) * ID(N)
  ISN 0005      150 IF(ITEST.GE.2.AND.ITEST.LE.224) GO TO 100
  ISN 0007             WRITE (6,200)
  ISN 0008      200 FORMAT ('1','ITEST OUT OF LIMITS')
  ISN 0009      300 RETURN
  ISN 0010             END
```

117

Figure 4.14   Portion of Assembly Language Listing (H-Level)

```
                   000000   47 F0 F 00C      COMP      BC      15,12(0,15)
                   000004   07                         DC      XL1'07'
                   000005   C3D6D4D7404040             DC      CL7'COMP   '
                   00000C   90 EC D 00C                STM     14,12,12(13)
                   000010   18 4D                      LR      4,13
                   000014   98 CD F 020                LM      12,13,32(15)
                   000018   50 40 D 004                ST      4,4(0,13)
                   00001A   50 D0 4 008                ST      13,8(0,4)
                   00001E   07 FC                      BCR     15,12

CONSTANTS
                   000098   00000002                   DC      XL4'00000002'
                   00009C   000000E0                   DC      XL4'000000E0'
ADCONS FOR VARIABLES AND CONSTANTS
ADCONS FOR COMMON
                   0000A8   FFFFFFFC                   DC      XL4'FFFFFFFC'
ADCONS FOR EXTERNAL REFERENCES
                   0000AC   00000000                   DC      XL4'00000000'        IBCOM#
                   0000C4   58 70 D 060      100        L       7,    96( 0,13)
                   0000C8   58 60 7 024                 L       6,    36( 0, 7)         M
                   0000CC   89 60 0 002                 SLL     6,     2( 0, 0)
                   0000D0   58 06 7 000                 L       0,     0( 6, 7)        ID
                   0000D4   50 00 D 068                 ST      0,   104( 0,13)       .S00
                   0000D8   58 60 7 028                 L       6,    40( 0, 7)         N
                   0000DC   89 60 0 002                 SLL     6,     2( 0, 0)
                   0000E0   58 06 7 000                 L       0,     0( 6, 7)        ID
                   0000E4   18 10                       LR      1, 0
                   0000E6   5C 00 D 068                 M       0,   104( 0,13)       .S00
                   0000EA   50 10 7 02C                 ST      1,    44( 0, 7)       ITEST
```
A → `0000FA   58 50 D 078`   and   B → `150` appear as:
```
                   0000EE   58 70 D 060   B→ 150       L       7,    96( 0,13)
                   0000F2   58 00 7 02C                 L       0,    44( 0, 7)       ITEST
                   0000F6   59 00 D 050                 C       0,    80( 0,13)         2
          A→       0000FA   58 50 D 078                 L       5,   120( 0,13)
                   0000FE   07 45                       BCR     4, 5
                   000100   58 70 D 060      200001     L       7,    96( 0,13)
                   000104   58 00 7 02C                 L       0,    44( 0, 7)       ITEST
                   000108   59 00 D 054                 C       0,    84( 0,13)        E0
                   00010C   58 50 D 070                 L       5,   112( 0,13)       100
                   000110   07 D5                       BCR     13, 5                 100
                   000112   58 F0 D 064   E→ 100002    L       15,  100( 0,13)    F→ IBCOM#
                   000116   18 00                       LR       0, 0
          D→       000118   45 E0 F 004                 BAL     14,    4( 0,15)
                   00011C   00000006                    DC      XL4'00000006'          6
                   000120   00000028                    DC      XL4'00000028'
                   000124   45 E0 F 010                 BAL     14,   16( 0,15)
                   000128   1B FF            300         SR      15,15
                   00012A   58 E0 D 000                 L       14,    0( 0,13)
                   00012E   07 FE                       BCR     15,14
ADDRESS OF EPILOGUE
                   000130   58 80 D 004                 L       8,     4( 0,13)
                   000134   58 E0 8 00C                 L       14,   12( 0, 8)
                   000138   58 10 8 018                 L       1,    24( 0, 8)
                   00013C   18 D8                       LR      13, 8
                   00013E   98 2C D 01C                 LM      2,    28(12,13)
                   000142   92 FF D 00C                 MVI     15,   12(15,13)
                   000146   07 FE                       BCR     15,14
ADDRESS OF PROLOGUE
                   000148   58 F0 D 070                 L       15,  112( 0,13)
```

to be 118, for example, reference to the Assembly Language listing would be made in Figure 4.14, letter 'D'. Moving two columns to the right and up, the compiler-generated label, 100002, would be encountered. See letter 'E'. As a result, a programmer may have difficulty determining to which source statement the machine instruction at Address 118 applies. The right-most column contains programmer-coded and compiler-generated reference names. The term IBCOM is generated for Input/Output operations. See letter 'F'. As a result, it more likely applies to Source Statement #7, WRITE (6,200), rather than to the preceding IF Statement located previously. See Figure 4.13, letter 'G'.

As can be seen, a bit of applied intuition may occasionally be necessary when locating FORTRAN H-Level statements. A close approximation of the source statement can always be made, however.

7. Extended Error Handling Facility

The FORTRAN Extended Error Handling Facility is a software feature available at many installations. It is essentially a debugging aid, and on many occasions cancels the dump routine. As such, it should be covered in addition to storage dump procedures.

The FORTRAN Extended Error Handling Facility 'flags' storage dump conditions by printing a brief error message accompanied by an appropriate Entry Point Address (EPA) and Interrupt Address (IA). A standard corrective action is taken, if possible, and processing continues. If a standard corrective action cannot be safely undertaken, or the number of times a particular error has occurred exceeds a specified limit, the job will abnormally terminate, many times without a storage dump.

Traceback information is provided, however, including the EPA, IA, and Return Address (RA). Its main disadvantage is the frequent lack of an accompanying dump. This loss of information is particularly detrimental if the programmer should desire to determine the value of pertinent program variables. As will be seen in the next chapter, in lieu of special debugging packages or program statements inserted for test purposes, values cannot be determined without the benefit of a dump.

Procedures for modifying the FORTRAN Error Handling Facility can be found in the FORTRAN Programmer's Guide. A CALL Statement can be inserted at the beginning of the program to override default values for such items as the maximum number of errors allowed prior to termination, whether or not standard corrective action is to be taken, etc,.

Figure 4.15 on the following page depicts two FORTRAN Extended Error Handling Facility messages which have occurred in two separate jobs resulting in an abnormal termination in each.

Concentrating on the first message, Error Number IHN240I and its accompanying text is found to be ABEND CODE IS: SYSTEM 00C5, USER 0000. See Figure 4.15, letter 'A'. This message can be interpreted to mean that the problem is associated with Completion Code 0C5. An 0C5 refers to the calculation of an invalid address such as would be encountered with a bad index, run-away subscript, etc. This particular message is usually accompanied by a User 240 Storage Dump for more detail analysis. Regardless, the objective is to determine the source statement which was being executed when the error occurred.

Contents of pertinent registers are provided next. The first line indicates the name of the routine in which the error occurred, COMP, while the second line indicates the name of the module which called the routine, MAIN. See letter 'B'. The right-most three bytes in Register 15 contain the Entry Point Address (EPA) for the routine of interest. The EPA of Subroutine COMP is 0F2DE8. See letter 'C'. The Interrupt Address (IA) can be found in the right-most three bytes after the message PSW IS. The initials PSW stand for Program Status Word. The IA for the instruction being executed is 0F2F3A. See letter 'D'. Subtracting the EPA from the IA, a length into the executable routine of 152 is determined (0F2F3A - 0F2DE8 = 000152). The appropriate Source Program and Assembly Language listings for Subroutine COMP can now be referenced to determine the problem source statement.

Continuing on to the second error message in Figure 4.15, Error Number IHN217I and its accompanying text is found to be END OF DATA SET ON UNIT 5. See letter 'E'. This should be interpreted to mean that the program has attempted to read a record which is shorter than expected. This particular FORTRAN message is not accompanied by a storage dump. The primary objective of determining the problem source statement remains the same, however.

The first line of register contents indicates the name of the rou-

Figure 4.15   FORTRAN Extended Error Handling Facility (240 and 217)

```
IHN900I EXECUTION TERMINATING DUE TO ERROR COUNT FOR ERROR NUMBER  240

IHN240I STAE - ABEND CODE IS: SYSTEM 00C5, USER 0000. IO -    NONE    . SCB = 0FBA88. PSW IS FFD5000DA20F2F3A.

TRACEBACK  ROUTINE  CALLED FROM ISN    REG.  15    REG.  14    REG.  0    REG.  1

           COMP          0004        420F2D96    000F2DE8    FD000008    00000000

           MAIN                      00020510    010F2C00    FD000008    000FBFF8

ENTRY POINT= 010F2C00


IHN900I EXECUTION TERMINATING DUE TO ERROR COUNT FOR ERROR NUMBER  217

IHN217I FIOCS - END OF DATA SET ON UNIT    5

TRACEBACK  ROUTINE  CALLED FROM ISN    REG.  15    REG.  14    REG.  0    REG.  1

           IBCOM                     00061FCC    00061D84    00000008    000817F8

           MAIN                      00020510    01061C10    00000008    000817F8

ENTRY POINT= 01061C10
```

121

tine in which the error occurred, IBCOM, while the second line indicates the name of the module which called the routine, MAIN. See letter 'F'. It should now be noted that the message PSW IS followed by an Interrupt Address is not provided as in the first error message at letter 'D'. This means that IBCOM is a system-provided routine, not a programmer-written subroutine as was COMP in the previous example. In this situation, one would be interested in locating the source statement in MAIN which called routine IBCOM.

An EPA of 061C10 for MAIN can be found in Register 15. See letter 'G'. The Return Address (RA), that is, the address of the instruction which called IBCOM, can be found in Register 14 of the called routine. A Return Address of 061D84 is determined. See letter 'H'. Subtracting the EPA from the RA, a length into MAIN of 174 is determined (061D84 - 061C10 = 000174). The appropriate Source Program and Assembly Language listings for MAIN can now be referenced to determine the source statement which called IBCOM.

In summary, the presence of PSW IS indicates that the error occurred in a programmer-written routine. As such, the EPA can then be subtracted from the IA to determine the source statement being executed. The absence of the PSW IS message indicates that the error occurred in a system-provided routine. When this is the case, the EPA should be subtracted from the RA to determine the actual source statement which called the routine. In either case, once the problem source statement has been located, a review of program logis is necessary. Unless a dump is provided in lieu of special debugging packages or program statements inserted for test purposes, the value of variables cannot be determined.

E. PL1 CONSIDERATIONS

When debugging Internal Abends, the same set of step-by-step procedures should always be followed regardless of the programming language utilized.

To locate the problem source statement, as with all Internal Abends, the Entry Point Address (EPA) is subtracted from the Interrupt Address (IA) to determine the length into the executable module. The Control

Section is next referenced to verify the appropriate length into the executable routine. The Source Program and Assembly Language listings are then referenced to isolate the source statement being executed at the time of the abend. A problem analysis and review of program logic is next accomplished. The programming language utilized is of little consequence to the above procedures.

Differences among programming languages as related to storage dump debugging procedures center around Assembly Language listing format. Relative addresses, source statement numbers, program labels, and the like, are contained within an Assembly Language listing regardless of the original programming language. Their location within the listing varies, however. As such, a PL1 program example should be reviewed.

Although the PL1 programming language provides an excellent set of diagnostic error messages, situations do arise when one must rely on a storage dump for problem solving. When exceeding a CPU time limit the problem source statement must be determined along with the value of pertinent variables which may not be accounted for in the diagnostics. For this reason, PL1 storage dump format differences should be noted and compared with the previous COBOL and FORTRAN examples.

Figures 4.16 through 4.18 depict selected pertinent pages of a PL1 Source Program listing, Assembly Language listing, and Table of Offsets.

Suppose that after subtracting the EPA from the IA and referencing the Control Section, a length into the program module of 302 is determined. The Assembly Language listing can now be referenced. See Figure 4.17. Note that two columnar sets of source-related assembly and machine instructions are printed on each page of the listing. Source statement numbers have been indicated with an underline. Relative Address 302 can be found at letter 'A'. Moving up and to the right, it can be noted that Source Statement #27 was being executed when the abend occurred. See letter 'B'.

Referring to the PL1 Source Program listing, it is determined that Source Statement #27, IF BPFYR = ' ', was being executed. See Figure 4.16, letter 'C'. The remaining portion of the same line, THEN GO TO RD, refers to Source Statement #28 and is of no concern to the current problem. Note that the next line begins with Source Statement #29.

Figure 4.16   Portion of Source Program Listing (PL1)

```
              RS1:   PROC OPTIONS (MAIN);

  1                      RS1:   PROC OPTIONS (MAIN);
  2                          DCL 1 RECIN,
                                2    REGION      CHAR  (2),
                                2    STATE       CHAR  (17),
                                2    FILL1       CHAR  (3),
                                2    BPFYR       CHAR  (2),
                                2    BPP         CHAR  (5),
                                2    BPA         CHAR  (4),
                                2    WQP         CHAR  (4),
                                2    WQA         CHAR  (4),
                                2    BAP         CHAR  (4),
                                2    BAA         CHAR  (4),
                                2    FILLER      CHAR  (71);
  3                          DCL 1 RECIN1,
                                2    REGION1     CHAR  (2),
                                2    STATE1      CHAR  (17),
                                2    FILL2       CHAR  (3),
                                2    BPFYR1      CHAR  (2),
                                2    BPP1        CHAR  (5),
                                2    BPA1        CHAR  (4),
                                2    WQP1        CHAR  (4),
                                2    WQA1        CHAR  (4),
                                2    BAP1        CHAR  (4),
                                2    BAA1        CHAR  (4),
                                2    FILLER      CHAR  (71);
  4                          DCL 1 RECIN2,
                                2    REGION2     CHAR  (2),
                                2    STATE2      CHAR  (17),
                                2    FILL3       CHAR  (3),
                                2    BPFYR2      CHAR  (2),
                                2    BPP2        CHAR  (5),
                                2    BPA2        CHAR  (4),
                                2    WQP2        CHAR  (4),
                                2    WQA2        CHAR  (4),
                                2    BAP2        CHAR  (4),
                                2    BAA2        CHAR  (4),
                                2    FILLER      CHAR  (71);
  5              DCL (C,D,E,F,G,H,I,J,K,Z,CONV)   FIXED DEC (5);
  6              C,D,E,F,G,H,I,J,K,CONV=0;
  7                          DCL  YYMMDD   CHAR (6);
  8                          DCL 1 MMDDYY,
                                2 (MD,DA,YR)   CHAR (2);
  9                          YYMMDD = DATE;
 10                          GET STRING (YYMMDD) EDIT (YR,MD,DA) (A(2),A(2),A(2));
 11                          DCL    PAGENUM FIXED DEC (4);   PAGENUM=1;
 13                          DCL REG   CHAR (2);  REG=' ';
 15                          DCL (Y1,Y2,Y3,Y4)  CHAR (2);  Y1,Y2,Y3,Y4=' ';
 17              DCL A CHAR (7);  A=(7)'-';  DCL B CHAR (8); B=(8)'-';
 21                          DCL READIT FILE RECORD INPUT;
 22                          ON ENDFILE(READIT) GO TO FIN;
 24                          OPEN FILE (SYSPRINT) LINESIZE (132);
 25                          REGION2=' ';
 26              RD:  READ FILE (READIT) INTO (RECIN);
 27       ◄────C────►        IF BPFYR = ' ' THEN GO TO RD;
 29                          IF Y4 = ' ' THEN GO TO FORM1;
 31              RD1:     IF REG=REGION THEN GO TO FORM2;
 33              PUT SKIP EDIT (A,B,A,B,B,A,A,B,B,A,A,B,B,A) (A,A,X(2),A(9),A(10),A(1)),
```

124

Figure 4.17 Portion of Assembly Language Listing (PL1)

RS1: PROC OPTIONS (MAIN):

```
000290  05 EF                           BALR  14,15

* STATEMENT NUMBER 12
000292  D2 02 D 1D7 B 365        MVC    PAGENUM(3),C..0628

* STATEMENT NUMBER 14
000298  D2 01 D 1DA B 362        MVC    REG(2),C..062C

* STATEMENT NUMBER 16
00029E  D2 01 D 1DC B 35D        MVC    Y1(2),C..043C
0002A4  D2 01 D 1DE B 35D        MVC    Y2(2),C..043C
0002AA  D2 01 D 1E0 B 35D        MVC    Y3(2),C..043C
0002B0  D2 01 D 1E2 B 35D        MVC    Y4(2),C..043C

* STATEMENT NUMBER 18
0002B6  D2 06 D 1E4 B 356        MVC    A(7),C..0440

* STATEMENT NUMBER 20
0002BC  D2 07 D 1EB B 34E        MVC    B(8),C..0444

* STATEMENT NUMBER 22
0002C2  41 F0 D 058              LA     15,ON..ENDFILE..RE
                                        ADIT
0002C6  94 C7 F 004              NI     4(15),X'C7'
0002CA  D2 02 F 005 B 04D        MVC    5(3,15),A..01+1

* ON UNIT BLOCK
0014C0  90 EB D 00C              STM    14,11,12(13)
0014C4  18 AF                    LR     10,15
0014C6  58 B0 A 01C              L      11,28(0,10)
0014CA  58 F0 B 020              L      15,32(0,11)
0014CE  58 00 A 018              L      0,24(0,10)
0014D2  05 EF                    BALR   14,15
0014D4  47 F0 A 020              B      32(0,10)
0014D8  00000080                 DC     F'176'
0014DC  00000000                 DC     A(SI.)
0014E0  05 A0                    BALR   10,0
0014E2  05 A0                    BALR   10,0

* PROLOGUE BASE
0014E4  41 90 D 090      CL.70   LA     9,144(0,13)
0014E8                           EQU    *
0014E8  58 EC 0 000              L      14,PR..01(12)
0014EC  50 E0 0 05C              ST     14,92(0,13)
0014F0  41 EC 0 000              LA     14,PR..01(12)
0014F4  1B EC                    SR     14,12
0014F6  50 E0 0 058              ST     14,88(0,13)
0014FA  50 DC 0 000              ST     13,PR..01(12)
0014FE  92 94 D 000              MVI    0(13),X'94'
001502  41 A0 A 024              LA     10,CL.68
001506  07 00                    NOPR   0

* PROCEDURE BASE
001508              CL.68        EQU    *

* STATEMENT NUMBER 23
```

```
                                        BALR   14,15

001508  41 10 B 044              LA     1,A..FIN
00150C  58 F0 B 090              L      15,A..IHESAFC
001510  58 F0 B 030              L      15,A..IHESAFA
001516  05 EF                    BALR   14,15

* ON UNIT BLOCK END

* STATEMENT NUMBER 24
0002D0  41 10 B 53C              LA     1,SKPL..055C
0002D4  58 F0 B 080              L      15,A..IHEOCLA
0002D8  05 EF                    BALR   14,15

* STATEMENT NUMBER 25
0002DA  D2 01 D 2E4 B 35F        MVC    RECIN2,REGION2(2),
                                        C..0630

* STATEMENT NUMBER 26

* STATEMENT LABEL
0002E0  D2 13 D 088 B 5BC        MVC    WS1.I(20),SKPL..05
                                        40
0002E6  41 80 D 1A8              LA     8,RDV..RECIN
0002EA  50 80 D 08C              ST     8,WS1.I+4
0002EE  41 10 D 083              LA     1,WS1.I
0002F2  58 F0 B 08C              L      15,A..IHEIONA
0002F6  05 EF                    BALR   14,15

* STATEMENT NUMBER 27
0002F8  D5 00 D 209 B 361        CLC    RECIN.BPFYR(1),C..
                                        0438
0002FE  47 70 A 138              BC     7,CL.18
000302  D5 00 D 20A B 118        CLC    RECIN.BPFYR+1(1),C
                                        ..0530

000308              CL.18        EQU    *

* STATEMENT NUMBER 28
000308  47 90 A 110              BC     9,RD
00030C              CL.1         EQU    *

* STATEMENT NUMBER 29
00030C  D5 00 D 1E2 B 361        CLC    Y4(1),C..0438
000312  47 70 A 14C              BC     7,CL.19
000316  D5 00 D 1E3 3 118        CLC    Y4+1(1),C..0530
00031C              CL.19        EQU    *

* STATEMENT NUMBER 30
00031C  47 90 A 4AA              BC     9,FORM1
000320              CL.3         EQU    *

* STATEMENT NUMBER 31
000320  D5 01 D 1DA D 1FB        CLC    RD1
                                        REG(2),RECIN.REGIO
                                        N
```

A →   B →

Figure 4.18   Table of Offsets (PL1)

```
RS1:  PROC OPTIONS (MAIN);

TABLE OF OFFSETS AND STATEMENT NUMBERS WITHIN ON UNIT

OFFSET (HEX)  0000 0048 0052
STATEMENT NO    23   23

TABLE OF OFFSETS AND STATEMENT NUMBERS WITHIN PROCEDURE                    RS1

OFFSET (HEX)  0000 01D0 020C 0224 0292 0298 029E 0286 028C 02C2 02D0 02DA 02E0 02F8 0308 030C 031C 0320 0326 032A 0480
STATEMENT NO     5    6    9   10   12   14   16   18   20   22   24   25   26   27   28   29   30   31   32   33   34

OFFSET (HEX)  0628 0664 067A 0680 0674 078E 07CE 080E 0872 0938 0978 097E 0984 099C 09A2 0BDA 0C98 0DEE 0F4E
STATEMENT NO    35   36   37   38   39   40   41   42   43   44   45   46   47   48   49   50   51   52   53   54   55

OFFSET (HEX)  0F5E 0F62 0F78 0F7E 0F8E 0F92 0FA8 0FAE 0FBE 0FC2 0FD8 0FDE 0FEE 0FF2 1008 101E 1022 1038 103E 104E
STATEMENT NO    56   57   58   59   60   61   62   63   64   65   66   67   68   69   70   71   72   73   74   75   76

OFFSET (HEX)  1052 1068 106E 107E 1082 1098 10AA 10BA 10BE 10D4 10E6 10F6 1110 1116 111C 112C 1130 1136 113C 1140
STATEMENT NO    77   78   79   80   81   82   83   84   85   86   87   88   89   90   91   92   93   94   95   96   97

OFFSET (HEX)  1146 115E 116E 1172 1178 117C 118C 1190 11A8 11AC 130A 148A
STATEMENT NO    98   99  100  101  102  103  104  105  106  107  108  109
```

A Table of Offsets can optionally be obtained if a print of the Assembly Language listing is not desired. To locate Relative Address 302, compare the offset of each statement with the statement number itself. See Figure 4.18, letter 'D'. Moving to the right, an offset of 02F8 is encountered for Source Statement #27. See letter 'E'. Offset 02F8 is the closest one can come to Address 302 without exceeding it. Source Statement #28 with an offset of 0308 exceeds Address 302. See letter 'F'. Therefore, Source Statement #27 is the program instruction of interest.

Again, the principles of Internal storage dump analysis remain the same regardless of the programming language utilized. The only significant difference relates to the format of the Assembly Language listing itself.

F. INTERNAL ABEND SUMMARY

Internal Storage Dumps are those which occur internal to the program being executed. They are denoted by Completion Codes 322 and the OC Group. The following set of step-by-step procedures apply to all Internal Abends.

1. Determine Jobname, Stepname, and Completion Code from top of first page of storage dump.

2. Obtain detail description of Completion Code by referencing the IBM Messages and Codes Manual and/or Chapter 7 of this textbook.

3. Calculate Relative Length into executable module.

    a. Determine Entry Point Address (EPA) from first line of Contents Directory Entry.

    b. Determine Interrupt Address (IA) from:

        i. System 360/370 OS - APSW near top of first page of storage dump.

        ii. System 370 OS/VS - PSW AT ENTRY TO ABEND at top of first page of storage dump.

    c. Subtract EPA from IA giving Relative Length into module.

4. Reference Control Section to verify and/or recalculate Relative Length.

a. If programmer-written subroutines are not utilized and Relative Length falls within bounds of the main program, ignore Control Section information.

b. If programmer-written subroutines are utilized and Relative Length falls within bounds of a subroutine, subtract the Origin of the subroutine from Relative Length, giving length into the called routine.

c. If Relative Length falls outside bounds of main program and programmer-written subroutines, refer to SAVE AREA TRACE portion of storage dump. Subtract Return Address for system-provided routine from Entry Point Address of the program module which called the routine, giving length into the calling module.

5. Reference Assembly Language Listing of pertinent program module or subroutine.

a. Locate Length calculated above.

b. Determine appropriate Source Statement Number.

6. Reference Source Program Listing of pertinent program module or subroutine.

a. Locate Source Statement Number.

b. Determine actual Source Statement being executed at time of abend.

7. Complete thorough problem analysis. If necessary, determine value of pertinent variables utilizing the techniques to be covered in the next chapter.

A workshop is now provided to solidify a working knowledge of Internal Storage Dump debugging procedures.

Although the above procedures are specific to OS and OS/VS environments, the principle of debugging program problems resulting in internal abends, and locating the problem statement, can be applied to DOS applications as well. The specific language of the program being executed is of little concern. Program problems resulting in internal storage dumps are often encountered when attempting to execute COBOL, FORTRAN, PL1, and Assembly language programs in all application, system, and data base environments.

G. WORKSHOP PROBLEMS

1. OCB Storage Dump (COBOL)

a. Description

Figures 4.19 through 4.22 consist of pertinent pages of a job which has abended with an OCB Storage Dump.

Completion Codes of the OC Group refer to the calculation of invalid data and/or storage addresses. Attempting to execute privileged operations, exceeding the bounds of an array or program, as well as performing illogical arithmetic functions are examples which can cause an abend of the OC Group.

An OCB Storage Dump specifically refers to a situation in which the program is attempting to divide by zero. An OCB will also result if the quotient length, as defined by the programmer, has been exceeded. This could also be caused by dividing a very small decimal equivalent into a relatively large number. In either case, the problem source statement must be determined.

Procedures for debugging an OCB Dump are identical to that of any Internal Abend. A Relative Length is calculated by subtracting the Entry Point Address from the Interrupt Address. The Control Section is then referenced to verify and/or recalculate the above length into the pertinent program module. The Assembly Language and Source Program listings are then referenced to isolate the source statement being executed at the time of the abend.

A problem solution can be found in Appendix A.

Figure 4.19   Portion of COBOL Source Program Listing (OCB)

```
00039          01   CTL-CARD.
00040               02   DATA-ARRAY        OCCURS 8 TIMES        PICTURE 99.
00041               02   NUM                                     PICTURE 99.
00042               02   DEN                                     PICTURE 99.
00043               02   FILLER         PICTURE X(60),   VALUE IS SPACES.
00044          01   PRT-RECORD.
00045               02   CARRIAGE-CONTROL   PICTURE X.
00046               02   FILLER             PICTURE X(4), VALUE IS SPACES.
00047               02   VARIABLE-NAME      PICTURE X(8).
00048               02   VARIABLE-VALUE     OCCURS 8 TIMES, PICTURE XX.
00049               02   FILLER             PICTURE X(65), VALUE IS SPACES.
00050          PROCEDURE DIVISION.
00051          OPEN-FILES.
00052               OPEN INPUT DATA-FILE.
00053               OPEN OUTPUT MESSAGE-FILE.
00054          READ-CTL-CARD.
00055               MOVE SPACES TO CONTROL-CARD, PRINT-RECORD, VARIABLE-NAME.
00056               MOVE ZEROS TO NUM, DEN, SUB-M, SUB-N, ITEST.
00057               READ DATA-FILE INTO CTL-CARD,
00058                   AT END GO TO CLOSE-FILES.
00059               MOVE NUM TO SJB-M.
00060               MOVE DEN TO SUB-N.
00061          COMPUTE-ITEST.
00062               COMPUTE ITEST = DATA-ARRAY (SUB-M) / DATA-ARRAY (SUB-N).
00063               MOVE '   ID = ' TO VARIABLE-NAME.
00064               MOVE DATA-ARRAY (1) TO VARIABLE-VALUE (1).
00065               MOVE DATA-ARRAY (2) TO VARIABLE-VALUE (2).
00066               MOVE DATA-ARRAY (3) TO VARIABLE-VALUE (3).
00067               MOVE DATA-ARRAY (4) TO VARIABLE-VALUE (4).
00068               MOVE DATA-ARRAY (5) TO VARIABLE-VALUE (5).
00069               MOVE DATA-ARRAY (6) TO VARIABLE-VALUE (6).
00070               MOVE DATA-ARRAY (7) TO VARIABLE-VALUE (7).
00071               MOVE DATA-ARRAY (8) TO VARIABLE-VALUE (8).
00072               WRITE PRINT-RECORD FROM PRT-RECORD
00073                   AFTER ADVANCING TO-TOP-OF-PAGE.
00074               MOVE SPACES TO VARIABLE-VALUE (2), VARIABLE-VALUE (3),
00075                   VARIABLE-VALUE (4), VARIABLE-VALUE (5),
00076                   VARIABLE-VALUE (6), VARIABLE-VALUE (7),
00077                   VARIABLE-VALUE (8)
00078               MOVE '    M = ' TO VARIABLE-NAME.
00079               MOVE NUM TO VARIABLE-VALUE (1).
00080               WRITE PRINT-RECORD FROM PRT-RECORD
00081                   AFTER ADVANCING 2 LINES.
00082               MOVE '    N = ' TO VARIABLE-NAME.
00083               MOVE DEN TO VARIABLE-VALUE (1).
00084               WRITE PRINT-RECORD FROM PRT-RECORD
00085                   AFTER ADVANCING 2 LINES.
00086               MOVE 'ITEST = ' TO VARIABLE-NAME.
00087               MOVE ITEST TO VARIABLE-VALUE (1).
00088               WRITE PRINT-RECORD FROM PRT-RECORD
00089                   AFTER ADVANCING 2 LINES.
00090               MOVE 'NORMAL E' TO VARIABLE-NAME.
00091               MOVE 'OJ' TO VARIABLE-VALUE (1).
00092               WRITE PRINT-RECORD FROM PRT-RECORD
00093                   AFTER ADVANCING 4 LINES.
00094          CLOSE-FILES.
00095               CLOSE DATA-FILE, MESSAGE-FILE.
00096          STOP-RUN.
00097               STOP RUN.
```

130

Figure 4.20   Portion of Assembly Language Listing (OCB)

```
              0006FE                      BCR   15,1
              000700                      EQU   *
                                  GN=02

59  MOVE
              000700  F2 71 D 200 6 018   PACK  200(8,13),018(2,6)    TS=01        DNM=1-373
              000706  4F 30 D 200         CVB   3,200(0,13)           TS=01
              00070A  10 33               LPR   3,3
              00070C  40 30 D 210         STH   3,210(0,13)
60  MOVE
              000710  D2 01 6 000 D 210   MVC   000(2,6),210(13)      DNM=1-287     TS3=1
              000716  F2 71 D 200 6 01A   PACK  200(8,13),01A(2,6)    TS=01         DNM=1-386
              00071C  4F 30 D 200         CVB   3,200(0,13)           TS=01
              000720  10 33               LPR   3,3
              000722  40 30 D 210         STH   3,210(0,13)           TS3=1
              000726  D2 01 6 002 D 210   MVC   002(2,6),210(13)      DNM=1-302     TS3=1

61  *CCMPUTE-ITEST
62  COMPUTE
              00072C  41 40 6 008         LA    4,008(0,6)            LIT+8
              000730  D2 01 6 210 6 000   MVC   210(2,13),000(6)      DNM=1-353     TS3=1
              000736  48 20 D 210         LH    2,210(0,13)           TS3=1
              00073A  4C 20 C 04C         MH    2,04C(0,12)           LIT+4
              00073E  1A 42               AR    4,2
              000740  5B 40 C 050         S     4,050(0,12)           LIT+8
              000744  41 20 6 008         LA    2,008(0,6)            DNM=1-353
              000748  D2 01 D 210 6 002   MVC   210(2,13),002(6)      DNM=1-353     TS3=1
              00074E  48 10 D 210         LH    1,210(0,13)           TS3=1
              000752  4C 10 C 04C         MH    1,04C(0,12)           LIT+4
              000756  1A 21               AR    2,1
              0C0758  5B 20 C 050         S     2,050(0,12)
              00075C  F2 71 D 200 2 000   PACK  200(8,13),000(2,2)    DNM=1-353     TS=01
              000762  FD 31 D 208 4 000   DP    208(4,13),000(2,4)    TS=09         TS=07
              000768  F8 71 D 20C D 206   ZAP   20C(8,13),206(2,13)   TS=013        TS=013
              00076E  F3 11 6 004 D 20C   UNPK  004(2,6),20C(2,13)    DNM=1-317     TS=015
              000774  96 F0 6 005         OI    005(6),X'F0'          DNM=1-317+1
              00077A  50 F0 D 220         ST    4,220(0,13)           SBS=1
              00077E  50 20 D 224         ST    2,224(0,13)           SBS=2

63  MOVE
              000786  D2 07 6 05D C 058   MVC   05D(8,6),058(12)      DNM=1-479     LIT+19
64  MOVE
              00078C  D2 01 6 065 6 008   MVC   065(2,6),008(6)       DNM=2-0       DNM=1-353
65  MOVE
              000792  D2 01 6 067 6 00A   MVC   067(2,6),00A(6)       DNM=2-0       DNM=1-353
66  MOVE
              000798  D2 01 6 069 6 00C   MVC   069(2,6),00C(6)       DNM=2-0       DNM=1-353
67  MOVE
              00079E  D2 01 6 06B 6 00E   MVC   06B(2,6),00E(6)       DNM=2-0       DNM=1-353
68  MCVE
              0007A4  D2 01 6 06D 6 010   MVC   06D(2,6),010(6)       DNM=2-0       DNM=1-353
69  MOVE
              0007AA  D2 01 6 06F 6 012   MVC   06F(2,6),012(6)       DNM=2-0       DNM=1-353
70  MOVE
              0007B0  D2 01 6 071 6 014   MVC   071(2,6),014(6)       DNM=2-0       DNM=1-353
71  MOVE
              0007B6  D2 01 6 073 6 016   MVC   073(2,6),016(6)       DNM=2-0       DNM=1-353
72  WRITE
              0007BC  58 F0 C 008         L     15,008(0,12)          V(ILBODBG4)
              0007C0  05 EF               BALR  14,15
              0007C2  D2 5D 8 000 6 058   MVC   CC0(94,8),058(6)      DNM=1-265     DNM=1-416
              0007C8  92 40 8 05E         MVI   05E(8),X'40'          DNM=1-265+94
              0007CC  D2 25 8 C5F 8 05E   MVC   05F(38,8),05E(8)      DNM=1-265+95  DNM=1-265+94
              0007D2  D2 03 D 234 D 1F8   MVC   234(4,13),1F8(13)     PRM=1         BL =2
              0007D8  92 54 D 234         MVI   234(13),X'54'         PRM=1
              0007DC  92 01 D 23C C 040   MVC   23C(4,13),040(12)     PRM=3
              0007E2  92 01 D 23B         MVI   23B(13),X'01'         PRM=2+3       DCB=2
              0007E6  41 10 D 234         LA    1,234(0,13)           PRM=1
              0007EA  58 F0 C 014         L     15,014(0,12)          V(ILBOSPA0)
              0007EE  05 EF               BALR  14,15
              C007F0                GN=03 EQU   *

74  MOVE
              0007F0  92 40 6 067         MVI   067(6),X'40'          DNM=2-0
              0007F4  D2 00 6 068 6 067   MVC   068(1,6),067(6)       DNM=2-0+1     DNM=2-0
```

131

Figure 4.21 Control Section of Cross Reference Table (OCB)

```
F88-LEVEL LINKAGE EDITOR OPTIONS SPECIFIED LET,LIST,XREF,SIZE=(,),LET
    DEFAULT OPTIONS(S) USED - SIZE=(90142,8192)
    SYSPRINT DEFAULT BLOCKING USED  1 - 1
```

CROSS REFERENCE TABLE

CONTROL SECTION   ENTRY

NAME	ORIGIN	LENGTH	NAME	LOCATION	NAME	LOCATION	NAME	LOCATION	NAME	LOCATION
ACOMP	00	BA2								
ILBOCCMO*	BA8	BA	ILBOCOM	BA8						
ILBODBG *	C68	B60	ILBODBG0	C6A	ILBODBG1	C6E	ILBODBG2	C72	ILBODBG3	C76
			ILBODBG4	C7A	ILBODBG5	C7E				
ILBOERR *	17C8	27B	ILBOERR0	17CA	ILBOERR1	17CE	ILBOERR2	17D2	ILBOERR3	17D6
			ILBOERR4	17DA	ILBOERR5	17DE	ILBOERR6	17E2	ILBOERR7	17E6
ILBOEXT *	1A48	1C	ILBOEXT0	1A4A						
ILBOSPA *	1A68	3F2	ILBOSPA0	1A6A	ILBOSPA1	1A6E				
ILBOSRV *	1E60	1B7	ILBOSRV0	1E94	ILBOSRV1	1E98	ILBOSRV2	1E9C	ILBOSRV3	1EA0

LOCATION	REFERS TO SYMBOL	IN CONTROL SECTION	LOCATION	REFERS TO SYMBOL	IN CONTROL SECTION
590	ILBOSRV0		594	ILBODBG0	ILBODBG
598	ILBODBG4		59C	ILBOERR7	ILBOERR
5A0	ILBOEXT0		5A4	ILBOSPA0	ILBOSPA
5A8	ILBOSRV1		4E0	ILBOCOM0	ILBOCOMO
16FC	ILBOFLW0	$UNRESOLVED(W)	1700	ILBOFLW2	$UNRESOLVED(W)
1704	ILBOTEF3	$UNRESOLVED(W)	1708	ILBOSTNO	$UNRESOLVED(W)
2000	ILBOCOM	ILBOCOMO			

```
ENTRY ADDRESS    00
TOTAL LENGTH     2018
```

***MAIN   DOES NOT EXIST BUT HAS BEEN ADDED TO DATA SET

Figure 4.22 First Page of OCB Storage Dump

```
JOB  RZZ925          STEP GO          TIME 200518

COMPLETION CODE      SYSTEM = OCB

PSW AT ENTRY TO ABEND  FF75000D E020AF56

TCB  0356A0   RBP  0003D9F8     PIE  00000000    DEB  00035624   TIO  00035840   CMP  800CB000   TRN  00000000
              MSS  02046860     PK-FLG 70850400  FLG  0005F58    LLS  0003A5E8   JLB  00000000   JPQ  80038BD0
              FSA  01211768     TCB  00000000    TME  00000000   JST  00356A0    NTC  00000000   OTC  0003BF20
              LTC  00000000     IQE  00000000    ECB  00036ED4   TSF  20000000   D-PQE 00046E10  SQS  000349A8
              NSTAE 80042980    TCT  80035E20    USER 00000000   CAR  00000000   RESV 00000000   JSCB 87046A80
              RESV 00000000     IOB  00000000

ACTIVE RBS

PRB  042800   RESV  00000000    APSW E020AF56    WC-SZ-STAB 00040082   FL-CDE 00035C8   PSW FF75000D E020AF56
              Q/TTR 00000000    WT-LNK 00356A0

SVRB 041BB0   TAB-LN C0F80220   APSW F9F0F1C3    WC-SZ-STAB 0012D002   TQN 00000000     PSW 00040033 5001SC32
              Q/TTR 00004D0C    WT-LNK 00042800
              RG 0-7  0000000A  00000006   0020A87C   00000003   0020AEE8   0020A870   00211E8
              RG 8-15 0020AA88  0020824E   0020A7E8   0020A7E8   0020AD78   5020AECE   002FDDA8
              EXTSA   000021BE  8F211250   00000000   00000000   00041C2C   00041C34   E2E8E2C9
                      C5C1F0F1  C9C5C1A0   C1C2C5D5   C4F90CB3

SVRB 03C9F8   TAB-LN 003803D8   APSW F1F0F5C1    WC-SZ-STAB 0012D002   TQN 00000000     PSW FF04000C 4020F7A6
              Q/TTR 00003D11    WT-LNK 00041BB0
              RG 0-7  00105B0   0004lC10   8001984A   0001A318   00035A0    040356A0   00041BB0
              RG 8-15 00356A0   40019A92   8F211250   8F211250   0035898    40019854   00000000
              EXTSA   E2E8E2C9  C5C1F0F1   C9C7C3F5   F2F0F3C5   002D7B9E   0021FE8     5001A460
                      00004C68  00035624   0001B810   0020EE52   002115EC

LOAD LIST

NE 0003A5F0   RSP-CDE 023388D0        NE 0003FB58   RSP-CDE 01045898
NE 00042920   RSP-CDE 01045C8         NE 00042968   RSP-CDE 01045A98
NE 00042978   RSP-CDE 01045A28        NE 00046800   RSP-CDE 01045828
NE 00046880   RSP-CDE 01045C8         NE 00046AF8   RSP-CDE 01045958
NE 00000000   RSP-CDE 01045AF8

CDE

0435C8   ATR1 0B   NCDE 00C000   RDC-RB 00042800   NM MAIN      USE 01   EPA 20A7E8   ATR2 20   XL/MJ 042AD8
0388D0   ATR1 30   NCDE 038BA0   RDC-RB 00000000   NM IGC0A05A  USE 02   EPA 20F058   ATR2 28   XL/MJ 03A470
0458C8   ATR1 B0   NCDE 0458F8   RDC-RB 00000000   NM IGG019CF  USE 01   EPA 2FC8A0   ATR2 20   XL/MJ 045888
045898   ATR1 B0   NCDE 0458C8   RDC-RB 00000000   NM IGG019CL  USE 01   EPA 2FF008   ATR2 20   XL/MJ 045888
0455C8   ATR1 B0   NCDE 0459F8   RDC-RB 00000000   NM IGG019BA  USE 01   EPA 2FCE40   ATR2 20   XL/MJ 045988
045988   ATR1 B0   NCDE 0459C8   RDC-RB 00000000   NM IGG019BB  USE 01   EPA 2FD800   ATR2 20   XL/MJ 045978
045A98   ATR1 B0   NCDE 045AC8   RDC-RB 00000000   NM IGG019CC  USE 01   EPA 2FD4F8   ATR2 20   XL/MJ 045A88
045A28   ATR1 B0   NCDE 045A58   RDC-RB 00000000   NM IGG019CI  USE 01   EPA 2FD298   ATR2 20   XL/MJ 045A18
045BC8   ATR1 B0   NCDE 045BF8   RDC-RB 00000000   NM IGG019AA  USE 01   EPA 2FE808   ATR2 20   XL/MJ 045BB8
```

b. Workshop

1. Problem Overview

Completion Code _____

Jobname _____   Stepname _____

2. Relative Length Determination

Interrupt Address (IA) from APSW .... _____

Entry Point Address (EPA) from CDE .... _____

Relative Length (IA - EPA) .... _____

Control Section Verification:

Origin of ACOMP .... _____

Origin of ILBOCOMO .... _____

Does Relative Length fall inside or outside the bounds of
Program ACOMP? What is the significance of this
determination?

_____

_____

_____

_____

_____

_____

_____

_____

3. Source Statement Determination

Length into Assembly Language Listing ... _____

Problem Source Statement Number .... _____

Actual Source Statement:

_____

4. Problem Analysis

Summarize your findings. At this point, what action should
be taken?

_____

_____

_____

_____

_____

_____

2. 240 Core Dump (FORTRAN--0C5)

a. Description

Figures 4.23 through 4.26 consist of pertinent pages of a job which
has abended with a user 240 error detected by the FORTRAN Extended Error
Handling Facility.

This particular error message has been debugged in a previous example. See the first error message in Figure 4.15. It was determined
at that point that the accompanying User 240 Storage Dump should be
viewed as one abending with an 0C5 Completion Code. An 0C5 refers to
the calculation of invalid addresses such as would be encountered with
a bad index, run-away subscript, etc. As a result, the problem source
statement need be isolated.

Procedures for debugging an 0C5 Dump are identical to that of any
Internal Abend. In this particular storage dump, the Relative Length
need be recalculated based upon information contained within the Con-

trol Section as the abend has occurred in a programmer-written sub-routine. The Origin of the executing routine must be subtracted from the Relative Length to determine the length into the called module. The Assembly Language and Source Program listings can then be referenced to isolate the source statement being executed at the time of the abend.

A problem solution can be found in Appendix A.

Figure 4.23   FORTRAN Source Program Listing for MAIN and COMP (OC5)

```
FORTRAN IV G LEVEL   21                  MAIN

            C       PROGRAM TO CREATE CORE DUMPS
    0001            COMMON ID(8), M, N, ITEST
    0002            READ (5,100) ID, M, N
    0003        100 FORMAT (10I2)
    0004            CALL COMP
    0005            WRITE (6,200) ID, M, N, ITEST
    0006        200 FORMAT ('-', T6, '   ID = ', 8I2//,
                 1               T6, '    M = ', I2//,
                 2               T6, '    N = ', I2//,
                 3               T6, 'ITEST = ', I2////,
                 4               T6, 'END OF JOB')
    0007            STOP
    0008            END



FORTRAN IV G LEVEL   21                  COMP

    0001            SUBROUTINE COMP
    0002            COMMON ID(8)
    0003        100 ITEST = ID(M) * ID(N)
    0004        150 IF(ITEST.GE.2.AND.ITEST.LE.224) GO TO 100
    0005            WRITE (6,200)
    0006        200 FORMAT ('1','ITEST OUT OF LIMITS')
    0007        300 RETURN
    0008            END
```

Figure 4.24   Portion of Assembly Language Listing for COMP (OC5)

```
FORTRAN IV G LEVEL  21              COMP

LOCATION  STA NUM   LABEL   OP      OPERAND           BCD OPERAND
 000000                     BC      15,12(0,15)
 000004                     DC      06C3D6D4
 000008                     DC      D7404040
 00000C                     STM     14,12,12(13)
 000010                     LM      2,3,40(15)
 000014                     LR      4,13
 000016                     L       13,36(0,15)
 00001A                     ST      13,8(0,4)
 00001E                     STM     3,4,0(13)
 000022                     BCR     15,2
 000024                     DC      00000000          A4
 000028                     DC      00000000          A20
 00002C                     DC      00000000          A36
 000118          A20        BALR    2,0
 00011A                     L       3,6(0,2)
 00011E                     BCR     15,3
 000120                     DC      00000000          A52
 000124          A36        L       1,4(0,13)
 000128                     L       1,24(0,1)
 00012C                     L       13,4(0,13)
 000130                     L       14,12(0,13)
 000134                     LM      2,12,28(13)
 000138                     MVI     12(13),255
 00013C                     BCR     15,14
 00013E      3    100       L       8,120(0,13)       M
 000142                     SLA     8,2(0)
 000146                     A       8,216(0,13)
 00014A                     L       10,72(0,13)
 00014E                     L       1,0(8,10)         ID
 000152                     L       9,124(0,13)       N
 000156                     SLA     9,2(0)
 00015A                     A       9,216(0,13)
 00015E                     M       0,0(9,10)         ID
 000162                     ST      1,116(0,13)       ITEST
 000166      4    150       L       0,116(0,13)       ITEST
 00016A                     C       0,220(0,13)
 00016E                     L       0,224(0,13)
 000172                     BALR    14,0
 000174                     BC      11,6(0,14)
 000178                     SR      0,0
 00017A                     L       1,116(0,13)       ITEST
 00017E                     C       1,228(0,13)
 000182                     LA      1,1(0,0)
 000186                     BALR    14,0
 000188                     BC      13,6(0,14)
 00018C                     SR      1,1
 00018E                     NR      1,0
 000190                     LTR     1,1
 000192                     L       14,100(0,13)      100
 000196                     BCR     7,14
 000198      5              L       15,112(0,13)      IBCOM#
 00019C                     BAL     14,4(0,15)
 0001A0                     DC      00000006
 0001A4                     DC      000000B0
 0001A8                     BAL     14,16(0,15)
 0001AC      7    300       SR      15,15
 0001AE                     L       1,0(0,13)
```

137

Figure 4.25 Control Section of Cross Reference Table (OC5)

F88-LEVEL LINKAGE EDITOR OPTIONS SPECIFIED XREF,LET,LIST
DEFAULT OPTION(S) USED - SIZE=(90112,8192)

CONTROL SECTION

NAME	ORIGIN	LENGTH
MAIN	00	1E2
COMP	1E8	1B4
IHNECOMH*	3A0	F8C
IHNCOMH2*	1330	715
IHNFCVTH*	1A48	B6F
IHNEFNTH*	25B8	548
IHNEFIOS*	2800	FF8
IHNFIOS2*	3AF8	588
IHNUOPT *	40B0	318
IHNFCONI*	43C8	2E5
IHNFCONO*	46B0	4A2
IHNFRRM *	4858	5FC
IHNUATBL*	5158	638
IHNFTEN *	5790	198
IHNETRCH*	5928	2A6
$BLANKCOM	5BD0	2C

ENTRY

CROSS REFERENCE TABLE

NAME	LOCATION	NAME	LOCATION	NAME	LOCATION	NAME	LOCATION
IBCOM#	3CC	FDIOCS#	488	INTSWTCH	1306		
SEQDASD	175E						
ADCON#	1A48	FCVAQUTP	1AF2	FCVLQUTP	1882	FCVZQUTP	1CDE
FCVIOUTP	2086	FCVEQUTP	2178	FCVCQUTP	22C2	INT6SWCH	2538
ARITH#	25B8	ADJSWTCH	2954				
FIOCS#	2800	FIOCSREP	2806				
FQCONI#	43C8						
FQCONO#	46B0						
ERRMON	4858	IHNERRE	4B70				
FTEN#	5790						
IHNTRCH	5928	ERRTRA	5930				

LOCATION REFERS TO SYMBOL IN CONTROL SECTION

LOCATION	REFERS TO SYMBOL	IN CONTROL SECTION
1EC	COMP	COMP
78	IBCOM#	IHNECOMH
98	IHNECOMH	IHNCOMH2
288	IHNCOMH2	IHNCOMH2
4E0	FIOCS#	IHNEFIOS
1204	IHNEFNTH	IHNEFNTH
1230	ADJSWTCH	
1328	IHNCMSE	$UNRESOLVED(W)
1218	FCVLQUTP	IHNFCVTH
1220	FCVQOUTP	IHNFCVTH
1228	FCVZQUTP	IHNFCVTH
1E4	IHNCOMH2	IHNCOMH2

LOCATION	REFERS TO SYMBOL	IN CONTROL SECTION
1B0		IHNECOMH
94	IBCOM#	
260	SEQDASD	IHNCOMH2
120C	ADCON#	IHNFCVTH
1210	ARITH#	IHNEFNTH
122C	IHNUOPT	IHNUOPT
1214	FCVEQUTP	IHNFCVTH
121C	FCVIQUTP	IHNFCVTH
1224	FCVAQUTP	IHNFCVTH
1B8	IHNERRE	IHNERRM
1E8	IHNERRM	IHNERRM

138

Figure 4.26   First Page of OC5 Storage Dump

```
JOB  PZZO17        STEP GO          TIME 185344

COMPLETION CODE    USER = 0240

PSW AT ENTRY TO ABEND  FFD5000D 400F407A

TCB 035328  RBP   0003EBF8  PIE  00000000    DEB  000352AC  TIO 0035850  CMP  800000F0  TRN  00000000
            MSS   02037F20  PK-FLG D0850400   FLG  00005F5B  LLS 00037BE0  JLB  00000000  JPQ  00037AF8
            FSA   010FBF68  TCB  00000000     TME  00000000  JST 0003528   NTC  00000000  OTC  0003C070
            LTC   00000000  IQE  00000000     ECB  0035A8C   TSF 20000000  D-PQE 0043398  SQS  0003928
            NSTAE 03000000  TCT  80036278     USER 00000000  DAR 00000000  RESV 00000000  JSCB 87037870
            RESV  03000000  IOB  00000000

ACTIVE RBS

PRB 037AC8  RESV  00000000  APSW A20F2F3A  WC-SZ-STAB 00040082  FL-CDE 00037C18  PSW FFD5000D 400F407A
            Q/TTR 00000000  WT-LNK 00035328

SVRB 042478  TAB-LN 00980220  APSW F9F0F1C3  WC-SZ-STAB 0012D002  TQN 00000000  PSW 00040033 50018282
             Q/TTR  00004629  WT-LNK 00037AC8
             RG 0-7   FF000010  800000F0  420F2F02  00F2F26    00F3F30    000358E4  0003DEE0
             RG 8-15  6382441C  00036278  000F87D0  00037068   00F2E18    420F2D96  000F2DE8
             EXTSA    000021BE  8F0F8F10  00000000  00000000   000424F4   000424FC  E2E8E2C9
                      C5C1F0F1  C9C5C128  C1C2C5D5  C4F90000

SVRB 03EBF8  TAB-LN 00D803D8  APSW F1F0F5C1  WC-SZ-STAB 0012D002  TQN 00000000  PSW FF04000C 400FB7A6
             Q/TTR  00003801  WT-LNK 00042478
             RG 0-7   C0000007  000424D8  8001819A  0001A318   00042478   04035328  00042478
             RG 8-15  00035328  400180E2  00035328  8F0F8F10   000424FC   4001693C  00000000
             EXTSA    E2E8E2C9  C5C1F0F1  C9C7E7F0  F0F0F1F5   0000015C   000FC7D0  00035378
                      C0001944  000FC7A8  00035204  FDF1A9E0

LOAD LIST

NE 00037BE8  RSP-CDE 02037AF8   NE 00037C38  RSP-CDE 01045888   NE 00037D90  RSP-CDE 01045888
NE 00037EC8  RSP-CDE 010459C8   NE 00037AB8  RSP-CDE 01045988   NE 00000000  RSP-CDE 010379F8

CDE

037C18  ATR1 0B  NCDE 000000   ROC-RB 00037AC8  NM MAIN     USE 01  EPA 0F2C00  ATR2 20  XL/MJ 037DD8
037AF8  ATR1 30  NCDE 0379F8   ROC-RB 00000000  NM IGC0A05A USE 02  EPA 0F8058  ATR2 28  XL/MJ 037948
0458C8  ATR1 80  NCDE 0458C8   ROC-RB 00000000  NM IGG019CF USE 01  EPA 1FC590  ATR2 20  XL/MJ 045888
045888  ATR1 80  NCDE 0458C8   ROC-RB 00000000  NM IGG019CL USE 01  EPA 1FF810  ATR2 20  XL/MJ 045878
0459C8  ATR1 80  NCDE 0459F8   ROC-RB 00000000  NM IGG019BA USE 01  EPA 1FCE40  ATR2 20  XL/MJ 045988
045988  ATR1 80  NCDE 0459C8   ROC-RB 00000000  NM IGG019BB USE 01  EPA 1FCCC8  ATR2 20  XL/MJ 045978
0379F8  ATR1 03  NCDE 037C18   ROC-RB 00000000  NM IHNSTAE  USE 01  EPA 0F8BD8  ATR2 20  XL/MJ 037A48

XL                          LN       ADR      LN       ADR      LN      ADR

037DD8  SZ 00000010  NO 00000001  80005C00  00F2C00
```

139

b. Workshop

   1. Problem Overview

      User Code _____   Completion Code _____

      Jobname _____   Stepname _____

   2. Relative Length Determination

      Interrupt Address (IA) from APSW ....   _____

      Entry Point Address (EPA) from CDE ....   _____

      Relative Length (IA - EPA) ....   _____

      Control Section Recalculation:

      Origin of MAIN ....   _____

      Origin of COMP ....   _____

      Origin of IHNECOMH ....   _____

      Does Relative Length fall inside or outside bounds of
      MAIN?

      _____

      If outside, which routine does the Relative Length fall
      within?

      _____

      Relative Length obtained previously ....   _____

      Origin of Pertinent Routine ....   _____

      Relative Length minus Origin ....   _____

 3. Source Statement Determination

      Length into Assembly Language Listing ....   _____

      Problem Source Statement Number ....   _____

      Actual Source Statement:

      _____

4. Problem Analysis

>   Summarize your findings. At this point, what action
>   should be taken?

_____

_____

_____

_____

_____

_____

3. Extended Error Handling Facility (FORTRAN)

a. Description

Figures 4.27 through 4.29 consist of pertinent pages of a job in
which a data error has been encountered by the FORTRAN Extended Error
Handling Facility.

The job did not abend, but rather a standard corrective action was
taken, and processing continued to a normal end. Upon completion of
the job, a programmer would be interested in determining in which source
statement the error occurred. This could affect a programmer's apprais-
al of output file validity.

The data error relates to an invalid character which was encountered in a field defined to contain decimal characters only. The standard corrective action consists of converting the illegal character to
a zero, and continuing processing. This may or may not be a valid
assumption and could seriously affect the validity of an output file.

The source statement in which the error was encountered should be
isolated and anlyzed. Corrective action can then be taken and the
job rerun, if necessary.

A problem solution can be found in Appendix A.

b. Workshop

1. Problem Overview

Error Number _____

Error Message _____

2. Relative Length Determination

Name of System Routine _____

Name of Program Module _____

Return Address (RA) .... _____

Entry Point Address (EPA) .... _____

Relative Length (RA - EPA) .... _____

3. Source Statement Determination

Length into Assembly Language Listing ... _____

Problem Source Statement Number .... _____

Actual Source Statement:

_____

4. Problem Analysis

Summarize your findings. If the occurrence of this particular error jeopardizes the run and the validity of the output files, what alternative actions can be taken?

_____

_____

_____

_____

_____

_____

Figure 4.27   FORTRAN Source Program Listing for MAIN and COMP (215)

```
FORTRAN IV G LEVEL  21                    MAIN

               C      PROGRAM TO CREATE CORE DUMPS
     0001             COMMON ID(8), M, N, ITEST
     0002             READ (5,100) ID, M, N
     0003       100 FORMAT (10I2)
     0004             CALL COMP
     0005             WRITE (6,200) ID, M, N, ITEST
     0006       200 FORMAT ('-', T6, '   ID = ', 8I2//,
                   1                 T6, '    M = ', I2//,
                   2                 T6, '    N = ', I2//,
                   3                 T6, 'ITEST = ', I2////,
                   4                 T6, 'END OF JOB')
     0007             STOP
     0008             END




FORTRAN IV G LEVEL  21                    COMP

     0001             SUBROUTINE COMP
     0002             COMMON ID(8), M, N, ITEST
     0003       100 ITEST = ID(M) * ID(N)
     0004       150 IF(ITEST.GE.2.AND.ITEST.LE.224) GO TO 100
     0005             WRITE (6,200)
     0006       200 FORMAT ('1','ITEST OUT OF LIMITS')
     0007       300 RETURN
     0008             END
```

Figure 4.28   Portion of Assembly Language Listing for MAIN (215)

```
FORTRAN IV G LEVEL  21                      MAIN

LOCATION    STA NUM    LABEL    OP          OPERAND              BCD OPERAND
000000                          BC          15,12(0,15)
000004                          DC          06D4C1C9
000008                          DC          D5404040
00000C                          STM         14,12,12(13)
000010                          LM          2,3,40(15)
000014                          LR          4,13
000016                          L           13,36(0,15)
00001A                          ST          13,8(0,4)
00001E                          STM         3,4,0(13)
000022                          BCR         15,2
000024                          DC          00060000              A4
000028                          DC          00060000              A20
00002C                          DC          00000000              A36
000138             A36          L           13,4(0,13)
00013C                          L           14,12(0,13)
000140                          LM          2,12,28(13)
000144                          MVI         12(13),255
000148                          BCR         15,14
00014A             A20          L           15,100(0,13)          IBCOM#
00014E                          LR          12,13
000150                          LR          13,4
000152                          BAL         14,64(0,15)
000156                          LR          13,12
000158      2                   L           15,100(0,13)          IBCOM#
00015C                          BAL         14,0(0,15)
000160                          DC          00000005
000164                          DC          0000009C
000168                          BAL         14,12(0,15)
00016C                          DC          00000000
000170                          DC          04500008
000174                          L           10,72(0,13)
000178                          BAL         14,8(0,15)
00017C                          DC          0450A020
000180                          BAL         14,8(0,15)
000184                          DC          0450A024
000188                          BAL         14,16(0,15)
00018C      4                   LA          1,0(0,0)
000190                          L           15,104(0,13)          COMP
000194                          BALR        14,15
000198                          BC          0,4(0,0)
00019A      5                   L           15,100(0,13)          IBCOM#
00019E                          BCR         0,0
0001A0                          BAL         14,4(0,15)
0001A4                          DC          00000006
0001A8                          DC          000000A2
0001AC                          BAL         14,12(0,15)
0001B0                          DC          00000000
0001B4                          DC          04500008
0001B8                          BAL         14,8(0,15)
0001BC                          DC          0450A020
0001C0                          BAL         14,8(0,15)
0001C4                          DC          0450A024
0001C8                          BAL         14,8(0,15)
0001CC                          DC          0450A028
0001D0                          BAL         14,16(0,15)
0001D4      7                   L           15,100(0,13)          IBCOM#
0001D8                          BAL         14,52(0,15)
```

Figure 4.29   FORTRAN Extended Error Handling Facility (215)

```
IHN215I CONVERT - ILLEGAL   DECIMAL   CHARACTER X

 2 4 6 810121416 6 X

TRACEBACK  ROUTINE  CALLED FROM ISN   REG.  14    REG.  15    REG.   0    REG.   1

          IBCOM                       00136598    001367CC    00000008    00155FF8

          MAIN                        0002C510    01136410    00000008    00155FF8

ENTRY POINT= 01136410

STANDARD FIXUP TAKEN . EXECUTION CONTINUING
```

5

Variable Values

A. PERTINENT VARIABLES

Determining the value of pertinent variables at the time of abend
is an invaluable aid to storage dump problem solving. The value of programmer-defined variables can be determined for any program residing
in main storage. The technique of locating and interpreting the value
of pertinent variables is particularly applicable to Internal Abends,
i.e., program problems, but can also be valuable to the solution of
External Abends where the status of program variables may shed light on
a file problem.

Because of the many variables defined by a programmer in most programs, one must limit the search to those variables which will provide
a maximum amount of information in a minimum amount of time. Variables
which directly relate to the source statement being executed at the time
the abend occurred are considered pertinent. In the OC7 Internal
Storage Dump example of Chapter 4, STATE-DATA and STATE4 would be of
particular interest to the problem solver as they occur in the source
statement being executed. Likewise, the value of a program record
counter might be of interest to the programmer debugging the D37 External Storage Dump in Chapter 3. Knowledge of the number of records

processed at abend time gives an indication of how much more space to allocate for the problem file. It could also signify a program loop. The significance of determining the value of pertinent program variables is not necessarily limited to Internal Abends.

The value of pertinent variables can be determined for application, system, and data base programs for which the Source Program listing and a Map or Assembly Language listing is available.

B. SOURCE STATEMENT VARIABLES (COBOL)

1. Computer Run Overview (OC7)

The computer run depicted in Figures 5.1 through 5.4 consists of selected pages of the same run which had abended with a OC7 Completion Code in Chapter 4.

The COBOL problem source statement was found to be IF STATE-DATA = STATE4 GO TO PRO-3. See Figure 5.1, letter 'A'.

Because a OC7 Storage Dump signals that non-numeric data is erroneously present in a numeric field, a programmer would be interested in locating the values of STATE-DATA and STATE4 to determine which is the problem variable. Having done so, the programmer can then trace the variable to the problem source.

The optional Data Map (DMAP), which is used in determining the value of pertinent program variables, should always be specified when compiling COBOL programs. The following example utilizes an ANS COBOL DMAP. Differences in format among COBOL programming levels are not significant.

First, a base address for the variable of interest must be determined. A displacement is then added and the resulting address located in main storage. An appropriate length is marked off and the value interpreted. This procedure can be accomplished for as many program variables as desired.

Figure 5.1 Portion of COBOL Source Program Listing (OC7)

```
00023    2 1   FD  OUTPUT1
00024    2 2       RECORDING MODE F
00025    2 3       LABEL RECORD STANDARD
00026    2 31      BLOCK CONTAINS 4000 CHARACTERS
00027    2 4       DATA RECORD IS OUTRCD1.
00028    2 5   01  OUTRCD1 PIC X(80).
00029    2 71  FD  OUTPUT2
00030    2 72      RECORDING MODE F
00031    2 73      LABEL RECORD STANDARD
00032    2 74      DATA RECORD IS OUTRCD2.
00033    2 75  01  OUTRCD2 PIC X(80).
00034    217  FD  CDINPUT1
00035    218      RECORDING MODE F
00036    219      LABEL RECORDS OMITTED
00037    220      RECORD CONTAINS 080 CHARACTERS
00038    221      DATA RECORD IS CD-IN.
00039    222  01  CD-IN PIC X(80).
00040    276  FD  TERM-FILE
00041    277      LABEL RECORDS STANDARD
00042    278      RECORDING MODE F
00043    279      DATA RECORD IS TERM-RECORD.
00044    280  01  TERM-RECORD PIC X(80).
00045    3 1   WORKING-STORAGE SECTION.
00046    3 2   77  STATE4 PICTURE  9(7).
00047          01  INREC.
00048              02  IDENT1      PICTURE 9(7)   OCCURS  5 TIMES.
00049              02  STATE-DATA  PICTURE 9(7).
00050              02  IDENT2      PICTURE 9(7)   OCCURS  5 TIMES.
00051              02 FILLER PIC X(3).
00052          01  CARDIN.
00053              02  STATE2    PICTURE X(7).
00054              02  FILLER        PICTURE X(73).
00055    3 3   01  COUNTS.
00056    3 4       02  FILLER PICTURE X(21) VALUE ' RECORDS ON TAPE 1 = '.
00057    3 5       02  CNT1 PICTURE  9(7) VALUE ZEROS.
00058    3 6       02  FILLER PICTURE X(21) VALUE ' RECORDS ON TAPE 2 = '.
00059    3 7       02  CNT2 PICTURE  9(7) VALUE ZEROS.
00060    3 8       02  FILLER PICTURE X(24) VALUE ' NORMAL END OF JOB        '.
00061    4 1   PROCEDURE DIVISION.
00062    4 2       OPEN INPUT CDINPUT1 INPUT1 OUTPUT OUTPUT1 OUTPUT2 TERM-FILE.
00063    4 3       READ CDINPUT1 INTO CARDIN AT END GO TO NORMAL-EOJ.
00064    4 4       MOVE STATE2 TO STATE4.
00065    4 5   PRO-2.
00066    4 6       READ INPUT1 INTO INREC AT END GO TO NORMAL-EOJ.
00067    4 7   A→  IF STATE-DATA = STATE4 GO TO PRO-3.
00068    4 8       WRITE OUTRCD1 FROM INREC.
00069    4 9       ADD 1 TO CNT1.
00070    410       GO TO PRO-2.
00071    411   PRO-3.
00072    412       WRITE OUTRCD2 FROM INREC.
00073    413       ADD 1 TO CNT2.
00074    415       GO TO PRO-2.
00075    416   NORMAL-EOJ.
00076             WRITE TERM-RECORD FROM COUNTS.
00077    418       CLOSE INPUT1 OUTPUT1 OUTPUT2 TERM-FILE CDINPUT1.
00078    419       STOP RUN.
```

Figure 5.2 Data Map or DMAP (OC7)

INTRNL NAME	LVL	SOURCE NAME	BASE	DISPL	INTRNL NAME	DEFINITION	USAGE	R	O	Q	M
DNM=1-073	FD	INPUT1	DCB=01		DNM=1-073	DS 80C	QSAM				F
DNM=1-092	01	INRCD	BL=1	000	DNM=1-092		DISP				
DNM=1-107	FD	OUTPUT1	DCB=02		DNM=1-107	DS 80C	QSAM				F
DNM=1-127	01	OUTRCD1	BL=2	000	DNM=1-127		DISP				
DNM=1-144	FD	OUTPUT2	DCB=03		DNM=1-144	DS 80C	DISP				F
DNM=1-164	01	OUTRCD2	BL=3	000	DNM=1-164		DISP				
DNM=1-181	FD	CDINPUT1	DCB=04		DNM=1-181	DS 80C	QSAM				F
DNM=1-202	01	CD-IN	BL=4	000	DNM=1-202		DISP				
DNM=1-220	FD	TERM-FILE	DCB=05		DNM=1-220	DS 80C	QSAM				F
DNM=1-242	01	TERM-RECORD	BL=5	000	DNM=1-242		DISP				
DNM=1-263	77	STATE4	BL=6	000	DNM=1-263	DS 7C	DISP-NM				
DNM=1-279	01	INREC	BL=6	000	DNM=1-279	DS 0CL80	GROUP		O		
DNM=1-297	02	IDENT1	BL=6	008	DNM=1-297	DS 7C	DISP-NM				
DNM=1-313	02	STATE-DATA	BL=6	028	DNM=1-313	DS 7C	DISP-NM		O		
DNM=1-333	02	IDENT2	BL=6	032	DNM=1-333	DS 7C	DISP-NM				
DNM=1-349	02	FILLER	BL=6	055	DNM=1-349	DS 3C	DISP				
DNM=1-360	01	CARDIN	BL=6	058	DNM=1-360	DS 0CL80	GROUP				
DNM=1-379	02	STATE2	BL=6	058	DNM=1-379	DS 7C	DISP				
DNM=1-395	02	FILLER	BL=6	05F	DNM=1-395	DS 73C	DISP				
DNM=1-409	01	COUNTS	BL=6	048	DNM=1-409	DS 0CL80	GROUP				
DNM=1-428	02	FILLER	BL=6	0A8	DNM=1-428	DS 21C	DISP				
DNM=1-442	02	CNT1	BL=6	0BD	DNM=1-442	DS 7C	DISP-NM				
DNM=1-456	02	FILLER	BL=6	0C4	DNM=1-456	DS 21C	DISP				
DNM=1-470	02	CNT2	BL=6	0D9	DNM=1-470	DS 7C	DISP-NM				
DNM=1-484	02	FILLER	BL=6	0E0	DNM=1-484	DS 24C	DISP				

(Annotation callouts on figure: B, C, G, H, M)

148

Figure 5.3 Register Assignment Area (OC7)

```
                    PARAM CELLS                 00720
                    RPTSAV AREA                 00720
                    CHECKPT CTR                 00720
                    VCON TBL                    00720
                    DEBUG TABLE                 00720

    LITERAL POOL (HEX)

    007A0 (LIT+0)       1C480048   05EF


                        PGT                     00738

                    OVERFLOW CELLS              00738
                    VIRTUAL CELLS               00738
                    PROCEDURE NAME CELLS        00750
                    GENERATED NAME CELLS        0075C
                    DCB ADDRESS CELLS           0078C
                    VNI CELLS                   007A0
                    LITERALS                    007A0
                    DISPLAY LITERALS            007A6


    REGISTER ASSIGNMENT

    REG 6      BL  =6  ◄──── D
    REG 7      BL  =1
    REG 8      BL  =2
    REG 9      BL  =3
    REG 10     BL  =4
    REG 11     BL  =5

WORKING-STORAGE STARTS AT LOCATION 00088 FOR A LENGTH OF 000F8.
```

Figure 5.4   First Page of OC7 Main Storage

REGS AT ENTRY TO ABEND ──► **E**

```
FLTR 0-6    08036CB040000001    05036D2400000028    31036D1340000005

                                                              F  08036CC840000001

REGS 0-7    0000000A   0009D140   00096C6A   8009652C   00096H9E   0009D140
REGS 8-15   0009AOC0   0009C630   0009D04R   00096988   50096B84   001FDBE0

LOAD MODULE   MAIN

096240   F8404040 C1D5E2F4 0700989F F02407FF   90EC000C 195D05F0 4580F010 C1F5F5F5   *8   ANS4........0..0..A555*
096260   00096250 00096988 00096730            96021034 07FE41F0 000107FE 00096E9A   *R   ANS4.....0........0.....*
096280   40D5C9E3 D9C9E3C5 40404040 40404040   00096E5A C1D4D4D6 D5C9E4D4 40404040   *.6..AMMONIUM*
0962A0   40404040 40404040 40404040 40404040   40404040 00000000 F0F0F0F0 F0F0F140   *NITRITE.........0000001*
0962C0   F6F1F1F8 F8F1F4F3 F2F3F2F1 F4F3F6F7   F3F4F1F1 F1F1F1F1 F2F2F2F2            *611881432214367341111112 7222*
0962E0   F2F2F2F0 F0F0F0F0 F0F0F6F9 F3F9F1F4   F9F4F9F3 F4F1F3F5 F7F8F3F4 F1F9F4F4   *2220000069391449341357834 1944*
096300   F9F4F4F1 F3F4F2F9 F0F1F1F2 F3F4F5F9   F0F0F0F0 F0F0F140 40404040 40404040   *904134290112345900000001*
096320   40404040 40404040 40404040 40404040   4F404040 40404040 40404040 40404040
096340   SAME AS ABOVE
LINE 096360
096380   40D9C5C3 D6D9C4E2 40D6D540 E3C1D7C5   40F1407E 40F0F0F0 40D9C5C3            *  RECORDS ON TAPE 1 . 0000000 REC*
0963A0   D6D9C4E2 40D6D540 E3C1D7C5 40F2407E   40F0F0F0 F0F0F0F2 40D5D6D9 D4C1D340   *ORDS ON TAPE 2 . 0000002 NORMAL*
0963C0   C5D5C440 D6C640D1 D6C24040 40404040   F0F7F6F3 00000000 00000000 00000000   *END OF JOB   0763*
0963E0   00000000 05097E2A 08096276 00000001   00000001 00410000 0209D0E8 00004000
096400   00000000 00000000 00000001 00000000   00000000 00036B4C 121FE880 06097BC6
096420   80000000 46096A98 800963D4 00404800   00000000 00000050 00000000 00000000
096440   00090050 28022828 0009C770 00090190   00090140 00000050 30060050 00000000
096460   001FD4F8 00000000 00000000 00000000   00000001 00000000 001FD830 05EF0000
096480   00000000 00000000 80000000 00000000   00000000 00800040 00000000 00000000
0964A0   00000000 00000001 46096B9C 08096276   00000000 00000001 00410000 02090190
0964C0   0029336D 0209A0B8 001FDAD0 0009FA00   00544800 000368CC 121FE880 001FDBE0
0964E0   921FCC48 00000001 00000000 001FD830   00090238 0009D1E8 00000050 00000001
096500   00000050 00000000 0209000C8 00000000   05EF0000 00000000 00000000 00000001
096520   00096276 00000000 0009000C8 00000000   00000000 05097E2A 08096276 00000000
096540   00000000 00480000 0209D040 00004000   80000000 46000001 80096684 00900048
096560   38000000 000F000E 0201C394 002931BF   00000001 46000001 28022828 4209C6D0 0009D098
096580   8009652C 007C0048 00036720 921FCC48   00090050 05EF0000 0009D380 50096EA0
0965A0   0009C478 0009C680 0009C680 00000050   001FDAD0 0D097BC6 00090050 0009D380 0009D380
0965C0   00000000 00000000 00000000 05097E2A   00000001 00000040 00000000 00000000
0965E0   00000000 00000000 00000001 08096276   00000001 00800040 00000000 00000000
096600   00000000 80000000 46096B5C 800965D8   00000000 00000000 00410000 02090190
096620   00004000 00000001 46096B5C 800965D8   00544800 000368CC 121FE880 001FDBE0
096640   06097BC6 0009D050 28022828 0009C7D0   00090238 0009D1E8 00000050 00000001
096660   00000000 001FD4F8 00000000 00000000   00000000 00000050 08096276 00000001
096680   00800040 00000000 00000000 00000000   00000000 00000000 00000000 00000001
0966A0   00000001 00000000 00480000 0209D040   80000000 46000001 80096684 00900048
0966C0   000366AC 921FCC48 07097BC6 00000040   00000001 46000001 28022828 00900048
0966E0   0009D098 00000050 00000000 00000040   00090050 05EF0000 00090380 0009D098
096720   00000000 00000000 00000000 00800040   0030C4C2 4209C6D0 0009D380 50096EA0
096740   0009704A 50096B84 121FE880 00000001   00096404 00096C68 8009652C 00000000
096760   00096B9E 000962D8 0009D0F0 0009A0C0   401FDBE0 001FDBE0 32028048 00000000
096780   00000000 000969F6 00000000 00000000   00097E7C FD000008 0009D7F8            *P8*
```

```
*          .....0..0..A555*
*R  ANS4..........0.....*
*......6...AMMONIUM*
*NITRITE...........0000001*     ◄─ N
*...611881432214367341111112 7222*
*2220000069391449341357834 1944*
*9041342901123459000000 01*
*  RECORDS ON TAPE 1 . 0000000 REC*
*ORDS ON TAPE 2 . 0000002 NORMAL*
*END OF JOB   0763................*
*...........................*
*.............E............*
*...............Q..........*
*..................H.......*
*.........M......Y...Y..F.*
*.M8....G...J..J....J......*
*.............C.........H..*
*......................C...*
*...............Q...........*
*.D...F...F......F....Q....*
*.....F...............F....*
*..................F...I...F.*
*.........DB..P...L........*
*..............Q...K..JY....*
*.F...M8.......Q...G...Y..J.*
*............6.......Y......*
*...........Q...0.....Y.....*
*....................F.....P8*
```

2. Variable Location

a. Base

The first step in determining the value of pertinent program variables is to find the contents of the specific base registers assigned to those variables. A Base Register contains a Base Address referring to many variables, such as STATE4 and STATE-DATA.

To determine the Base Address one must first reference the compiler output Data Map (DMAP). Looking under the heading SOURCE NAME (third column from the left), the variables STATE4 and STATE-DATA can be found. See Figure 5.2, letter 'B'. An indirect base register reference is printed to the right of the variable name under the heading BASE. For both variables of interest, that reference is BL=6. See letter 'C'. This should not be interpreted as the base register, however, because for that information one must refer to the Register Assignment Area. There it can be seen that BL=6 refers to Base Register 6. See Figure 5.3, letter 'D'. Note that in the Register Assignment Area the Base Reference number is not necessarily the same as the Base Register, although for variables STATE4 and STATE-DATA they do happen to be.

The next step is to determine the contents of the Base Register. The Base Registers are located in an area called REGS AT ENTRY TO ABEND, just before the print of main storage. See Figure 5.4, letter 'E'. A few lines below this heading can be found REGS 0-7, indicating that this line contains Base Registers 0 through 7. Base Register 6 can be located by counting to the right, up to six, starting with zero. See letter 'F'. The Base Address for the variables STATE4 and STATE-DATA is 0962D8. The sum of the Base Address plus a displacement will be used to locate the value of variables STATE4 and STATE-DATA.

b. Displacement

A Base Register contains a Base Address for many variables. Each variable is 'displaced', or located, a specified distance from the base. To determine the Displacement for pertinent program variables, the Data Map (DMAP) must again be referenced. Under the heading DISPL, a

Displacement of 000 for STATE4 and 02B for STATE-DATA can be found.
See Figure 5.2, letter 'G'. This is the distance, in bytes, from which
the variables are located from the Base.

In order to determine the exact location of pertinent program
variables, the Base Address must be added, in hexadecimal notation, to
Displacement as follows:

	STATE4	STATE-DATA
Base Register 6	0962D8	0962D8
Displacement	+ 000	+ 02B
Address of Variable	0962D8	096303

STATE4 is located at Address 0962D8 while STATE-DATA is located at
Address 096303. After determining the programmer-defined length of
each variable, the main storage portion of the dump can be referenced.

3. Variable Interpretation

   a. Length

   Before accessing main storage to determine the value of pertinent
   variables, the length of each variable should be determined by referencing, the Data Map (DMAP). Under the heading DEFINITION it can be
   found that the length of STATE4 and STATE-DATA is 7C. See Figure 5.2,
   letter 'H'. This can be interpreted as 7 characters, or, more pre-
   cisely, 7 bytes. Once the starting address for these variables is
   located in main storage a length of seven bytes will be marked off,
   comprising the entire field.

   b. Value

   Now that Base, Displacement, and Length have been determined for
   the pertinent program variables, their respective values can be located.
   Recall that Base plus Displacement for STATE4 and STATE-DATA is 0962D8
   and 096303 respectively, and each variable is seven bytes in length.

First, page down the left-hand side of the print of main storage until the nearest address is found which does not exceed the starting address of the variable. For STATE4 this would be 0962C0, as the next line with 0962E0 exceeds Address 0962D8. See Figure 5.4, letter 'I'. Reviewing Chapter 2's technique of address lookup, the first character encountered at Address 0962D8 is F. Counting off a length of seven bytes, the complete character string for the value of STATE4 is F0F0F0F0F0F0F1. See letter 'J'.

Using the same technique for STATE-DATA, the nearest address on the left-hand side of the dump which does not exceed the starting address of the variable is 096300. See letter 'K'. The first character encountered at Address 096303 is also F. Counting off a length of seven bytes, the complete character string for the value of STATE-DATA is F0F0F0F0F0F040. See letter 'L'.

The interpretation of character strings can be accomplished by referring to the Data Map (DMAP). Under the heading USAGE, the data representation for both STATE4 and STATE-DATA is found to be DISP-NM, or DISPLAY-NUMERIC. See Figure 5.2, letter 'M'. Reviewing Chapter 2's technique of data interpretation, it is found that the data is stored in Character Format (External Decimal). The value of STATE4, therefore, is ' +0+0+0+0+0+0+1 ' or six zeroes followed by a one. However, the value of STATE-DATA is ' +0+0+0+0+0+0 ' or six zeroes followed by a blank as represented by a 40 in the low order position. A blank is a non-numeric character, as are all alphabetic and special characters, and is the cause of the 0C7 Storage Dump. Tracing through program logic, one would find that the program did not create the erroneous value itself; rather it was read in as raw data. The technique of interpreting character strings will be expanded later in this chapter as well as in Chapter 6.

It is also worthy to note that data represented in External Decimal Unpacked Format is interpreted in the right-hand portion of the print of main storage. The values for STATE4 and STATE-DATA are found to be ' 0000001 ' and ' 000000 ', respectively. See Figure 5.4, letter 'N'. The blank which caused the problem is readily apparent. Alpha and special characters described in Character Format would also be displayed here.

A FORTRAN example, to be discussed next, utilizes the Binary form of Data Representation. This is comparable to COBOL's USAGE COMP, as opposed to USAGE DISPLAY found previously in the DMAP.

As can be seen, locating the value of pertinent variables is an invaluable aid in debugging storage dumps. Program logic can then be traced with specific variable values in mind.

C. FORTRAN COMPARISON

1. Computer Run Overview

The computer run depicted in Figures 5.5 through 5.8 consists of selected pages of the same run which had abended with a 322 Completion Code in Chapter 4.

The FORTRAN problem source statement in Subroutine COMP was found to be 100 ITEST = ID(M) * ID(N). See Figure 5.5, letter 'A'.

Because a 322 Storage Dump signifies that a specified CPU time limit has been exceeded and that the program may be in a loop, a programmer would be interested in locating the value of ITEST since it is this variable that may be causing the program to remain in an endless loop. Having determined the value, a programmer can then trace the variable to the problem source.

During the program review process, it would be discovered that Source Statement #4, 150 IF(ITEST.GE.2.AND.ITEST.LE.224) GO TO 100, compares the values of ITEST. See Figure 5.5, letter 'B'. In addition to ITEST, the values located in the Mth and Nth positions of the ID Array would appear to be of interest.

Contrary to the utilization of a DMAP in COBOL, a FORTRAN programmer should use the Assembly Language listing to determine the Base Register and Displacement. Although a MAP option is available with FORTRAN compilers, the proper Base Register cannot always be assured. An Assembly Language listing provides complete assurance of Base and Displacement indications.

Figure 5.5 FORTRAN Source Program Listing for MAIN and COMP (322)

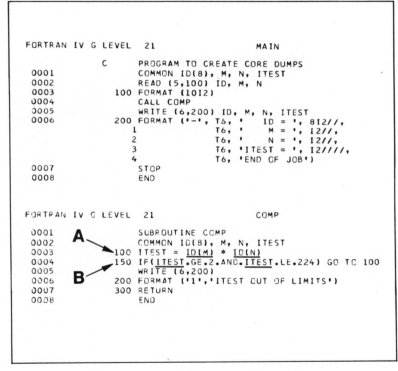

```
FORTRAN IV G LEVEL  21                 MAIN

          C       PROGRAM TO CREATE CORE DUMPS
     0001          COMMON ID(8), M, N, ITEST
     0002          READ (5,100) ID, M, N
     0003     100 FORMAT (10I2)
     0004          CALL COMP
     0005          WRITE (6,200) ID, M, N, ITEST
     0006     200 FORMAT ('-', T5, '    ID = ', 8I2//,
               1               T6, '     M = ', I2//,
               2               T6, '     N = ', I2//,
               3               T6, 'ITEST = ', I2////,
               4               T6, 'END OF JOB')
     0007          STOP
     0008          END


FORTRAN IV G LEVEL  21                 COMP

     0001          SUBROUTINE COMP
     0002          COMMON ID(8), M, N, ITEST
     0003     100 ITEST = ID(M) * ID(N)
     0004     150 IF(ITEST.GE.2.AND.ITEST.LE.224) GO TO 100
     0005          WRITE (6,200)
     0006     200 FORMAT ('1','ITEST OUT OF LIMITS')
     0007     300 RETURN
     0008          END
```

155

Figure 5.6 Portion of Assembly Language Listing for COMP (322)

```
FORTRAN IV G LEVEL  21                    COMP

LOCATION  STA NUM   LABEL   OP    OPERAND              BCD OPERAND
 000000                     BC    15,12(0,15)
 000004                     DC    06C3D6D4
 000008                     DC    D7404040
 00000C                     STM   14,12,12(13)
 000010                     LM    2,3,40(15)
 000014                     LR    4,13
 000016                     L     13,36(0,15)
 00001A                     ST    13,8(0,4)
 00001E                     STM   3,4,0(13)
 000022                     BCR   15,2
 000024                     DC    00000000            A4
 000028                     DC    00000000            A20
 00002C                     DC    00000000            A36
 000108            A20       BALR  2,0
 00010A                     L     3,6(0,2)
 00010E                     BCR   15,3
 000110                     DC    00000000            A52
 000114            A36       L     1,4(0,13)
 000118                     L     1,24(0,1)
 00011C                     L     13,4(0,13)
 000120                     L     14,12(0,13)
 000124                     LM    2,12,28(13)
 000128                     MVI   12(13),255
 00012C                     BCR   15,14
 00012E      3    100       L     10,72(0,13)
 000132                     L     8,32(0,10)          M
 000136                     SLA   8,2(0)
 00013A                     A     8,200(0,13)
 00013E                     L     8,0(8,10)           ID
 000142                     L     8,36(0,10)          N
 000146                     SLA   9,2(0)
 00014A                     A     9,200(0,13)
 00014E                     M     0,0(9,10)           ID
 000152                     ST    1,40(0,10)          ITEST
 000156      4    150       L     0,40(0,10)          ITEST
 00015A                     C     0,204(0,13)
 00015E                     L     0,208(0,13)
 000162                     BALR  14,0
 000164                     BC    11,6(0,14)
 000168                     SR    0,0
 00016A                     L     1,40(0,10)
 00016E                     C     1,212(0,13)
 000172                     LA    1,1(0,0)
 000176                     BALR  14,0
 000178                     BC    13,6(0,14)
 00017C                     SR    1,1
 00017E                     NR    1,0
 000180                     LTR   1,1
 000182                     L     14,100(0,13)        100
 000186                     BCR   7,14
 000188      5             L     15,112(0,13)        IBCOM#
 00018C                     BAL   14,4(0,15)
 000190                     DC    00000006
 000194                     DC    000000A4
 000198                     BAL   14,16(0,15)
 00019C      7    300       SR    15,15
 00019E                     L     1,0(0,13)           ITEST
```

156

REGS AT ENTRY TO ABEND

```
FLTR 0-6    4040404040 40014A    2224F0000000066    FEA766E24675224F    0000000000000000

REGS 0-7    00000001   00000001   42084F26            00084C40   0003E48    0003E4D0
REGS 8-15   00000014   00000008   00BA7D0             00084C40   00084E28   00084DF8
```

LCAD MODULE   MAIN

```
                                        E→
0B4C00                                         47F0F00C 0604C1C9 D5404040 90ECD00C  *0538818 21.6564.CO..MAIN ....*
0B4C20  9823F028 184D58D0 F0245000 40089034    D00007F2 00DB4C40 00DB4D5A 00DB4D48  *..0.....0.... .....2......*
0B4C40  00084D48 000BDF68 00038E48 00036D64    00DBDF68 FD000008 00DB4D5A 00DB4D5A  *......0...........8.......*
0B4C60  00084D48 000BDF68 00038E48 00036D64    0003E4D0 0003C0E0 000357D8 00DBA7D0  *...............U...Q......*
0B4C80  0003E588 00084C40 000BA7D0 00084C40    00DB5C30 000B6C20 00DB7C10 CA0C8008  *...V.............Q........*
0B4CA0  5044540E 000B4FCC 000B4FCC 02060A10    0222021A 01601206 1A084040 40C9C440  *..................8......ID*
0B4CC0  7E400608 1002E1E  12061A08 C9E3C5E2    D4407E40 10021E1E 12061A08 40404040  *..............8...........*
0B4CE0  D5407E40 1002E1E  12061A08 C9E3C5E2    E3407E40 10021E1E 1E1E1206 1A0AC5D5  *.......M...........M....EN*
0B4D00  C440D6C6 40D1D6C2 22265622 34026C00    00000000 00000000 00000000 D06418CD  *N..........ITEST.........*
0B4D20  4E000000 4E000000 00C00000 58E0D00C    4E000000 00000000 00000000 00DBA7D0  *D OF JOB..................*
0B4D40  00C00000 00000000 00000000 58E0F000    982CD01C 00DB4CAC 45E0F00C 41100000  *.............0............*
0B4D60  1BD445E0 F04018DC 45E0F000 45E0F000    0C000005 0450A024 45E0F010 45E0F00C  *.M..0.......0..0..........*
0B4D80  04500008 58A0D048 45E0F008 0450A020    45E0F008 0450A024 45E0F008 0450A028  *.......0.....0.....0......*
0B4DA0  58F0D068 05EF4700 04500008 D0640700    45E0F004 00000006 45E0F008 0450A028  *........0.....0.....0.....*
0B4DC0  00DBA7D0 04500008 45E0F008 0450A020    40F0C000 47F0F00C 06C3D6D4 00DB4E28  *.........0.....0.....0..COM*
0B4DE0  45E0F010 58F0D064 45E0F034 05404040    F0245000 40089034 D00007F2 00DB4E28  *.P..........0......0......*
0B4E00  D7404040 90ECD00C 9823F028 184D58D0    540A4208 CA0C5803 CACC1601 D230C8AE  *....P............2.....2..*
0B4E20  00DB4F00 000B4F0C 840FB20E 1C0E9807    CC04CC14 C832A009 0425B618 1255CC04  *..............K.H.........*
0B4E40  CA14CA0C 6C165620 CA0C1602 4C4C58EC    CA0C340C 00DB4E28 00DB5E18 00DB6E08  *.........H.............H..*
0B4E60  3A30CC14 CA0C340C 0538CA0C D6E4E340    16014400 58D0A100 00DB4FCC 021A01F1  *........1.................*
0B4E80  00DB7DF8 47F09E8C D6E4E340 D6C64026    C9D4C9E3 E2224780 00000000 00000000  *..8.0.....................*
0B4EA0  1A13C9E3 C5E2E340 D6C640D3 00000000    FFFFFFFC 00000002 4E000000 00000000  *.ITEST OUT OF LIMITS......*
0B4EC0  00030000 00000000 4E000000 00000000    00000000 00000001 00000000 000000E0  *.........................*
0B4EE0  00000000 00000000 00000000 00000000    58D0D004 58D0D004 58D0D00C 000000E0  *..........3...............*
0B4F00  05205830 200607F3 00084F26 5810D004    58101018 58D0D004 58E0D00C 982CD01C  *.........................*
0B4F20  92FFD00C 07FE58A0 D0485880 A0208B80    00025A80 D0C85B18 A0005890 A0248B90  *............H.............*
0B4F40  00025A90 D0C85C09 A0005010 A0285800    A0285900 DDD005E0 DDD005E0 47B0E006  *.......H.....M...........*
0B4F60  1B005810 A0285910 D0D44110 000105E0    4700E006 1B111410 12115BE0 D064077E  *....M.....................*
0B4F80  58F0D070 45E0F004 00000006 000B4E9C    45E0F010 1BFF5810 D00007F1 91504740  *.............0....l.......*
0B4FA0  40F5F7F3 F46D03D4 F140C3D6 D7E8D9C7    C7D6D440 C9C2D440 C3D6D9D7 4840F1F9  * 5734,LMI COPYRIGHT IBM CORP. 19*
0B4FC0  F7F04040 F2F0F0F1 F5F14B40 F5F14B40    47F0F516 47F0F54E 47F0F690 47F0F690  *70 200151 .01..05..05..06.*
0B4FE0  47F0FAF8 F2FDF0F0 47F0FB46 47F0FB94    47F0FCE8 47F0FD5F 47F0FD84 47F0FD98  *.0.8..0...0...Y.0...0.....*
0B5000  47F0FDAC 47F0FDC0 00000005 47F0FDD4    47F0FDE4 00005810 FE385810 FE5C5810  *.0........0.M.0.U.......0..*
0B5020  FE505810 FE485810 FE485810 FE4C5810    FE545810 FE580700 0008A1C4 000192FF  *...............M.O.U.....D.*
0B5040  FF3A9200 FFDBA0E8 FFDB4D9C 0003E4D0    F0000008 000BDFF8 000B4D5A 00DB4D48  *..........Y.........8.....*
0B5060  00DBDF68 00DB3E48 00036D64 0003E4D0    003C0E0  00145040 00DBA7D0 0003E588  *.............U........Q...*
0B5080  00DB4C40 00084C40 0008635E 01084C10    0008510C F11E45A0 F13E45A0 F4689110  *............V..............V.*
0B50A0  F3E84780 F10E45A0 F09645A0 F2289120    F3E84780 F07A45A0 F07445A0 F2289140  *.3Y..l...0...2..3Y..l...0..*
0B50C0  F3E84780 F12E45A0 F0B245A0 F2289101    F3E84780 F13E45A0 00000000 00000000  *3Y..l..0...2..3Y..l...0....*
0B50E0  00DB6388 0008CBC0 45000050 92F0F1A9    47F0F12C 92FFF1A9 95FFF07C 4770F1F8  *..............01..01...l...0...18*
0B5100  90EDF07C 41300008 41D0F1A2 50E0FE0C    9200FE37 18111B22 9012F10C 5810FE38  *...............0.....l..0..1*
0B5120  182ED207 FE94E000 9180FE94 4780F16C    5810F08C 41303004 9110FE94 4780F180  *..........K....l....l.0....*
0B5140  58532000 5050F10C 41303004 9120FE94    4780F194 58532000 5050F110 41303004  *..............l....l.......1*
0B5160  41E23000 50E0F07C 5010FE3C 07FD41F0    F1BA0501 00F047F0 F1D85020 FEA44183  *.S..0..........l....0.0IQ..*
0B5180  200P1892 07FE1B77 5070FF08 5070FE28    5070FF0C 58A0FE98 91FFFE98 4750FFE8  *......l...........0.0IQ...7Y*
```

Figure 5.7   First Page of 322 Main Storage

Figure 5.8 Intermediate Page of 322 Main Storage

```
0BA5E0    00024E60 F270F332 201FF275 96F02022    41502025 41C00004 18354120 900C4570   *....2.3...2..0..................*
0BA600    F1581A9A 4150500B 46C0F0C8 4B90F20E    4570F166 D5C39010 80C04780 F10E4150   *1..........0H..2...1.N........1...*
0BA620    002C875A F1041BCC 86CAF132 599CF190    4770F0F8 D2132016 F2784570 F166D20B   *....1.....1...1...08K...2...1.K.*
0BA640    2001F28C 4132000D 412800C0 4570F158    4570F166 58D0D004 9200F20C 98ECD00C   *..2............1...1.......2.....*
0BA660    07FE509B F194589C 900418BC 47F0F06E    41600005 4150F25E 47F0F09A 41600005   *....1.........00........2..00.....*
0BA680    4150F263 47F0F09A 5810F184 5811005C    0501040A 07F74820 F26C5810 F18C0501   *..2..00...1............7..2...1...*
0BA6A0    02004700 000092F0 20004030 F26C07F7    000B4FCC 000B6648 00000000 000B7706   *........0.. .2..7.................*
0BA6C0    04000000 00000001 00000000 00000000    00000000 00000000 00000000 00000000   *................................*
0BA6E0    00000000 00000000 00000000 00000000    00000000 B0649620 B00191C0 C9134740   *.............................I.. *
0BA700    C27A5840 C9A0910F 40014780 C3684150    B05059B0 CA204770 C0F0943F C9139640   *B.. I... ...C...............0..I.. *
0BA720    C9139201 B0989502 B0644770 C1769202    B0989240 B06A9200 B0829220 00000010   *I.............A....... .............*
0BA740  K E3D9C1C3 C5C2C1C3 D24040D9 D6E4E3C9    D5C54040 C3C1D3D3 M C440C6 D9D6D440   *TRACEBACK  ROUTINE  CALLED FROM *
0BA760    C9E2D540 404040C5 C74B4040 F1F44040    40D9C5C7 4B4040F1 F5404040 D9C5C74B   *ISN   REG.  14   REG.  15   REG.*
0BA780    404040F0 404040D9 C5C74B40 4040F1C9    C2C3D6D4 D3C4C6C9 D5470000 0000B010   *   0   REG.   1IBCOMLDFIO........*
0BA7A0    00000000 00000000 E3D9C1C3 C5C2C1C3    D240E3C5 D9D4C9D5 C1E3C5C4 C5D5E3D9   *.........TRACEBACK TERMINATEDENTR*
0BA7C0    E840D7D6 C9D5E37E D200200C 50014348    00000002 00000004 00000006 00000008   *Y POINT.K..........................*
0BA7E0    0000000A 0000000C 0000000E 00000010    00000006 00000003 00000048 00000000   *................................*

LOAD MODULE    IGC0A05A

          G        N                             L        I        J        H
0BD040                                                                 41800099 1B114313   *................................*
0BD060    00001A81 41330001 95FF3000 47806068    1BEE1BFF 1B001B11 43E30000 43030001   *..........................T.......*
0BD080    8CE00004 88F0001C 8C000004 8810001C    1A2044E0 60701A1E 41818001 44F06076   *......0...........................0..*
0BD0A0    F384D069 D069DC07 D06962C6 41FFF001    44F0607C 47F066F8 413E3003 47F06010   *3...........F..0..0...0.8......0..*
0BD0C0    41330001 47F060E2 D2008000 3002D200    D0692000 C2008000 D0695050 D08C5000   *......0.SK......K......K..............*
0BD0E0    D12094FC D1235B00 D1201A10 5800D120    41110003 5010D064 94FCD067 D703D06C   *J...J...J......J..................P...*
0BD100    D06C1810 54006290 19014780 608C1B10    4010D06C 5810D064 4A10D06C 1B005D00   *.................. ................*
0BD120    66804000 D06A1211 4770611C 4810D06A    12114770 60E85850 D08C5860 D12407F5   *.. ....................Y......J..5*
0BD140    4120D121 45B06236 582CD120 413062C4    48A0D06A 4BA0D06C 88A00002 45B0623E   *..J.........J.....D......................*
0BD160    46A06104 9640D112 455062DA 94BFD112    47F060DE 18A15810 D1204B10 D06C5010   *..... J.........J..0........J........*
0BD180    00704120 D07145B0 62364810 D06C8810    00011A31 5820D120 45B0623E 5020D120   *............................J.........J.*
0BD1A0    9640D112 455062DA 94BFD112 4810D06C    12114770 61984700 615E4110 0001191A   *. J.........J............................*
0BD1C0    47B061A6 18125B10 6680D51F 10002000    477061A6 4810D06E 41110001 4010D06E   *............N......................... ...*
0BD1E0    41220020 5020D120 46A0615E 47F061B0    1B114010 D06C46A0 611E47F0 60D44810   *.......J........0..... ...........0.M..*
0BD200    D06E1211 4780619E 5810D120 4800D06E    89000005 1B105010 D0704120 D0714810   *...........J...............................*
0BD220    D06E0610 12114770 6202D203 D09F629D    41306294 45B0623E D20DD0AA 62A29640   *...........K..................K....... *
0BD240    D1124550 62DA94BF D112D701 D06ED06E    12AA4780 60D447F0 619ED204 D09F629D   *J.........J.P..............M.0..K......*
0BD260    41306297 45B0623E 9260D0AB 5810D120    5B106680 5010D070 41200071 4130629A   *..................J.........................*
0BD280    45B0623E D20DD0B2 62A247F0 61E64130    62BC47F0 65744180 D09995FF 30004780   *.....K........0.W......0...............*
0BD2A0    627C1B00 43030000 1B114313 00011A80    44106284 F384D070 D070DC07 D07062C6   *.........................3..........F*
0BD2C0    41111001 4410628A 41330002 41220004    47F0623E 41330001 07FBD078 D200D070   *.......................0............K...*
0BD2E0    2000D200 8000D070 FFFFFFE0 0B02FF0C    02FF1302 FFD3C9D5 C5E240E2 C1D4C540   *..K........................LINES SAME *
0BD300    C1E240C1 C2D6E5C5 0002FF09 0312031B    03240330 03390342 034B03FF 0903FF12   *AS ABOVE...............................*
0BD320    03FF1B03 FF2403FF 3003FF39 03FF4203    FF0098E0 D08012EE 47806310 D27CF000   *.............................K.0.*
```

2. Assembly Language Listing

a. Base

The first step in determining the value of pertinent variables is to determine the contents of each base register assigned to the variables. The variables of interest are ITEST, M, N, and the Mth and Nth positions of the ID Array.

To determine the appropriate base register, one must first locate the variable names ITEST, M, N, and ID in the Assembly Language listing for the source statements of interest; that is, #3 and #4. See Figure 5.6, letter 'C'. Any occurrence of the variable name within a pertinent source statement is sufficient. The Base Register can be found as the right-most number within the parentheses to the left of the variable of interest. As can be seen, Base Register 10 has been assigned to all four variables. See letter 'D'.

Next, the contents of the base register must be determined. Recall that the base registers are located in an area of the dump called REGS AT ENTRY TO ABEND, just before the printing of main storage. The Base Address located in Base Register 10 is 0BA7D0. This is the base address for the variables ITEST, M, N, and the ID Array. See Figure 5.7, letter 'E'.

In this example, Base Register 10 has been assigned by the compiler to all four variables. For larger programs it is usually the case that two or more base registers will be utilized. The exact base register can always be determined from the appropriate Assembly Language statement for the variables of interest.

b. Displacement

Each variable is 'displaced', or located, a specified distance from a base address. To locate Displacement, the Assembly Language listing must again be referenced.

The Displacement for each variable is located to the left of the parentheses. See Figure 5.6, letter 'F'. The Displacement for the variables ITEST, M, N, and ID are Decimal 40, 32, 36, and 0, respectively. Because the base address to which displacement is to be added is represented in hexadecimal form, a conversion of the Displacement from decimal to hexadecimal is necessary. Reviewing Chapter 2's technique of decimal to hexadecimal conversion, the respective Displacements become 28, 20, 24, and 0.

The starting address of each variable is calculated by adding the Base Address to the Displacement as follows:

	ITEST	M	N	ID
Base Register 10	0BA7D0	0BA7D0	0BA7D0	0BA7D0
Displacement	+ 28	+ 20	+ 24	+ 0
Address of Variable	0BA7F8	0BA7F0	0BA7F4	0BA7D0

The starting address of the program variables ITEST, M, N, and the ID Array are 0BA7F8, 0BA7F0, 0BA7F4, and 0BA7D0, respectively. Once these locations are found in main storage, a four byte field will be marked off because FORTRAN variables are stored internally as four byte fields unless the programming technique of double precision to eight bytes is utilized. Two byte (halfword) fields can also be described.

The main storage portion of the dump can now be accessed.

3. Variable Location

a. Single Value Variables

The variables ITEST, M, and N are single value variable items just like STATE4 and STATE-DATA in the previous example. As determined from the source statement, they do not represent an array or group of values. As such, when the Address of the Variable is located, a four byte field can be directly marked off.

First, page down the left-hand side of the print of main storage until the nearest address is found which does not exceed the starting address of interest. For ITEST, M, and N this would be 0BA7E0, as Address 0BA7F8, 0BA7F0, and 0BA7F4 are located on that print line. See Figure 5.8, letter 'G'.

160

Reviewing Chapter 2's technique of address lookup, the first character encountered at Address OBA7F8 for ITEST is a zero. See letter 'H'.
Counting off a length of four bytes, the complete character string for
variable ITEST is 00000048. Likewise, the first character encountered
at Address OBA7F0 for M is a zero. See letter 'I'. Counting off a
length of four bytes, the complete character string for variable M is
00000006. Finally, the first character encountered at Address OBA7F4
for N is a zero. See letter 'J'. Counting off a length of four bytes,
the complete character string for variable N is 00000003.

FORTRAN Integer variables are those which begin with the letter I
through N. All others are Real. Non-numeric variables can begin with
any letter. FORTRAN language conventions allow a programmer to modify
the above rules, however. A check of the program should be made.

An interpretation of the above character strings can be easily
accomplished. Because all FORTRAN Integer variables are internally
stored as Binary, a direct hexadecimal interpretation of the above
values can be made. Utilizing Chapter 2's technique of converting to
decimal notation, the values for ITEST, M, and N are found to be 72, 6,
and 3, respectively.

Fields described as Binary in COBOL programs are denoted as USAGE
COMP in the DMAP. Regardless of the programming language utilized,
Binary fields referenced in main storage can be converted directly from
hexadecimal to decimal.

b. Variable Arrays

An array represents a multi-occurrence of values associated with a
given variable name. Positions to be accessed within an array, such as
the ID Array, are determined by program logic.

In the preceding example, the Mth and Nth positions of the ID
Array are multiplied by each other to determine ITEST. See Figure 5.5,
letter 'A'. With M equal to six and N equal to three, it can be determined that the sixth and third positions of the ID Array were being
accessed, i.e., ITEST = ID(6) * ID(3). The number or variable indicating
the position within an array is referred to as a subscript or index.

Paging down the left-hand side of the print of main storage, the nearest address which does not exceed Address OBA7D0 of the ID Array is OBA7C0. See Figure 5.8, letter 'K'. The first character encountered at Address OBA7D0 is a zero. See letter 'L'. Counting off a length of four bytes, the complete character string for the first position of the ID Array is 00000002. Because interest is in the third and sixth position of the ID Array, another two fields of four bytes each must be counted off. The complete character string for the third position of the ID Array is 00000006. See letter 'M'. Continuing to count and moving to the next line, the complete character string for the sixth position of the ID Array is 0000000C. See letter 'N'. Converting to decimal, it can be seen that a C (or 12) was multiplied by 6 giving an ITEST value of 72 as follows:

$$ITEST = ID(M) * ID(N)$$
$$72 = ID(6) * ID(3)$$
$$72 = 12 \quad * 6$$

The value of any program variable at the time of abend can be determined, regardless of the programming language utilized. A thorough review of program logic can now be accomplished. It will be seen that the values for M, N, and the ID Array were read into the program from an input file. An appropriate correction to prevent the loop from occurring can then be made.

To determine the value of pertinent PL1 program variables, a breakdown and analysis of machine instructions are necessary. This subject will be covered in Chapter 6.

D. PROGRAM DATA DEFINITION

Once the location of a given address in main storage has been determined, an interpretation of the respective field must be accomplished. Programmers define data fields in many forms. As a result, character strings found at any particular location in storage must be related to their usage as defined in the program being executed. A synopsis of Chapter 2's data interpretation techniques as relates to programmer-defined fields follows.

Figure 5.9 Synopsis of Data Representation Forms

Data Representation	Program Definition		Character String	Interpretation (Decimal)
	COBOL	FORTRAN		
CHARACTER FORMAT (External Decimal, Zoned Decimal, Unpacked Format)	USAGE DISPLAY	ALPHA and INTEGER Formats	F1F2F3F4	1234
INTERNAL DECIMAL (Packed Format)	USAGE COMP-3	Not Applicable	1234F	1234
BINARY	USAGE COMP	INTEGER Un-format	4D2	1234
EXTERNAL FLOATING POINT	USAGE DISPLAY E Picture	REAL E Format	+12.34Eb02	1234.
INTERNAL FLOATING POINT	USAGE COMP-1 or COMP-2	REAL Un-format	460004D2	1234.

The length of a variable as it resides in main storage is dependent upon two factors:

1. Programmer Definition
2. Program Language Conventions

A check of the source program can usually be made to verify the length of a given variable. On occasion however, the length is not defined in the program because various programming conventions are in effect. For example, field lengths are not defined when the Internal

Floating Point form of data representation is utilized. FORTRAN REAL
variables and COBOL USAGE COMP-1 items default to a length of four bytes.
A FORTRAN Double Precision of the above or utilization of COBOL's
USAGE COMP-2 defines a length of eight bytes to the above field. In
other words, Internal Floating Point field lengths are not directly
specified in the program itself.

Field lengths for all other forms of COBOL data representation are
programmer defined via the Picture Clause. For FORTRAN programs, however, program language conventions take on more significance. All
FORTRAN variables are automatically converted by the compiler to four
byte fields. If the Double Precision feature is utilized, eight byte
field lengths will result. Two byte fields can also be defined. In
addition, Integer and Real fields are converted to Binary and Internal
Floating Point, respectively, even though they may not have been originally defined as such.

In the breakdown and analysis of machine instructions to be covered
in the next chapter, some COBOL variables will be found to be represented in Internal Decimal even though they were defined as External
Decimal in the program. This is because the compiler generates instructions to automatically convert from the Unpacked to Packed Format prior
to the execution of various test and arithmetic operations.

In summary, actual data representation of program variables as
found in main storage depends upon the programming language utilized
and its conventions, as well as programmer-defined fields within the
program itself. The exact length of a COBOL variable can always be
determined from the DMAP. FORTRAN variables are usually four bytes
but can be two or eight bytes if the halfword or doubleword feature
has been utilized.

E. VARIABLE VALUE SUMMARY

After isolating the problem source statement, the value of pertinent variables should be determined. The following set of step-by-
step procedures apply specifically to COBOL and FORTRAN programs;
however, the principles utilized apply to all programming languages.

Determining the value of PL1 program variables is discussed in detail in the next chapter.

1. Determine Pertinent Variables.

   Those variables coded directly in the problem source statement or related to the problem are considered pertinent.

2. Locate Variable Name.
   a. COBOL   -- In DMAP under heading SOURCE NAME.
   b. FORTRAN -- In right-hand portion of Assembly Language Listing at or near problem statement.

3. Determine Base Register and Base Address.
   a. COBOL   -- Base Register assignment in DMAP under heading BASE. Go to Register Assignment Area and note Base Register.
   b. FORTRAN -- Note Base Register (right-hand number in parentheses) to left of Variable Name in Assembly Language Listing.
   c. Obtain Base Address from appropriate register in REGS AT ENTRY TO ABEND Area just prior to the print of Main Storage.

4. Determine Displacement.
   a. COBOL   -- In DMAP under heading DISPL.
   b. FORTRAN -- In Assembly Language Listing to the left of parentheses. Convert from Decimal to Hexadecimal.

5. Determine Variable Length.
   a. COBOL   -- In DMAP under heading DEFINITION.
   b. FORTRAN -- Four bytes; eight bytes if Double Precision; two bytes if Halfword defined.

6. Determine Data Representation Form.
   a. COBOL   -- In DMAP under heading USAGE.

      Character Format, i.e., External Decimal, for DISPLAY Variables;
      Internal Decimal for COMP-3 Variables;
      Binary for COMP Variables;

External Floating Point for DISPLAY E Picture
Variables;

Internal Floating Point for COMP-1 and COMP-2
Variables.

b.   FORTRAN -- From Source Program Listing.

Character Format, i.e., Unpacked Format, for Alpha
Variables;

Binary for INTEGER Variables;

Internal Floating Point for REAL Variables.

7.   Add Base Address to Displacement giving Address of Variable in
Main Storage.

8.   Page down left-hand side of the print of Main Storage and locate Address.

9.   Delineate data field using appropriate Length.

10. Determine Variable Value by interpreting character string in
relation to form of data representation utilized.

Although the above procedures are specific to OS and OS/VS environments, the principle of locating and interpreting pertinent program variables can be applied to DOS applications as well. The specific
language of the program to be executed is of little concern. Problems resulting in storage dumps are often encountered when attempting
to execute COBOL, FORTRAN, PL1, and Assembly language programs in all
application, system, and data base environments.

F. WORKSHOP PROBLEMS

1. COBOL Variables (OCB)

   a. Description

   Figures 5.10 through 5.13 consist of selected pages of the same run
which abended with a OCB Completion Code in Chapter 4's workshop. The
problem source statement was found to be COMPUTE ITEST = DATA-ARRAY
(SUB-M) / DATA-ARRAY (SUB-N). The value of pertinent variables at the
time of the abend can now be determined.

   Recall that a OCB Storage Dump refers to a situation in which the
program is attempting to divide by zero. A OCB will also result if
the quotient length, as defined by the programmer, has been exceeded.
This could also be caused by dividing a very small decimal equivalent
into a relatively large number. In either case, with the problem source
statement having been isolated, the value of pertinent program variables
should be determined.

   Procedures for determining COBOL variables are identical regardless
of programming level utilized. Register Assignment, Displacement,
Length, and Data Representation are determined from the DMAP. The Base
Register is determined from the Register Assignment Area. The Base
Address is found in the Registers At Entry To Abend. After Base is
added to Displacement, main storage is accessed, and the appropriate
length marked off. An interpretation of the character string can then
be made depending upon the form of data representation utilized.

   A problem solution can be found in Appendix A.

Figure 5.10 Portion of COBOL Source Program Listing (OCB)

```
00039              01   CTL-CARD.
C0040                   02   DATA-ARRAY        OCCURS 8 TIMES        PICTURE 99.
00041                   02   NUM                                     PICTURE 99.
00042                   02   DEN                                     PICTURE 99.
00043                   02   FILLER           PICTURE X(30),  VALUE IS SPACES.
00044              01   PRT-RECORD.
00045                   02   CARRIAGE-CONTROL      PICTURE X.
00046                   02   FILLER               PICTURE X(4), VALUE IS SPACES.
00047                   02   VARIABLE-NAME        PICTURE X(8).
00048                   02   VARIABLE-VALUE       OCCURS 8 TIMES, PICTURE XX.
00049                   02   FILLER               PICTURE X(55), VALUE IS SPACES.
00050              PROCEDURE DIVISION.
00051              OPEN-FILES.
00052                   OPEN INPUT DATA-FILE.
00053                   OPEN OUTPUT MESSAGE-FILE.
00054              READ-CTL-CARD.
00055                   MOVE SPACES TO CONTROL-CARD, PRINT-RECORD, VARIABLE-NAME.
00056                   MOVE ZEROS TO NUM, DEN, SUB-M, SUB-N, ITEST.
00057                   READ DATA-FILE INTO CTL-CARD,
00058                        AT END GO TO CLOSE-FILES.
00059                   MOVE NUM TO SUB-M.
00060                   MOVE DEN TO SUB-N.
00061              COMPUTE-ITEST.
00062                   COMPUTE ITEST = DATA-ARRAY (SUB-M) / DATA-ARRAY (SUB-N).
C0063                   MOVE '   ID = ' TO VARIABLE-NAME.
00064                   MOVE DATA-ARRAY (1) TO VARIABLE-VALUE (1).
00065                   MOVE DATA-ARRAY (2) TO VARIABLE-VALUE (2).
00066                   MOVE DATA-ARRAY (3) TO VARIABLE-VALUE (3).
00067                   MOVE DATA-ARRAY (4) TO VARIABLE-VALUE (4).
00068                   MOVE DATA-ARRAY (5) TO VARIABLE-VALUE (5).
00069                   MOVE DATA-ARRAY (6) TO VARIABLE-VALUE (6).
00070                   MOVE DATA-ARRAY (7) TO VARIABLE-VALUE (7).
00071                   MOVE DATA-ARRAY (8) TO VARIABLE-VALUE (8).
00072                   WRITE PRINT-RECORD FROM PRT-RECORD
00073                        AFTER ADVANCING TO-TOP-OF-PAGE.
00074                   MOVE SPACES TO VARIABLE-VALUE (2), VARIABLE-VALUE (3),
00075                        VARIABLE-VALUE (4), VARIABLE-VALUE (5),
00076                        VARIABLE-VALUE (6), VARIABLE-VALUE (7),
00077                        VARIABLE-VALUE (8)
00078                   MOVE '    M = ' TO VARIABLE-NAME.
00079                   MOVE NUM TO VARIABLE-VALUE (1).
00080                   WRITE PRINT-RECORD FROM PRT-RECORD
00081                        AFTER ADVANCING 2 LINES.
00082                   MOVE '    N = ' TO VARIABLE-NAME.
00083                   MOVE DEN TO VARIABLE-VALUE (1).
00084                   WRITE PRINT-RECORD FROM PRT-RECORD
00085                        AFTER ADVANCING 2 LINES.
00086                   MOVE 'ITEST = ' TO VARIABLE-NAME.
00087                   MOVE ITEST TO VARIABLE-VALUE (1).
00088                   WRITE PRINT-RECORD FROM PRT-RECORD
00089                        AFTER ADVANCING 2 LINES.
00090                   MOVE 'NORMAL E' TO VARIABLE-NAME.
00091                   MOVE 'OJ' TO VARIABLE-VALUE (1).
00092                   WRITE PRINT-RECORD FROM PRT-RECORD
00093                        AFTER ADVANCING 4 LINES.
00094              CLOSE-FILES.
00095                   CLOSE DATA-FILE, MESSAGE-FILE.
00096              STOP-RUN.
00097                   STOP RUN.
```

Figure 5.11 Data Map on DMAP (OCB)

INTRNL NAME	LVL	SOURCE NAME	BASE	DISPL	INTRNL NAME	DEFINITION	USAGE	R	O	Q	M	F
DNM=1-122	FD	DATA-FILE	DCB=01		DNM=1-122	DS OCL80	QSAM					F
DNM=1-144	01	CONTROL-CARD	BL=1	000	DNM=1-144	DS 16C	GROUP					
DNM=1-169	02	DATA-VALUE	BL=1	000	DNM=1-169	DS 2C	DISP					
DNM=1-189	02	NUMERATOR	BL=1	013	DNM=1-189	DS 2C	DISP					
DNM=1-208	02	DENOMINATOR	BL=1	012	DNM=1-208	DS 2C	DISP					
DNM=1-229	02	FILLER	BL=1	014	DNM=1-229	DS 60C	DISP					
DNM=1-240	FD	MESSAGE-FILE	DCB=02		DNM=1-240		QSAM					F
DNM=1-265	01	PRINT-RECORD	BL=2	000	DNM=1-265	DS 133C	DISP					
DNM=1-287	77	SUB-M	BL=3	000	DNM=1-287	DS 2C	COMP					
DNM=1-302	77	SUB-N	BL=3	002	DNM=1-302	DS 2C	COMP					
DNM=1-317	77	ITEST	BL=3	004	DNM=1-317	DS 2C	DISP-NM					
DNM=1-332	01	CTL-CARD	BL=3	003	DNM=1-332	DS OCL80	GROUP		O			
DNM=1-353	02	DATA-ARRAY	BL=3	008	DNM=1-353	DS 2C	DISP-NM					
DNM=1-373	02	NUM	BL=3	018	DNM=1-373	DS 2C	DISP-NM					
DNM=1-386	02	DEN	BL=3	01A	DNM=1-386	DS 2C	DISP-NM					
DNM=1-402	02	FILLER	BL=3	01C	DNM=1-402	DS 60C	DISP					
DNM=1-416	01	PRT-RECORD	BL=3	058	DNM=1-416	DS OCL94	GROUP					
DNM=1-439	02	CARRIAGE-CONTROL	BL=3	058	DNM=1-439	DS 1C	DISP					
DNM=1-465	02	FILLER	BL=3	059	DNM=1-465	DS 4C	DISP					
DNM=1-479	02	VARIABLE-NAME	BL=3	05D	DNM=1-479	DS 8C	DISP					
DNM=2-000	02	VARIABLE-VALUE	BL=3	065	DNM=2-000	DS 2C	DISP		O			
DNM=2-024	02	FILLER	BL=3	075	DNM=2-024	DS 65C	DISP					

Figure 5.12 Register Assignment Area (OCB)

```
              PARAM CELLS              0055C
              RPTSAV AREA              0056C
              CHECKPT CTR              0056C
              VCON TBL                 00570
              DEBUG TABLE              00570

LITERAL POOL (HEX)

005D8 (LIT+0)     F0F00000  00020000  00000002  48004805  EF07C040  4040C9C4
005F0 (LIT+24)    407E4040  4040D440  7E404040  40D5407E  40C9E3C5  E2E3407E
00608 (LIT+48)    4CD5D6D9  D4C1D340  C5D6D1


              PGT                      00590

              OVERFLOW CELLS           00590
              VIRTUAL CELLS            00590
              PROCEDURE NAME CELLS     005AC
              GENERATED NAME CELLS     005B0
              DCB ADDRESS CELLS        005CC
              VNI CELLS                005D4
              LITERALS                 005D8
              DISPLAY LITERALS         00613


   REGISTER ASSIGNMENT

   REG 6    BL =3
   REG 7    BL =1
   REG 8    BL =2

WORKING-STORAGE STARTS AT LOCATION 00088 FOR A LENGTH OF 00088.
```

Figure 5.13 First Page of OCB Main Storage

```
REGS AT ENTRY TO ABEND

   FLTR 0-6   CCCCCCCCCCCCCCCC   000000000000000    00000000080018E14   0003533000000000C8

   REGS 0-7   0000000A   00000006   0020A87C   00000003   0020A882   0000024E   0020AEE8   00211IE8
   REGS 8-15  0020A88    0020A24E   0020A7E8   0020A7E8   0020AD78   0020AB10   5020AECE   002FDDA8

LOAD MODULE    MAIN

20A7E0   40404040 40404040 40404040 40404040   40404040 4040C4040 40404040 40404040   *..............*
20A800   40404040 40404040 40404040 40404040   40404040 40404040 40404040 40404040   *..............*
20A820   40404040 40404040 40404040 40404040   40404040 40404001 12116CF1 12116CF1   *..........1..*
20A840   D4C5E309 D6404040 C1F7F2F0 40404040   40404001 12117CF1 D4C5E3D9 ....1METR*  *METRO A720  ....1METR*
20A860   D6404040 C1F7F2F1 40404040 00000000   F0F0B0FL 40F240F4 40F040F8 00.1 2 4 0 8* *G  A721 .....00.1 2 4 0 8*
20A880   F1F0F1F2 F1F4F1F6 40F640F3 40404040   40404040 40404040 40404040 40404040   *10121416 6 3 ....*
20A8A0   40404040 40404040 12404040 40404040   40404040 40404040 40404040 40404040   *...... 725 .......*
20A8C0   40404040 12404040 40404040 40404040   40404040 40F7F2F5 40404040 40404040   *.. . 725 ......*
2CA8E0   40404040 40404040 40404040 40404040   40404040 40404040 40404040 40404040   *..............*
20A900   40404040 40408277 D202B25D 00000000   00000000 00000000 0520C232 .....B..   *..........B..*
20A920   40404040 40408277 D202B25D 00000000   00000000 80000000 05200232 .....B..   *.....K......B.*
20A940   0820A80E 00000001 00000000 00000000   00000000 80000000 4620AEE2 ....S.     *......S..*
20A960   CCC00C00 CCC0C0C0 CCC0C0C0 00410000   02211190 00000001 4620AEE2 ....S.     *.......S*
20A980   9020A92C 00404800 000355A4 122FEE08   0020F00Ab J620BFCE 28022828 ....Y.     *......Y...*
2CA9A0   00211160 00211238 0021IIE8 00000050   00000001 CC2FD4F8 00000000 ...M8...   *......M8....*
20A9C0   CCC0C0C0 CCC0C0C0 00000000 00000000   00000000 00130000 00000000           *..........*
20AA00   CCC0C0C0 00000000 0520C232 00000000   00000001 CCC00000 00480000 ...B...    *.........B....*
20AAA20  00004000 00000000 46C00001 8420A908   0680048 00035524 922FCDC0 002FDC98 ...J.   *........J......*
20AA40   0720BFCE 04090085 28022828 42210F90   0021195 J0211020 00000001           *..........*
20AA60   CCC0C000 002FC8A0 C5EF0700 00000000   00000003 CCC00000 00000000 ...H...    *.....H.......*
20AA80   00940076 91012008 40404040 40404040   40404040 40404040 40404040           *..........*
20AAA0   40404040 40404040 40404040 40404040   40404040 40404040 40404040           *..........*
LINES 20AAC0-20AAEC SAME AS ABOVE
20AB00   40404040 40404040 40404040 4C995090   00030402 00211168 CC2113B0 50208254 ...DB...  *.....DB......*
20AB20   00208452 5020AECE 122FEB08 0020A95C   0020A95C 5C136ED8 0020A908          *......Y......Q*
20AB40   5020B280 0020AB70 0020A7E8 C020AA88   422FE840 002FDDA8 32023048 00000000 ...Y.. Y ... *.......Y.......*
20AB60   00000000 0020AUFC 00000000 00000000   00223FCE 0020067C FDC00008 00211778 ...F...8*  *..........F...8*
20AB80   CCC38888 5CC36EC8 00C38D78 00211768   00035300 J003D018 8C20A7F4 00210B24E ...Q....4  *....Q....4*
20ABA0   0020A7E8 0020A7E8 0020A2J78 7000472U   B1E22401 F03CF03C 4730B1E2 5890201C SM.0..S... *...Y..Y...SM.0..S...*
20ABC0   4A9OF03C 58E02040 43AQF010 06A044AA   B9E44780 31E202C1 2C10B6CA 96032008 .0...U...SK  *...0....U...SK...*
20ABE0   41E0R2C8 1255478E 0620B98C 0020B390   22009200 00009200 5C3450C0 501C1B11 .0...0...0  *.0.....0...0..*
20AC00   40105010 07FE9101 20084780 B21E1255   4780333C 96205CC3 47F0B38C 1B994390 9..0...0...0  *.0......0...0...*
20AC20   7C004110 202C948F 20084FF5 323047FD   B24D47FD 328047FD 323047FD A3A49104 .0...0  *.9...0...0...0*
20AC40   40084780 B26A9110 F0244780 B26A9602   1004922U J00558F1 0085B0FF 005805EF .0...1  *....0..1...*
```

b. Workshop

    1. Pertinent Variables

Variable Name	Single Value or Array?
_____	_____
_____	_____
_____	_____
_____	_____

    2. DMAP Reference

	Single Value Variables		Variable Array	
Variable Name	_____	_____	_____	_____
Base Register Assignment	_____	_____	_____	_____
Base Register Number	_____	_____	_____	_____
Base Address	_____	_____	_____	_____
Displacement	_____	_____	_____	_____
Field Length (bytes)	_____	_____	_____	_____
Form of Data Representation	_____	_____	_____	_____

    3. Single Value Variable Location and Interpretation

        Variable Name .... _____ _____ _____

        Base + Displacement .... _____ _____ _____

        Character String .... _____ _____ _____

        Decimal Interpretation .... _____ _____ _____

        How do you account for the value of ITEST?

        _____

    4. Variable Array Location and Interpretation

        Variable Name .... _____

        Base + Displacement ...... _____

        Position or Index .... _____ _____

        Character String .... _____ _____

        Decimal Interpretation ... _____ _____

        Which of the above positions of the DATA-ARRAY is equal to

        zero? _____ If a zero is not found, recheck data

        locations and respective interpretations.

5. Problem Analysis

Summarize your findings. Assuming that the erroneous data was read in from an input file, what would your problem solution be?

_____

_____

_____

_____

_____

_____

_____

_____

_____

_____

2. FORTRAN Variables (OC5)

a. Description

Figures 5.14 through 5.16 consist of selected pages of the same run which abended with User Code 240 and was interpreted as a OC5 Storage Dump in Chapter 4's workshop. The problem source statement in Subroutine COMP was found to be 100 ITEST = ID(M) * ID(N). The value of pertinent variables at the time of abend can now be determined.

Recall that a OC5 Storage Dump refers to the calculation of invalid addresses. This is generally caused by faulty program logic or invalid program variable indexes. With the source statement having been isolated, the value of pertinent program variables should be determined. Variables M and N are the two subscripts considered pertinent.

Procedures for determining FORTRAN G-Level variables are similar to H-Level. As discussed in Chapter 4, H-Level Assembly Language listings consist of a modified format. The same procedures can be followed, however. The following example utilizes the FORTRAN G-Level compiler. Base Register, Displacement, and Length are determined from the Assembly

Language listing. The form of data representation is Binary for Integer variables and Internal Floating Point for Real variables. Unless specified otherwise, variables beginning with the letters I through N are Integer while all others are Real. They are also four bytes in length.

The Base Address is found in the Registers At Entry To Abend. After Base is added to Displacement, main storage is accessed, and the appropriate length marked off. An interpretation of the character string can then be made depending upon the form of data representation utilized.

A problem solution can be found in Appendix A.

Figure 5.14 FORTRAN Source Program Listing for MAIN and COMP (OC5)

```
FORTRAN IV G LEVEL  21                    MAIN

           C       PROGRAM TO CREATE CORE DUMPS
   0001             COMMON ID(8), M, N, ITEST
   0002             READ (5,100) ID, M, N
   0003         100 FORMAT (10I2)
   0004             CALL COMP
   0005             WRITE (6,200) ID, M, N, ITEST
   0006         200 FORMAT ('-', T6, '   ID = ', 8I2//,
                  1              T6, '    M = ', I2//,
                  2              T6, '    N = ', I2//,
                  3              T6, 'ITEST = ', I2////,
                  4              T6, 'END OF JOB')
   0007             STOP
   0008             END



FORTRAN IV G LEVEL  21                    COMP

   0001             SUBROUTINE COMP
   0002             COMMON ID(8)
   0003         100 ITEST = ID(M) * ID(N)
   0004         150 IF(ITEST.GE.2.AND.ITEST.LE.224) GO TO 100
   0005             WRITE (6,200)
   0006         200 FORMAT ('1','ITEST OUT OF LIMITS')
   0007         300 RETURN
   0008             END
```

Figure 5.15 Portion of Assembly Language Listing for COMP (OC5)

```
FORTRAN IV G LEVEL   21                    COMP

LOCATION   STA NUM    LABEL    OP       OPERAND              BCD OPERAND
 000000                        BC       15,12(0,15)
 000004                        DC       06C3D6D4
 000008                        DC       D7404040
 00000C                        STM      14,12,12(13)
 000010                        LM       2,3,40(15)
 000014                        LR       4,13
 000016                        L        13,36(0,15)
 00001A                        ST       13,8(0,4)
 00001E                        STM      3,4,0(13)
 000022                        BCR      15,2
 000024                        DC       00000000             A4
 000028                        DC       00000000             A20
 00002C                        DC       00000000             A36
 000118            A20         BALR     2,0
 00011A                        L        3,6(0,2)
 00011E                        BCR      15,3
 000120                        DC       00000000             A52
 000124            A36         L        1,4(0,13)
 000128                        L        1,24(0,1)
 00012C                        L        13,4(0,13)
 000130                        L        14,12(0,13)
 000134                        LM       2,12,28(13)
 000138                        MVI      12(13),255
 00013C                        BCR      15,14
 00013E     3      100         L        8,120(0,13)          M
 000142                        SLA      8,2(0)
 000146                        A        8,216(0,13)
 00014A                        L        10,72(0,13)
 00014E                        L        1,0(8,10)            ID
 000152                        L        9,124(0,13)          N
 000156                        SLA      9,2(0)
 00015A                        A        9,216(0,13)
 00015E                        M        0,0(9,10)            ID
 000162                        ST       1,116(0,13)          ITEST
 000166     4      150         L        0,116(0,13)          ITEST
 00016A                        C        0,220(0,13)
 00016E                        L        0,224(0,13)
 000172                        BALR     14,0
 000174                        BC       11,6(0,14)
 000178                        SR       0,0
 00017A                        L        1,116(0,13)          ITEST
 00017E                        C        1,228(0,13)
 000182                        LA       1,1(0,0)
 000186                        BALR     14,0
 000188                        BC       13,6(0,14)
 00018C                        SR       1,1
 00018E                        NR       1,0
 000190                        LTR      1,1
 000192                        L        14,100(0,13)         100
 000196                        BCR      7,14
 000198     5                  L        15,112(0,13)         IBCOM#
 00019C                        BAL      14,4(0,15)
 0001A0                        DC       00000006
 0001A4                        DC       00000080
 0001A8                        BAL      14,16(0,15)
 0001AC     7      300         SR       15,15
 0001AE                        L        1,0(0,13)
```

Figure 5.16 First Page of OC5 Main Storage

```
REGS AT ENTRY TO ABEND

  FLTR 0-6     4040404OC2C2C2C1   C6D5C3F0C3C4C2C3   0000000000000000

  REGS 0-7     FF000010   800000F0   420F2F02   000F2F26   000F2C30   000F3F30   00358E4    0003DEE0
  REGS 8-15    6382441C   00036278   000F87D0   00037068   000F2C30   000F2E18   420F2D96   000F2DE8

LOAD MODULE   MAIN

0F2C00   47F0F00C 06D4C1C9 D5404040 90ECD00C   9823F028 184D58D0 F02450D0 40089034   *.00..MAIN ......0....*
0F2C20   D00007F2 000F2C30 000F2D4A 000F2D38   000F2038 000FBF68 000F2E18 420F2096   *...2.........0......*
0F2C40   000F2DE8 FD000008 00000000 000F2D4A   000F2038 000FBF68 0003C070 000358E4   *...Y...............U*
0F2C60   0003DEE0 00035A68 00036278 000F87D0   00037068 000F2C30 000F87D0 000F2C30   *........Y...........*
0F2C80   000F3C20 000F4C10 000F5C00 CA0C8008   5044540E 000F2FCC 000F2DE8 02060A10   *.............Y......*
0F2CA0   0222021A 01601206 1A084040 40C9C440   7E400608 10021E1E 12061A08 40404040   * ........ ID .......*
0F2CC0   D440 7E40 10021E1E 12061A08 40404040   D5407E40 10021E1E 12061A08 C9E3C5E2   *M .N ......ITES*
0F2CE0   E340 7E40 10021E1E 1E1E1206 1A0AC5D5   C440C6C6 40D1D6C2 22265622 34026C00   *T ........END OF JOB..*
0F2D00   00000000 00000000 00000000 00000000   4E000000 00000000 00000000 58E0D00C   *....+...............*
0F2D20   4E000000 00000000 00000000 00000000   00000000 00000000 58D00004 58E0D00C   *+...................*
0F2D40   982CD01C 000F2C9C 07FE58F0 D06418CD   18D445E0 F04018DC 58A0D048 45E0F000   *.......0......0 ..0..*
0F2D60   00000005 000F2C9C 45E0F00C 45E0F010   04500008 58A0D048 45E0F008 0450A020   *..............0 ..0..*
0F2D80   45E0F008 0450A024 45E0F010 41100000   58F0D068 05EF4700 00458F0 D064Q700   *............0..0..*
0F2DA0   45E0F004 00000006 000F2CA2 45E0F00C   000F87D0 04500008 45E0F008 0450A020   *..........0......0..*
0F2DC0   45E0F008 0450A024 45E0F008 0450A028   45E0F010 58F0D064 45E0F034 05404040   *......0......00..0.*
0F2DE0   40F0C000 90180538 47F0F00C 06C3D6D4   D7404040 90ECD00C 000F2F0C 184D5800   *..0.......00.COMP...*
0F2E00   F0245000 40089034 D00007F2 000F2E18   000F2FOC 000F2FOC 840FB20E 1C0E9807   *0..........2.......*
0F2E20   540A4208 CA0C5803 CA0C1601 D230C8AE   CA14CA0C 6C165620 840FB20E 4C4C58E0   *...........K.H......*
0F2E40   CC04CC14 C832A009 0425B618 1255CC04   3A30CC14 CA0C340D 0538CA0C 000F2F26   *..............H....*
0F2E60   000F87D0 000F2E18 000F3E08 000F4DF8   000F50E8 47F09E8C 0538CA0C 000F2F26   *........8..Y.0......*
0F2E80   16014400 58D0A108 000F2FCC 5AD04004   58E09108 58F09008 021A01F1 1A13C9E3   *.......1..0...1.IT*
0F2EA0   C5E2E340 D6E4E340 D6C640D3 C9D4C9E3   E2224780 9EAE4530 00000000 00000000   *EST OUT OF LIMITS....*
0F2EC0   00000000 00000000 4E000000 00000000   00000000 00000002 4E000000 000000E0   *....+..........+....*
0F2EE0   00000000 00000000 00000000 00000000   FFFFFFFC 00000000 00000001 000000E0   *....................*
0F2F00   05205830 200607F3 000F2F26 5810D004   5810101B 5800D004 58E0D00C 982CD01C   *...........3........*
0F2F20   92FFD00C 07FE5880 D0788880 000025A80   DOD858A0 D0485818 A0005890 47B0E006   *...............Q....*
0F2F40   00025A90 D0D85C09 A0005010 D0745800   D0745900 D0DC5800 DOE005E0 47B0E006   *............Q.......*
0F2F60   1B005810 D0745910 D0E44110 000105E0   47D0E006 1B111410 12115BE0 D064077E   *.........U..........*
0F2F80   58F0D070 45E0F004 00000006 000F2E98   45E0F010 18FF5810 D0007F1 D2031000   *......0.......0....1K*
0F2FA0   40F5F7F3 F460D3D4 F140C3D6 D7E8D9C9   C7C8E340 C9C2D440 C3D609D7 4B40F1F9   * 5734-LMI COPYRIGHT IBM CORP. 19*
0F2FC0   F7F04040 F2F0F0F1 F5F14840 47F0F120   47F0F128 47F0F516 47F0FD5E 47F0F690   *70 20015L .01.05..05..06.*
0F2FE0   47F0FAF8 47F0FB00 47F0FB46 47F0FB94   47F0FCE8 47F0FD5E 47F0FD84 47F0FD98   *.0.8.0...0...0.Y.0...0..*
0F3000   47F0FDAC 47F0FDC0 00000005 47F0FDD4   00005810 FE385810 FE5C5810 000192FF   *.0...0...0.M.0.U...*
0F3020   FE505810 FE485810 FE4C5810 000F2FCC   FE545810 FE580700 000F31C4 000F2D38   *.................D...*
0F3040   FF3A9200 FF3A00E8 FFOF2D8C 000F2FCC   FD000008 000FBFF8 000F2D4A 000F2D38   *........Y.......8....*
0F3060   000FBF68 0003C070 000358E4 0003DEE0   00035A68 00036278 000F87D0 00037068   *.............U......*
0F3080   000F2C30 000F2C30 000F435E 010F2C00   000F310C 00145040 000F787C 440F3FDC   *.0.................*
0F30A0   000F7758 440F7A8E 440F7A8E 000FBD90   00000085 00000010 000F3F30 000F2FCC   *..............Q.....*
0F30C0   00000082 000F6DD8 840F79C0 840F7A4C   000F2C30 000F7758 00000000 00000000   *.........01..01...0...18*
0F30E0   000FBBC0 000FBBC0 00000050 92FFF1A9   47F0F12C 92FFF1A9 95FFF07C 4770F1F8   *..........1.1.0.....*
0F3100   90EDF07C 41300008 41D0F1A2 50E0FE0C   9200FE37 1B111B22 9012F10C 5810FE38   *.0...............1....*
0F3120   182ED207 FE94E000 9180FE94 4780F16C   5810F08C 41303004 9110FE94 4780F180   *...K.......1........*
0F3140   58532000 5050F10C 41303004 9120FE94   4780F194 58532000 5050F110 41303004   *........1.......1....*
0F3160   41E23000 50E0FE7C 5010FE3C 07FD41E0   F1BA0501 00F047F0 F1D85020 FEA44183   *.S.....1....0.0IQ.....*
0F3180   20001892 07FE1B77 5070FF08 5070FE28   5070FF0C 58A0FE98 91FFFE98 4750F7E8   *..................7Y*
```
```
                                                                                     176
```

b. Workshop

   1. Pertinent Variables

      Subscript Name   Single Value or Array?

      _____   _____

      _____   _____

   2. Assembly Language Listing Reference

      Variable Name .... _____ _____

      Base Register Number .... _____ _____

      Base Address .... _____ _____

      Decimal Displacement .... _____ _____

      Hexadecimal Displacement ..... _____ _____

      Field Length (bytes) .... _____ _____

      Form of Data Representation ... _____ _____

   3. Variable Location and Interpretation

      Variable Name .... _____ _____

      Base + Displacement .... _____ _____

      Character String .... _____ _____

      Decimal Interpretation .... _____ _____

      Can the above character strings be interpreted? Why not?

      _____

      _____

      _____

   4. Problem Analysis

      Summarize your findings. Assuming limited FORTRAN pro-
      gramming experience, what general alternative solutions
      should be sought?

      _____

      _____

      _____

      _____

      _____

      _____

6

Machine Instructions

The breakdown and analysis of machine instructions can be a valuable aid in debugging storage dumps, however, the technique need not be employed for all abends. An analysis of machine instructions is only necessary for Internal Abends when one of the following conditions exist.

COBOL Programs:

The source statement being executed cannot be determined because the Assembly Language listing is not available. The value of pertinent variables cannot be determined because the Data Map (DMAP) is not available.

FORTRAN Programs:

The source statement being executed, as well as the value of pertinent variables, cannot be determined because the Assembly Language listing is not available.

PL1 Programs:

The source statement being executed cannot be determined because the Assembly Language listing or Table of Offsets are not available. The value of pertinent variables cannot be determined because the Assembly Language listing is not available.

As will be seen in this chapter, knowledge of machine instruction format is necessary when referencing PL1 Assembly Language listings. One lesson to be learned, however, is to ensure that an Assembly or Condensed listing is generated for all programs regardless of language whenever they are recompiled. For COBOL a DMAP is also required. If this is accomplished, the breakdown and analysis of machine instructions will very seldom be necessary during the process of debugging storage dumps.

Figure 6.1 on the following page depicts the first and second panels of the Reference Data Card. These pages must be referenced when a breakdown of machine instruction statements is necessary. The remaining panels of the Reference Data Card are used primarily by programmers and analysts for data interpretation purposes.

A. INSTRUCTION FORMAT

Machine instructions are generated in one of five formats, and all are two, four, or six bytes in length. Each format and respective length is displayed on the second panel of the Reference Data Card. See Figure 6.1, letter 'A'.

1. RR Format

Machine instructions in Register To Register (RR) Format require the least amount of storage. They are only two bytes, or one half-word, in length. See letter 'B'.

Figure 6.1 Reference Data Card (panels 1 and 2)

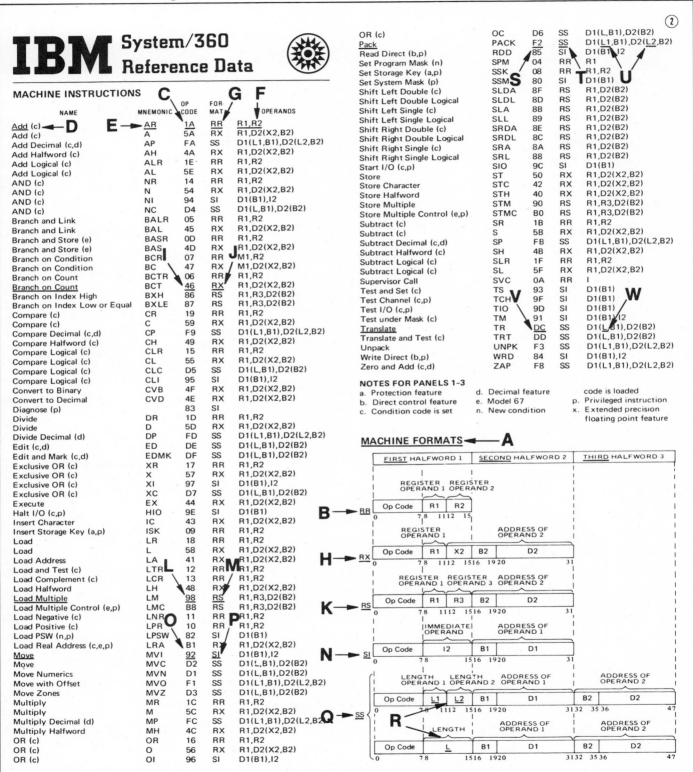

Note that the first byte of each of the five formats contains an Operation Code (Op Code). The Op Code indicates the function to be performed; i.e., Add, Branch, Compare, etc. An Op Code is followed by two or three Operands containing the actual data or location of the two or three fields to be operated upon.

Suppose the instruction, 1A68, as found in main storage was determined to be the actual machine instruction being executed at the time of the abend. It could then be broken down as follows:

OP Code	R1	R2
1A	6	8

where 1A represents the Op Code; 6 is the Register (R1) which contains the First Operand; and 8 refers to the Register (R2) which contains the Second Operand.

In order to determine which of the five formats to use, however, one must first locate the Op Code in the Machine Instruction List of the Reference Data Card. Op Code 1A can be found at the top of the first panel under the heading OP CODE. See letter 'C'. The Function to be performed can be found under the heading NAME. See Letter 'D'. Op Code 1A then, refers to an Add Instruction. The Assembly Language Code for the operation can be found under the heading MNEMONIC. The Op Code for this operation in Assembly Language is AR. See letter 'E'. The format for coding the Operands in Assembly Language can be found under the heading OPERANDS. See letter 'F'. The Second Operand must be coded after the First Operand separated by a comma.

Most important, the format of the machine instruction can be found under the heading FORMAT. Here it is determined that the instruction which contains Op Code 1A is in Register To Register (RR) Format. See letter 'G'. The machine instruction can now be broken down using the appropriate format. See letter 'B'. It is thus determined that the machine instruction, 1A68, refers to Registers 6 and 8 for the First and Second Operands, respectively.

One would next go to the Registers At Entry To Abend portion of the storage dump. In Registers 6 and 8 would be found the value of the First and Second Operands, respectively. This particular instruction adds the value of the Second Operand to the value of the First Operand. The resulting sum is placed in the First Operand overlaying its contents.

2. RX Format

The Register To Index (RX) Format is four bytes, two halfwords, or one word in length. See Figure 6.1, letter 'H'. The Op Code is located in the first byte followed by two Operands. Suppose the instruction, 46246280, as found in main storage was determined to be the actual machine instruction being executed at the time of the abend. It could then be broken down as follows:

Op Code	R1	X2	B2	D2
46	2	4	6	280

where 46 represents the Op Code; and 2 is the Register (R1) which contains the First Operand. The address of the value for the Second Operand is determined by adding together the contents of Index Register (X2) 4, Base Register (B2) 6, and the hexadecimal Displacement (D2) 280 as found in the instruction itself.

In order to determine which of the five formats to use, however, one must first locate the Op Code in the Machine Instruction List of the Reference Data Card. Op Code 46 can be found near the top of the first panel under the heading OP CODE. See letter 'I'. The function to be performed is Branch On Count. The format to use is Register To Index (RX). See letter 'J'.

One can now refer to the Registers At Entry To Abend portion of a storage dump to determine respective addresses and values for the two Operands. This particular instruction causes a branch to the address as indicated by the Second Operand when the value of the First Operand is zero.

3. RS Format

The Register To Storage (RS) Format is also four bytes, two half-words, or one word in length. See Figure 6.1, letter 'K'. The Op Code is located in the first byte, and in this case is followed by three Operands. Suppose the instruction, 988A6060, as found in main storage was determined to be the actual machine instruction being executed at the time of the abend. It could then be broken down as follows:

Op Code	R1	R3	B2	D2
98	8	A	6	060

where 98 represents the Op Code; 8 is the Register (R1) which contains the First Operand; and A (or 10) refers to the Register (R3) which contains the Third Operand. The address of the value for the Second Operand is determined by adding the contents of Base Register (B2) 6 to the hexadecimal Displacement (D2) 060.

In order to determine which of the five formats to use, however, one must again locate the Op Code in the Machine Instruction List of the Reference Data Card. Op Code 98 can be found near the bottom of the first panel under the heading OP CODE. See letter 'L'. The function to be performed is Load Multiple. The format to use is Register To Storage (RS). See letter 'M'.

The Registers At Entry To Abend portion of a storage dump can now be referenced to determine respective addresses and values for the three Operands. This particular instruction loads the value of the Second Operand into the First and Third Operands.

4. SI Format

The Storage Immediate (SI) Format is also four bytes, two halfwords, or one word in length. See Figure 6.1, letter 'N'. The Op Code is located in the first byte followed by two Operands. Suppose the instruction, 922E4320, as found in main storage, was determined to be the actual machine instruction being executed at the time of the abend. It could then be broken down as follows:

Op Code	I2	B1	D1
92	2E	4	320

where 92 represents the Op Code, and 2E is the actual hexadecimal value for the Second Operand (I2). The address of the value for the First Operand is determined by adding the contents of Base Register (B1) 4 to the hexadecimal Displacement (D1) 320.

In order to determine which of the five formats to use, however, one must locate the Op Code in the Machine Instruction List of the Reference Data Card. Op Code 92 can be found near the bottom of the first panel under the heading OP CODE. See letter 'O'. The function to be performed is Move. The format to use is Storage Immediate (SI). See letter 'P'.

The Registers At Entry To Abend portion of a storage dump can now be referenced to determine the address and value for the First Operand. This particular instruction moves the value of the Second Operand to the address specified by the First Operand.

5. SS Format

The Storage To Storage (SS) Format is six bytes, three halfwords, or one and one half words in length. See Figure 6.1, letter 'Q'. The Op Code is located in the first byte followed by two Operands. Two types of operand length specifications are available in SS Format depending upon the actual machine instruction being executed. See letter 'R'. Suppose the instruction, F212A2808080, as found in main storage was found to be the machine instruction being executed at the time of the abend. It could then be broken down as follows:

Op Code	L1	L2	B1	D1	B2	D2
F2	1	2	A	280	8	080

Where F2 represents the Op Code, 1 + 1 or 2 is the Length (L1) of the First Operand, and 2 + 1 or 3 is the Length (L2) of the Second Operand. With other formats, Length was assumed to be four bytes, unless the Halfword or Double Word feature was utilized.

184

The address of the value for the First Operand is determined by adding the contents of Base Register (B1) A (or 10) to the hexadecimal Displacement (D1) 280. The address of the value for the Second Operand is determined by adding the contents of Base Register (B2) 8 to the hexadecimal Displacement (D2) 080.

A one is always added to the length indication to determine the actual field length utilized. This is because hexadecimal numbers 0 through F are generated to represent field lengths of 1 through 16 bytes, respectively, in the source program. A two character field length of 16 can be represented by a one-character code, F, if one is subtracted from the coded length (16 - 1 = F). A field length of two bytes is represented in main storage as a one (2 - 1 = 1), and so on. Therefore, when determining operand length, a one must be added back to the stored indication.

In order to determine which of the five formats to use, however, one must reference the Machine Instruction List of the Reference Data Card. Op Code F2 can be found near the top of the second panel in the appropriate column. See letter 'S'. The function to be performed is Pack. The format to use is Storage To Storage (SS). See letter 'T'.

Note that L1 and L2 can be found in the operand portion of the appropriate Assembly Language statement. See letter 'U'. If the Op Code would have been DC, for example, a Translate instruction of SS Format would have been executed. See letter 'V'. Only one length is specified, however. See letter 'W'. As a result, the second form of the SS Format would be utilized. See letter 'R'. With the Translate instruction, the Length (L) refers to the actual number of bytes to be translated.

The Registers At Entry To Abend portion of a storage dump can now be referenced to determine respective addresses and values for the two Operands. A Pack Instruction converts the value of the Second Operand from External Decimal (Unpacked Format) to Internal Decimal (Packed Format). The result is stored at the address specified by the First Operand.

An attempt has been made to delineate a basic understanding of the formats of machine language instructions, as opposed to the actual

coding and execution of the instructions themselves. Operand values
for any machine instruction can be located in main storage once the
appropriate format has been determined.

B. MACHINE INSTRUCTION BREAKDOWN

The technique of machine instruction location, breakdown, and
analysis need only be accomplished when appropriate listings for the
techniques described in the previous chapters are not available. The
complete process of machine instruction breakdown should be discussed,
however, as all OS, OS/VS, and DOS programmers and analysts will
occasionally find themselves in situations when this procedure is
necessary.

1. Computer Run Overview (OC7)

Recall from the OC7 Storage Dump example in Chapters 4 and 5 that
the COBOL problem source statement was found to be IF STATE-DATA=
STATE4. The value of the pertinent variable STATE4 was found to be
equal to a one with leading zeroes; STATE-DATA contained zeroes along
with a blank in the low order position. If an Assembly Language listing and Data Map had not been available, the above items could not
have been determined. The only alternative would have been to locate,
breakdown, and analyze the actual machine instruction being executed at
the time of the abend.

Figures 6.2 through 6.5 consist of selected pages of the same run
which abended with a OC7 Completion Code in Chapters 4 and 5. Because
a OC7 Storage Dump signals that non-numeric data is erroneously present
in a numeric field, and assuming that pertinent listings are not available,
a programmer would be interested in determining the Op Code and locating
the value of the Operands in the machine instruction being executed.

Figures 6.6 through 6.9 depict panels 1, 2, 3, 7, 11, 12, 13, and
14 of the Reference Data Card. They will be utilized in the discussion
to follow.

Figure 6.2 Portion of Assembly Language Listing (OC7)

```
65   *PRO-2
66   READ      00091C                    EQU   *                         PN=01
               00091C  58 F0 C 008       L     15,008(0,12)              V(ILBODBG4)
               000920  05 EF             BALR  14,15
               000922  58 10 C 054       L     1,054(0,12)               DCB=1
               000926  18 21             LR    2,1
               000928  D2 02 2 021 C 02D MVC   0213,2),02D(12)           GN=03+1
               00092E  58 F0 1 030       L     15,030(0,1)
               000932  05 EF             BALR  14,15
               000934  50 10 D 1F8       ST    1,1F8(0,13)               RL =1
               000938  58 70 D 1F8       L     7,1F8(0,13)               RL =1
               00093C  D2 4F 6 008 7 000 MVC   00R(80,6),000(7)          DNM=1-279
               000942  58 50 C 030       L     5,030(0,12)               DNM=1-92   GN=04
               000946  07 F5             BCR   15,5
66   GO        000948                    EQU   *
               000948  58 10 C 020       L     1,020(0,12)               PN=03
               00094C  07 F1             BCR   15,1
67   IF        00094E  GN=04             EQU   *
               00094E  F2 76 D 210 6 028 PACK  210(8,13),028(7,6)        TS=01   DNM=1-313
               000954  F2 76 D 218 6 000 PACK  218(8,13),000(7,6)        TS=09   DNM=1-263
               00095A  F9 33 D 214 D 21C CP    214(4,13),21C(4,13)       TS=05   TS=013
               000960  58 F0 C 034       L     15,034(0,12)              GN=05
               000964  07 7F             BCR   7,15
               000966  58 10 C 01C       L     1,01C(0,12)
               00096A  07 F1             BCR   15,1                      PN=02
67   GO        00096C  GN=05             EQU   *
68   WRITE     00096C  58 F0 C 008       L     15,008(0,12)              V(ILBODBG4)
               000970  05 EF             BALR  14,15
               000972  D2 4F 8 000 6 008 MVC   000(80,8),008(6)          DNM=1-127   DNM=1-279
               000978  58 10 C 058       L     1,058(0,12)               DCB=2
               00097C  18 21             LR    2,1
               00097E  92 00 2 07A       MVI   07A(2),X'00'
               000982  5A 40 2 024       A     4,024(0,2)
               000986  92 00 4 014       MVI   014(4),X'00'              DCB=2
               00098A  58 10 C 058       L     1,058(0,12)
               00098E  58 00 1 04C       L     0,04C(0,1)
               000992  58 00 1 030       L     15,030(0,1)
               000996  44 00 1 060       EX    0,060(0,1)
               00099A  58 20 C 058       L     2,058(0,12)               DCB=2
               00099E  91 40 2 07A       TM    07A(2),X'40'
               0009A2  92 00 2 07A       MVI   07A(2),X'00'
               0009A6  58 30 C 044       L     3,044(0,12)               GN=09
               0009AA  07 13             BCR   1,3
               0009AC  50 10 D 1FC       ST    1,1FC(0,13)               BL =2
               0009B0  58 A0 D 1FC       L     8,1FC(0,13)               RL =2
69   ADD       0009B4  GN=09 / GN=06     EQU   *
               0009B4  F2 76 D 218 6 0AD PACK  21A(8,13),0AD(7,6)        TS=09   DNM=1-442
               0009BA  FA 40 D 21B C 068 AP    21B(5,13),068(1,12)       TS=012  LIT+0
               0009C0  F3 64 6 0AD D 21B UNPK  0AD(7,6),21B(5,13)        DNM=1-442   TS=012
               0009C6  96 F0 6 0C3       OI    0C3(6),X'F0'              DNM=1-442+6
```

D E

Figure 6.3 First Page of OC7 Storage Dump

```
JOB  RZZ765        STEP GO        TIME 132747

COMPLETION CODE    SYSTEM = 0C7

PSW AT ENTRY TO ABEND  FFF5000D C0096BB0 ──►B     ILC 6

TCB 036CD8  RBP   00042520  PIE    00000000  DEB  00036BB4  TIO  00037B80  CMP   800C7000  TRN  00000000
            MSS   0203F670  PK-FLG F0850400  FLG  00005F5B  LLS  0003ACE0  JLB   00000000  JPQ  80037F10
            FSA   01090768  TCB    000369D0  TME  00000000  JST  00036CD8  NTC   00000000  OTC  0003D078
            LTC   00000000  IQE    00000000  ECB  00037A64  TSF  20000000  D-PQE 00043B50  SQS  00036IE8
            NSTAE 8003E088  TCT    8003A7D8  USER 00000000  DAR  00000000  RESV  00000000  JSCR 8703D928
            RESV  00000000  IOB    00000000

ACTIVE RBS

PRB 03D30A  RESV 00000000  APSW   C0096BB0 ──►  WC-SZ-STAB 00040082  FL-CDE 0003E748  PSW FFF5000D C0096BB0
            RESV 00000000  WT-LNK 00036CD8 ──►
                           H      A

SVRB 042250 TAB-LN 00080220  APSW   F9F0F1C3  WC-SZ-STAB 0012D002  TQN 00000000  PSW 00040033 50015BFA
            Q/TTR  00004629  WT-LNK 0003D30A
            RG 0-7   0000000A 0009D140 00096404 00096C68 8009652C 000969E  000962D8 0009D140
            RG 8-15  0009A0C0 0009C630 0009D1E8 0009D048 00096988 00096730 5096R84  001FDAE0
            EXTSA    000021BE 8F09D250 00000000 C4F90C70 FF030000 000422CC 000422D4 E2E8E2C9
                     C5C1F0F1 C9C5C1D8

SVRR 042520 TAB-LN 00A803D8  APSW   F1F0F5C1  WC-SZ-STAB 0012D002  TQN 00000000  PSW FF04000C 40099FA6
            Q/TTR  00003R01  WT-LNK 00042250
            RG 0-7   00000007 000422R0 80015B12 0001A318 00042250 04036CD8 00042250
            RG 8-15  00036CD8 40015A5A 00036CD8 9F09D250 00037C28 40017FA4 00000000
            EXTSA    E2E8E2C9 C5C1F0F1 1509DDE0 0009D5EC 0009DFC8 0009DFE8 00000000
                     00004C08 00036BB4 80015BF8 000325F0

LOAD LIST
NE 0003ADC0  RSP-CDE 02037F10   NE 0003AF28   RSP-CDE 01045AC8   NE 0003B548  RSP-CDE 01045888
NE 0003RD88  RSP-CDE 010459C8   NE 0003D9D8   RSP-CDE 01045988   NE 0003DAB0  RSP-CDE 02045ACA
NE 0003DF98  RSP-CDE 02045A28   NE 0003E080   RSP-CDE 0203D488   NE 0003E3B8  RSP-CDE 01045AFA
NE 0003E6C8  RSP-CDE 02045A98   NE 0003E6F0   RSP-CDE 02045BB8   NE 0003F598  RSP-CDE 02045R2A
NE 0003F6EA  RSP-CDE 01045888   NE 00040EF0   RSP-CDE 03045958   NE 00000000  RSP-CDE 03045AFA

CDE
03E748  ATR1 0A  NCDE 000000  ROC-RB 00000000  NM MAIN      USE 01  EPA 096250 ──►C  ATR2 20  XL/MJ 03E0A8
037F10  ATR1 30  NCDE 03CE00  ROC-RB 00000000  NM IGC0A05A  USE 02  EPA 099858        ATR2 28  XL/MJ 037AE8
045ACA  ATR1 A0  NCDE 045AFA  ROC-RB 00000000  NM IGG019CF  USE 01  EPA 1FC590        ATR2 20  XL/MJ 045A88
0458AA  ATR1 A0  NCDE 045RCA  ROC-HB 00000000  NM IGG019CL  USE 01  EPA 1FF810        ATR2 20  XL/MJ 045A78
0459CA  ATR1 A0  NCDE 0459FA  ROC-RB 00000000  NM IGG019BA  USE 01  EPA 1FCE40        ATR2 20  XL/MJ 04598A
045988  ATR1 B0  NCDE 0459CA  ROC-RB 00000000  NM IGG019BB  USE 01  EPA 1FCCC8        ATR2 20  XL/MJ 045978
045AC8  ATR1 B0  NCDE 045AF8  ROC-RB 00000000  NM IGG019CD  USE 01  EPA 1FD830        ATR2 20  XL/MJ 045A8A
045A2A  ATR1 H0  NCDE 045A5A  ROC-RB 00000000  NM IGG019CI  USE 01  EPA 1FD298        ATR2 20  XL/MJ 045A18
```

Figure 6.4 First Page OC7 Main Storage

```
              R7 0009A89E   R8 00096208   R9 0009D0F0   R10 0009A0C0   R11 401FE888   R12 001FDBE0

REGS AT ENTRY TO ABEND

FLTR 0-6  W→ 08036C8040000001   05036D2400000028   3103601340000005  →08036CC840000001

REGS 0-7   W→ 0000000A  0009D140  00096404  00096C68  8009652C  0009A89E  00096208  0009D140
REGS 8-15     0009A0C0  0009C630  0009D1E8  0009D048  00096988  00096730→ 50096B84  001FDBE0

LOAD MODULE   MAIN

096240  F8404040 C1D5E2F4 0700989F F02407FF  90ECD00C 1A5D05F0 4580F010 C1F5F5F5   *8  ANS4....0......0..0.A555*
096260  00096250 00096988 00096730 40404040  96021034 07FE41F0 000107FE 0009A89E   *........ ................*
096280  40D5C9E3 D9C9E3C5 40404040 40404040  0009696 00096E5A C1D4D4D6 D5C9E4D4   * NITRITE          ...AMMONIUM*
0962A0  40D5C9E3 D9C9E3C5 40404040 40404040  40404040 40404040 40404040 40404040   * NITRITE                     *
0962C0  F6F1F1F8 F8F1F4F3 F2F3F6F1 F4F3F6F7  F3F4F1F1 F1F1F1F1 F2F2F2F2 F0F0F0F140  *6118814323143673411111122220000001*
0962E0  F2F2F2F0 F0F0F0F0 F0F0F6F9 F3F9F1F4  F9F4F9F3 F4F1F3F5 F7F8F3F4 F1F9F4F4    *2220000069391494934135783419 44*
096300  F9F0F4F1 F3F4F2F9 F0F1F1F2 F3F4F5F9  F0F0F0F0 F0F0F140 40404040 40404040    *90413429011234590000001        *
096320  40404040 40404040 40404040 40404040  40404040 40404040 40404040 40404040   *                               *

LINE 096360 SAME AS ABOVE

096380  40D9C5C3 D6D9C4E2 40D6D540 E3C1D7C5  40F0F0F0 F0F0F0F2 F0D5D6D9 D4C1D340    * RECORDS ON TAPE  1 . 0000000 REC*
0963A0  D6D9C4E2 40D6D540 E3C1D7C5 40F2407E  F0F0F0F0 F0F0F0F2 40D5D6D9 D4C1D340    *ORDS ON TAPE  2 . 0000002 NORMAL *
0963C0  C5D5C440 D6C640D1 D6C24040 40404040  F0F7F6F3 00000000 00000000 00000000    *END OF JOB    0763...............*
0963E0  00000000 05097E2A 08096276 08096276  00000001 00000000 00000000 00000000   *....... ............ .......*
096400  80000000 00000000 00000000 00000000  00410000 0209D0E8 00004000 00000000   *...................Y.........*
096420  00000001 46096898 800963D4 00404800  0003684C 121FE880 06097BC6 00000000   *......M.....M.....M.....F....*
096440  00090050 28022828 0009C770 0009D190  0009D140 00000001 00000000 00000000   *.......G....J.....J.....H*
096460  001FD4F8 00000000 00000000 00000000  001FD4F8 00000001 00000000 08000CC8   *..M8...................M8....H*
096480  00000000 00000000 00000000 00000000  05097E2A 08096276 00000001 00000000   *............................*
0964A0  00000000 00000000 00000000 80000000  00000000 38000000 00060000 0001C394   *.................................C.*
0964C0  0029336D 0209A0H8 00004000 00000001  46000001 90096480 00680048 000367BC   *.................F...........*
0964E0  921FCC48 001FDAD0 0D097BC6 0009DFA0  30060050 4209C550 0009B060 0009A110   *...........F....E.........*
096500  00000050 00000000 00000000 001FD830  05EF0000 00000000 00000000 00000000   *.........................*
096520  00000000 00000000 00000000 009000C8  00000000 00000000 00000000 05097E2A   *.................H...........*
096540  00096276 00000001 00000001 00000001  00000000 00004000 00000000 00000000   *...........................*
096560  38000000 00F000E0 0201C394 0029318F  00000001 46000001 46000000 46000001   *.....0....C.............F.........*
096580  8009652C 007C0048 0003672C 921FCC48  001FDAD0 0D097BC6 00090050 30060050   *......C...........F....Q.........*
0965A0  0009C478 0009C680 00096680 00000050  00000001 00000000 001FD830 05EF0000   *...D..F...F........Q.........*
0965C0  00000000 00000000 00000000 08096276  00000000 00800040 00000000 00000000   *........................*
0965E0  00000000 00000000 05097E2A 08096276  00000001 00000000 00000000 00000000   *...........................*
096600  00000000 80000000 00000000 00000000  00000040 00410000 0209D190 00000000   *.....................J*
096620  00004000 00000001 46096B5C 800965D8  0003684C 121FE880 001FDBE0 00000000   *.......Q......Q.....Y.....*
096640  06097BC6 00090050 28022828 0009C7D0  0009D1E8 0009D1E8 00000000 00000001   *...F.......G...JY...JY.*
096660  00000000 001FD4F8 00000000 00000000  0009D238 0009D1E8 00000000 00000000   *.....M8.......K..JY.*
096680  00800040 00000000 00000000 00000000  05097E2A 08096276 00000001 00000000   *..............................*
0966A0  00000001 00000000 0209D040 00004000  80000000 46000001 80096684 00900048   *.....................F....*
0966C0  00000000 00480000 921FCC48 00000050  0009D050 28022828 4209C6D0 0009D098   *...........C....Q..Q....F....*
0966E0  000366AC 921FDAD0 07097BC6 00000000  001FC998 05EF0000 00000000 50096EA0   *.F.......F....I.........F*
096700  0009D098 00000001 00000000 00800040  0030C4C2 0009D768 0009D3B0 50096E5C   *.Q..............DB..P..L....F*
096720  00000000 00000000 121FE880 00000001  00096404 00096404 00096C68 8009652C   *.......Q.......Y.....*
096740  00097044 50096B84 00000000 0009A0C0  401FE888 001FDBE0 32028048 00000000   *...Y.0....Y....*
096760  00096B9E 000962D8 0009D0F0 00000000  00096B9E 001FDBE0 00097E7C FD000008   *.......Q....6...........F.*
096780  00000000 000969F6 00000000 00000000  00097BC6 00000000 00000000 0009D7F8   *...................P8*
```

Figure 6.5 - Intermediate Page of OC7 Main Storage

```
0966E0   00033744 922FCDC0 002FDC98 07162BC6   CC090050 2E022828 4217FED0 00180898   *..............F.................*
096700   0018C898 C0000050 00000001 C0000000   002FC810 05EFC000 C0000000 00000000   *................................*
096720   00000000 C0000000 00000000 00800000   0030C4C2 00180F68 00180BB0 50161EA0   *....................DB..........*
096740   0016204A 5C161B84 122FE808 CC000001   00161404 00161404 00161C68 8016152C   *..........Y.....................*
096760   00161B9E 001612D8 001808F0 C0170BC0   402FEE4C CC2FCDAE 3202804B CC000000   *.......Q...0..Q. .Y ............*
096780   00000000 001619F6 00000000 00000000   00162BC6 00162E7C 00000008 00180FF8   *.......6............F..........8*
0967A0   00033EEC C003B438 00000000 C0180F68   CC03B3F4 0C03DC64 8016125C 00161E9A   *..................4.............*
0967C0   00161250 00161250 00161988 70BC9400   7C785860 7C7847F0 928C9110 60024770   *........................0.......*
0967E0   92AC9124 60034770 92AC9608 60C247F0   92ACD205 AC766004 47F09420 91046002   *................0..K.......0.....*
096800   47FC93E6 D5C56004 06162584 00161F88   2C00D048 50F0DCC8 50D0F004 18DF9500   *.0.WN...................0....0..*
096820   B05D478C C1585850 B0401255 4770C046   58F0C166 180F4510 C0300A0A 41501000   *....A.... ........0A............*
096840   50FC5010 5010B040 41FC5058 50F0501C   1BEE58F0 B0044100 50381B11 90E15000   *.0...... .0...0......0..........*
096860   D7175020 502C58F0 501C41E0 F02450E0   5C1E5CFC ECC0D202 A1ECA1C6 5810A1E0   *P......0....0.......0..K........*
096880   881C0C08 D223F000 100058F0 C24205EF   5000A1E0 D202A105 A1E058F0 C24605EF   *....K.0.....0B........K.......0B...*
0968A0   9120B05D 4780C0DC D20CA1E0 AC87940F   A1EC58EC 501C41F0 82904100 A1E04110   *........K...............0.......*
0968C0   000CCCCC CCC00000 C24A12FF 4780C0DC   4110A130 05EF5900 00161B72 C0DC9620   *.........B......................*
0968E0   00161250 CCCC0720 00161F88 E2E8E2D6   E4E34040 E3E1D202 A115A1E5 9110BC5D   *..............SYSOUT  T.K....V....*
096900   4780C158 D72BA548 A5489214 A54DD2C7   A54EA1E0 5810B040 5810101C D203A556   *..A.P..........K........ ....K...*
096920   1010D20F A55A1000 00180940 0017D8C0   0017FE30 0018C9E8 CC1EC848 001612D8   *..K........ ..Q.........Y.......Q*
096940   000CCCCC C0C00004 00000000 C0C0001F   CC000000 0CCC0000 00161608 00161404   *................................*
096960   0F161480 0F16155C 8F1616B4 07FE4780   CCC0CCCA CCCCCCCC CC161F10 00161F79   *................................*
096980   00161F83 95052008 00162E7C 0016204A   0016205A 00162EC6 00162E2A 00162E80   *........................F.......*
0969A0   00161B6C C0161C20 00161C84 0C161B5C   CC161B62 CC161898 0016189E 00161EBC   *................................*
0969C0   00161C04 00161C68 00161CCC 00161CC4   CC161C68 00161CCC 00161E54 00161404   *................................*
0969E0   001614B0 0016155C 00161608 001616B4   1C48CC4E C5EF5EFC CCC805EF 5810C060   *........................0.......*
096A00   D203DC6C C0CCD202 1039D061 581CCC60   C2011032 C0695840 1024D202 4011C011   *K.....K.........K....... ..K. ...*
096A20   501CD228 9200D228 5810C054 D2C3DC60   CCCCD2C2 1C39D061 5810C054 D2C11032   *..K...K......K......K..........K...*
096A40   C0695840 1024D202 4011C011 5010D22C   9200D22C 5E10C058 D203D060 C00CD202   *... ..K. ......K...K......K......K.*
096A60   1039DC61 5810C058 D2011032 C06AD2C1   1C60C06C 58401024 D2024011 C0115010   *.........K......K....... ..K. .....*
096A80   D230920F C2305810 C05CD203 DC60C00C   C2021C39 DC615810 C05CD2C1 1032C06A   *K...K......K......K..........K.....*
096AA0   D2011060 C06C5840 1024D202 4011C011   5010D234 920FC234 5810C064 D203D060   *K....... ..K. ......K...K......K...*
096AC0   C00CD202 1C39D061 5810C064 D2011032   CC6AC2C1 1C60C06C 58401024 D2024011   *..K...........K......K........ ..K. .*
096AE0   C0115010 D238920F D2389680 D2384110   C228CA13 5E10CC58 1E2158F0 103005EF   *....K...K...K...K...............0....*
096B00   501CD1FC 5880D1FC 5810C05C 182158F0   1030C5EF 5C10C200 5890D200 5810C064   *..J...J..........0........K...K......*
096B20   182158F0 103005EF 5010D208 58BCD2C8   58FCCCC8 05EF5810 C0601821 D2022021   *...0........K...K..0..............K...*
096B40   C02558F0 103005EF 5010D204 58A0D204   D24F6058 ACC05E50 CC28C7F5 5810C020   *...0........K...K.K..............5....*
096B60   07F1D206 60C06058 96F06006 58FCCCC8   05EF5810 C0541821 D2022021 C02D58F0   *.1K.........0...0..............K.......0*
096B80   103CC5EF 5010D1F8 5870D1F8 D24F6CC8   7CCC5E5C CC30C7F5 581CCC2C 07F1F276   *.......J8..J8K..............5.....12.*
096BA0   D210602E F276D218 6000F933 D214D21C   58F0C034 077F5E10 C01C07F1 58F0C008   *K...2.K...9.K.K..0.............1.0..*
096BC0   05EFD24F 8CCC6CC8 5810C058 18219200   2C7A5E40 20249200 40145810 C0585800   *..K................... .... ........*
096BE0   104C58F0 10304400 10605820 C0589140   2C7A92C0 2C7A5830 C044C713 5010D1FC   *...0............. ..................J.*
096C00   5880D1FC F276D218 60BCFA40 D21BCC68   F3E460BD D21B96F0 60C35810 C018C7F1   *..J.2.K..... K...3...K..0.C.....1*
096C20   58FCCC08 05EFD24F 90C06008 5810CC5C   182192C0 2C7A5840 20249200 40145810   *.0....K..................... .... ...*
096C40   C05C58C0 104C58F0 10304400 10605820   C05C9140 2C7A9200 207A5E30 C0480713   *........0............. .............*
096C60   501CD20C 589CD200 F276D218 60D9FA40   C21BC068 F3646009 C21396F0 60DF5810   *..K...K.2.K..R. K...3..RK..0.....*
096C80   C01E07F1 58F0C008 05EFD24F B0CC60A8   581CCC64 18219200 2C7A5840 20249200   *...1.0....K.................... ....*
096CA0   40145810 C0645800 104C58F0 10304400   10605820 C0649140 207A9200 207A5830   * ...........0............. ........*
096CC0   CC4CC713 5010D208 58B0D208 58FCCCC8   C5EF581C C0545830 102C910F 300C0550   *.......K...K..0...................*
096CE0   47EC5010 5820104C 4B201052 5020104C   581CCC54 5010D228 9240D228 5810C058   *...........................K.. K.....*
```

Figure 6.6 Reference Data Card (panels 1 and 2)

IBM System/360 Reference Data

②

MACHINE INSTRUCTIONS

NAME	MNEMONIC	OP CODE	FORMAT	OPERANDS
Add (c)	AR	1A	RR	R1,R2
Add (c)	A	5A	RX	R1,D2(X2,B2)
Add Decimal (c,d)	AP	FA	SS	D1(L1,B1),D2(L2,B2)
Add Halfword (c)	AH	4A	RX	R1,D2(X2,B2)
Add Logical (c)	ALR	1E	RR	R1,R2
Add Logical (c)	AL	5E	RX	R1,D2(X2,B2)
AND (c)	NR	14	RR	R1,R2
AND (c)	N	54	RX	R1,D2(X2,B2)
AND (c)	NI	94	SI	D1(B1),I2
AND (c)	NC	D4	SS	D1(L,B1),D2(B2)
Branch and Link	BALR	05	RR	R1,R2
Branch and Link	BAL	45	RX	R1,D2(X2,B2)
Branch and Store (e)	BASR	0D	RR	R1,R2
Branch and Store (e)	BAS	4D	RX	R1,D2(X2,B2)
Branch on Condition	BCR	07	RR	M1,R2
Branch on Condition	BC	47	RX	M1,D2(X2,B2)
Branch on Count	BCTR	06	RR	R1,R2
Branch on Count	BCT	46	RX	R1,D2(X2,B2)
Branch on Index High	BXH	86	RS	R1,R3,D2(B2)
Branch on Index Low or Equal	BXLE	87	RS	R1,R3,D2(B2)
Compare (c)	CR	19	RR	R1,R2
Compare (c)	C	59	RX	R1,D2(X2,B2)
Compare Decimal (c,d)	CP	F9	SS	D1(L1,B1),D2(L2,B2)
Compare Halfword (c)	CH	49	RX	R1,D2(X2,B2)
Compare Logical (c)	CLR	15	RR	R1,R2
Compare Logical (c)	CL	55	RX	R1,D2(X2,B2)
Compare Logical (c)	CLC	D5	SS	D1(L,B1),D2(B2)
Compare Logical (c)	CLI	95	SI	D1(B1),I2
Convert to Binary	CVB	4F	RX	R1,D2(X2,B2)
Convert to Decimal	CVD	4E	RX	R1,D2(X2,B2)
Diagnose (p)		83	SI	
Divide	DR	1D	RR	R1,R2
Divide	D	5D	RX	R1,D2(X2,B2)
Divide Decimal (d)	DP	FD	SS	D1(L1,B1),D2(L2,B2)
Edit (c,d)	ED	DE	SS	D1(L,B1),D2(B2)
Edit and Mark (c,d)	EDMK	DF	SS	D1(L,B1),D2(B2)
Exclusive OR (c)	XR	17	RR	R1,R2
Exclusive OR (c)	X	57	RX	R1,D2(X2,B2)
Exclusive OR (c)	XI	97	SI	D1(B1),I2
Exclusive OR (c)	XC	D7	SS	D1(L,B1),D2(B2)
Execute	EX	44	RX	R1,D2(X2,B2)
Halt I/O (c,p)	HIO	9E	SI	D1(B1)
Insert Character	IC	43	RX	R1,D2(X2,B2)
Insert Storage Key (a,p)	ISK	09	RR	R1,R2
Load	LR	18	RR	R1,R2
Load	L	58	RX	R1,D2(X2,B2)
Load Address	LA	41	RX	R1,D2(X2,B2)
Load and Test (c)	LTR	12	RR	R1,R2
Load Complement (c)	LCR	13	RR	R1,R2
Load Halfword	LH	48	RX	R1,D2(X2,B2)
Load Multiple	LM	98	RS	R1,R3,D2(B2)
Load Multiple Control (e,p)	LMC	B8	RS	R1,R3,D2(B2)
Load Negative (c)	LNR	11	RR	R1,R2
Load Positive (c)	LPR	10	RR	R1,R2
Load PSW (n,p)	LPSW	82	SI	D1(B1)
Load Real Address (c,e,p)	LRA	B1	RX	R1,D2(X2,B2)
Move	MVI	92	SI	D1(B1),I2
Move	MVC	D2	SS	D1(L,B1),D2(B2)
Move Numerics	MVN	D1	SS	D1(L,B1),D2(B2)
Move with Offset	MVO	F1	SS	D1(L1,B1),D2(L2,B2)
Move Zones	MVZ	D3	SS	D1(L,B1),D2(B2)
Multiply	MR	1C	RR	R1,R2
Multiply	M	5C	RX	R1,D2(X2,B2)
Multiply Decimal (d)	MP	FC	SS	D1(L1,B1),D2(L2,B2)
Multiply Halfword	MH	4C	RX	R1,D2(X2,B2)
OR (c)	OR	16	RR	R1,R2
OR (c)	O	56	RX	R1,D2(X2,B2)
OR (c)	OI	96	SI	D1(B1),I2

J → K →

NAME	MNEMONIC	OP CODE	FORMAT	OPERANDS
OR (c)	OC	D6	SS	D1(L,B1),D2(B2)
Pack	PACK	F2	SS	D1(L1,B1),D2(L2,B2)
Read Direct (b,p)	RDD	85	SI	D1(B1),I2
Set Program Mask (n)	SPM	04	RR	R1
Set Storage Key (a,p)	SSK	08	RR	R1,R2
Set System Mask (p)	SSM	80	SI	D1(B1)
Shift Left Double (c)	SLDA	8F	RS	R1,D2(B2)
Shift Left Double Logical	SLDL	8D	RS	R1,D2(B2)
Shift Left Single (c)	SLA	8B	RS	R1,D2(B2)
Shift Left Single Logical	SLL	89	RS	R1,D2(B2)
Shift Right Double (c)	SRDA	8E	RS	R1,D2(B2)
Shift Right Double Logical	SRDL	8C	RS	R1,D2(B2)
Shift Right Single (c)	SRA	8A	RS	R1,D2(B2)
Shift Right Single Logical	SRL	88	RS	R1,D2(B2)
Start I/O (c,p)	SIO	9C	SI	D1(B1)
Store	ST	50	RX	R1,D2(X2,B2)
Store Character	STC	42	RX	R1,D2(X2,B2)
Store Halfword	STH	40	RX	R1,D2(X2,B2)
Store Multiple	STM	90	RS	R1,R3,D2(B2)
Store Multiple Control (e,p)	STMC	B0	RS	R1,R3,D2(B2)
Subtract (c)	SR	1B	RR	R1,R2
Subtract (c)	S	5B	RX	R1,D2(X2,B2)
Subtract Decimal (c,d)	SP	FB	SS	D1(L1,B1),D2(L2,B2)
Subtract Halfword (c)	SH	4B	RX	R1,D2(X2,B2)
Subtract Logical (c)	SLR	1F	RR	R1,R2
Subtract Logical (c)	SL	5F	RX	R1,D2(X2,B2)
Supervisor Call	SVC	0A	RR	I
Test and Set (c)	TS	93	SI	D1(B1)
Test Channel (c,p)	TCH	9F	SI	D1(B1)
Test I/O (c,p)	TIO	9D	SI	D1(B1)
Test under Mask (c)	TM	91	SI	D1(B1),I2
Translate	TR	DC	SS	D1(L,B1),D2(B2)
Translate and Test (c)	TRT	DD	SS	D1(L,B1),D2(B2)
Unpack	UNPK	F3	SS	D1(L1,B1),D2(L2,B2)
Write Direct (b,p)	WRD	84	SI	D1(B1),I2
Zero and Add (c,d)	ZAP	F8	SS	D1(L1,B1),D2(L2,B2)

NOTES FOR PANELS 1-3

a. Protection feature
b. Direct control feature
c. Condition code is set
d. Decimal feature
e. Model 67
n. New condition
    code is loaded
p. Privileged instruction
x. Extended precision
    floating point feature

MACHINE FORMATS

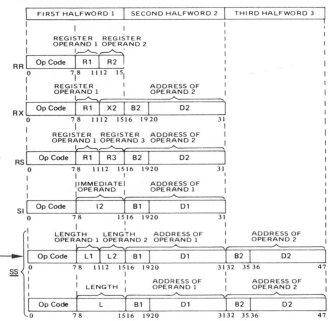

Figure 6.7 Reference Data Card (panels 3 and 7)

FLOATING-POINT FEATURE INSTRUCTIONS ← V ③

Add Normalized, Extended (c,x)	AXR	36	RR	R1,R2
Add Normalized, Long (c)	ADR	2A	RR	R1,R2
Add Normalized, Long (c)	AD	6A	RX	R1,D2(X2,B2)
Add Normalized, Short (c)	AER	3A	RR	R1,R2
Add Normalized, Short (c)	AE	7A	RX	R1,D2(X2,B2)
Add Unnormalized, Long (c)	AWR	2E	RR	R1,R2
Add Unnormalized, Long (c)	AW	6E	RX	R1,D2(X2,B2)
Add Unnormalized, Short (c)	AUR	3E	RR	R1,R2
Add Unnormalized, Short (c)	AU	7E	RX	R1,D2(X2,B2)
Compare, Long (c)	CDR	29	RR	R1,R2
Compare, Long (c)	CD	69	RX	R1,D2(X2,B2)
Compare, Short (c)	CER	39	RR	R1,R2
Compare, Short (c)	CE	79	RX	R1,D2(X2,B2)
Divide, Long	DDR	2D	RR	R1,R2
Divide, Long	DD	6D	RX	R1,D2(X2,B2)
Divide, Short	DER	3D	RR	R1,R2
Divide, Short	DE	7D	RX	R1,D2(X2,B2)
Halve, Long	HDR	24	RR	R1,R2
Halve, Short	HER	34	RR	R1,R2
Load and Test, Long (c)	LTDR	22	RR	R1,R2
Load and Test, Short (c)	LTER	32	RR	R1,R2
Load Complement, Long (c)	LCDR	23	RR	R1,R2
Load Complement, Short (c)	LCER	33	RR	R1,R2
Load, Long	LDR	28	RR	R1,R2
Load, Long	LD	68	RX	R1,D2(X2,B2)
Load Negative, Long (c)	LNDR	21	RR	R1,R2
Load Negative, Short (c)	LNER	31	RR	R1,R2
Load Positive, Long (c)	LPDR	20	RR	R1,R2
Load Positive, Short (c)	LPER	30	RR	R1,R2
Load Rounded, Extended to Long (x)	LRDR	25	RR	R1,R2
Load Rounded, Long to Short (x)	LRER	35	RR	R1,R2
Load, Short	LER	38	RR	R1,R2
Load, Short	LE	78	RX	R1,D2(X2,B2)
Multiply, Extended (x)	MXR	26	RR	R1,R2
Multiply, Long	MDR	2C	RR	R1,R2
Multiply, Long	MD	6C	RX	R1,D2(X2,B2)
Multiply, Long/Extended (x)	MXDR	27	RR	R1,R2
Multiply, Long/Extended (x)	MXD	67	RX	R1,D2(X2,B2)
Multiply, Short	MER	3C	RR	R1,R2
Multiply, Short	ME	7C	RX	R1,D2(X2,B2)
Store, Long	STD	60	RX	R1,D2(X2,B2)
Store, Short	STE	70	RX	R1,D2(X2,B2)
Subtract Normalized, Extended (c,x)	SXR	37	RR	R1,R2
Subtract Normalized, Long (c)	SDR	2B	RR	R1,R2
Subtract Normalized, Long (c)	SD	6B	RX	R1,D2(X2,B2)
Subtract Normalized, Short (c)	SER	3B	RR	R1,R2
Subtract Normalized, Short (c)	SE	7B	RX	R1,D2(X2,B2)
Subtract Unnormalized, Long (c)	SWR	2F	RR	R1,R2
Subtract Unnormalized, Long (c)	SW	6F	RX	R1,D2(X2,B2)
Subtract Unnormalized, Short (c)	SUR	3F	RR	R1,R2
Subtract Unnormalized, Short (c)	SU	7F	RX	R1,D2(X2,B2)

NOTES

CODES FOR PROGRAM INTERRUPTION ⑦

Interruption Code		Program Interruption Cause	Interruption Code		Program Interruption Cause
Dec	Hex		Dec	Hex	
1	0001	Operation	10	000A	Decimal overflow
2	0002	Privileged operation	11	000B	Decimal divide
3	0003	Execute	12	000C	Exponent overflow
4	0004	Protection	13	000D	Exponent underflow
5	0005	Addressing	14	000E	Significance
6	0006	Specification	15	000F	Floating-point divide
7	0007	Data	16*	0010	Segment translation
8	0008	Fixed-point overflow	17*	0011	Page translation
9	0009	Fixed-point divide			

*Model 67

HEXADECIMAL AND DECIMAL CONVERSION

From hex: locate each hex digit in its corresponding column position and note the decimal equivalents. Add these to obtain the decimal value.

From decimal: (1) locate the largest decimal value in the table that will fit into the decimal number to be converted, and (2) note its hex equivalent and hex column position. (3) Find the decimal remainder. Repeat the process on this and subsequent remainders.

Note: Decimal, hexadecimal, (and binary) equivalents of all numbers from 0 to 255 are listed on panels 11-14.

HEXADECIMAL COLUMNS

6 HEX = DEC	5 HEX = DEC	4 HEX = DEC	3 HEX = DEC	2 HEX = DEC	1 HEX = DEC
0 0	0 0	0 0	0 0	0 0	0 0
1 1,048,576	1 65,536	1 4,096	1 256	1 16	1 1
2 2,097,152	2 131,072	2 8,192	2 512	2 32	2 2
3 3,145,728	3 196,608	3 12,288	3 768	3 48	3 3
4 4,194,304	4 262,144	4 16,384	4 1,024	4 64	4 4
5 5,242,880	5 327,680	5 20,480	5 1,280	5 80	5 5
6 6,291,456	6 393,216	6 24,576	6 1,536	6 96	6 6
7 7,340,032	7 458,752	7 28,672	7 1,792	7 112	7 7
8 8,388,608	8 524,288	8 32,768	8 2,048	8 128	8 8
9 9,437,184	9 589,824	9 36,864	9 2,304	9 144	9 9
A 10,485,760	A 655,360	A 40,960	A 2,560	A 160	A 10
B 11,534,336	B 720,896	B 45,056	B 2,816	B 176	B 11
C 12,582,912	C 786,432	C 49,152	C 3,072	C 192	C 12
D 13,631,488	D 851,968	D 53,248	D 3,328	D 208	D 13
E 14,680,064	E 917,504	E 57,344	E 3,584	E 224	E 14
F 15,728,640	F 983,040	F 61,440	F 3,840	F 240	F 15
0 1 2 3	4 5 6 7	0 1 2 3	4 5 6 7	0 1 2 3	4 5 6 7
BYTE		BYTE		BYTE	

POWERS OF 2

2^n	n
256	8
512	9
1 024	10
2 048	11
4 096	12
8 192	13
16 384	14
32 768	15
65 536	16
131 072	17
262 144	18
524 288	19
1 048 576	20
2 097 152	21
4 194 304	22
8 388 608	23
16 777 216	24

$2^0 = 16^0$	
$2^4 = 16^1$	
$2^8 = 16^2$	
$2^{12} = 16^3$	
$2^{16} = 16^4$	
$2^{20} = 16^5$	
$2^{24} = 16^6$	
$2^{28} = 16^7$	
$2^{32} = 16^8$	
$2^{36} = 16^9$	
$2^{40} = 16^{10}$	
$2^{44} = 16^{11}$	
$2^{48} = 16^{12}$	
$2^{52} = 16^{13}$	
$2^{56} = 16^{14}$	
$2^{60} = 16^{15}$	

POWERS OF 16

16^n	n
1	0
16	1
256	2
4 096	3
65 536	4
1 048 576	5
16 777 216	6
268 435 456	7
4 294 967 296	8
68 719 476 736	9
1 099 511 627 776	10
17 592 186 044 416	11
281 474 976 710 656	12
4 503 599 627 370 496	13
72 057 594 037 927 936	14
1 152 921 504 606 846 976	15

Figure 6.8   Reference Data Card (panels 11 and 12)

Panel ⑪

Decimal	Hexa-decimal	Instruction Mnemonic (RR Format)	Graphic & Control Symbols (5) BCDIC	EBCDIC	7-Track Tape BCDIC	Punched Card Code	System/360 8-bit Code
0	00			NUL		12-0-1-8-9	0000 0000
1	01			SOH		12-1-9	0000 0001
2	02			STX		12-2-9	0000 0010
3	03			ETX		12-3-9	0000 0011
4	04	SPM		PF		12-4-9	0000 0100
5	05	BALR		HT		12-5-9	0000 0101
6	06	BCTR		LC		12-6-9	0000 0110
7	07	BCR		DEL		12-7-9	0000 0111
8	08	SSK				12-8-9	0000 1000
9	09	ISK				12-1-8-9	0000 1001
10	0A	SVC		SMM		12-2-8-9	0000 1010
11	0B			VT		12-3-8-9	0000 1011
12	0C			FF		12-4-8-9	0000 1100
13	0D	BASR (4)		CR		12-5-8-9	0000 1101
14	0E			SO		12-6-8-9	0000 1110
15	0F			SI		12-7-8-9	0000 1111
16	10	LPR		DLE		12-11-1-8-9	0001 0000
17	11	LNR		DC1		11-1-9	0001 0001
18	12	LTR		DC2		11-2-9	0001 0010
19	13	LCR		TM		11-3-9	0001 0011
20	14	NR		RES		11-4-9	0001 0100
21	15	CLR		NL		11-5-9	0001 0101
22	16	OR		BS		11-6-9	0001 0110
23	17	XR		IL		11-7-9	0001 0111
24	18	LR		CAN		11-8-9	0001 1000
25	19	CR		EM		11-1-8-9	0001 1001
26	1A	AR		CC		11-2-8-9	0001 1010
27	1B	SR		CU1		11-3-8-9	0001 1011
28	1C	MR		IFS		11-4-8-9	0001 1100
29	1D	DR		IGS		11-5-8-9	0001 1101
30	1E	ALR		IRS		11-6-8-9	0001 1110
31	1F	SLR		IUS		11-7-8-9	0001 1111
32	20	LPDR		DS		11-0-1-8-9	0010 0000
33	21	LNDR		SOS		0-1-9	0010 0001
34	22	LTDR		FS		0-2-9	0010 0010
35	23	LCDR				0-3-9	0010 0011
36	24	HDR		BYP		0-4-9	0010 0100
37	25	LRDR		LF		0-5-9	0010 0101
38	26	MXR		ETB		0-6-9	0010 0110
39	27	MXDR		ESC		0-7-9	0010 0111
40	28	LDR				0-8-9	0010 1000
41	29	CDR				0-1-8-9	0010 1001
42	2A	ADR		SM		0-2-8-9	0010 1010
43	2B	SDR		CU2		0-3-8-9	0010 1011
44	2C	MDR				0-4-8-9	0010 1100
45	2D	DDR		ENQ		0-5-8-9	0010 1101
46	2E	AWR		ACK		0-6-8-9	0010 1110
47	2F	SWR		BEL		0-7-8-9	0010 1111
48	30	LPER				12-11-0-1-8-9	0011 0000
49	31	LNER				1-9	0011 0001
50	32	LTER		SYN		2-9	0011 0010
51	33	LCER				3-9	0011 0011
52	34	HER		PN		4-9	0011 0100
53	35	LRER		RS		5-9	0011 0101
54	36	AXR		UC		6-9	0011 0110
55	37	SXR		EOT		7-9	0011 0111
56	38	LER				8-9	0011 1000
57	39	CER				1-8-9	0011 1001
58	3A	AER				2-8-9	0011 1010
59	3B	SER		CU3		3-8-9	0011 1011
60	3C	MER		DC4		4-8-9	0011 1100
61	3D	DER		NAK		5-8-9	0011 1101
62	3E	AUR				6-8-9	0011 1110
63	3F	SUR		SUB		7-8-9	0011 1111

Panel ⑫

Decimal	Hexa-decimal	Instruction Mnemonic (RX Format)	Graphic & Control Symbols (5) BCDIC	EBCDIC	7-Track Tape BCDIC (1)	Punched Card Code	System/360 8-bit Code
64	40	STH		SP	(2)	no punches	0100 0000
65	41	LA				12-0-1-9	0100 0001
66	42	STC				12-0-2-9	0100 0010
67	43	IC				12-0-3-9	0100 0011
68	44	EX				12-0-4-9	0100 0100
69	45	BAL				12-0-5-9	0100 0101
70	46	BCT				12-0-6-9	0100 0110
71	47	BC				12-0-7-9	0100 0111
72	48	LH				12-0-8-9	0100 1000
73	49	CH				12-1-8	0100 1001
74	4A	AH	·	¢	BA8 21	12-2-8	0100 1010
75	4B	SH	.	.	BA8 2 1	12-3-8	0100 1011
76	4C	MH	⌐)	<	BA8 4	12-4-8	0100 1100
77	4D	BAS (4)	[	(	BA8 4 1	12-5-8	0100 1101
78	4E	CVD	<	+	BA8 42	12-6-8	0100 1110
79	4F	CVB	‡	!	BA8 421	12-7-8	0100 1111
80	50	ST	& +	&	BA	12	0101 0000
81	51					12-11-1-9	0101 0001
82	52					12-11-2-9	0101 0010
83	53					12-11-3-9	0101 0011
84	54	N				12-11-4-9	0101 0100
85	55	CL				12-11-5-9	0101 0101
86	56	O				12-11-6-9	0101 0110
87	57	X				12-11-7-9	0101 0111
88	58	L				12-11-8-9	0101 1000
89	59	C				11-1-8	0101 1001
90	5A	A		!		11-2-8	0101 1010
91	5B	S	$	$	B 8 21	11-3-8	0101 1011
92	5C	M	*	*	B 8 4	11-4-8	0101 1100
93	5D	D	]	)	B 8 4 1	11-5-8	0101 1101
94	5E	AL	;	;	B 8 42	11-6-8	0101 1110
95	5F	SL	∆	⌐	B 8 421	11-7-8	0101 1111
96	60	STD	−	−	B	11	0110 0000
97	61		/	/	A 1	0-1	0110 0001
98	62					11-0-2-9	0110 0010
99	63					11-0-3-9	0110 0011
100	64					11-0-4-9	0110 0100
101	65					11-0-5-9	0110 0101
102	66					11-0-6-9	0110 0110
103	67	MXD				11-0-7-9	0110 0111
104	68	LD				11-0-8-9	0110 1000
105	69	CD				0-1-8	0110 1001
106	6A	AD		¦		12-11	0110 1010
107	6B	SD	,	,	A 8 21	0-3-8	0110 1011
108	6C	MD	% (	%	A 8 4	0-4-8	0110 1100
109	6D	DD	⋎	_	A 8 4 1	0-5-8	0110 1101
110	6E	AW	\	>	A 8 42	0-6-8	0110 1110
111	6F	SW	⧻	?	A 8 421	0-7-8	0110 1111
112	70	STE				12-11-0	0111 0000
113	71					12-11-0-1-9	0111 0001
114	72					12-11-0-2-9	0111 0010
115	73					12-11-0-3-9	0111 0011
116	74					12-11-0-4-9	0111 0100
117	75					12-11-0-5-9	0111 0101
118	76					12-11-0-6-9	0111 0110
119	77					12-11-0-7-9	0111 0111
120	78	LE				12-11-0-8-9	0111 1000
121	79	CE				1-8	0111 1001
122	7A	AE	6	:	A	2-8	0111 1010
123	7B	SE	# =	#	8 21	3-8	0111 1011
124	7C	ME	@ '	@	8 4	4-8	0111 1100
125	7D	DE	:	'	8 4 1	5-8	0111 1101
126	7E	AU	>	=	8 42	6-8	0111 1110
127	7F	SU	⋎	"	8 421	7-8	0111 1111

U

NOTES FOR PANELS 11-14

1. Add C (check bit) for odd or even parity as needed, except as noted
2. For even parity use CA
3. Decimal feature
4. Model 67
5. EBCDIC graphics shown are standard bit pattern assignments. For specific print train/chain see printer manual.

RR FORMAT

Op Code	R₁	R₂

0   78 1112 15

RX FORMAT

Op Code	R₁	X₂	B₂	D₂

0   78 1112 1516 1920   31

R1, D2 (X2, B2) or R1, S2 (X2)
R1, D2 (0, B2) or R1, S2

Figure 6.9 Reference Data Card (panels 13 and 14)

⑬

Deci-mal	Hexa-deci-mal	Instruction Mnemonic (Var. Formats)	Graphic & Control Symbols (5) BCDIC	EBCDIC	7-Track Tape BCDIC	Punched Card Code	System/360 8-bit Code
128	80	SSM				12-0-1-8	1000 0000
129	81			a		12-0-1	1000 0001
130	82	LPSW		b		12-0-2	1000 0010
131	83	(Diagnose)		c		12-0-3	1000 0011
132	84	WRD		d		12-0-4 ·	1000 0100
133	85	RDD		e		12-0-5	1000 0101
134	86	BXH		f		12-0-6	1000 0110
135	87	BXLE		g		12-0-7	1000 0111
136	88	SRL		h		12-0-8	1000 1000
137	89	SLL		i		12-0-9	1000 1001
138	8A	SRA				12-0-2-8	1000 1010
139	8B	SLA				12-0-3-8	1000 1011
140	8C	SRDL				12-0-4-8	1000 1100
141	8D	SLDL				12-0-5-8	1000 1101
142	8E	SRDA				12-0-6-8	1000 1110
143	8F	SLDA				12-0-7-8	1000 1111
144	90	STM				12-11-1-8	1001 0000
145	91	TM		j		12-11-1	1001 0001
146	92	MVI		k		12-11-2	1001 0010
147	93	TS		l		12-11-3	1001 0011
148	94	NI		m		12-11-4	1001 0100
149	95	CLI		n		12-11-5	1001 0101
150	96	OI		o		12-11-6	1001 0110
151	97	XI		p		12-11-7	1001 0111
152	98	LM		q		12-11-8	1001 1000
153	99			r		12-11-9	1001 1001
154	9A					12-11-2-8	1001 1010
155	9B					12-11-3-8	1001 1011
156	9C	SIO				12-11-4-8	1001 1100
157	9D	TIO				12-11-5-8	1001 1101
158	9E	HIO				12-11-6-8	1001 1110
159	9F	TCH				12-11-7-8	1001 1111
160	A0					11-0-1-8	1010 0000
161	A1			~		11-0-1	1010 0001
162	A2			s		11-0-2	1010 0010
163	A3			t		11-0-3	1010 0011
164	A4			u		11-0-4	1010 0100
165	A5			v		11-0-5	1010 0101
166	A6			w		11-0-6	1010 0110
167	A7			x		11-0-7	1010 0111
168	A8			y		11-0-8	1010 1000
169	A9			z		11-0-9	1010 1001
170	AA					11-0-2-8	1010 1010
171	AB					11-0-3-8	1010 1011
172	AC					11-0-4-8	1010 1100
173	AD					11-0-5-8	1010 1101
174	AE					11-0-6-8	1010 1110
175	AF					11-0-7-8	1010 1111
176	B0	STMC (4)				12-11-0-1-8	1011 0000
177	B1	LRA (4)				12-11-0-1	1011 0001
178	B2					12-11-0-2	1011 0010
179	B3					12-11-0-3	1011 0011
180	B4					12-11-0-4	1011 0100
181	B5					12-11-0-5	1011 0101
182	B6					12-11-0-6	1011 0110
183	B7					12-11-0-7	1011 0111
184	B8	LMC (4)				12-11-0-8	1011 1000
185	B9					12-11-0-9	1011 1001
186	BA					12-11-0-2-8	1011 1010
187	BB					12-11-0-3-8	1011 1011
188	BC					12-11-0-4-8	1011 1100
189	BD					12-11-0-5-8	1011 1101
190	BE					12-11-0-6-8	1011 1110
191	BF					12-11-0-7-8	1011 1111

⑭

Deci-mal	Hexa-deci-mal	Instruction Mnemonic (SS Format)	Graphic & Control Symbols (5) BCDIC	EBCDIC	7-Track Tape BCDIC (1)	Punched Card Code	System/360 8-bit Code
192	C0		?	{	B A 8 2	12-0	1100 0000
193	C1		A	A	B A 1	12-1	1100 0001
194	C2		B	B	B A 2	12-2	1100 0010
195	C3		C	C	B A 2 1	12-3	1100 0011
196	C4		D	D	B A 4	12-4	1100 0100
197	C5		E	E	B A 4 1	12-5	1100 0101
198	C6		F	F	B A 4 2	12-6	1100 0110
199	C7		G	G	B A 4 2 1	12-7	1100 0111
200	C8		H	H	B A 8	12-8	1100 1000
201	C9		I	I	B A 8 1	12-9	1100 1001
202	CA					12-0-2-8-9	1100 1010
203	CB					12-0-3-8-9	1100 1011
204	CC		♪			12-0-4-8-9	1100 1100
205	CD					12-0-5-8-9	1100 1101
206	CE		Ψ			12-0-6-8-9	1100 1110
207	CF					12-0-7-8-9	1100 1111
208	D0	MVN	!	}	B 8 2	11-0	1101 0000
209	D1		J	J	B 1	11-1	1101 0001
210	D2	MVC	K	K	B 2	11-2	1101 0010
211	D3	MVZ	L	L	B 2 1	11-3	1101 0011
212	D4	NC	M	M	B 4	11-4	1101 0100
213	D5	CLC	N	N	B 4 1	11-5	1101 0101
214	D6	OC	O	O	B 4 2	11-6	1101 0110
215	D7	XC	P	P	B 4 2 1	11-7	1101 0111
216	D8		Q	Q	B 8	11-8	1101 1000
217	D9		R	R	B 8 1	11-9	1101 1001
218	DA					12-11-2-8-9	1101 1010
219	DB					12-11-3-8-9	1101 1011
220	DC	TR				12-11-4-8-9	1101 1100
221	DD	TRT				12-11-5-8-9	1101 1101
222	DE	ED (3)				12-11-6-8-9	1101 1110
223	DF	EDMK (3)				12-11-7-8-9	1101 1111
224	E0		*	\	A 8 2	0-2-8	1110 0000
225	E1					11-0-1-9	1110 0001
226	E2		S	S	A 2	0-2	1110 0010
227	E3		T	T	A 2 1	0-3	1110 0011
228	E4		U	U	A 4	0-4	1110 0100
229	E5		V	V	A 4 1	0-5	1110 0101
230	E6		W	W	A 4 2	0-6	1110 0110
231	E7		X	X	A 4 2 1	0-7	1110 0111
232	E8		Y	Y	A 8	0-8	1110 1000
233	E9		Z	Z	A 8 1	0-9	1110 1001
234	EA					11-0-2-8-9	1110 1010
235	EB					11-0-3-8-9	1110 1011
236	EC		⌐			11-0-4-8-9	1110 1100
237	ED					11-0-5-8-9	1110 1101
238	EE					11-0-6-8-9	1110 1110
239	EF					11-0-7-8-9	1110 1111
240	F0		0	0	8 2	0	1111 0000
241	F1	MVO	1	1	1	1	1111 0001
242	F2	PACK	2	2	2	2	1111 0010
243	F3	UNPK	3	3	2 1	3	1111 0011
244	F4		4	4	4	4	1111 0100
245	F5		5	5	4 1	5	1111 0101
246	F6		6	6	4 2	6	1111 0110
247	F7		7	7	4 2 1	7	1111 0111
248	F8	ZAP (3)	8	8	8	8	1111 1000
249	F9	CP (3)	9	9	8 1	9	1111 1001
250	FA	AP (3)				12-11-0-2-8-9	1111 1010
251	FB	SP (3)				12-11-0-3-8-9	1111 1011
252	FC	MP (3)				12-11-0-4-8-9	1111 1100
253	FD	DP (3)				12-11-0-5-8-9	1111 1101
254	FE					12-11-0-6-8-9	1111 1110
255	FF					12-11-0-7-8-9	1111 1111

RS FORMAT

| Op Code | R₁ | R₃ | B₂ | D₂ |

bits: 0   7 8   11 12   15 16   19 20   31

R1, R3, D2 (B2) or R1, R3, S2: BXH, BXLE, LM, LMC, STM, STMC
R1, D2 (B2) or R1, S2: All shift instructions

SI FORMAT

| OP Code | I₂ | B₁ | D₁ |

bits: 0   7 8   15 16   19 20   31

D1 (B1) or S1: LPSW, SSM, HIO, SIO, TIO, TCH, TS
D1 (B1), I2 or S1, I2: MVI, CLI, NI, OI, XI, TM, WRD, RDD

SS FORMAT

| Op Code | L₁ | L₂ | B₁ | D₁ | B₂ | D₂ |

bits: 0   7 8   11 12   15 16   19 20   31 32   35 36   47

D1 (L, B1), D2 (B2) or S1 (L), S2: { NC, OC, XC, CLC, MVC, MVN, MVZ, TR, TRT, ED, EDMK }

D1 (L1, B1), D2 (L2, B2) or S1 (L1), S2 (L2): { PACK, UNPK, MVO, AP, CP, DP, MP, SP, ZAP }

2. Address Location

Recall from Chapter 4 that the Interrupt Address (IA) in the Active Program Status Word (APSW) for OS System 360/370 was found to be 096BB0. See Figure 6.3, letter 'A'. For System 370 OS/VS the appropriate IA would have been located in the PSW AT ENTRY TO ABEND. See letter 'B'. The Entry Point Address (EPA) was found to be 096250. See letter 'C'. Subtracting the EPA from the IA, a Relative Length into the program module of 960 was determined. Accessing the Assembly Language listing by Relative Length 960, the problem source statement was found to be #67, an IF Statement. See Figure 6.2, letter 'D'. The Source Program listing was then referenced to determine the actual source statement being executed at the time of the abend.

The compiler-generated Assembly Language listing takes on even more significance than determined previously because machine instructions are also listed. Realizing that the IA is the address of the next machine instruction to be executed, one need only back up one instruction to determine the actual machine instruction being executed at the time of the abend. As is evident, this instruction is located at Relative Address 95A. See Figure 6.2, letter 'E'. The actual machine instruction is F933D214D21C. It can now be appropriately broken down and analyzed. With an Assembly Language listing available, main storage need not ever be accessed, if desired, to analyze machine instructions.

Assuming the unavailability of an Assembly Language listing, this same instruction can be found in main storage. The Interrupt Address, 096BB0 can be referenced directly. Paging down the left-hand side of the print of main storage, Address 096BA0 is found to come closest to the address of interest without exceeding it. See Figure 6.5, letter 'F'. Counting to the right the required number of bytes, the Op Code for the next instruction to be executed is found to be 58. See letter 'G'.

To locate the actual instruction being executed, one must back up a number of bytes equivalent to the length of the instruction. What is the length of the instruction being executed? The left-most byte of the APSW now becomes significant to the storage dump analyst. It is found to be equal to C0. See Figure 6.3, letter 'H'. To determine

the length of the instruction being executed, this left-most byte of
the APSW is converted to Binary as follows:

Hexadecimal -   C   0

Binary   -   1100   0000

Hexadecimal C0 is equal to Binary 11000000. Instruction length is
determined by the status of the two left-most bits as follows:

01 = One Halfword, or two bytes.

10 = Two Halfwords, or four bytes.

11 = Three Halfwords, or six bytes.

With the two left-most bits equal to 11 in this example, Instruction
Length is three halfwords, or six bytes. One can now refer to main
storage and back up six bytes from the Interrupt Address to locate the
appropriate instruction. The machine instruction being executed at the
time of the abend is found to be F933D214D21C. See Figure 6.5, letter
'I'. This corresponds to the same instruction previously found in the
Assembly language listing, had it been obtained!

For System 370 OS/VS the determination of Instruction Length is
much simpler. The following message is provided to the right of the
PSW AT ENTRY TO ABEND:

ILC x

where x is equal to Instruction Length in bytes. See Figure 6.3, to
the right of letter 'B'.

ILC 2, ILC 4, and ILC 6, refer to Instruction Lengths of two, four,
and six bytes, respectively. In this example, the length of the
machine instruction being executed at the time of the abend is six bytes.

3. Delineation

a. Operation Code

F933D214D21C, the machine instruction being executed, can now be
broken down using the appropriate format. Recall that the Op Code

can be found as the first byte of the instruction itself. Op Code F9
can now be used to determine appropriate Instruction Format.

b. Format

Moving down the OP CODE column on the Reference Data Card, F9 can
be found approximately a third of the way from the top of the first
panel. See Figure 6.6, letter 'J'. The instruction is found to be
Compare Decimal with SS Format. See letter 'K'. Operand length fields
L1 and L2 can be found to the right of the format specification under
the heading OPERANDS. It is therefore determined that the SS Format
with two length specifications is to be utilized for instruction
breakdown purposes. See letter 'L'.

Instruction F933D214D21C can now be broken down as follows:

Op Code	L1	L2	B1	D1	B2	D2
F9	3	3	D	214	D	21C

where F9 represents the Op Code; 3 + 1 or 4 is the Length (L1) of the
First Operand; and 3 + 1 or 4 is the Length (L2) of the Second Operand.
Register (B1) D with hexadecimal Displacement (D1) 214 refers to the
location of the First Operand and Register (B2) D with hexadecimal Displacement (D2) 21C refers to the location of the Second Operand.

4. Operand Value

a. Address

This particular instruction compares the First Operand with the
Second Operand. The next step, therefore, is to locate both Operands
in main storage such that their values can be determined. The contents
of Base Register D or 13 as found in the instruction can be located in
the Registers At Entry To Abend area of the dump. The contents of the
Base Register is found to be 096730. See Figure 6.4, letter 'M'. Recall that the Displacements for the First and Second Operands were

found to be 214 and 21C, respectively. The address of both Operands
can be calculated as follows:

	First Operand	Second Operand
Base Address	096730	096730
Displacement	+ 214	+ 21C
Address of Operand	096944	09694C

The starting address in main storage of the First and Second Operands
is found to be 096944 and 09694C, respectively.

b. Length

Paging down the left-hand side of the print of main storage Address
096940 is found to come closest to the addresses of interest without
exceeding them. See Figure 6.5, letter 'N'. Moving to the right C bytes
for the Second Operand, the first character encountered at Address 09694C
is a zero. Marking off a length of 3 + 1 or 4 bytes, as determined previously, the character string for the Second Operand is found to be
0000001F. See letter 'O'. Moving to the right 4 bytes from Address
096940, the first character encountered for the First Operand at
Address 096944 is a zero. Marking off a length of 3 + 1 or 4 bytes,
as determined previously, the character string for the First Operand is
found to be 00000004. See letter 'P'.

The character string for each Operand can now be interpreted.

c. Interpretation

It is difficult to relate machine instructions to specific source
statements when an Assembly Language listing is not available. If it
were available the program could be referenced as well as the Data Map
to determine the form of data representation utilized. Without these
listings, only two clues as to data representation are possible.

1. Nature of the Op Code.
2. The Character String itself.

The nature of the Op Code can assist in determining the form of data representation utilized. As can be determined from the Reference Data Card, Op Code 1A along with a few others refer to an Add function. If the source program only contains one Add statement, the likelihood is that this is the problem statement. If the program contains 10 Add functions, the problem has been narrowed to 10 source statements, etc. The same holds true for Op Codes such as 1B, 1C, and 1D, for the functions of Subtraction, Multiplication, and Division, respectively. Having narrowed the problem to a reasonable number of source statements, the program variables defined within those statements can each be analyzed in terms of the character string found in main storage. A bit of applied logic is necessary when analyzing character strings for which the form of data representation is not known with complete assurance.

In the current example, a Compare Instruction which is generated from tests within the source program was being executed. It just so happens that this particular program contains only one IF Statement, IF STATE-DATA = STATE4, and is the problem source statement. Most programs contain more than one test statement; nevertheless, narrowing the problem to a small group of source statements can be an aid in problem solving. Attention can then be centered upon variables such as STATE-DATA and STATE4. A programmer would know by reviewing the source listing that the variables STATE-DATA and STATE4 are defined as External Decimal, i.e., USAGE DISPLAY. Remember, it is possible they could have been defined as Binary or some other form of data representation and thus interpreted quite differently.

One question remains - how do the character strings 0000001F and 00000004 for the Second and First Operands, respectively, relate to the External Decimal form of Data Representation? Recall from the presentation in Chapter 5 on this subject that the compiler generates instructions to automatically convert from Unpacked to Packed form prior to the execution of tests and arithmetic operations. Most abends do not occur until after External Decimal data has been packed. Assuming the Operands to be in Packed form, an Unpacking operation on the right-most byte of each string in this example would proceed as follows:

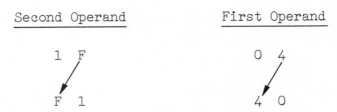

Second Operand   First Operand

The resulting character strings are now in External Decimal form and should be interpreted as such.

5. Problem Analysis

Recall that F1 is equivalent to +1 or 1, while a 40 is equivalent to a blank which is a non-numeric character. As determined in Chapter 5, it is being stored in a numeric field, thus causing the OC7 Storage Dump.

Character Format representation can be interpreted from the Reference Data Card, panels 11 - 14. Looking in the columns under the headings Hexadecimal and Punched Card Code, F1 is found to be equal to a one punch as expected. See Figure 6.9, letter 'Q'. When desired, this area of the card can also be used to convert to decimal or binary. If the Binary form of data representation were utilized, Hexadecimal F1 would be converted to Decimal 241. See letter 'R'. This can also be verified in the Hexadecimal Decimal Conversion Table where F (or 240) plus 1 (or 1) equals F1 (or 241). See Figure 6.7, letter 'S'. Hexadecimal F1 is also equivalent to Binary 11110001. See Figure 6.9, letter 'T'. Looking in the columns under the headings Hexadecimal and Punched Card Code, a 40 is found to be equal to a blank (no punches). See Figure 6.8, letter 'U'. This non-numeric character is the cause of the dump as discovered in Chapter 5.

It should also be noted that it is quite possible that a programmer could have defined various program variables in Internal Floating Point. FORTRAN Real Variables as well as COBOL COMP-1 and COMP-2 Variables are stored in Internal Floating Point form. Floating Point Feature Instructions are displayed on panel 3 of the Reference Data Card. See Figure 6.7, letter 'V'. Internal Floating Point is an extension of the basic Machine Instruction List on panels 1 and 2 of the Reference Data Card. The Floating Point Registers are also located in the Registers

At Entry To Abend area of a storage dump. See Figure 6.4, letter 'W'.
If a programmer utilized this form of data representation they would
need to be converted and interpreted as described in Chapter 2.

As can be seen, the breakdown and analysis of machine instructions
is not the most preferred method for effective debugging of storage
dumps. When compiler-generated Assembly Language listings and Data
Maps are not available, this is the only technique remaining to the
programmer and analyst.

Although an OS COBOL example was utilized in this chapter, the
machine instruction principles discussed apply to all programming languages, software, and operating systems.

C. PL1 VARIABLES

In order to determine the value of pertinent PL1 program variables,
an understanding of machine instruction formats is necessary. In
addition, a compiler-generated Assembly Language listing must be
available.

Similar to FORTRAN procedures, the name of the variable of interest
is printed in the Assembly Language listing. Actual machine instructions are also displayed. The value of appropriate Operands can therefore be determined.

If an Assembly Language listing is not available, the source statement being executed at the time of the abend cannot be determined unless
a Table of Offsets has been generated. In addition, the value of pertinent program values cannot be determined. In this case, one can only
proceed as described previously in this chapter. The actual machine
instruction being executed at the time of the abend must be located,
broken down, and analyzed. Operand values need be determined. Without
an Assembly Language listing or Table of Offsets, machine instruction
information can only provide a clue as to the actual cause of a storage dump.

Figures 6.10 and 6.11 on the following pages consist of selected
portions of the same PL1 source program and compiler-generated Assembly Language listing as described in Chapter 4.

Figure 6.10 Portion of PL1 Source Program Listing

```
2                        DCL 1 RECIN,
                             2    REGION    CHAR  (2),
                             2    STATE     CHAR  (17),
                             2    FILL1     CHAR  (3),
                             2    BPFYR     CHAR  (2),          ◄── F
                             2    BPP       CHAR  (5),
                             2    BPA       CHAR  (4),
                             2    WQP       CHAR  (4),
                             2    WQA       CHAR  (4),
                             2    BAP       CHAR  (4),
                             2    BAA       CHAR  (4),
                             2    FILLER    CHAR  (71);
3                        DCL 1 RECIN1,
                             2    REGION1   CHAR  (2),
                             2    STATE1    CHAR  (17),
                             2    FILL2     CHAR  (3),
                             2    BPFYR1    CHAR  (2),
                             2    BPP1      CHAR  (5),
                             2    BPA1      CHAR  (4),
                             2    WQP1      CHAR  (4),
                             2    WQA1      CHAR  (4),
                             2    BAP1      CHAR  (4),
                             2    BAA1      CHAR  (4),
                             2    FILLER    CHAR  (71);
4                        DCL 1 RECIN2,
                             2    REGION2   CHAR  (2),
                             2    STATE2    CHAR  (17),
                             2    FILL3     CHAR  (3),
                             2    BPFYR2    CHAR  (2),
                             2    BPP2      CHAR  (5),
                             2    BPA2      CHAR  (4),
                             2    WQP2      CHAR  (4),
                             2    WQA2      CHAR  (4),
                             2    BAP2      CHAR  (4),
                             2    BAA2      CHAR  (4),
                             2    FILLER    CHAR  (71);
5                DCL (C,D,E,F,G,H,I,J,K,Z,CONV)  FIXED DEC (5);
6                C,D,E,F,G,H,I,J,K,CONV=0;
7                        DCL  YYMMDD  CHAR (6);
8                        DCL 1 MMDDYY,
                             2  (MO,DA,YR)  CHAR (2);
9                        YYMMDD = DATE;
10                       GET STRING (YYMMDD) EDIT (YR,MO,DA) (A(2),A(2),A(2));
11                       DCL    PAGENUM FIXED DEC (4);  PAGENUM=1;
13                       DCL REG    CHAR (2); REG=' ';
15                       DCL (Y1,Y2,Y3,Y4) CHAR (2);  Y1,Y2,Y3,Y4=' ';
17               DCL A CHAR (7);  A=(7)'-';  DCL B CHAR (8); B=(8)'-';
21                       DCL READIT FILE RECORD INPUT;
22                       ON ENDFILE(READIT) GO TO FIN;
24                       OPEN FILE (SYSPRINT) LINESIZE (132);
25                       REGION2=' ';
26               RD:     READ FILE (READIT) INTO (RECIN);
27                       IF BPFYR = ' ' THEN GO TO RD;
29                       IF Y4 = ' ' THEN GO TO FORM1;
31               RD1:      IF REG=REGION THEN GO TO FORM2;
```

Figure 6.11 Portion of Assembly Language Listing (PL1)

```
000290 05 EF                        BALR  14,15

* STATEMENT NUMBER 12
000292 D2 02 D 1D7 B 365            MVC   PAGENUM(3),C..062C

* STATEMENT NUMBER 14
000298 D2 01 D 1DA B 362            MVC   REG(2),C..062C

* STATEMENT NUMBER 16
00029E D2 01 D 1DC B 35D            MVC   Y1(2),C..043C
0002A4 D2 01 D 1DE B 35D            MVC   Y2(2),C..043C
0002AA D2 01 D 1E0 B 35D            MVC   Y3(2),C..043C
0002B0 D2 01 D 1E2 B 35D            MVC   Y4(2),C..043C

* STATEMENT NUMBER 18
0002B6 D2 06 D 1E4 B 356            MVC   A(7),C..0440

* STATEMENT NUMBER 20
0002BC D2 07 D 1EB B 34E            MVC   B(8),C..0444

* STATEMENT NUMBER 22
0002C2 41 F0 D 058                  LA    15,ON..ENDFILE..READIT
0002C6 94 C7 F 004                  NI    4(15),X'C7'
0002CA D2 02 F 005 B 04D            MVC   5(3,15),A..01+1

* ON UNIT BLOCK
0014C0 90 EB D 00C                  STM   14,11,12(13)
0014C4 18 AF                        LR    10,15
0014C6 58 B0 A 01C                  L     11,28(0,10)
0014CA 58 F0 B 020                  L     15,32(0,11)
0014CE 58 00 A 018                  L     0,24(0,10)
0014D2 05 EF                        BALR  14,15
0014D4 47 F0 A 020                  B     32(0,10)
0014D8 00000080                     DC    F'176'
0014DC 00000000                     DC    A(SI.)
0014E0 05 A0                        BALR  10,0
0014E2 05 A0                        BALR  10,0

* PROLOGUE BASE
0014E4 41 90 D 090                  LA    9,144(0,13)
0014E8                     CL.70    EQU   *
0014E8 58 EC 0 000                  L     14,PR..01(12)
0014EC 50 E0 0 05C                  ST    14,92(0,13)
0014F0 41 EC 0 000                  LA    14,PR..01(12)
0014F4 1B EC                        SR    14,12
0014F6 50 E0 0 058                  ST    14,88(0,13)
0014FA 50 DC 0 000                  ST    13,PR..01(12)
0014FE 92 94 0 000                  MVI   0(13),X'94'
001502 41 A0 A 024                  LA    10,CL.68
001506 07 00                        NOPR  0

* PROCEDURE BASE
001508                     CL.68    EQU   *

* STATEMENT NUMBER 23

001508 41 10 B 044                  LA    1,A..FIN
00150C 58 F0 B 090                  L     15,A..IHESAFC
001510 05 EF                        BALR  14,15
001512 58 F0 B 030                  L..   15,A..IHESAFA
001516 05 EF                        BALR  14,15

* ON UNIT BLOCK END

* STATEMENT NUMBER 24
0002D0 41 10 B 53C                  LA    1,SKPL..055C
0002D4 58 F0 B 080                  L     15,A..IHEOCLA
0002D8 05 EF                        BALR  14,15

* STATEMENT NUMBER 25
0002DA D2 01 D 2E4 B 35F            MVC   RECIN2.REGION2(2),C..0630

* STATEMENT NUMBER 26

* STATEMENT LABEL
0002E0 D2 13 D C88 B 58C            MVC   WS1.1(20),SKPL..05
                                          40
0002E6 41 80 D 1A9                  LA    8,RDV..RECIN
0002EA 50 80 D 08C                  ST    8,WS1.I+4
0002EE 41 10 D 089                  LA    1,WS1.1
0002F2 05 EF                        L..   15,A..IHEIONA
                                    BALR  14,15

* STATEMENT NUMBER 27
0002F8 D5 00 D 209 B 361            CLC   RECIN.BPFYR(1),C..
                                          0438
0002FE 47 70 A 138                  BC    7,CL.18
000302 D5 00 D 20A B 118            CLC   RECIN.BPFYR+1(1),C
                                          ..0530

000308                     CL.13    EQU   *

* STATEMENT NUMBER 28
000308 47 90 A 110                  BC    9,RD
00030C                     CL.1     EQU   *

* STATEMENT NUMBER 29
00030C D5 00 D 1E2 B 361            CLC   Y4(1),C..0438
000312 47 70 A 14C                  BC    7,CL.19
000316 D5 00 D 1E3 B 118            CLC   Y4+1(1),C..0530
00031C                     CL.19    EQU   *

* STATEMENT NUMBER 30
00031C 47 90 A 4AA                  BC    9,FORM1
000320                     CL.3     EQU   *

* STATEMENT LABEL
000320 D5 01 D 1DA D 1F8            CLC   REG(2),RECIN.REGIO
                                          N
```

203

1. Assembly Language Listing

     In the determination of the problem source statement in Chapter 4, a relative length of 302 bytes into the program module was assumed. From the Assembly Language listing it was found that Source Statement #27 was being executed at the time of the abend. See Figure 6.11, letter 'A'. The Source Program listing was then referenced where the problem source statement was found to be IF BPFYR = ' '. See Figure 6.10, letter 'B'. Variable BPFYR is considered pertinent as it is contained within the problem source statement. See letter 'C'.

     In order to determine the value of BPFYR at the time of the abend, the variable name must be located in the Assembly Language listing at or near the machine instruction being executed. See letter 'D'. For PL1 program variables, it is significant to note that the same variable name also occurs earlier in the same set of machine instructions at Address 2F8. See letter 'E'. The value in the parentheses behind BPFYR indicates the length of the character string being referenced. This number may be less than or equal to the total length of the field as defined in the program.

     From the Source Program listing it can be seen that the length of Variable BPFYR is two characters, or two bytes. See Figure 6.10, letter 'F'. Referring back to the Assembly Language listing in Figure 6.11, letter 'E', the variable name indication BPFYR(1) means that only the first character of the two byte field is being tested. Likewise, the variable name indication BPFYR+1(1) at letter 'D' means that the first character of the string is being skipped as denoted by a +1, and that the remaining characters, for a length of one in parentheses, are being tested. This concept is depicted below. Assume that the value of BPFYR is equal to 28.

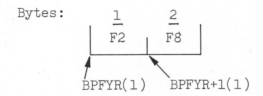

Assume for the moment that BPFYR is a four byte field with a value of 2480. The variable name as depicted in an Assembly Language listing would reference the field as follows:

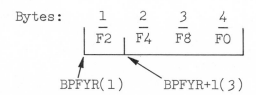

Bytes: BPFYR(1)   BPFYR+1(3)

In other words, only selected portions of a complete field may be referenced in a given machine instruction.

It is also important to note which Operand pertains to the variable of interest. Those to the left of the comma refer to the First Operand, while those to the right refer to the Second Operand, etc. This is determined by the actual format of the Assembly Language instruction itself. See Figure 6.11, letter 'G'. As can be seen, variable BPFYR to the left of the comma is referenced by the First Operand.

2. Instruction Analysis

The two machine instructions for the variable of interest can now be located, broken down, and the value of pertinent Operands determined. The machine instructions for the first and second characters of the variable BPFYR are D500D209B361 and D500D20AB118, respectively. See Figure 6.11, letter 'H'. From the Reference Data Card it can be determined that Op Code D5 refers to a Compare Logical instruction of SS Format. The two machine instructions can therefore be broken down as follows:

	Op Code	L1	L2	B1	D1	B2	D2
BPFYR(1)	D5	0	0	D	209	B	361
BPFYR+1(1)	D5	0	0	D	20A	B	118

The value of the First Operand in the first instruction, and in this case the first character of BPFYR, can be found and interpreted in main storage by adding the contents of Base Register D to Displacement 209. Once this address is located, a Length of 0 + 1, or 1, would be marked off. Similarly, the value of the First Operand in the second instruction, and in this case the second character of BPFYR, can be found and interpreted by adding the contents of Base Register D to Displacement 20A. Once this address is located, a Length of 0 + 1, or 1, would be marked off.

As can be seen, a knowledge of machine instruction breakdown and analysis within an Assembly Language listing is necessary when determining the value of pertinent PL1 program variables.

D. MACHINE INSTRUCTION SUMMARY

When appropriate listings are not available, the location, breakdown, and analysis of machine instructions should be accomplished. Op Code and Operand Values can then be determined.

1. Determine Address of Next Machine Instruction to be executed.
   a. System 360/370 OS -- Right-most three bytes of APSW.
   b. System 370 OS/VS -- Right-most three bytes of PSW AT ENTRY TO ABEND.
2. Determine Length of Machine Instruction.
   a. System 360/370 OS -- Convert left-most byte of APSW to Binary. Two left-most bits indicate Length.
      01 - 2 bytes
      10 - 4 bytes
      11 - 6 bytes
   b. System 370 OS/VS -- See 'ILC x' message to right of PSW AT ENTRY TO ABEND, where x = Length in bytes.
3. Determine Machine Instruction being executed.
   a. Locate Address in Main Storage.
   b. Back up required Number of Bytes as determined from Length.
4. Note Op Code, Function, and Format.
   a. Determine Op Code from First Byte of Machine Instruction.
   b. Determine Function from Reference Data Card.
   c. Determine Format from Reference Data Card.

5. Determine Operand Addresses.
   a. Breakdown Instruction utilizing appropriate Format.
   b. Calculate Operand Addresses utilizing appropriate Base Registers, Index Registers, and Displacements, as required.
6. Locate and Interpret Operand Value.
   a. Locate Operand Address in Main Storage except for Immediate Operands which are located in the Instruction itself.
   b. Delineate Operand using appropriate Length.

   For SS Format, Length is determined by adding one to Length Indication in Machine Instruction. For other Formats, Length equals four bytes, except for occasional Halfword (2 bytes) and Double Word (8 bytes) instruction use as determined from the Reference Data Card or the program itself.

   c. Interpret Character String based upon nature of Op Code and Data Representation techniques.

A workshop is now provided to solidify a working knowledge of Machine Instruction location, breakdown, and analysis.

E. WORKSHOP PROBLEM (OCB)

1. Description

The following workshop depicts selected pages of the same run which abended with a OCB Completion Code in Chapters 4 and 5.

Recall that a OCB Storage Dump refers to a type of problem in which an attempt has been made to divide by zero, or, the quotient length as defined in the program has been exceeded. The problem source statement was found to be #62, COMPUTE ITEST = DATA-ARRAY (SUB-M) / DATA-ARRAY (SUB-N). The value for DATA-ARRAY (SUB-N) was found to be zero as read in from the input file.

If an Assembly Language listing and Data Map were not available, the above information could not have been determined. Assuming their unavailability, locate the machine instruction being executed at the time of the abend. Breakdown the instruction utilizing the appropriate format. Determine the value for the First and Second Operands. A problem analysis can then be made.

Figures 6.12 through 6.14 depict selected pages for machine instruction purposes of the same OCB Storage Dump described in the workshops in Chapters 4 and 5. Figure 6.15 displays panels 1 and 2 of the Reference Data Card.

A problem solution can be found in Appendix A.

Reference Data Card reprinted by permission from GX20-1703-9 © by International Business Machines Corporation.

Figure 6.12 First Page of OCB Storage Dump

```
JOB  RZZ925        STEP GC        TIME 200518

COMPLETION CODE        SYSTEM = 0C3

PSW AT ENTRY TO ABEND  FF75000D E020AF56

TCB  0356A0  RBP  0003D5F8  PIE  00000000  DEB  0003B524  TIO 0003B840  CMP 800CB000  TRN 00000000
             MSS  02046B60  PK-FLG 70850400  FLG 0003F5B  LLS 0C03A5E8  JLB 00000000  JPQ 80038BD0
             FSA  01211768  TCB  00000000  TME 00000000  JST 00356A0  NTC 00000000  OTC 0003BF20
             LTC  00000000  IQE 00000000  EC8 0003BED4  TSF 20000000  D-PQE 00046E10  SQS 000349A8
             NSTAE 80042980 TCT 80035E20  USER 00000000  DAR 00000000  RESV 00000000  JSCB 87046A80
             RESV CC000000  IOB 00000000

ACTIVE RBS

FRB  042800  RESV 00000000  APSW E020AF56  WC-SZ-STAB 00040382  FL-CDE 0004B5C8  PSW FF75000D E020AF56
             Q/TTR CC000000  WT-LNK 00356A0

SVRB 041EE0  TAB-LN 00F80220  APSW F9F0F1C3  WT-LNK 0004280Q  WC-SZ-STAB 0012D002  TQN 00000000  PSW 00040033 5019C32
             Q/TTR CC004DDC  0C000006  0020A87C  00000003  0020AEE8  0020A870  00211E8
             RG 0-7 0000000A  0020B24E  0020A7E8  00000000  0020AB10  5020AECE  002FDDA8
             RG 8-15 0020AA88  8F211250  00000000  FF030000  00041C2C  00041C34  E2E8E2C9
             EXTSA C5C1F0F1  C9C5C1A0  C4F90CB0

SVRB 03D5F8  TAB-LN 0038D3D8  APSW F1F0F5C1  WT-LNK 00041BB0  WC-SZ-STAB 0012D002  TQN 00000000  PSW FF0400QC 4020F7A6
             Q/TTR 0003D11  0CC41C1C  80C19B44  0001A318  00356A0  04035640  00041BB0
             RG 0-7 001C58B0  40019A92  0003554D  8F211250  00041C34  40019854  00000000
             RG 8-15 000356A0  C5C1F0F1  C9C1C3F0  F2F0F3C5  0020D789E  00211FE8  5001A46C
             EXTSA E2E8E2C9  00035624  84018B10  002DEB52

LOAD LIST

NE 0003A5F0  RSP-CDE 02038BD0  NE 0003AFA0  NE 0003F858  RSP-CDE 01045898
NE 00042920  RSP-CDE 01045BC8  NE 00042960  RSP-CDE 01045988  NE 00042968  RSP-CDE 01045A98
NE 00042978  RSP-CDE 01045BC8  NE 00042AD0  RSP-CDE 01045BC8  NE 00046800  RSP-CDE 01045B28
NE 00046880  RSP-CDE 01045BC8  NE 00046968  RSP-CDE 01045898  NE 00046AF8  RSP-CDE 01045958
NE 00000000  RSP-CDE 01045AF8

CDE

0435C8  ATR1 08  NCDE 000000   ROC-RB 03043800  NM MAIN    USE 01  EPA 20A7E8  ATR2 20  XL/MJ 042AD8
038BD0  ATR1 30  NCDE 038BA0   ROC-RB 00033000  NM IGCOA05A USE 02  EPA 20F058  ATR2 28  XL/MJ 03A470
0458C8  ATR1 B0  NCDE 0458F8   ROC-RB 00000000  NM IGG019CF USE 01  EPA 2FC8A0  ATR2 20  XL/MJ 045888
045898  ATR1 B0  NCDE 0458C8   ROC-RB 00000000  NM IGG019CL USE 01  EPA 2FF008  ATR2 20  XL/MJ 045888
0459C8  ATR1 B0  NCDE 0459F8   ROC-RB 00000000  NM IGG019BA USE 01  EPA 2FCE40  ATR2 20  XL/MJ 045988
045988  ATR1 B0  NCDE 0459C8   ROC-RB 00000000  NM IGG019BB USE 01  EPA 2FD800  ATR2 20  XL/MJ 045978
045A58  ATR1 B0  NCDE 045AC8   ROC-RB 00000000  NM IGG019CC USE 01  EPA 2FD4F8  ATR2 20  XL/MJ 045A88
045A28  ATR1 B0  NCDE 045A58   ROC-RB 00000000  NM IGG019CI USE 01  EPA 2FD298  ATR2 20  XL/MJ 045A18
045BC8  ATR1 B0  NCDE 045BF8   ROC-RB 00000000  NM IGG019AA USE 01  EPA 2FE808  ATR2 20  XL/MJ 045B88
```

209

Figure 6.13 First Page of OCB Main Storage

```
PROCEEDING BACK VIA REG 13

MAIN   WAS ENTERED VIA CALL       AT EP 03  C9 08   03 083 09  09      0J80 0 600 J0    < I  Z  J   -

SA  20AB10 WD1 0030C4C2  HSA 03211768   LSA 00211380   RET 5020B254   EPA 00208452   R0  5020AECE
           R1  122FE808  R2  00000030   R3  002JA95C   R4  0020A95C   R5  5C036ED8   R6  0020A9D8
           R7  5C2B280   R8  JU2CA870   R9  0020A7E8   R10 0020AA88   R11 402FE840   R12 002FDDA8

REGS AT ENTRY TO ABEND

FLTR 0-6   CCCCCC0000CJJJ   0000000J0J00JJ000   0000000J0J00JJ000     0000000C080018E14   00035330000000C8

REGS 0-7   0000000A  0000006   0020A37C  3000JJ03    0020A882  0020AEE8   0020A870  00211E8
REGS 8-15  0020AA88  0020B24E   0020A7E8  JJ20A7E8    0020AD78  0020AB10   5020AECE  002FDDA8

LOAD MODULE   MAIN

20A7E0   40404040 40404040   40404040 40404040   *................*
20A800   40404040 4C4C4C40   4040J340 40404040   *................*
20A820   4C4C4C40 D6404340   4040J340 40404040   *..............1*
20A840   D4C5E3D9 C1F7F2F0   4040J001 12116CF1   *METRO A720....1*
20A860   D6404040 C1F7F2F1   40F240F4 40F040F8   *O  A721 .00.1 2 4 0 8*
20A880   F1F0F1F2 F1F6J3F3   40404040 40404040   *10121416 63   *
20A8A0   40404040 12404040   4040J340 40404040   *................*
20A8C0   40404040 40404040   40F7F2F5 40404040   *........725*
20A8E0   40404040 12404040   4C4C4040 40404040   *................*
20A900   40404040 40404040   40404043 40404040   *................*
20A920   40404040 40408277   02028250 CC000000   *.......B.*
20A940   0820A80E 00000001   00000001 00000000   *................*
20A960   CC00C00C 00000003   0D000J31 00010000   *................*
20A980   9020A92C 00404800   02211190 0000400J   *.........S*
20A9A0   00211160 00211238   02EFJ3A8 J6208FCE   *................Y*
20A9C0   CC00C000 00000000   00000000 000000CC   *..........M8*
20A9E0   00000000 05200232   CC000001 0000000J   *................*
20AA00   00000000 80000000   00000000 0C4800000   *................*
20AA20   00000001 46000001   00680048 00035524   *.......B.*
20AA40   0720BFCE 28022828   0211JA5 J0211020     *................Q*
20AA60   CC000000 002FC8A0   CC000000 0C000000    *........H*
20AA80   00940076 91012008   40404043 40404040   *................*
20AAA0   40404040 40404340   4J404J40 40404040   *................*

LINES 20AAC0-2CAAE0 SAME AS ABOVE

20AB00   40404040 40404340   CJ30C4C2 00211768   *.......CB.*
20AB20   0020B452 5020AECE   0020A95C 5C036ED8   *.....Y....Q..Q*
20AB40   5020B280 0020A870   4J2FE840 J02FDDA8   *.....Y....Y*
20AB60   00000000 0020ADFC   0203FCE  F0000008    *................8*
20AB80   0C038888 5C036ED8   0J0358C0 J0003D018   *.......Q.....4*
20ABA0   0020A7E8 58E02040   B1220401 F03CF03C    *.Y..Y....SM.0...*
20ABC0   4A90F03C 58E02040   B3E44780 31E2D2C1    *.0.....0...U..SK*
20ABE0   41F0B2C8 1255478E   2J002CC0 50045CC0    *.0.........0*
20AC00   40105010 07FE9101   4I8033BC J62050C0    *.9.0..0.0*
20AC20   70004110 202C94BF   B243I7F0 328047FJ    *.0.1*
20AC40   4C084780 B26A9110   F0244780 B26A9602    *.0*
```

210

Figure 6.14   Intermediate Page of OCB Main Storage

```
20AC60  96402008  47F0B3BC  9602100+  92801005  5B+1D008  58FF0058  05EF47F0  83BC5880   *....0.........1....0..*
20AC80  20384188  00105890  20IC43A0  202012AA  47T0B2A8  96032008  96205000  D2012012   *.....K........K......*
20ACA0  00000000  00000000  F052D401  F03CF03C  4J70B302  1BAA43C0  0020AEBC  7004770    *...O.M.0.0..........*
20ACE0  0020A7E8  C0C00570  0020B390  E2E8E2D6  E+E34040  E381E8A  5C02038   1E1A1F8A   *...Y........SYSOUT T..*
20ACE0  06A044A0  B6C85080  2040IE81  41AA0001  5J9201C  9110F024  4780B302  1BEA1E8A   *.....Q......0........*
20AD00  48A02C20  00211IE8  0020AA88  0020A870  CJ000000  J000000F  00000000  0000012F   *.....Y.............*
20AD20  00031005  58F10008  00000003  00000050  BJ3C9602  L0049208  8F20AA08  000858FF   *....1.........1......*
20AD40  005805EF  47F0B38C  96021034  92201005  5JF10008  J0000001  0000JA26  00000000   *...........1.....0...*
20AD60  0020B2B8  0020B380  0020B38A  4780B37A  4J8034F4  +7F0B598  0020C67C  0020B452   *............B...4.0..F*
20AD80  0020B462  0020BFCE  0020C232  0020C252  0J20C680  J020817C  0020AEE2  0020AEE8   *........B..B..F...S..Y*
20ADA0  0020AFD8  0020B07C  0C20BJDA  0020B138  0J203208  J020A95C  0020AA08  47915E76   *...Q...............*
20ADC0  F0F00000  00020000  00000002  48004805  EF070040  +040C9C4  407E4040  40400440   *00.......  ID .. M *
20ADE0  7E404040  40D5407E  40C9E3C5  E2E3407E  4J0536D9  04C1D340  C5D6D100  58F0C008   *00..  N ITEST  NCRMAL EOJ...0.*
20AE00  05EF5810  C03C0203  D060C00C  D2021039  DJ15310  C03CD0C   1032C054  58401024   *....K.......K....K..0.*
20AE20  D2024011  C0115010  D2289200  D2289680  D2284110  J2280413  58F0C008  05EF5810   *.K....K.....K..K...0.*
20AE40  C04D0203  D060C00C  D2021J39  D061581O  C04D2201  L032C055  D2231060  C0575840   *.K....K...K.....K...*
20AE60  10240202  4011C011  5010C228  920FD228  9J80J228  +1100223  0AL39240  7000D24E   *.K....K...K....K.....*
20AE80  70017000  924080OO  D2838JJ1  00009240  6J5DJ206  605E605D  D2J16018  C048D201   *..........K..K...K..*
20AEA0  601AC048  D2C16000  C04AD201  6002C04A  C2215J04  C0485BF0  CC0805EF  5810C03C   *.K....K..0......*
20AEC0  18210202  2021C021  58F01030  C5EF5010  DLF45370  J1F4024F  50087000  5850C024   *.......0....J4.J4K...*
20AEE0  C7F55810  C01C07F1  F27ID200  60184F30  D2J1033  +0300210  D2J16000  D210F271   *.5....12.K...K.K.K.2.*
20AF00  D200601A  4F30D200  1033433O  .21D0201  6J22210  J2013210  D2104C10  C04C1A21   *K...K..K.K..K.K...K..*
20AF20  D2104C20  C04C1A42  5B40C053  41206008  D2013210  J0024810  D2104C10  F3116004   *...K..2.K...K.K.8.K.K.3*
20AF40  5B20C050  F271D200  2000F271  2208J240  FB31020C  D206F871  C238D20C  6067600A   *..K...2.K....K.K...K..*
20AF60  D20E96F0  60C55040  D2205J20  D224D207  6J5C05B  D2016065  5008D201  6067600A   *K..0...........0.....*
20AF80  D2016069  600C0201  6066J0JE  D2016060  6J1J2J0   90F6012  D2316071  6014D201   *....K........K......K.*
20AFA0  60736C16  58F0C008  05EFD25D  80006058  9240J5E  D225805F  805ED203  D234D1F8   *.K...0...K...K.K.J8*
20AFC0  925+0234  D203D23C  C04092J01  D2384110  D23458=0  C0L405EF  924006067  D2006068   *.K.K.K...0...K.K..0....*
20AFE0  60679240  6069D200  606A6J63  60BF9240  C2C06J6C  J0689240  606DD200  606E606D   *.K...K....K....K..K..*
20B000  9240006F  D2006070  C2006070  6071D200  6J72J071  92406073  D2006074  6073D207   *K.......K....K....K..*
20B020  6050C062  D2016065  601858F0  C00805EF  D25CB300  6058924J  805ED225  805F605E   *.K....0...K.K...K.K..*
20B040  92F08000  5810C040  18219200  207A5840  2J49J200  +0145810  C04058OO  104C58F0   *.0........K....0...*
20B060  10304400  10600284  10008C0J  5810C040  1J211B12  28F01030  44001062  D2076050   *.0.........0....K..0.*
20B080  C069D201  6065601A  58F0C008  05EFD250  8J306358  J2408050  D225805F  805E92F0   *.K.K...0...K.....K..0*
20B0A0  80CC5810  C0401821  52302J7A  58402024  9J0409J4  J810C040  5830104C  58F01030   *...K...O.....K.K...0*
20B0C0  44001060  D2841000  80005810  C0401821  1J125B=0  10304400  10622J07  605DC071   *.K.....0....K..0...*
20B0E0  D2016065  600458F0  C0080C5EF  D250B000  6J5BJ24J  J05ED225  835F805E  92F08000   *K.......0....K.K...0*
20B100  5810C040  18219200  207A584J  2J249200  4J143313  J0405803  104C58F0  10304400   *.........K..0...K..*
20B120  10600284  10008000  5810C040  18211B12  5JF01030  44001062  D2J76050  C079D201   *.........0.....K..K*
20B140  6C65C81  58F0C008  05EFD250  80006058  9243J5E  D225805F  805ED203  D234D1F8   *K..K...0..0.....K.K.J8*
20B160  9214D234  D203D23C  C04C4110  00045010  D2384110  J23458F0  C0L405EF  58F0C008   *.K.K......K.K.K..0*
20B180  05EF5810  C03C5830  102C91UF  300C0550  4JE05010  J820104C  48201052  5020104C   *....K..K....K..0..*
20B1A0  5810C03C  50100228  9240D228  5810C040  5J1D22C  J240D22C  963D022C  4110D228   *..K...K...K....K.K.K.*
20B1C0  0AL45820  C03C5810  20149J01  201F1B44  4J401005  +C401006  41004008  41101000   *.K...K..K...0.K..0.*
20B1E0  0A0A5820  C040581O  20149601  201F1B44  4J4J1005  +C401005  41004008  41101000   *.K...K..K..K..0.*
20B200  0A0A58F0  CC0805EF  58F0C018  07FF5000  5J085020  J0045OED  D0549120  D04847E0   *...0....0.K...0.*
20B220  F02E5820  D1889140  D0947EJ3  90C09604  2J0058F0  203841F0  FJ407FF  94EFD048   *.0..J....0.00....*
20B240  58F0CC00  05FF1220  C7899610  D0485BF0  CJJ405EF  J5F09120  C04847E0  F0165800   *..........0.0O.*
20B260  B0469820  B05058E0  D05407FE  96200048  46600JC4  +110C01C  4170C048  06700550   *.0..........*
20B280  58401000  1E4B5040  10038716  50004180  DLF44170  J1FF0510  58038000  1E0B5000   *........J4.J...*
20B2A0  8CCC8786  10C05660  0360007E  D1FC5870  DLF853E0  J09C0023  91J08A00  00000341   *......J4.J8...*
20B2C0  0CCC0003  51003C00  03600J7E  DJ011800  7=000381  J09C0003  9130BA00  03A100E6   *....J.......*
20B2E0  00C3B10C  EC00003C1  01020003  DD011800  0JE1J118  J003F101  6A0J0401  01780004   *...A......*
20B300  11017E00  04210184  00C43101  8A000441  01902034  J1019603  0461019C  00047101   *.........1....*
20B320  A2C00481  C1A80004  A1010C00  04E10222  CJ04=102  28J0J501  0225D005  21028000   *.........W..*
```

Figure 6.15 Reference Data Card (panels 1 and 2)

IBM System/360 Reference Data

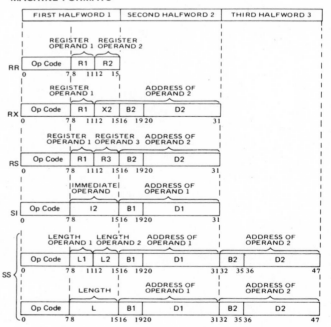

MACHINE INSTRUCTIONS

NAME	MNEMONIC	OP CODE	FOR-MAT	OPERANDS
Add (c)	AR	1A	RR	R1,R2
Add (c)	A	5A	RX	R1,D2(X2,B2)
Add Decimal (c,d)	AP	FA	SS	D1(L1,B1),D2(L2,B2)
Add Halfword (c)	AH	4A	RX	R1,D2(X2,B2)
Add Logical (c)	ALR	1E	RR	R1,R2
Add Logical (c)	AL	5E	RX	R1,D2(X2,B2)
AND (c)	NR	14	RR	R1,R2
AND (c)	N	54	RX	R1,D2(X2,B2)
AND (c)	NI	94	SI	D1(B1),I2
AND (c)	NC	D4	SS	D1(L,B1),D2(B2)
Branch and Link	BALR	05	RR	R1,R2
Branch and Link	BAL	45	RX	R1,D2(X2,B2)
Branch and Store (e)	BASR	0D	RR	R1,R2
Branch and Store (e)	BAS	4D	RX	R1,D2(X2,B2)
Branch on Condition	BCR	07	RR	M1,R2
Branch on Condition	BC	47	RX	M1,D2(X2,B2)
Branch on Count	BCTR	06	RR	R1,R2
Branch on Count	BCT	46	RX	R1,D2(X2,B2)
Branch on Index High	BXH	86	RS	R1,R3,D2(B2)
Branch on Index Low or Equal	BXLE	87	RS	R1,R3,D2(B2)
Compare (c)	CR	19	RR	R1,R2
Compare (c)	C	59	RX	R1,D2(X2,B2)
Compare Decimal (c,d)	CP	F9	SS	D1(L1,B1),D2(L2,B2)
Compare Halfword (c)	CH	49	RX	R1,D2(X2,B2)
Compare Logical (c)	CLR	15	RR	R1,R2
Compare Logical (c)	CL	55	RX	R1,D2(X2,B2)
Compare Logical (c)	CLC	D5	SS	D1(L,B1),D2(B2)
Compare Logical (c)	CLI	95	SI	D1(B1),I2
Convert to Binary	CVB	4F	RX	R1,D2(X2,B2)
Convert to Decimal	CVD	4E	RX	R1,D2(X2,B2)
Diagnose (p)		83	SI	
Divide	DR	1D	RR	R1,R2
Divide	D	5D	RX	R1,D2(X2,B2)
Divide Decimal (d)	DP	FD	SS	D1(L1,B1),D2(L2,B2)
Edit (c,d)	ED	DE	SS	D1(L,B1),D2(B2)
Edit and Mark (c,d)	EDMK	DF	SS	D1(L,B1),D2(B2)
Exclusive OR (c)	XR	17	RR	R1,R2
Exclusive OR (c)	X	57	RX	R1,R2
Exclusive OR (c)	XI	97	SI	D1(B1),I2
Exclusive OR (c)	XC	D7	SS	D1(L,B1),D2(B2)
Execute	EX	44	RX	R1,D2(X2,B2)
Halt I/O (c,p)	HIO	9E	SI	D1(B1)
Insert Character	IC	43	RX	R1,D2(X2,B2)
Insert Storage Key (a,p)	ISK	09	RR	R1,R2
Load	LR	18	RR	R1,R2
Load	L	58	RX	R1,D2(X2,B2)
Load Address	LA	41	RX	R1,D2(X2,B2)
Load and Test (c)	LTR	12	RR	R1,R2
Load Complement (c)	LCR	13	RR	R1,R2
Load Halfword	LH	48	RX	R1,D2(X2,B2)
Load Multiple	LM	98	RS	R1,R3,D2(B2)
Load Multiple Control (e,p)	LMC	B8	RS	R1,R3,D2(B2)
Load Negative (c)	LNR	11	RR	R1,R2
Load Positive (c)	LPR	10	RR	R1,R2
Load PSW (n,p)	LPSW	82	SI	D1(B1)
Load Real Address (c,e,p)	LRA	B1	RX	R1,D2(X2,B2)
Move	MVI	92	SI	D1(B1),I2
Move	MVC	D2	SS	D1(L,B1),D2(B2)
Move Numerics	MVN	D1	SS	D1(L,B1),D2(B2)
Move with Offset	MVO	F1	SS	D1(L1,B1),D2(L2,B2)
Move Zones	MVZ	D3	SS	D1(L,B1),D2(B2)
Multiply	MR	1C	RR	R1,R2
Multiply	M	5C	RX	R1,D2(X2,B2)
Multiply Decimal (d)	MP	FC	SS	D1(L1,B1),D2(L2,B2)
Multiply Halfword	MH	4C	RX	R1,D2(X2,B2)
OR (c)	OR	16	RR	R1,R2
OR (c)	O	56	RX	R1,D2(X2,B2)
OR (c)	OI	96	SI	D1(B1),I2

NAME	MNEMONIC	OP CODE	FOR-MAT	OPERANDS
OR (c)	OC	D6	SS	D1(L,B1),D2(B2)
Pack	PACK	F2	SS	D1(L1,B1),D2(L2,B2)
Read Direct (b,p)	RDD	85	SI	D1(B1),I2
Set Program Mask (n)	SPM	04	RR	R1
Set Storage Key (a,p)	SSK	08	RR	R1,R2
Set System Mask (p)	SSM	80	SI	D1(B1)
Shift Left Double (c)	SLDA	8F	RS	R1,D2(B2)
Shift Left Double Logical	SLDL	8D	RS	R1,D2(B2)
Shift Left Single (c)	SLA	8B	RS	R1,D2(B2)
Shift Left Single Logical	SLL	89	RS	R1,D2(B2)
Shift Right Double (c)	SRDA	8E	RS	R1,D2(B2)
Shift Right Double Logical	SRDL	8C	RS	R1,D2(B2)
Shift Right Single (c)	SRA	8A	RS	R1,D2(B2)
Shift Right Single Logical	SRL	88	RS	R1,D2(B2)
Start I/O (c,p)	SIO	9C	SI	D1(B1)
Store	ST	50	RX	R1,D2(X2,B2)
Store Character	STC	42	RX	R1,D2(X2,B2)
Store Halfword	STH	40	RX	R1,D2(X2,B2)
Store Multiple	STM	90	RS	R1,R3,D2(B2)
Store Multiple Control (e,p)	STMC	B0	RS	R1,R3,D2(B2)
Subtract (c)	SR	1B	RR	R1,R2
Subtract (c)	S	5B	RX	R1,D2(X2,B2)
Subtract Decimal (c,d)	SP	FB	SS	D1(L1,B1),D2(L2,B2)
Subtract Halfword (c)	SH	4B	RX	R1,D2(X2,B2)
Subtract Logical (c)	SLR	1F	RR	R1,R2
Subtract Logical (c)	SL	5F	RX	R1,D2(X2,B2)
Supervisor Call	SVC	0A	RR	I
Test and Set (c)	TS	93	SI	D1(B1)
Test Channel (c,p)	TCH	9F	SI	D1(B1)
Test I/O (c,p)	TIO	9D	SI	D1(B1)
Test under Mask (c)	TM	91	SI	D1(B1),I2
Translate	TR	DC	SS	D1(L,B1),D2(B2)
Translate and Test (c)	TRT	DD	SS	D1(L,B1),D2(B2)
Unpack	UNPK	F3	SS	D1(L1,B1),D2(L2,B2)
Write Direct (b,p)	WRD	84	SI	D1(B1),I2
Zero and Add (c,d)	ZAP	F8	SS	D1(L1,B1),D2(L2,B2)

NOTES FOR PANELS 1-3

a. Protection feature
b. Direct control feature
c. Condition code is set

d. Decimal feature
e. Model 67
n. New condition

code is loaded
p. Privileged instruction
x. Extended precision floating point feature

MACHINE FORMATS

2. Workshop

1. Address of Next Machine Instruction to be Executed .. _____

2. Length of Machine Instruction

    APSW left-most Byte .... _____

    Convert to Binary .... _____

    Length in Bytes .... _____

3. Instruction being executed

    Op Code of Next Machine Instruction .... _____

    Back up required Number of Bytes and record Machine Instruction.

    _____

4. Op Code, Function, and Format

    Op Code .... _____

    Function Performed .... _____

    Format .... _____

5. Machine Instruction Breakdown

    Op Code .... _____

	1st Operand	2nd Operand
Length Indication	_____	_____
Length + 1	_____	_____
Base Register	_____	_____
Displacement	_____	_____

6. Operand Values

Base Register Contents ..	_____	_____
Base + Displacement	_____	_____
Length in Bytes	_____	_____
Character String	_____	_____

    Given the above character strings, interpret the value of the
    First and Second Operands. How did you arrive at this
    interpretation?

    _____

    _____

    _____

    _____

_____

_____

_____

_____

_____

_____

_____

_____

_____

7. Problem Analysis
    Summarize your findings. How do the values obtained in this
    workshop compare to that obtained in Chapter 5?

_____

_____

_____

_____

_____

_____

_____

_____

7

Completion Codes (A Desk Reference)

All storage dumps can be classified into three general categories based upon completion codes.

A. EXTERNAL ABENDS
    1. 001 Completion Code
    2. 13 Group
    3. 22 Group (excluding 322)
    4. 37 Group
B. INTERNAL ABENDS
    1. 0C Group (includes User Code 240)
    2. 322 Completion Code
C. UNGROUPED ABENDS
    1. 00 Group (excluding 001)
    2. 01 Group
    3. 02 Group
    4. 03 Group
    5. 04 Group
    6. 05 Group
    7. 06 Group

8.   09 Group

9.   0A Group

10.   0B Group

11.   0D Group

12.   0F Group

13.   14 and 17 Groups

14.   23 Group

15.   28 and 2A Groups

16.   2C Group

17.   2D Group

18.   2F Group

19.   30 Group

20.   31 Group

21.   38 Group

22.   40 Group

23.   F Group

24.   Other Completion Codes

An External Abend is one in which the program within the step the abend occurred was not being executed, i.e., external to the program. Conversely, an Internal Abend is one in which the program within the step the abend occurred was being executed, i.e., internal to the program. A distinct set of debugging procedures need be followed for each class.

The Ungrouped Abends, though most often external by nature, have not been classified as such because debugging procedures for them are generally minimal in addition to occurring on an infrequent basis.

Following is a detailed description of the most frequently obtained Completion Codes and a brief description of others not so common to the application and system programmer and analyst environment. Additionally, the IBM Messages and Codes Manual provides a good technical reference.

A. EXTERNAL ABENDS

1. 001 Completion Code

A 001 Completion Code refers to an uncorrectable Input/Output (I/O) error. Determine the problem ddname and file along with pertinent DCB characteristics. The most probable causes of a 001 Completion Code follow.

a. Dirty or Damaged Tape or Disk

A dirty or damaged tape or disk is a most frequent cause of a 001 Completion Code. In some instances, a data error message occurs in the JCL listing to verify this problem. The tape should be cleaned and the job resubmitted. Experience has shown that in most cases, however, the file will have to be recreated.

b. Tape or Disk Drive Malfunction

A tape or disk drive malfunction is also a frequent cause of a 001 Completion Code. In some instances, an equipment error message occurs in the JCL listing to verify this problem. The actual device assigned to the file can be found in the allocation messages. A check with the installation should be made to determine if I/O problems have been re-occurring on the device allocated.

c. Conflicting DCB Information

Conflicts between specific DCB attributes as coded in the program and the JCL, as well as stored in the Label, can cause a 001 Completion Code. A check of program and JCL specifications for the problem file, along with a breakdown of pertinent DCB characteristics as they reside in main storage, should be made.

d. Attempted Program READ After an AT END Execution

Attempting to execute a Program READ Statement after an End Of File (EOF) condition has been reached can also cause a 001 Completion

217

Code. A complete review of program logic as it applies to the problem
file should be made.

Suppose that a thorough problem analysis has been accomplished,
Items c and d have been eliminated from further consideration, but the
problem cannot be narrowed specifically to either Items a or b. A
tape or disk drive malfunction could be assumed, and the job resubmitted. A different device will most likely be allocated to the problem file. If the problem does not re-occur, concern no longer need be
given to the storage dump problem. The installation should be notified
of a possible defective device. If the problem does re-occur, a dirty
or damaged tape or disk can be assumed and it must be cleaned and/or
recreated. If time is of essence, the file should be recreated along
with job resubmission to ensure a successful run.

An example of a 001 Storage Dump can be found in Chapter 3.

2. 13 Group

All completion codes ending with 13 refer to data definition
errors. Determine the problem ddname and file along with pertinent
DCB characteristics. The most probable causes of Completion Codes in
the 13 Group follow.

013:

A 013 Completion Code is caused by conflicting DCB information
between specific DCB attributes as coded in the program and the JCL,
as well as stored in the Label. The most probable causes are:

a. DCB Program, JCL, and Label Conflicts.
b. Required DCB Information not specified.

A 013 Completion Code is usually accompanied by an error message
in the JCL listing which describes the problem in more detail. The
Completion Code is qualified by a Return Code, i.e., 013-20, 013-68,
etc. Following is an interpretation of frequent Return Codes as found
with a 013 Completion Code.

Return Code:

  18 -- System could not locate specified member of a Partitioned
      Data Set.

  20 -- Blocksize is not a multiple of Fixed Record Length.

  4C -- Invalid Blocksize Specification.

  60 -- Blocksize not equal to Record Length for Unblocked files.

  68 -- Blocksize greater than 32,767.

A thorough analysis of DCB attributes for the problem file should
be accomplished.

An example of a 013 Storage Dump can be found in Chapter 1.

213:

A 213 Completion Code is caused by an illogical DD Statement in
the JCL. The system cannot locate a specified disk data set. The
most probable causes are:

  a. The disk data set as referred to on a specific volume does
not exist. Perhaps it has not been created or passed from the previous step.

  b. Data Set Name specification incorrect.

  c. Volume Serial Number specification incorrect.

  d. Disk file has been accidently scratched.

A complete review of JCL associated with the problem file should
be accomplished.

An example of a 213 Storage Dump can be found in Chapter 3.

413:

A 413 Completion Code is usually caused by an illogical DD Statement in the JCL. The system cannot locate a specified data set (usually
tape). The most probable causes are:

  a. Data set not created in previous step.

b. Data set not passed from previous step.

c. JCL and Label conflicts exist.

A complete review of JCL associated with the problem file should be accomplished.

613:

A 613 Completion Code is caused by a tape-related I/O error. The most probable causes are:

a. Tape Drive Malfunction.

b. Error in Tape Positioning.

c. I/O Error during Label Processing.

A check with the installation should be made to verify possible tape drive problems associated with the device specified in the allocation messages of the JCL listing. If the error re-occurs, the tape should be cleaned and/or recreated.

713:

A 713 Completion Code occurs most frequently in installations with automated library systems. The most probable causes are:

a. Attempting to process an output Data Set for which the Expiration Date has not been reached.

b. Erroneous Volume Request.

A check of the programmer's File Log should be made.

813:

An 813 Completion Code is caused by Data Set Name or Volume Serial Number conflicts. The Data Set Name and/or Volume Serial Number as specified in the JCL does not agree with internally stored Header Label specifications. The most probable causes are:

a. Incorrect Data Set Name specification.

b. Incorrect Volume Serial Number specification.

c. Wrong Volume mounted.

d. Incorrect or Erroneous Entries in programmer's File Log.

e. File was accidently scratched.

An example of an 813 Storage Dump can be found in Chapter 3.

Other less frequent occurrences of Completion Codes in the 13 Group are:

a. System Input/Output Error -- 113, 313, B13, and C13.

b. Open File Error -- 513, A13, D13, and E13.

c. Security or Password Error -- 913.

3. 22 Group (excluding 322)

Completion codes ending with 22 refer, in general, to the violation of installation standards and/or system limitations. Determine the problem ddname and file. Isolating DCB characteristics for the problem file may not be necessary. The most probable causes of a storage dump with a Completion Code in the 22 Group follow.

122:

A 122 Completion Code results when the operator simply cancels a job and requests a dump. The job is usually terminated external to the program being executed. The most probable causes are:

a. Job violated Installation Standards.

b. System waiting for resources to be allocated, but were not readily available.

c. Program Loop detected.

d. Job was accidently terminated.

A check with the installation and computer operations should be made.

222:

A 222 Completion Code results when the operator cancels a job and does not request a dump. The most probable causes for the cancelation are identical to the 122 Completion Code mentioned previously. A check with the installation and computer operations should be made, however, to ensure that if the problem re-occurs a storage dump will be issued.

422:

A 422 Completion Code results when a job is too large for current installation standards. Space must be allocated in the job queue for various OS tables, control blocks, and system messages as they relate to each job. When this area fills up, the job is terminated with a 422 Completion Code. The most probable causes are:

a. Too many Job Steps.
b. Too many DD Statements per Job and/or Step.

Most installations allocate enough job queue space to handle at least 20 job steps of average length. If a job requires more queue space than is available at a particular installation, it must be split into two or more separate jobs.

522:

A 522 Completion Code indicates that the System was in a Wait State. Whenever a command or request is made by the Operating System, and a response is not forthcoming within 30 minutes, the job is auto- matically terminated with a 522 Storage Dump. The most probable causes are:

a. Operator missed Mount Request message.
b. Operator failed to respond to other System requests.
c. Invalid User Request.
d. Operating System error.

A check with the installation and computer operations should be made to determine specific problem causing the Wait State.

722:

A 722 Completion Code results when the number of print records routed through the output stream for a given job exceeds the limit established at a particular installation. The most probable causes are:

a. Program Loop.
b. Number of Print Records underestimated.

A thorough review of program logic should be accomplished. If a program loop cannot be detected, the job will need to be split into two or more separate jobs.

4. 37 Group

All completion codes ending with 37 refer to End Of File (EOF) or End of Volume (EOV) problems. Determine the problem ddname and file along with pertinent DCB characteristics. The most probable causes of a storage dump with a Completion Code in the 37 Group follow.

137:

A 137 Completion Code results when an Input/Output (I/O) error is encountered during Trailer Label tape processing. The dump occurred during positioning of the Trailer Label, or when actually reading Trailer Label records and tape marks. The most probable causes are:

a. Undetected error during Trailer Label creation.
b. System error when positioning and/or reading Trailer Label records and tape marks.

The tape should be cleaned and the job resubmitted. If error re-occurs the file must be recreated.

237:

A 237 Completion Code results when a verification error is encountered during Trailer Label processing. The actual number of blocks processed must agree with the block count internally stored within the Trailer Label. The most probable causes are:

a. One or more blocks of data inadvertently skipped during processing.

b. Erroneous Data Set Name or Volume Serial Number specification for multi-volume files.

A complete check of JCL associated with the problem file should be accomplished. If no errors are found the tape should be cleaned and the job resubmitted. If the error re-occurs the file must be recreated.

B37:

A B37 Completion Code results when the system is requested to demount a volume for End Of Volume (EOV) processing but cannot do so. The most probable causes are:

a. Incorrect Space Allocation.

b. Program Loop encompassing a Write Statement.

c. Volume reserved and/or permanently resident.

D37:

A D37 Completion Code results when the system requires more space for a given file than that allocated by the programmer. The most probable causes are:

a. Program Loop encompassing a Write Statement.

b. Underestimated Space Allocation.

A thorough review of problem logic should be accomplished. If a program loop cannot be detected, a recalculation of space requirements need be made.

An example of a D37 Storage Dump can be found in Chapter 3.

Other less frequent occurrences of Completion Codes in the 37 Group are:

   a. End of File or Space -- 337, E37.
   b. End of Volume I/O Error -- 437, 737, 837.
   c. End of Volume Concatenation Error -- 537, 637.
   d. Security or Password Error -- 937.

B. INTERNAL ABENDS

1. 0C Group (includes User Code 240)

Completion Codes beginning with 0C refer to the calculation and/or reference of invalid data or storage addresses during program execution. User Code 240 as generated by the FORTRAN Extended Error Handling Facility also falls into the 0C Group, and is indicated as such in the appropriate error message. Determine the problem source statement along with the value of pertinent program variables. Machine instructions need not be located and analyzed unless appropriate compiler output listings are not available. The most probable causes of a storage dump with a Completion Code in the 0C Group follow.

0C1:

A 0C1 Completion Code is called an Operation Exception. An invalid operation has been requested. The most probable causes are:

   a. Read or Write attempt on file not Opened or Closed.
   b. Incorrect or Missing DD Statement.
   c. Run-away Subscript.

A thorough review of program logic and JCL file specifications should be accomplished.

OC2:

A OC2 Completion Code is called a Privileged Operation. An unavailable operation has been requested. The most probable causes are:

a. Incorrect or Missing DD Statement.
b. Run-away Subscript.

A thorough review of program logic and JCL file specifications should be accomplished.

OC3:

A OC3 Completion Code is called an Execute Exception. An invalid Execute operation has been encountered. The most probable cause is faulty program logic.

A thorough review of program logic should be accomplished.

OC4:

A OC4 Completion Code is called a Protection Exception. An invalid address has been calculated by the program. The most probable causes are:

a. Run-away Subscript.
b. Invalid Index.
c. Incorrect or Missing DD Statement.

A thorough review of program logic and JCL file specifications should be accomplished.

OC5:

A OC5 Completion Code is called an Addressing Exception. An address outside the bounds of available storage has been calculated. The most probable causes are:

a. Run-away Subscript.
b. Invalid Index.
c. Close Attempt on file already closed.
d. Incorrect or Missing DD Statement.

A thorough review of program logic and JCL file specifications should be accomplished.

An example of a OC5 Storage Dump can be found in Chapters 4 and 5.

OC6:

A OC6 Completion Code is called a Specification Exception. This type of problem is caused by an address which does not align on a proper boundary. The most probable causes are:

a. Incorrectly defined Fields and/or Program Tables.
b. Run-away Subscript.
c. Incorrect or Missing DD Statement.

A thorough review of program logic and JCL file specifications should be accomplished.

OC7:

A OC7 Completion Code is called a Data Exception. Non-numeric characters have been referenced in a field defined to contain numeric characters only. The most probable causes are:

a. Numeric Data Field in Arithmetic Statement contains non-numeric character(s).

b. Numeric Data Field in an IF Statement contains non-numeric character(s).

c. Run-away Subscript.

d. Invalid Index.

It is important to note that a blank is considered to be a non-numeric character in most business-oriented programming languages. A thorough review of program logic should be accomplished. An example of a OC7 Storage Dump can be found in Chapters 4, 5, and 6.

OC8, OCA, OCC:

OC8, OCA, and OCC Completion Codes are called Fixed Point Overflow, Decimal Overflow, and Exponent Overflow, respectively. A value has been calculated which is larger than program defined field length. The most probable causes are:

a. Division by too small of a number.

b. Multiplication by too large of a number.

c. Program Loop.

A thorough review of program logic should be accomplished.

OC9, OCB, OCF:

OC9, OCB, and OCF Completion Codes are called Fixed Point Divide, Decimal Divide, and Floating Point Divide, respectively. A quotient which has been calculated is larger than the program defined field length. The most probable causes are:

a. Division by zero.

b. Division by too small of a number.

c. Program Loop.

A thorough review of program logic should be accomplished. An example of a OCB Storage Dump can be found in Chapters 4, 5, and 6.

OCD:

A OCD Storage Dump is called an Exponent Underflow. A value has
been calculated to be so fractionally small that it cannot be accurately
represented. The most probable causes are:

a. Division by too large of a number.
b. Multiplication by too small of a number.
c. Program Loop.

A thorough review of program logic should be accomplished.

OCE:

A OCE Storage Dump is called a Significance Exception. An absolute zero resulted from an arithmetic operation upon data represented
in Internal Floating Point form. The most probable causes are:

a. Program Loop.
b. Incorrect Arithmetic Logic.

A thorough review of program logic should be accomplished.

User Code 240:

This is a program generated code. Refer to FORTRAN Extended Error
Handling Facility message to determine appropriate Completion Code of
the OC Group.

An example of a User Code 240 for a OC5 Storage Dump can be found
in Chapters 4 and 5.

2. 322 Completion Code

A 322 Completion Code results when a specified CPU time limit has
been exceeded. The program was being executed at the time of the abend.
The most probable causes are:

a.   Program Loop.

b.   Job Time Parameter exceeded.

c.   Step Time Parameter exceeded.

If a Time Parameter for a given step has not been specified, a most frequent default, though it varies among installations, is 10 minutes.

A thorough review of program logic should be accomplished. If a program loop cannot be found, the appropriate Time Parameter need be increased.

An example of a 322 Storage Dump can be found in Chapters 4 and 5.

C.   UNGROUPED ABENDS

1.   00 Group (excluding 001)

Completion Codes beginning with the number 00, i.e., 002, 003, 004, and 008, are caused by uncorrectable Input/Output (I/O) errors. They are similar to the 001 Completion Code discussed earlier in that the cause is related to system I/O problems; however, programmer DCB conflicts occasionally result in 002 and 004 Storage Dumps.

Probable System or Operations error.

Completion Codes ending with the number 00, i.e., 100, 200, 300, 400, and 500, are also caused by errors encountered during I/O processing.

Probable System or Operations error.

2.   01 Group

Completion Codes ending with 01, i.e., 101, 201, and 301, occur during a Wait condition and are usually caused by reference to invalid addresses.

Probable System error.

3. 02 Group

    Completions Codes beginning with 02, i.e., 020, 025, and 026, refer
specifically to DCB problems on direct access files. This problem is
caused by invalid DCB specifications as well as possible system I/O
errors.

        Probable System error.

    Completion Codes ending with 02, i.e., 102, and 202, are signified by
the existence of invalid addresses for control program reference. An
address which points to an area outside the bounds of main storage is
one such example.

        Probable System error.

4. 03 Group

    Completion Codes beginning with 03 are caused by DCB conflicts,
space problems, and occasional I/O errors. Codes 030, 032, 034, 035,
037, and 03D, all refer to erroneous DCB specifications during the
opening of an Input/Output file. Codes 036 and 038 relate to incorrect space allocations. An 039 denotes end of data problems during the
scan process. An 03B is caused by opening a file already open. An
03E occurs during load activities for Index Sequential files. System
I/O errors cause the remaining completion codes of the 03 Group, that
is, 031, 033, and 03A.

        Probable User error.

    Completion Codes ending with 03, i.e., 103, A03, C03, and D03, are
characterized by the existence of invalid return addresses to a calling routine.

        Probable User error.

5. 04 Group

Completion Codes beginning with 04, i.e., 041, 042, 043, 044, 045, and 046, generally occur during the file opening process. An invalid or missing DCB specification is a most frequent cause, along with possible system I/O errors.

Probable User error.

Completion Codes ending with 04 signify main storage specification problems. Codes 104, 804, and E04 result from a shortage of main storage availability. Codes 504, 604, 704, B04, and C04 are caused by reference to invalid main storage addresses.

Probable User error.

6. 05 Group

Completion Codes beginning with 05, i.e., 056, and 057, relate to erroneous DCB file specifications for graphic output.

Probable User error.

Completion Codes ending with 05, i.e., 305, 505, 605, 705, 905, A05, B05, and D05, are characterized by reference to invalid addresses during the freeing of main storage.

Probable System error.

7. 06 Group

Completion Codes beginning with 06, i.e., 061, and 062, relate to errors encountered during the file closing process as well as terminations due to return code values.

Probable User error.

Completion Codes ending with 06 occur during the process of locating a program module. Codes 406 and 706 indicate that the module is non-executable. Codes 506 and 606 mean that not enough main storage is available for the requested program module. Code 806, the most frequent of the 06 Group, occurs when the program module cannot be located. Perhaps the requested module does not exist, or, a JOBLIB or STEPLIB DD Statement has not been provided to 'open-the-door' of a private library. Codes 906 and A06 occur while the system is waiting for the requested module. Codes B06 and C06 mean that the request for a program module has been cancelled.

Probable User error.

8. 09 Group

Completion Codes beginning with 09, i.e., 090, 091, 092, 093, 094, 095, 096, 097, and 098, occur during the file opening process. All relate to communication, transmission, or terminal problems with the exception of an 090. Codes 090, 091, 092, 093, and 094 are caused specifically by invalid UCB specifications.

Probable System or Operations error.

9. 0A Group

Completion Codes beginning with 0A relate to file problems. A 0A0 and 0A1 are caused by missing DCB information. Ddname conflicts cause a 0A2 Completion Code. A 0A3 results when the system message queue is filled. A 0A4 occurs during Checkpoint and Restart activity. Codes 0A5, 0A6, and 0A7 are caused by opening a file which is already open. Input/Output errors can also cause abends of the 0A Group.

Probable User error.

Completion Codes ending with 0A refer to main storage allocation problems. Codes 10A and 20A are caused by the unavailability of main storage. Codes 30A, 40A, and 60A occur during the freeing of main storage. An 80A, the most frequent of the OA Group, indicates that the total amount of main storage specified by a Region parameter or the core allocation default procedure has been exceeded. Main storage specifications need be reviewed and increased. Codes 90A and AOA are caused by invalid main storage addresses and boundary alignment problems.

Probable User error.

10. OB Group

Completion Codes beginning with OB refer to job queue problems. A OB1 is caused by an Input/Output (I/O) error while reading the job queue. A OB2 is caused by invalid addresses when referencing the job queue.

Probable System or Operations error.

11. OD Group

Completion Codes ending with OD, i.e., DOD, EOD, relate to system and/or space problems during Abend processing.

Probable System error.

12. OF Group

Completion Codes beginning with OF relate to system program problems. Codes OF1, OF2, and OF5 are called Program Interruptions. An OF3 is called a Machine Check Interruption and is caused by hardware error.

Probable System error.

13. 14 and 17 Groups

Completion Codes ending with 14, i.e., 214, 314, 414, 514, 614,

714, A14, B14, and D14, as well as those ending with 17, i.e., 117, 217, 317, 417, and 717, are caused by I/O errors during the file closing process.

Probable System or Operations error.

14. 23 Group

Completion Codes ending with 23, i.e., D23, and E23, are caused by invalid parameters being passed to a utility program.

Probable User error.

15. 28 and 2A Groups

Completion Codes ending with 28, i.e., 128, 228, and 328, as well as those ending with 2A, i.e., 12A, 22A, 32A, 42A, and 62A, relate to invalid addresses resulting in boundary alignment problems.

Probable User error.

16. 2C Group

Completion Codes ending with 2C, i.e., 12C, and 22C, are caused by the reference of invalid addresses.

Probable User error.

17. 2D Group

Completion Codes ending with 2D, i.e., 12D, 22D, 32D, and C2D, are caused by the creation of invalid Segment Table addresses when using the overlay program option.

Probable User error.

18. 2F Group

Completion Codes beginning with 2F generally refer to system problems. Code 2F3 is caused by a system failure, usually during the Restart process. Code 2FE is caused by an Input/Output error during the program roll procedure. Code 2FF results from an abend requested by the user.

Probable System error.

19. 30 Group

Completion Codes ending with 30, i.e., 130, 230, 330, 430, and 530, refer to erroneous resource specifications. Invalid or privileged resource requests have been made.

Probable User error.

20. 31 Group

Completion Codes ending with 31, i.e., 131, 331, 431, and 531, refer to problems encountered during the linkage process. They are caused by invalid Control Section addresses, entry points, and return addresses, as well as Input/Output errors.

Probable User error.

21. 38 Group

Similar to the 30 Group, completion codes ending with 38, i.e., 138, 238, 338, and 438, refer to erroneous resource specifications.

Probable User error.

22. 40 Group

Completion Codes ending with 40, i.e., 140, and 240, are caused by erroneous DCB Address specifications and Input/Output errors.

Probable User error.

NOTE: Completion Code 240 should not be confused with User Code 240 as generated by the FORTRAN Extended Error Handling Facility for the OC Group.

23. F Group

Completion Codes beginning with F refer to the presence of invalid operands in a supervisor call. The last two digits of the completion code contain the erroneous operand in hexadecimal.

Probable User error.

24. Other Completion Codes

13F -- Error during Checkpoint and Restart procedures.

Probable System error.

155 -- User has requested a privileged supervisor call.

Probable User error.

207 -- Attempt to exit routine with no return specified.

Probable User error.

308 -- Invalid entry point address in a called load module.

Probable User error.

425 -- Error occurred during the program overlay process.

Probable User error.

Reference can also be made to the IBM Messages and Codes Manual for a detailed description of completion codes, including a more technical presentation relating to the nature of a specific problem, if desired.

The description of completion codes as presented in this chapter lists their most frequent and probable causes. If kept at an application or system programmer's or analyst's desk, the text provides a most helpful and handy reference in all ADP environs.

APPENDIX
A

Workshop Answers

CHAPTER 2 - DATA IDENTIFICATION

Utilizing the Reference Data Card where appropriate, perform the following hexadecimal arithmetic, conversions, and data representation interpretations.

Arithmetic

1. Hexadecimal Addition

2	4	3	5	B
4	7	B	F	D
6	B	E	14	18

E	42	4CF	ABCD	A94FC
F	8F	BAD	EFAB	ACB1
1D	D1	107C	19B78	B41AD

2. Hexadecimal Subtraction

6	D	D	A0	B3
4	6	B	4	D
2	7	2	9C	A6

DA	C72	F123	1ABCD	C4000
AD	AB8	ABC	CDEF	C3ABC
2D	1BA	E667	DDDE	544

Conversion

1. Hexadecimal to Decimal

C = _____12_____   35 = _____53_____   6B = _____107_____

54C = _____1356_____   DEF = _____3567_____   7CB3 = _____31923_____

5AD2 = _____23250_____   46C4C = _____289868_____   FBFCA = _____1032138_____

2. Decimal to Hexadecimal

11 = _____B_____   48 = _____30_____   237 = _____ED_____

1035 = _____40B_____   2000 = _____7D0_____   3484 = _____D9C_____

12380 = _____305C_____   65535 = _____FFFF_____   200000 = _____30D40_____

3. Hexadecimal to Binary

4 = _0100_   F = _1111_   1B = _00011011_

ABC = _101010111100_   D7E = _110101111110_

F159D = _____1111000101011001110 1_____

Decimal Interpretation

1. External Decimal

F9 = ___9___   C4 = ___+4___   40 = _blank_

C1C8 = _+18_   D6D2 = _-62_   F3F4 = ___34___

40F4F7 = _47_   C9C7C5 = _+975_   40D9D8 = _-98_

2. Internal Decimal

8F = ___8___   6D = ___-6___   04 = _blank_

24C = _+24_   37F = ___37___   64D = _-64_

267F = _267_   814D = _-814_   974C = _+974_

3. Binary

04 = ___4___   0F = ___15___   F1 = ___-15___

40 = ___64___   06D = ___109___   7BC = ___1980___

03F4 = _1012_   F23B = _-3525_   A67F = _-22913_

4. External Floating Point

+01.00Eb00 = _+1.00_   -123.4Eb01 = _-1234._

+4.567E-01 = _.4567_   -.74620E-02 = _-.0074620_

+01.000Eb05 = _+100000._   -12.120Eb05 = _-1212000._

+000.310E-04 = _+.0000310_   -187224.E-06 = _-.187224_

+.999999Eb10 = _+9999990000._

5. Internal Floating Point

44A45B40 = _42075.25_   43AB4800 = _2740.50_

C2FB0000 = _-251.0000_   C35CC120 = _-1484.075_

213 Storage Dump

1. Problem Overview

Completion Code <u>213</u>

Jobname <u>RZZ414</u>   Stepname <u>GO</u>

2. Short Hand Method

Valid UCB <u>3DC4</u>   Problem Ddname <u>READIT</u>

Problem File JCL DD Statement:

<u>//GO.READIT DD UNIT=3330,DISP=(OLD,KEEP),</u>

<u>//   DSN=GOODDATA,VOL=SER=TS0001,</u>

<u>//   DCB=(RECFM=FB,LRECL=120,BLKSIZE=3120)</u>

3. Problem Analysis
    Summarize your findings. Analyzing all JCL associated with the
    problem file; and assuming the Data Set Name and Volume Serial
    Number to be correctly specified, what would your problem
    solution be?

    <u>Problem File - READIT. System cannot locate</u>

    <u>GOODDATA on TS0001. Check for errors in previous job</u>

    <u>to ensure data set as specified was created.</u>

D37 Storage Dump

1. Problem Overview

Completion Code <u>D37</u>

Jobname <u>RZZ455</u>   Stepname <u>STEP1</u>

2. Short Hand Method

Valid UCB   3984   Problem Ddname   SYSUT2

Problem File JCL DD Statement:

    //SYSUT2 DD UNIT=3330,DISP=(NEW,PASS),

    //   DSN=GOODDATA,VOL=SER=TS0001,

    //   SPACE = (1600,4),

    //   DCB=(RECFM=FB,LRECL=080,BLKSIZE=1600)

3. Long Hand Method

DCB Address 085C3C

DCB + Hexadecimal 28 ....   085C64

Hexadecimal TIOT Offset Value 002C

Decimal TIOT Offset Value   44

Subtract 24, Divide 20   1

Truncate, Add 1   2

Problem Ddname SYSUT2

Is the Problem Ddname the same as that obtained in the Short
Hand Method?   Yes   If not, recheck both methods.

4. DCB Characteristics

Maximum Blocksize:

DCB Address 085C3C

DCB + Hexadecimal 3E 085C7A

Hexadecimal Blocksize Value   0640

Decimal Blocksize   1600

Logical Record Length:

DCB + Hexadecimal 52 ....   085C8E

Hexadecimal Record Length Value   0050

Decimal Record Length Value   80

Block Count:

DCB + Hexadecimal 0 .... <u>085C3C</u>

Hexadecimal Block Count Value .... <u>00000000</u>

Decimal Block Count Value .... <u>0</u>

What is the significance of the obtained value for Block
Count?

<u>A complete block of data had not yet been processed at</u>

<u>the time of the abend. This could affect your analysis</u>

<u>of space requirements.</u>

5. Problem Analysis

Summarize your findings. Analyzing all JCL associated with
the problem file; and assuming that the program is not in a
loop, what would your problem solution be?

<u>Problem File - SYSUT2. Maximum Blocksize = 1600;</u>

<u>Logical Record Length = 080; Block Count = 0. Recalculate</u>

<u>and increase space allocation after thorough review of</u>

<u>program logic for possible loop.</u>

CHAPTER 4 - INTERNAL ABENDS

OCB Storage Dump

1. Problem Overview

Completion Code <u>OCB</u>

Jobname <u>RZZ925</u>   Stepname <u>GO</u>

2. Relative Length Determination

Interrupt Address (IA) from APSW .... <u>20AF56</u>

Entry Point Address (EPA) from CDE .... <u>20A7E8</u>

Relative Length (IA - EPA) .... <u>76E</u>

Control Section Verification:

Origin of ACOMP   00

Origin of ILBOCOMO BA8

Does Relative Length fall inside or outside the bounds of
Program ACOMP? What is the significance of this
determination?

    Inside. If Relative Length were outside bounds of ACOMP

    and the problem routine were programmer-written, the

    Origin would need to be subtracted from Relative Length to

    determine length into called module. If the problem routine

    were system-generated, the Return Address in SAVE AREA

    TRACE would need to be subtracted from the Entry Point

    Address to determine length into calling module.

3. Source Statement Determination

    Length into Assembly Language listing 76E

    Problem Source Statement Number   62

    Actual Source Statement:

    COMPUTE ITEST = DATA-ARRAY (SUB-M) / DATA-ARRAY (SUB-N)

4. Problem Analysis

    Summarize your findings, At this point, what action should be
taken?

    Relative Length 76E; Source Statement #62. The determi-

    nation of the value of pertinent variables such as DATA-

    ARRAY (SUB-N) to be covered in the next chapter, would be a

    logical step. In lieu of this action, a critical review of

    program logic for erroneous zeroed data and/or calculations

    should be accomplished.

240 Storage Dump

1. Problem Overview

   User Code _____240_____   Completion Code _____0C5_____

   Jobname _____RZZ017_____   Stepname _____GO_____

2. Relative Length Determination

   Interrupt Address (IA) from APSW .... _____0F2F3A_____

   Entry Point Address (EPA) from CDE .... _____0F2C00_____

   Relative Length (IA - EPA) .... _____33A_____

   Control Section Recalculation:

   Origin of MAIN .... _____00_____

   Origin of COMP .... _____1E8_____

   Origin of IHNECOMH .... _____3A0_____

   Does Relative Length fall inside or outside bounds of MAIN?

   _____Outside._____

   If outside, which routine does the Relative Length fall within?

   _____COMP._____

   Relative Length obtained previously .... _____33A_____

   Origin of Pertinent Routine .... _____1E8_____

   Relative Length minus Origin .... _____152_____

3. Source Statement Determination

   Length into Assembly Language Listing .... _____152_____

   Problem Source Statement Number .... _____3_____

   Actual Source Statement:

   _____100 ITEST = ID(M) * ID(N)_____

4. Problem Analysis

   Summarize your findings. At this point, what action should be
   taken?

Relative Length 33A; Length into COMP 152; Source Statement #3. The determination of the value of pertinent variables such as ID(M) and ID(N), to be covered in the next chapter would be a logical step. In lieu of this action, a critical review of program logic for erroneous address and data references should be accomplished.

Data Error

1. Problem Overview

    Error Number   IHN215I

    Error Message   CONVERT - ILLEGAL DECIMAL CHARACTER X

2. Relative Length Determination

    Name of System Routine .... IBCOM

    Name of Program Module .... MAIN

    Return Address (RA) 136598

    Entry Point Address (EPA) 136410

    Relative Length (RA - EPA) 188

3. Source Statement Determination

    Length into Assembly Language Listing 188

    Problem Source Statement Number 2

    Actual Source Statement:

        READ (5,100) ID, M, N

4. Problem Analysis

    Summarize your findings. If the occurrence of this particular error jeopardizes the run and the validity of the output files, what alternative actions can be taken?

    Relative Length 188; Source Statement #2. A critical review of program logic for erroneous data sources should

be accomplished. If desired, a CALL Statement can be
inserted into the program module to alter standard corrective action. In either case, the job would have to
be rerun.

CHAPTER 5 - VARIABLE VALUES

COBOL Variables

1. Pertinent Variables

Variable Name	Single Value or Array?
ITEST	Single Value
SUB-M	Single Value
SUB-N	Single Value
DATA-ARRAY	Array

2. DMAP Reference

	Single Value Variables			Variable Array
Variable Name	ITEST	SUBM	SUB N	DATA-ARRAY
Base Register Assignment ...	BL=3	BL=3	BL=3	BL=3
Base Register Number	6	6	6	6
Base Address	20A870	20A870	20A870	20A870
Displacement	004	000	002	008
Field Length (bytes)	2	2	2	2
Form of Data Representation .	External Decimal	Binary	Binary	External Decimal

3. Single Value Variable Location and Interpretation

Variable Name	ITEST	SUB-M	SUB-N
Base + Displacement	20A874	20A870	20A872
Character String	F0F0	0006	0003
Decimal Interpretation .	+0+0 or 0	6	3

How do you account for the value of ITEST?

Value initialized to zero by program; not yet calculated.

4. Variable Array Location and Interpretation

Variable Name	DATA-ARRAY	
Base + Displacement	20A878	
Position or Index	6	3
Character String	F1F2	40F0
Decimal Interpretation	+1+2 or 12	blank+0 or 0

Which of the above positions of the DATA-ARRAY is equal to zero?
___3rd___ If a zero is not found, recheck data locations and
respective interpretations.

5. Problem Analysis

Summarize your findings. Assuming that the erroneous data
was read in from an input file, what would your problem
solution be?

ITEST = DATA-ARRAY (SUB-M) / DATA-ARRAY (SUB-N)

0   = DATA-ARRAY (6)   / DATA-ARRAY (3)

0   =   12   /   0

The sixth position of the Data Array is equal to 12.

It is being divided by a zero found in the third position

of the Data Array, thus causing a OCB Storage Dump. One

alternative solution is to run the input data through a

pre-edit utility program, thus 'cleaning up' the data prior

to execution. Another solution is to change the program

such that erroneous data will be edited and/or modified

prior to the execution of arithmetic operations.

FORTRAN Variables

1. Pertinent Variables

Subscript Name	Single Value or Array
M	Single Value
N	Single Value

2. Assembly Language Listing Reference

	M	N
Variable Name	M	N
Base Register Number	13	13
Base Address	OF2E18	OF2E18
Decimal Displacement	120	124
Hexadecimal Displacement	78	7C
Field Length (bytes)	4	4
Form of Data Representation	Binary	Binary

3. Variable Location and Interpretation

	M	N
Variable Name	M	N
Base + Displacement	OF2E90	OF2E94
Character String	58E09108	58F09008
Decimal Interpretation	?	?

Can the above character strings be interpreted? Why not?

Not under the Binary Form of Data Representation as

expected. They are essentially 'nonsense' values

inadvertently accessed in main storage.

4. Problem Analysis

> Summarize your findings. Assuming limited FORTRAN programming experience what general alternative solutions should be sought?

> Subscripts M and N are invalid. A complete review of program logic should be accomplished checking for a program loop or invalid variable specifications. An experienced FORTRAN programmer would find that the Variables M and N as well as the ID Array have not been placed in COMMON between MAIN and Subroutine COMP. Thus, the variables take on incoherent values when referenced in COMP from MAIN, causing the OC5 Storage Dump.

CHAPTER 6 - MACHINE INSTRUCTIONS

OCB Storage Dump

1. Address of Next Machine Instruction to be Executed   20AF56

2. Length of Machine Instruction

   APSW left-most Byte ....   EO

   Convert to Binary   11100000

   Length in Bytes   6

3. Instruction being Executed

   Op Code of Next Machine Instruction F8

   Back up required Number of Bytes and record Machine Instruction.

   FD31D20CD206

4. Op Code, Function, and Format

   Op Code ....   FD

Function Performed .... <u>Divide Decimal</u>

Format .... <u>SS</u>

5. Machine Instruction Breakdown

   Op Code .... <u>FD</u>

	1st Operand	2nd Operand
Length Indication	3	1
Length + 1	4	2
Base Register	D	D
Displacement	20C	206

6. Operand Values

	1st Operand	2nd Operand
Base Register Contents	20AB10	20AB10
Base + Displacement	20AD1C	20AD16
Length in Bytes	4	2
Character String	0000012F	000F

Given the above character strings, interpret the value of the
First and Second Operands?   How did you arrive at this
interpretation?

First Operand = Decimal 12; Second Operand = Decimal 0.

Although 12F and 0F could be interpreted as Hexadecimal

and converted to Decimal 303 and 15 respectively, the

presence of F in the low order position is suspicious

of Packed Format. Reference to the Source Listing would

verify the variable as USAGE DISPLAY (External Decimal

Unpacked Format). Realizing that the compiler generates

instructions to pack all unpacked data fields prior to

tests and arithmetic operations, 0000012F and 000F are

equivalent to F0F0F0F0F0F0F1F2 and F0F0F0F0 respectively

in Unpacked Form. Thus, the First Operand is equal to

+0+0+0+0+0+0+1+2 or twelve. The Second Operand is equal

to +0+0+0+0 or zero.

7. Problem Analysis

Summarize your findings. How do the values obtained in this workshop compare to that obtained in Chapter 5?

Op Code	L1	L2	B1	D1	B2	D2
FD	3	1	D	20C	D	206

Value of First Operand = 12. Value of Second Operand = 0.

Division by zero caused the OCB Storage Dump as determined

by the Second Operand and the value of pertinent values in

Chapter 5's workshop where DATA-ARRAY (SUB-M) equals twelve

and DATA-ARRAY (SUB-N) equals zero.

CHAPTER 1 - STORAGE DUMP CONCEPTS

013 Storage Dump

A problem solution for the Storage Dump depicted in Figures 1.1 through 1.6 of Chapter 1 follows.

1. Problem Overview

Completion Code ___013___

Jobname ___RZZ022___   Stepname ___GO___

2. Short Hand Method

Valid UCB ___45E8___   Problem Ddname ___CARDIN___

3. Long Hand Method

    DCB Address 04E95C

    DCB + Hexadecimal 28 ....   04E984

    Hexadecimal TIOT Offset Value   0040

    Decimal TIOT Offset Value   64

    Subtract 24, Divide 20   2

    Truncate, Add 1   3

    Problem Ddname ....   CARDIN

The problem ddname obtained in the Long Hand Method should be the same
as that obtained in the Short Hand Method.

4. DCB Characteristics

Block Count:

    DCB Address 04E95C

    DCB + Hexadecimal 0 ....   04E95C

    Hexadecimal Block Count Value   00000000

    Decimal Block Count Value   0

Maximum Blocksize:

    DCB + Hexadecimal 3E 04E99A

    Hexadecimal Blocksize Value 012C

    Decimal Blocksize Value   300

Logical Record Length:

    DCB + Hexadecimal 52 ....   04E9AE

    Hexadecimal Record Length Value   0050

    Decimal Record Length Value   80

5. Problem Analysis

    Problem File - CARDIN. Block Count = 0 (A complete

    block has not been processed). Maximum Blocksize = 300,

    Logical Record Length = 80 (Blocksize is not a multiple

of Record Length). A conflict thus exists for fixed

length records between Maximum Blocksize and Logical

Record Length specifications. A check of DCB attributes

specified in the Source Program and JCL Listing must be

made to determine programmer's original intent.

APPENDIX
B

Storage Dump Glossary

The following glossary is intended to clarify terminology frequently used in discussing storage dump debugging procedures.

Abend -- an abnormal termination of the execution of a given job; accompanied by a storage dump and/or error handling facility message.

Abend Dump -- a type of storage dump which displays only that portion of main storage pertinent to a user's program and files for the step within which the abnormal termination occurred; similar to a Snap Dump.

Array -- a contiguous series of data fields arranged in one or more directions (dimensions), which has been assigned a program defined variable name.

Base -- a reference point in main storage referring to the starting location of pertinent instructions and/or data. Also refers to the number of allowable codes within a numbering system.

Binary -- a Base 2 numbering system utilizing two valid codes, i.e., 0 and 1. Also a form of data representation.

Bit -- the smallest unit of measurement referring to main storage usage, i.e., a ferrite core magnetized in a clockwise or counter-clockwise direction, that is, on or off, 1 or 0.

Byte -- a unit of measurement referring to main storage; equivalent to eight contiguous bits; represented in print form by two hexa-decimal characters.

Character String -- a series of one or more contiguous codes re-siding in main storage interpreted in terms of a particular form of data representation.

Completion Code -- a code issued by the Operating System in-dicating the nature of a problem which has caused an abnormal termination.

Data Interpretation -- the process of translating character strings into a meaningful form, usually decimal, based upon the form of data representation utilized.

Data Representation -- a form or method of storing and portraying data, i.e., Character Format (External Decimal), Internal Decimal, Binary, External Floating Point, Internal Floating Point.

Displacement -- a relative length on location, in bytes, from a given base.

Entry Point Address (EPA) -- the starting address of a program module which resides in main storage.

Error Handling Routine -- a program utilized as a debugging aid to detect and/or correct system and program errors, either in addition to or in lieu of a storage dump being issued.

Executable Module -- a set of machine language instructions executed as a program under the control of the Operating System. Also referred to as Load module, Program Module, and Executable Routine.

External Abend -- an abnormal termination of the execution of a given job resulting in a storage dump which occurs when the program, within the step in which the abend occurred, was not being executed.

Hexadecimal -- a Base 16 numbering system utilizing sixteen valid codes, i.e., 0 through F.

Internal Abend -- an abnormal termination of the execution of a given job resulting in a storage dump which occurs when the program, within the step in which the abend occurred, was being executed.

Interrupt Address (IA) -- the address of the next machine instruction to be executed at the time an abend occurs.

Machine Instruction -- a contiguous series of bits comprised of an Operation Code and two or three Operands for reference and execution purposes. Consists of five formats -- Register To Register, Register To Index, Register To Storage, Storage Immediate, and Storage To Storage.

Main Storage Print -- that portion of a storage dump which depicts main storage contents in contiguous hexadecimal form. Accompanied by decimal interpretations when appropriate.

Operand -- the right-most portion of a machine instruction, one to four bytes in length; contains data and/or references to data to be tested, moved, manipulated, or otherwise referred to and/or operated upon.

Operating System -- a series of programs which allows a data processing system to automatically control its own operations.

Operation Code -- the first byte, or eight bits, of a machine instruction; indicates the function to be performed.

Register -- a unit of reference for addresses and data. The Registers At Entry To Abend area of a storage dump contains 16 General

Registers four bytes in length. When utilized as base and index registers, they contain references to storage addresses. When utilized as data registers, they contain actual data values (character strings).

Relative Address -- the length, in bytes, into a given executable module at which point an abend occurred.

Storage Dump -- a printed representation of the contents of main storage at a given moment in time. Actual format and range of addresses printed depends upon the type of storage dump issued -- Abend or Snap, Indicative, or Stand-alone.

Subscript -- a number or variable specifying a specific position within an array.

User Code -- a code issued by a program or error handling routine indicating the nature of a problem which has caused an abnormal termination.

Variable -- a name assigned by a programmer to an area of main storage, the contents of which may vary, as determined by program processing logic.

Virtual Storage -- a feature of the Operating System in which main storage requirements are allocated by segments (or pages) as needed by the processing program, thus creating an appearance to the user of unlimited or 'virtual' storage.

Word -- a unit of measurement referring to main storage usage; equivalent to four contiguous bytes, 32 bits, or eight hexadecimal characters.

Index